Controversies in
Juvenile Justice
and Delinquency

Peter J. Benekos, Ph.D.
Mercyhurst College

Alida V. Merlo, Ph.D.
Indiana University of Pennsylvania

 LexisNexis®

 anderson publishing
A member of the LexisNexis Group

Controversies in Juvenile Justice and Delinquency, Second Edition

Controversies in Juvenile Justice and Delinquency/Peter J. Benekos and Alida V. Merlo
p. cm.
Includes bibliographical references and index.
ISBN: 978-1-59345-5705 (softbound)
Transferred to Digital Printing 2010

Cover design by Tin Box Studio, Inc./Cincinnati, OH

EDITOR   Janice Eccleston
ACQUISITIONS EDITOR   Michael C. Braswell

Dedication

To our parents, John and Lillian Benekos,
and Nicholas and Clara Merlo.

Acknowledgments

This project could not have happened without the contributions of our authors. We are very fortunate to have had the opportunity to work with such distinguished colleagues. We appreciate their scholarly contributions and are honored by their participation in this second edition.

We also appreciate the assistance of Mickey Braswell, who helped us develop and refine our ideas for the first edition of this book. Special thanks to Janice Eccleston, our Editor, whose commitment to the successful completion of this project was exemplary. Kelly Grondin was a supportive and reassuring presence at LexisNexis/Anderson throughout the project. We have fond memories of Anderson Publishing Co.

We also appreciate the help and conscientious work of our Research Assistants, Audry Passetti and Abby Bloomquist from Mercyhurst College, and Katie Herman from Indiana University of Pennsylvania. Their work was instrumental in our efforts. A special thanks to Douglas Ritson and the Butler County Pennsylvania Probation Department and John Daley, Director of the Erie County Pennsylvania Edmund L. Thomas Adolescent Center, for their willingness to provide us with photographs for this edition.

All of this could not have happened without the love and support of our families. My mother, Lil Benekos, has taught me tolerance and compassion, and has supported me in my efforts. My wife, Pat, is patient and encouraging, and her support and love make me a better person.

My mother, Clara Merlo, is wise, thoughtful, and generous. I feel fortunate to have experienced her love. My husband, Kevin Ashley, demonstrates his intelligence, good humor, and love each day. He makes it possible for me to do what I do. Finally, I cherish the love and kindness of our daughter, Alexandra Ashley.

Peter J. Benekos
Alida V. Merlo

Table of Contents

CHAPTER 1

Reflections on Youth and Juvenile Justice

Alida V. Merlo
Peter J. Benekos

Introduction

Since the 1980s, juvenile justice policies have been both punitive and progressive. Most notable among harsh sanctions were changes to state statutes which not only made it easier to try juveniles as adults, but also resulted in more youth being incarcerated in adult institutions. Simultaneously, there are signs of an emergent reaffirmation of the juvenile court's original mission; specifically, a more rehabilitative and community-based response to youthful offending. For example, California's SB 81, signed into law in 2007, designates a different direction in the treatment of youth. The legislation precludes counties from committing nonviolent juvenile offenders to the Division of Juvenile Justice, and authorizes block grant funds to local jurisdictions to create alternative treatment options (*Commonweal*, 2007). Although this is one state's recent response, it is indicative of a greater emphasis on the community's role in preventing and rehabilitating youth and a policy that focuses on deinstitutionalization of juveniles.

While additional developments in juvenile justice will be reviewed, it is useful to examine trends in juvenile crime as a context for understanding youth policies and legislative reforms. Contrary to general impressions, a snapshot of juvenile arrests in 2006 illustrates that juveniles accounted for 16 percent of all arrests and 17 percent of violent crime arrests (Figure 1.1). In 2004, juveniles accounted for 16 percent of all arrests and 12 percent of all violent crimes cleared by arrest (Snyder, 2006). As demonstrated in Figure 1.2, since 1980, with the exception of the late 1980s until mid 1990s, the rate of juvenile arrests for violent crime has been fairly stable. The impact of this "crime wave" is underscored by the murder rate and the visibility of juveniles in driving up violent crime rates (Figure 1.3). It was during this period of time that much of the get-tough legislation that focused on adultification and punitive sanctions was introduced.

Figure 1.1 **Juvenile Proportion of Arrests by offense, 2006**

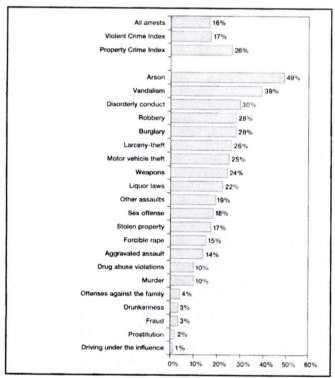

Source: *OJJDP Statistical Briefing Book*. Online. Available: http://ojjdp.ncjrs.gov/ojstatbb/crime/qa05102.asp?qaDate=2006. Released on December 13, 2007.

Figure 1.2 **Arrests per 100,000 Juveniles ages 10-17, 1980 - 2006**

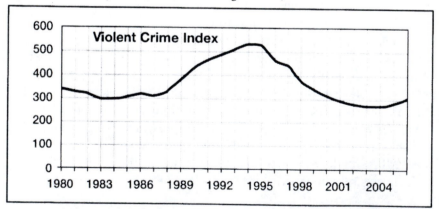

Source: *OJJDP Statistical Briefing Book*. Online. Available: http://ojjdp.ncjrs.org/ojstatbb/crime/JAR_Display.asp?ID=qa05201. December 13, 2007.

Figure 1.3 **Arrests per 100,000 Juveniles ages 10-17, 1980 - 2006**

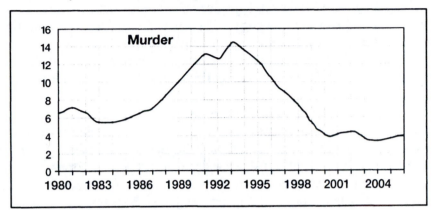

Source: *OJJDP Statistical Briefing Book*. Online. Available: http://ojjdp.ncjrs.org/ojstatbb/crime/JAR_
Display.asp?ID=qa05202. December 13, 2007.

Arguably, the increase in juvenile violence indicated in Figures 1.2 and 1.3 was attributed to the confluence of gangs, guns, and drugs (Blumstein, 1996).

After a period of a sustained decline in youth crime, the FBI *Uniform Crime Report* data illustrate that juvenile arrests for murder in 2006 increased about 3 percent from 2005 arrests, with 764 youth under the age of 18 arrested for murder. Arrests of youth under the age of 18 for armed robbery also increased 18.9 percent from 2005 to 2006 (*Uniform Crime Reports*, 2007). Although the increases are troubling, in their analysis of 2005 data, Butts and Snyder caution us to refrain from drawing conclusions that react to a "relatively small increase" reported in a few major cities (2006:8). In short, it is too soon to conclude that youth are becoming more violent.

These statistics and the analysis of crime trends suggest conflicting images. Increases in juvenile arrests for murder and armed robbery do not fit with perceptions of youth being less violent than in the previous decade. Nonetheless, the incidence of arrests for youth under the age of 18 in 2006 was 1.9 percent more than 2005, but 26 percent less than 1997 (*Uniform Crime Reports*, 2007). These comparisons suggest that a slight increase in juvenile arrests does not portend a new wave of youth violence.

Understanding Juvenile Justice

Since its founding in 1899, the juvenile court has become increasingly more procedural and formal, and public attitudes toward youthful offenders also have changed. Although the juvenile justice system was originally intended to provide youth with an alternative to adult criminal court (i.e., diversion), there has been a significant transformation in policies toward youth. Specifically, society is inclined toward accountability of youth and more punitive approaches to delinquent behavior.

Even though the juvenile crime wave of the 1980s and 1990s has ended, its continuing impact on juvenile justice policies is evident. Images of young, violent, armed offenders engaged in gang and drug activities undermine the notion of innocent children and developing adolescents, and support arguments against the need for a separate jurisdiction for youth (Merlo & Benekos, 2003). It is difficult for society to reconcile these diverse perceptions of youth.

A review of juvenile justice history suggests at least three salient developments that have had a dynamic impact on the juvenile justice system. Media coverage of youth violence resulted in exaggerated public fear of crime and fostered emotional reactions that bordered on hysteria. Stories of unprecedented youth violence and victimization of innocent citizens contributed to inaccurate perceptions and misunderstanding about juvenile delinquency and the juvenile justice system (Benekos & Merlo, 2006; Merlo & Benekos, 2000a; Kappeler, Blumberg & Potter, 2000).

A second and related emotional response to the fear of youth crime was anger and frustration which promoted a "demonization" of youth (Vogel, 1994). In her review of this phenomenon, Triplett used Tannenbaum's concept of the "dramatization of evil" to explain how reactions to violent youth were generalized to all youths and, in particular, to inner city minority males (2000:132). As a result, adolescent offenders were portrayed as "super predators" who were dangerous and remorseless (DiIulio, 1995; Bazelon, 2000). In his treatise on youth crime and moral panics, Schissel described the tendency to overstate the youth crime problem (especially gangs) and to "create and foster a collective enmity towards youth" that results in making youth into 'folk devils'" (1997:51).

These responses of anger and frustration were not only directed toward youth; the juvenile justice system was also criticized for its perceived failure to effectively treat youth and its inability to control youth crime. In their national assessment of juvenile offenders who were housed in adult correctional facilities, Austin, Johnson, and Gregoriou summarized the impact of public attitudes and concluded that "This concept of a distinct justice system for juveniles focused upon treatment has come under attack in recent years" (2000:ix).

These developments – exaggerated media coverage, demonization of youth, and loss of faith in the juvenile justice system – were used by legislators to drive policies that resulted in a shift of discretion from judges to prosecutors, reduced the individualization of sanctions, and further adultified the juvenile justice system. As a result, convergence of the juvenile and criminal justice systems prompted some to contend that the juvenile justice system should be abolished. With a cooptation of the therapeutic goals that guided the founding of the juvenile justice system, deterrence, incapacitation, and punishment became the reality of juvenile justice (Feld, 1993; 1999).

The conservative "get-tough" attitude that characterized criminal justice policy since the late 1970s has been incorporated into policies for youth. By revising juvenile statutes, most legislatures have re-evaluated perceptions of youth and reformulated policies toward youthful offenders. Overall, these policies have tended to treat youth more harshly.

One measure of these changes is the increase in the number of youth in out-of-home placements. According to Snyder and Sickmund (2006:199), the number of youth in public and private facilities increased 41 percent from 1991 to 1999 and then decreased 10 percent between 1999 and 2003. Overall, the increase between 1991 and 2003 was 27 percent. Even though crime rates for adults and juveniles have continued to decline, punitive attitudes persist and fear of crime remains a salient public concern.

Simultaneously, politicians have seized the crime issue and proposed harsher sanctions for juvenile offenders. Candidates for public office understand the importance of shibolleths that emphasize strict sanctions for youth, and they embrace them. The media have also influenced perspectives on youth and helped to solidify the belief that youth are "mini-adults" who should be held to the same standards and subject to the same punishments. For example, findings from a Canadian survey suggest the widespread nature of these changes and the "considerable pressure to impose harsher penalties on juvenile offenders" (Tufts & Roberts, 2002:46). In her study, Sprott found that a majority of respondents opposed a separate system for youthful offenders and perceived that youth in the juvenile justice system received sanctions that were too lenient (Sprott, 1998). While studies such as these also find that the public is not well informed about juvenile justice policy, nonetheless, the "views of the public and the reaction of politicians are clearly linked in a spiral of punitiveness" (Tufts & Roberts, 2002:48). In this prevailing climate of intolerance, zero-tolerance policies have become popular solutions to the complex problems of adolescent behaviors. A survey of college students found that a majority supported zero-tolerance policies and drug testing in high schools (Merlo, Benekos & Cook, 2001).

School policies that mandate expulsions for weapons (i.e., mandatory sentences for youth) have captured media attention, often for their excessiveness in punishing youth for innocent behaviors (e.g., bringing nail clippers to school; sharing mints). Students who have minor violations can be punished as severely as students who bring weapons to school (*New York Times*, 2002). Incidents such as these prompted one parent to say that "Zero tolerance doesn't mean zero judgment or rights" (CNN, 2002:par 4). This underscores that reactionary policies that restrict discretion and emphasize punishment may actually distort justice and be an *iatrogenesis* that does more harm than good (Miller, 1996).

In this introductory chapter on the controversies in juvenile justice, the authors review the evolution of juvenile justice, examine the influence of ideology, politics, and the media on juvenile justice policy, consider recent trends that reaffirm rational policies and therapeutic interventions, provide a context for assessing future initiatives for the juvenile justice system, and offer support for policies that seek to expand innovations that maintain emphasis on prevention, early intervention, and jurisdictional separation.

History and Development of the Juvenile Court

The classic interpretation of the juvenile court is that a special court was established through the efforts of child savers and concerned citizens in order to protect children from the harms of criminal court and to use social welfare programs to save wayward youth (Taylor, Fritsch & Caeti, 2007; Bortner, 1988; Platt, 1977). The *parens patriae* doctrine that the state would act as a kind and benevolent parent underscored a different philosophy and a therapeutic system to care for the best interests of children. Not surprisingly, "the juvenile court corresponded with the rise of positivism" which Albanese describes as an emphasis on environmental influences as opposed to rational, calculated criminality (1993:9). Ferdinand and McDermott also discussed this presumption of the new court: "Under *parens patriae*, juveniles, for example, have a right to treatment for their offenses instead of full punishment . . ." (2002:91).

Concepts such as paternalism, best interests, informality, and treatment characterized this early period. A different perspective, however, of this separate system criticized the increased social control over poor, immigrant children and the justification that it presented for removing children from their homes and families (Albanese, 1993:9). For example, Bernard observed that "like the new idea of juvenile delinquency, the juvenile court was probably popular in part because it sounded new and different but it actually wasn't" (1992:101). This new legal philosophy justified institutionalization to control children for their "own good" but at the same time helped to "increase the power of the state" over poor urban youth (Bernard, 1992:106).

Eventually, abuses of this new court's informal authority reached the attention of the Supreme Court and its resulting decisions began to transform the juvenile court. In his assessment of the state of juvenile justice, Feld examined the outcomes of the Court's decisions: the juvenile court relied less on informal procedures; the philosophy shifted from therapeutic to crime control; and the separate jurisdiction for children and youth was eroded by the diversion of status offenders and the transfer of serious adolescent offenders to criminal court (1993; 1999). Essentially, this created a convergence of procedure, jurisprudence, and jurisdiction, and prompted Feld to ask: What was the justification for separate but parallel systems of justice? His critique of the resulting transformation suggested that youth received neither due process protections nor treatment, and as a result, Feld proposed the abolition of the juvenile court (1993; 1999).

Butler County, Pennsylvania Juvenile Court: Adjudication Hearing

While the mission of the juvenile court may have reflected an admirable objective, the reality of how youth were treated was condemned. In the context of hardening attitudes toward youth and with a system depicted by deficit performance, juvenile justice at the beginning of the twenty-first century was bleak.

Ideology, Politics, the Media, and Juvenile Justice

The developments and transformation of the juvenile justice system summarized above did not occur unilaterally. A general shift in criminal justice from rehabilitation to retribution, from determinism to free will, and from treatment to punishment coincided with social and political changes in the 1970s and 1980s. Merlo and Benekos have reviewed how the interaction of ideology, politics, and the media affected the criminal justice system and removed the development of crime policies from professionals to politicians (2000a). In this sociopolitical context of getting tough with crime by getting tough on criminals, the war on drugs also extended to youth who were demonized as "godless, fatherless, jobless" and dangerous offenders who deserved no special treatment due to age (DiIulio, 1995). Magill examined how youth in the 1980s-1990s were portrayed as "Public Enemy #1" that needed more severe, adult-like sanctions in order to instill deterrence and to apply appropriate punishment (1998). This reaction was reminiscent of the Willie Horton incident: present images and language of crime and criminals that provoke emotional reactions; announce and promote moral imperatives; and propose more and longer prison sentences (Benekos & Merlo, 2006:16).

With these changes in images and ideology, state legislators further transformed the juvenile justice system by enacting policies that essentially adultified youthful offenders (Sickmund, Snyder & Poe-Yamagata, 1997). Characteristic of this national trend was the 1995 special legislative session in Pennsylvania. Convened by the governor to address the problem of violent youth crime, lawmakers targeted crimes committed with weapons and lowered to age 14 the statutory transfer of youth to adult court (Juvenile Court Act, 1995; Torbet & Thomas, 1997). This type of get-tough legislation resulted in an increase in the incarceration of youth. More than 14,000 youth under age 18 were confined in state and local adult institutions in 1997. In 1997, 7,400 youth under age 18 were sentenced to adult prisons, up from 3,400 in 1985 (Strom, 2000). In his review of these trends, Strom concluded, "relative to the number of arrests, the likelihood of incarceration in state prison increased for offenders under 18" (2000:1).

While the number of youth incarcerated in state prisons increased throughout the 1990s, data from mid-year 2006 indicate a decline in the number of inmates under age 18: from 3,896 in state prisons in June, 2000, to 2,364 in June, 2006 (Sabol, Minton & Harrison, 2007:4-5). Consistent with the dramatic decrease in reported arrests for violent offending, Snyder and Sickmund found that there was also a decrease in the number of youth under 18 admitted to prison between 1996 and 2002 (Snyder & Sickmund, 2006: 237). However, the 2006 data reflect an increase over the 2005 count in the number of youth held in jail (as juveniles) and the number of juveniles in adult prisons (Sabol, Minton & Harrison, 2007:5).

With respect to the number of youth in adult jails, Sabol et al. (2007:4-6) reported that there were 7,615 youth housed in adult jails in June, 2000, and 6,104 youth in jail in June of 2006. Jails hold juveniles who are unable to make bail as well as those who are awaiting consideration for transfer back to juvenile court or sentenced as adults to shorter terms. In some instances, youth can be incarcerated in jails for months before a decision to send their case back to juvenile court is made (Banks, 2007). These stays are not inconsequential; there is a greater likelihood of suicide of youth in jails than adults and there is an increased risk of victimization (Mumola, 2005:5; Hartney, 2006:1).

Because the public's views and understanding of crime are largely influenced by the media, it is not surprising that "the role of the media in informing pubic opinion and influencing citizen reaction to crime issues is central to understanding the framing of crime policy" (Merlo & Benekos, 2000a:4). In a study of public perceptions of youth crime by Dorfman and Schiraldi, 62 percent of respondents believed that youth crime was on the rise (2001:1). This is not unanticipated considering that network news coverage of homicide increased 473 percent from 1990 to 1998. However, during the same period, homicide arrests actually dropped 33 percent. The researchers concluded that the "news media unduly connects youth to crime and violence" (2001:1).

In their study of the role of media, Kappeler and Potter describe the "social construction of crime myths" and they attempt to "deconstruct" the media's role in reporting crime (2005). The authors conclude that "social policy should not be developed based on distortion, sensationalism, or a few newsworthy events" which is typically characteristic of the media industry (2005:9). In a similar perspective, Schissel's critique of media accounts of youth crime prompted this observation: "the portraits of young criminals that public crime accountants paint are largely nihilistic, pathological criminals . . . who are devoid of a moral base" (1997:150).

Notwithstanding their critique of media and crime policy, the dynamics of ideology, politics, and media influence have increased the reach of juvenile justice and reduced the discretion in handling youthful offenders (Merlo & Benekos, 2000b). With attention to zero tolerance and the fear of school violence, youth have lost the presumption of innocence and court decisions have diminished youth rights. In this context, Schwartz observes that "the rights of young people are shredded when they walk through the schoolhouse gates" (2002:2). Even as an exaggeration, Schwartz's concern reflects the dichotomous views that confound juvenile justice policy and the treatment of youth: in one sense, youth are recognized as being immature and impulsive, and therefore are denied adult privileges and receive reduced privacy; however, when youth commit crime, there is an expectation reflected in public policy that they should be held accountable to adult consequences (2002:2).

This abbreviated review underscores that juvenile justice policies have been influenced by neoconservative ideology that emphasizes deterrence and punishment. As youth have become demonized, tolerance and discretion have been replaced with increased focus on accountability and incapacitation. At the same time that politicalization of juvenile justice has transformed the system, researchers have demonstrated that prevention and intervention are viable strategies that can reduce youthful offending and also offer a balance to the hardening attitudes toward youth. Some of those promising strategies are considered later in the chapter. In the next section, recent legislation and policies are discussed.

Juvenile Justice Policies

By the end of the 1990s, juvenile justice policies were more exclusive and punitive than in the past. Most notably, this transformation occurred in juvenile justice statutes. In 17 states, legislators revisited juvenile court legislation and revised the language regarding the purpose of the juvenile court. Although it had previously focused on the best interests of the child, by 1997, Torbet and Szymanski (1998) found that the language was altered to highlight public safety (community protection), punishment for youthful offenders, specific sanctions, and/or offender accountability.

Simultaneously, states decided that confidential proceedings designed to provide guidance to troubled youth while shielding them from the stigma associated with criminal or delinquent activity were no longer necessary. In 47 states, legislators revised statutes that had previously mandated the confidentiality of juvenile records (Snyder & Sickmund, 1999:89). Today, in many states, the media identify and publicize the names of youth alleged to be involved in delinquent activity (Snyder & Sickmund, 2006:109).

Statutes that lower the age when juveniles can be transferred to the adult court, mandate transfer for certain offenses, and authorize alternatives to judicial waiver demonstrate how the exclusion of juveniles from the juvenile justice system can occur. The changes in the purpose clause and the confidentiality of records were accompanied by a third reaction: 45 states endorsed legislation that changed the process and made it easier to transfer juveniles from the juvenile justice system to the adult criminal court (Snyder & Sickmund, 1999:89). As previously discussed, this legislative revision also resulted in more juveniles sentenced to adult prisons.

Concurrently, some positive developments occurred. Despite the harsh sanctions, there was evidence that prevention and intervention approaches were being implemented. By comparing some of the more preventive approaches with the more punitive and reactive responses, there is an opportunity to examine the changes that have transpired. In this section, the policies and programs are delineated as those that emphasize prevention, education, and treatment (PET), balanced and restorative justice (BARJ), or retribution, adultification, and punishment (RAP) (Benekos & Merlo, 2002).

Secure Detention Facility: Erie County, Pennsylvania

A series of highly publicized school shootings were responsible for some of the public's perceptions that youth were becoming more violent and that schools were unsafe for children and youth. School officials, shocked by the tragedies, were eager to find some "quick fix" to address the problem. School boards hurriedly reacted by adopting zero-tolerance initiatives.

Instituting Zero-Tolerance Policies

Zero-tolerance initiatives are neither novel nor innovative; federal and state governments had employed them in the 1980s as a part of a drug enforcement strategy (Skiba & Peterson, 1999:372). In the 1990s, they were simply modified to deal with school violence. Their popularity is demonstrated by the fact that by 1993, schools across the country had implemented zero-tolerance policies to deal with behaviors that ranged from smoking on a school campus to school disruptions (Skiba & Peterson, 1999:372-373).

Utilizing zero-tolerance initiatives as a primary defense against school violence exemplifies an ideology that emphasizes retribution, adultification, and punishment (RAP). Policies are harsh and arbitrary; and there seems to be no latitude in applying and enforcing the sanctions. Every infraction is handled as a threat to school safety. These policies preclude an examination of the students' intentions, level of understanding, or specific behaviors (Bogos, 1997; Levick, 2000).

However, official data demonstrate that violence in school began decreasing in 1992. Schools are safer places than they were before 1992, and there has been a decline in the incidence of school-related violent deaths (Brooks, Schiraldi & Zeidenberg, 2000; Justice Policy Institute, 1999; Repenning, Powell, Doane & Dunkle, 2000; Powell, 1999). In short, school is one of the safest environments for a child. In 1998, ". . . students were twice [more] likely to be victims of serious violent crime away from school than at school" (Girouard, 2001:1).

Schools can play an important role in preventing school violence. Unfortunately, most (94%) of the resources designed to address violence are utilized after rather than before the violent offending occurs (Burns, Howell, Wiig, Augimeri, Welsh, Loebe & Petechuk, 2003:8). School curriculums, teaching techniques, and the approach used by teachers and administrators to manage the school environment have the potential to enhance or prevent youthful offending (Burns et al., 2003:8). However, as Kenney and McNamara found in their study of six Kentucky high schools' efforts to institute student-based problem-solving programs, administrative support and teacher training and assistance in integrating the materials into the curriculum are vital components of any endeavour (2003:61). The next section focuses on three contemporary issues regarding juveniles in the system that merit consideration.

Disproportionate Minority Contact in the System

One major area of research on juvenile justice policies has focused on minority youth. Specifically, studies have examined various stages of the juvenile justice process and whether a particular racial or ethnic group is over-represented in that stage. For example, are more black youth waived to adult court versus white youth? By contrast, other researchers have examined the actual proportion of minority youth who are incarcerated. In their analysis, Snyder and Sickmund (2006:213) found that custody rates tend to be highest for black youth. In 2003, for every 100,000 black youth in the United States, 754 were in custody in a juvenile facility (Snyder & Sickmund, 2006:213). In addition, these data indicate that African-American youth were more likely to be detained than white youth. For every 100 white youth ages 10-17 in the U.S. population, there were 18 youth detained under the age of 18. For every 100 African-American youth ages 10-17 in the U.S. population, 25 youth under the age of 18 were detained (Snyder & Sickmund, 2006:189).

Disproportionate minority contact has been documented in a number of states. For example, evidence from California, Connecticut, Florida, Illinois, North Carolina, Virginia, and Wisconsin illustrates a pattern in which minority youth are more likely to be transferred to adult court, more likely to be in the county jail, and more likely to be in adult prisons (Ryan & Zeidenberg, 2007:11-12). Similarly, Stahl (2008) reported that detention was more likely for black youth (28%) than white youth (15%) who were involved in drug offenses in 2004. Disproportionate minority contact remains an important component of the Juvenile Justice and Delinquency Prevention Act re-authorizations, and federal and state governments continue to evaluate and address the issue.

Correctional Institutions for Youth

States confront a number of challenges in residential programs for youthful offenders. Kupchik (2007) interviewed 95 young adult offenders incarcerated in juvenile correctional institutions and adult correctional institutions. Although the youth in the juvenile facilities reported more positive staff-inmate interaction and mentoring, youth in the adult facilities rated the availability of institutional services more positively (2007:265). These data suggest that juvenile facilities for youth may be reducing the number of treatment and educational programs offered to youth in confinement.

The size of the institution and overcrowding are also controversial issues. Large institutions for juvenile offenders continue to be the dominant model. For example, juvenile facilities that accommodate more than 100 youth held 48 percent of all youthful offenders in custody in 2002. By contrast, facilities designed to hold no more than 10 youth held 5 percent of all the youth in custody in 2002 (Sickmund, 2006:7). In addition, 14 percent of all the juveniles held were in facilities where the administrators reported that their population exceeded the rated capacity of their institution (Sickmund, 2006:8).

Sexual victimization by other juveniles or staff members is also a significant concern in juvenile institutions. In 2004, administrators indicated that there were more than 2,800 allegations of sexual violence reported in juvenile facilities. Based on Bureau of Justice Statistics calculations, there were 18.1 sexual violence incidents for every 1,000 juvenile beds in the United States (Snyder & Sickmund, 2006:230). These data suggest that youth are more likely to be sexually victimized by other youth and staff in juvenile facilities than adults in adult institutions (Snyder & Sickmund, 2006:231).

In California, conditions of youth in confinement have resulted in both legal action and a plan to change the current system. Legal advocates assert that the Division of Juvenile Justice (formerly the California Youth Authority) has not complied with previous court-ordered deadlines in a number of areas (Rothfeld, 2008). Nonetheless, the state is moving toward closing two of these institutions and is attempting to move from a punitive to a rehabilitative model (Rothfeld, 2008).

Although there have been improvements in youth facilities, there are persistent issues that states will have to address. These include strategies to ensure that there is adequate funding available to provide services to youth in custody, training for staff, and the development and support of alternative sanctions. A commitment of resources is critical to ascertain that youth receive adequate treatment, care, and protection.

Sentencing Youth to Life without Parole

The third issue involves Life Without Parole sentences for youthful offenders. In order to assess the extent of the life without parole sanction, Amnesty International and Human Rights Watch (Amnesty International and Human Rights Watch, 2005) investigated "child offenders" sentenced to life without parole (JLWOP). They found 2,225 inmates who "have been sentenced to spend the rest of their lives in prison for the crimes they committed as children" (2005:1). According to Hartney (2006:3), in each year from 1990 to 2003, about 98 youth under the age of 18 have been admitted to prison who were sentenced to life without possibility of parole.

While the implementation of life sentences varies in the 41 states and federal courts that utilize them, the average is "1.80 per 100,000 children nationwide" (Amnesty International and Human Rights Watch, 2005:1). Relying on state youth populations per 100,000 youth who are 14-17 years old, the rate nationally of youthful offenders serving life without parole is 14.20. The states with the highest rates are (2005:36):

109.6	Louisiana
52.9	Michigan
49.3	Pennsylvania
38.2	Iowa
35.1	Missouri

In fact, four states account for more than half (55%) of the 2,225 LWOP offenders sentenced for felonies committed before the youth were 18 years of age (2005:35):

Pennsylvania	332
Louisiana	317
Michigan	306
Florida	273

Recent reports suggest that more offenders are currently serving LWOP in Pennsylvania than the data published by Amnesty International and Human Rights Watch in 2005 identified. According to Levin (2007), there were 440 such inmates in Pennsylvania prisons in February of 2007.

This sanction continues to be utilized more frequently than in the past. In 2003, although there were 54 "life without parole" sentences recorded, the rate was "three times higher today than it was fifteen years ago" (2007:2). These youth do not typically have a serious prior record; 59 percent of youthful offenders serving life without parole sentences received them on their "first-ever criminal conviction" (Amnesty International and Human Rights Watch, 2005:1). Even more troubling is the number of offenders who were sentenced to life without parole at the age of 13 or 14. According to a report published by the Equal Justice Initiative, there are 73 inmates in nineteen states who are serving such sentences. Pennsylvania leads the nation with 18 inmates now incarcerated for life who were sentenced for crimes committed when they were age 13 or 14 (Liptak, 2007:A24). As Liptak observed, "the United States stands alone in the world in convicting young adolescents as adults and sentencing them to live out their lives in prison" (2007:A24).

Assessing Life without Parole for Youthful Offenders

Despite the fact that the legal issue of the death penalty for young offenders has been resolved, the policy issue of harsh penalties remains. As reported by Amnesty International and Human Rights Watch, "Although it has never ruled on the constitutionality of life without parole for children, the U. S. Supreme Court has often highlighted the inherent differences between youth and adults in the criminal law context" (2005:86). For example, in *Roper* (2005), the justices acknowledged the immaturity and reduced culpability of youth.

The reliance on harsh sanctions like life without parole suggests that "commitment to a juvenile justice system and the youth rehabilitation principles embedded in it" have been relinquished (Amnesty International and Human Rights Watch, 2005:2). As Kurlychek and Johnson (2004) noted, tougher sentencing reflects a focus on public safety, a minimization of rehabilitation, and a lack of consideration of the diminished culpability or blameworthiness of youthful offenders (Benekos & Merlo, 2008).

Based on this review of trends in juvenile justice policy, it appears that the castigatory legislative reforms of the 1990s are well-established. Urbina observed that "young criminals today are being punished for the behavior of their counterparts who committed serious offenses 15 to 20 years ago" (2005:148). While harsh, punitive, and lengthy sanctions appear to conflict with the rationale used by the Court in *Roper* (2005), it is premature to measure if *Roper* will have a significant effect on juvenile justice. In a subsequent survey of undergraduate students, Kalbeitzer and Sevin Goldstein (2006) found that the undergraduate students in their sample did not perceive younger offenders as less culpable than older offenders. Their data suggest that public opinion might contravene the Supreme Court's decision. However, some developments may foreshadow a "softening" or "balancing" in policy.

Understanding and Preventing Youth Victimization

The nature and extent of youth victimization are integral to prevention programs. It is estimated that 2 million youth between the ages of 12 and 17 have experienced posttraumatic stress disorder which is believed to be linked to their experience with violence in the past (Kracke, 2001a:1). In their sample of 3,907 adolescents, Stevens, Ruggiero, Kilpatrick, Resnick, and Saunders (2005) found that 1 in 10 adolescents reported having experienced a number of incidents of sexual or physical assault (2005: 219). Adolescents who are 12 to 17 years of age have a greater risk of being victimized by crime than children who are 11 years of age or younger. Finkelhor and Ormrod (2000) analyzed 1997 FBI data from 12 states and found that family members were the more likely offenders when the children were under the age of 5 but youth had a greater likelihood of being victimized by adolescent peers (2000:8). Thus, unlike younger children, both peers and adults victimize them during this phase of their development (Finkelhor & Ormrod, 2000:7).

Not only is youth victimization a significant problem in its own right, but research suggests that it results in more victimization, violent offending, and drug use in later life. Previously, researchers studied the effects of child maltreatment on subsequent delinquent and criminal behavior. However, until recently, little research focused on adolescent maltreatment as distinct; i.e., not simply a part of the larger problem of child maltreatment (Widom, 1995). Menard (2002) analyzed data from the National Youth Survey and reported that adolescent violent victimization augments the victim's chances of being a violent offender or an adult victim, increases the probability of becoming a property offender as an adult, and "doubles the odds of problem drug use in adulthood" (Menard, 2002:14).

In analyzing data from the Rochester Youth Development Study, Ireland, Smith, and Thornberry reported that maltreatment experienced only during adolescence, and continuing maltreatment which victimized a youth during childhood and adolescence, were related to delinquency and drug use (2002:383). The research illustrates the importance of understanding the long-term effects of substantiated maltreatment (2002:366). In their sample, adolescent victims of maltreatment had a greater likelihood of arrest than those who had not experienced victimization (Ireland, Smith & Thornberry, 2002:387).

To provide assistance and services to victims of domestic violence and child maltreatment, the National Council of Juvenile and Family Court Judges collaborated with an advisory group to develop effective intervention programs (Kracke, 2001b:1). The "Green Book" provides a format for establishing a comprehensive and cooperative strategy to deal with domestic violence and child maltreatment among the juvenile and criminal courts, agencies involved in child welfare and protection, and various interested groups in the community (Kracke, 2001b:1; Ireland, Smith & Thornberry, 2002). Over the course of five years, six communities were funded and assisted in their efforts to implement the recommendations of the "Green Book." By collaborating with other agencies and organizations, there is evidence of a more integrated systemic approach and the opportunity to treat the entire family (Caliber Associates, 2004:i).

In 2000, the Office of Juvenile Justice and Delinquency Prevention created the Child Protection Division to safeguard and prevent the victimization of children and youth (Cullen, 2001:1). A promising initiative, The Safe Kids/Safe Streets project was designed to service youth and families at five different sites in the United States. This project attempted to lower the incidence of child and adolescent victimization by implementing a collaborative strategy that incorporated assisting the family, developing programs in neighborhoods, enhancing services provided by child protection and welfare organizations, instituting court reforms, and engaging child advocacy center teams that were comprised of law enforcement, court, medical, and social service agency professionals who jointly investigated abuse and neglect and interceded in the lives of child and adolescent victims (Cullen, 2001:6). The Safe Kids/Safe Streets initiative exemplified a comprehensive collaborative approach to child maltreatment. Results from the five program sites illustrate that more cooperation is possible; and their success demonstrates that collaborations in prevention and treatment can also occur in other areas (Cronin, Gragg, Schultz & Eisen, 2006:9).

Research on violence prevention programs requires a thorough assessment of the implementation of the program components. Such an evaluation was conducted on violence prevention programs and drug prevention programs for children from infancy to age 19 in 147 sites with funding from the federal government (Mihalic, Irwin, Fagan, Ballard & Elliot, 2004). The researchers evaluated "implementation fidelity...a determination of how well the program is being implemented in comparison with the original program design" (Mihalic et al., 2004:8) and found that high fidelity was attained. They also found, however, that some sites experienced difficulties in other areas such as providing adequate exposure to the program and being able to offer the number of sessions intended. Their findings illustrate the importance of not only replicating successful strategies but also making sure that there is adequate support to deliver them to the intended population (Mihalic et al., 2004:9).

Programs for Children and Parents

Child abuse and neglect continue to affect the victims long after the actual incidences have occurred. However, research evidence demonstrates the value of early intervention and delinquency prevention programs and the public support for such endeavors (Merlo, 2000). When Cullen, Wright, Brown, Moon, Blankenship, and Applegate (1998) surveyed the public, they found that "a clear majority" of citizens still prefer "governmental efforts designed to intervene with families and children" (1998:197). Similarly, in Tennessee, Moon, Sundt, Cullen, and Wright found that the public enthusiastically supported allotting money for programs that focused on prevention rather than for building new prisons (2000:55).

Programs that have been particularly successful work with families whose children are in preschool, elementary, and middle school. One early intervention initiative, "The Incredible Years: Parents, Teachers, and Children Training Series," assists parents with children from ages 3 to 12. The short term program endeavors to re-enforce and enhance the parents' supervision and parenting skills and ameliorate their confidence (Alvarado & Kumpfer, 2000:12). Program staff also engages parents in their children's academic activities. Research demonstrates that this program is successful in reducing children's inappropriate behaviors and involving them in academic pursuits (Alvarado & Kumpfer, 2000:12).

Early intervention and parenting programs emphasize the prevention, education, and treatment approach (PET). In economic costs and outcome measures, as well as in humanitarian costs, these initiatives are viewed as preferable to the reactive policies characterized by retribution, adultification, and punishment (RAP). It would appear that programs which stress collaboration among parents, schools, the juvenile justice system, and child welfare agencies, and have clear goals (i.e., informed by prior research), have the greatest likelihood of success.

Juvenile Justice Legislation

As previously discussed, in 1995, Pennsylvania legislators enacted Act 33. It prioritized the protection of the public interest and mandated programs that focused on community protection, offender accountability, and competency development to insure that youth would develop into responsible and constructive members of the community (Juvenile Court Act, 42 PA.C.S.A., Sec. 6301; Torbet & Thomas, 1997:2). The legislation stipulates that the victim, the community, and the offender are to be given "balanced attention" and that the resources of the Commonwealth are to be distributed to all three of these groups to attain the goals (Juvenile Court Judges' Commission, 1997:3). Restorative justice emphasizes the importance of actively and extensively involving the offender, the victim, and the community, in the juvenile justice process (Bazemore & Umbreit, 2001:1). It is believed that through the commitment and activities of these diverse groups, reintegration of the offender and the restoration of the community can be attained.

In an effort to effectively develop the principles and objectives of the Balanced and Restorative Justice model (see Bazemore & Umbreit, 1995), the Pennsylvania Commission on Crime and Delinquency (PCCD) has funded training for juvenile justice professionals, assisted the juvenile court judges in the state to successfully institute the goals and services, established services for victims, including juvenile who are the victims of crime, and helped to evaluate the programs (PCCD, 7/27/02).

Balanced and Restorative Justice (BARJ) appeals to conservative, moderate, and liberal groups. With an emphasis on community safety and accountability, BARJ is enthusiastically supported by conservatives because it emphasizes a tougher stance toward juvenile offenders and a concern for the harm that their behaviors caused for victims and communities. Moderates find it appealing because it is an attempt to focus on the victim and the offender without being too lopsided in its approach. It is perceived as neither too harsh nor too lenient. Liberals endorse BARJ because it stresses competency development which underscores treatment programs for youth. As Urban, St. Cyr, and Decker (2003) note, "Putting restorative justice programs into practice does not occur quickly or easily, as it involves systemic changes that often conflict with existing practices and philosophies" (2003:475). Typically, the actual operation and support of BARJ vary from jurisdiction to jurisdiction. Most commonly, BARJ is applied to juveniles on probation or unofficial supervision.

Balanced and Restorative Justice stresses the value of victim-offender mediation, community conferencing, and other strategies intended to make the youthful offender accountable and cognizant of the harm done to the victim and community. For over twenty years, these kinds of victim offender mediation programs have been utilized in the United States, Canada, and Europe (Bazemore & Umbreit, 2001:2). Research to determine effects on juvenile recidivism, victims, and community safety has been undertaken.

For example, in her study of restorative justice in Arizona, Rodriguez (2005) found that restorative justice participants had lower recidivism rates than juveniles who were in traditional supervision programs (2005:121). These data suggest that restorative justice programs play an important part in juvenile justice.

Conclusion

The juvenile court in the early part of the twenty-first century bears little resemblance to the juvenile court of 1899. Today, youth are perceived as miniature adults and many current policies are designed to punish rather than prevent youthful offending. Society appears to be an intransigent and stern parent rather than a loving and understanding one.

Although the spike in juvenile violence in the late 1980s and early 1990s did not continue, legislators responded to youth violence with new legislation, revisions of existing juvenile law, and plenty of hyperbolic language advocating a get-tough approach to youth. Legislative actions resulted in a harsh, adult-like stance and states hurriedly put the new sanctions in place. One manifestation was the decision to try more youth as adults. The largest number transferred to adult court occurred in 1994, when 12,100 youth were waived (Puzzanchera, 2003:1).

Unfortunately, elected officials neglected to ask, "Where are the data?" (Merlo, 2000). Many of these legislative provisions went into effect when juvenile crime was decreasing. The short-term consequences are troubling: an understanding of the cognitive development of youth and adolescence has largely disappeared, schools routinely suspend or expel youth for behavior that would not have warranted such a draconian response ten years ago, and the jail and prison population of youth as well as the use of life without parole sentences have increased significantly.

There is no evidence that one agency or organization can effectively prevent youth from engaging in criminal activity or treat all youthful offenders. Relying on the juvenile justice system to prevent juvenile delinquency by implementing harsher sanctions is an untenable goal. In the OJJDP Study Group on Very Young Offenders (under the age of 13), there was consensus about the need to provide comprehensive and coordinated services to youth who are experiencing difficulty (Burns et al. 2003:12). The Study Group advocated the integration of agencies and services to prevent juvenile delinquency or to provide appropriate interventions for youth who have engaged in such activities and their families (Burns et al., 2003:12).

Early intervention programs that involve parents and tend to be home-or school-based are emphasized by Burns and colleagues (2003:3). Parenting programs, mental health services, and educational programs are examples of successful and cost effective strategies. As Burns et al. indicate, these kinds of programs prevent or reduce delinquent involvement, enhance educational achievement, reduce welfare costs, and improve family relationships (2003:5). Similarly, Welsh, Loeber, Stevens, Stouthamer-Loeber, Cohen, and Farrington (2008) substantiate these findings and point out that "…these non-punitive interventions need only produce a modest level of crime reduction to pay back program costs and produce a dividend for society" (2008:20).

Research suggests that the public endorses these strategies. In an analysis of data on public attitudes conducted in Tennessee, Moon, Cullen, and Wright found that ". . . 80% to more than 90% of the sample favored programs to support at-risk youths, even if it meant raising taxes. This included programs such as preschool interventions, family interventions, drug education and school-based initiatives" (2003:42). A majority of these same respondents expressed their support for Big Brothers/Big Sisters programs which they viewed as more effective in reducing delinquency than imprisoning youth, transferring them to adult court, and putting them on probation (Moon, Cullen & Wright, 2003:42-43). In addition, Applegate and Davis (2006) found some evidence among Florida respondents of a softening in public attitudes toward sentencing of juvenile offenders. Similarly, Nagin, Piquero, Scott, and Steinberg (2006) found Pennsylvania respondents more willing to pay for rehabilitation rather than incarceration. Taken together, Cullen (2006) contends that there is ample evidence to support the rehabilitation of youthful offenders.

It is not clear if the emphasis on punishing youthful offenders will affect the impetus to establish programs designed to identify and treat adolescents who may be victims of abuse or neglect (Ireland, Smith & Thornberry, 2002:387). Although there is evidence of society's concern for child victims, the public has not focused its attention and interest on adolescent victims of abuse and neglect.

Presently, the juvenile justice system's response to youthful delinquent and pre-delinquent behavior is somewhat equivocal. Legislators have developed and endorsed punitive approaches but they also appear poised to support preventive strategies. With a decrease in the incidence of school shootings, extensive media coverage has dissipated. Clearly, terrorism and the economy have replaced youth violence as the *cause celebre*. Bernard's research on the cyclical nature of juvenile justice would seem to indicate that the United States is currently shifting (albeit slowly) in the direction of a more prevention oriented and liberal approach toward youth (Benekos & Merlo, 2008; Bernard, 1992; Merlo, 2000). That shift may help to usher in a new era in juvenile justice. A comprehensive approach might involve more diverse perspectives, a greater appreciation of and understanding of youth, and the prevention of child and youth victimization and offending.

This book provides the reader with an insightful understanding of juvenile delinquency and juvenile justice policies. The contributors discuss the major theories of juvenile delinquency along with biological and psychological theories, the relationship between drugs and delinquency, school violence, status offenders and the juvenile justice system, waiver to adult criminal court, disproportionate minority contact in the system, girls and juvenile justice, juveniles in institutional settings, capital punishment and juveniles, and comparative juvenile justice. As the authors present and discuss the controversies in juvenile justice and delinquency, consider how the juvenile justice system functions and how agencies and even countries might work together collaboratively to address juvenile delinquency and youth crime in a more proactive way. A comprehensive approach might involve more diverse perspectives, a greater appreciation and understanding of youth, and the prevention of child and youth victimization and offending.

References

Albanese, J. (1993). *Dealing With Delinquency: The Future of Juvenile Justice*. Chicago, IL: Nelson-Hall Publishers.

Alvarado, R. & K. Kumpfer (2000). "Strengthening America's Families." *Juvenile Justice*, 7:8-18.

Amnesty International/Human Rights Watch (2005). *The Rest of Their Lives: Life Without Parole for Children Offenders in the United States*. New York, NY: Human Rights Watch.

Applegate, B.K. & R.K. Davis (2006). "Public Views on Sentencing Juvenile Murderers: The Impact of Offender, Offense, and Perceived Maturity." *Youth Violence and Juvenile Justice*, 4:55-74.

Austin, J., K.D. Johnson & M. Gregoriou (2000). *Juveniles in Adult Prisons and Jails: A National Assessment*. Washington, DC: Bureau of Justice Assistance.

Banks, G. (2007). "Juveniles Languish in Adult Jails." *Pittsburgh Post-Gazette*, (November 19):A-1, A-4.

Bazelon, L.A. (2000). "Exploding the Superpredator Myth: Why Infancy is the Preadolescent's Best Defense in Juvenile Court." *New York University Law Review*, 75:159-198.

Bazemore, G. & M. Umbreit (2001). "A Comparison of Four Restorative Conferencing Models." *Juvenile Justice Bulletin*. Washington, DC: U.S. Department of Justice, Office of Juvenile Justice and Delinquency Prevention, (February):1-19.

Bazemore, G. & M. Umbreit (1995). *Balanced and Restorative Justice for Juveniles. A National Strategy for Juvenile Justice in the 21st Century. The Balanced and Restorative Justice Project*. Washington, DC: U.S. Department of Justice, Office of Juvenile Justice and Delinquency Prevention.

Benekos, P.J. & A.V. Merlo (2008). "Juvenile Justice: The Legacy of Punitive Policy." *Youth Violence and Juvenile Justice*, 6:28-46.

Benekos, P.J. & A.V. Merlo (2006). *Crime Control, Politics & Policy*, Second Edition. Newark, NJ: LexisNexis/Matthew Bender & Company, Inc.

Benekos, P.J. & A.V. Merlo (2002). "Reaffirming Juvenile Justice." In R. M. Muraskin & A. R. Roberts (eds.) *Visions for Change: Criminal Justice in the 21st Century*, Third Edition, pp. 265-286. Upper Saddle River, N.J: Prentice Hall.

Bernard, T.J. (1992). *The Cycle of Juvenile Justice*. New York, NY: Oxford University Press.

Blumstein, A. (1996). *Youth Violence, Guns, and Illicit Drug Markets*. Washington, DC: National Institute of Justice, Research Preview (June).

Bogos, P.M. (1997). *"Expelled. No Excuses. No Exceptions." – Michigan's Zero Tolerance Policy in Response to School Violence:* MCLA Section 380.1311. *University of Detroit Mercy Law Review,* 74d:357-387.

Bortner, M.A. (1988). *Delinquency and Justice: An Age of Crisis.* New York, NY: McGraw-Hill.

Brooks, K., V. Schiraldi & J. Ziedenberg (2000). "School House Hype: Two Years Later." (November 6). Available at www.cjcj.org.

Burns, B.J., J.C. Howell, J.K. Wiig, L.K. Augimeri, B.C. Welsh, R. Loeber & D. Petechuck (2003). *Treatment, Services, and Intervention Programs for Child Delinquents.* Washington, DC: U.S. Department of Justice, Office of Juvenile Justice and Delinquency Prevention.

Butts, J.A. & H.N. Snyder (2006). *Too Soon to Tell: Deciphering Recent Trends in Youth Violence.* Chicago, IL: Chapin Hall Center for Children at the University of Chicago.

Caliber Associates Inc. (2004). *The Greenbook Demonstration Initiative: Interim Evaluation Report.* Fairfax, VA.

CNN (2002). "Zero Tolerance under Fire after Expulsion over Bread Knife." http://cnnstudent-news.cnn.com/2002/fyi/teachers.ednews/03/20/bread.knife.expulsion.ap/index.html (March 20) [Retrieved March 7, 2008].

Commonweal (2007). "Special Report: California Governor Signs Major Juvenile Justice Reform Bill – Nearly Half of the State's Youth Corrections Population Will Now Be 'Realigned' to County Programs and Facilities." http://www.iecomm.org/CALJuvJusticeReformsigned byGovernorSep4.pdf/ [Retrieved October 15, 2007].

Cronin, R.F. Gragg, D. Schultz & K. Eisen (2006). *Lessons Learned From Safe Kids/Safe Streets.* Washington, DC: U.S. Department of Justice, Office of Juvenile Justice and Delinquency Prevention.

Cullen, F.T. (2006). "It's Time to Reaffirm Rehabilitation." *Criminology & Public Policy,* 5(4):665-672.

Cullen, F.T., J.P. Wright, S. Brown, M. Moon, M.B. Blankenship & B.K. Applegate (1998). "Public Support for Early Intervention Programs: Implications for a Progressive Policy Agenda." *Crime & Delinquency,* 44:187-204.

Cullen, T. (2001). *Keeping Children Safe: OJJDP's Child Protection Division.* Washington, DC: U.S. Department of Justice, Office of Juvenile Justice and Delinquency Prevention.

DiIulio, J.J. (1995). "The Coming of the Superpredators." *Weekly Standard,* (November 27):23.

Dorfman, L. & V. Schiraldi (2001). *Off Balance: Youth, Race & Crime in the News.* Washington, DC: Youth Law Center, Building Blocks for Youth.

Feld, B. (1999). *Bad Kids: Race and the Transformation of the Juvenile Court.* New York, NY: Oxford University Press.

Feld, B. (1993). *Justice for Children: The Right to Counsel and the Juvenile Court.* Boston, MA: Northeastern University Press.

Ferdinand, T.N. & M.J. McDermott (2002). "Joining Punishment and Treatment in Substantive Equality." *Criminal Justice Policy Review,* 13:87-116.

Finkelhor, D. & R. Ormrod (2000). *Characteristics of Crimes Against Juveniles.* Washington, DC: U.S. Department of Justice, Office of Juvenile Justice and Delinquency Prevention.

Girouard, C. (2001). "School Resource Officer Training Program." *OJJDP Fact Sheet*. Washington, DC: Office of Juvenile Justice and Delinquency Prevention.

Hartney, C. (2006). *Youth Under Age 18 in the Adult Criminal Justice System*. Oakland, CA: National Council on Crime and Delinquency.

Ireland, T.O., C.A. Smith & T.P. Thornberry (2002). "Developmental Issues in the Impact of Child Maltreatment on Later Delinquency and Drug Use." *Criminology*, 40:359-400.

Justice Policy Institute (1999). "New Report Shows No Increase in School Shooting Deaths over Six-Year Period." cjcj.org/jpi/schoolhousepr.html

Juvenile Court Act (1995). 42 PA. C.S.A., Sec. 6301.

Juvenile Court Judges' Commission (1997). *Balanced and Restorative Justice in Pennsylvania: A New Mission and Changing Roles within the Juvenile Justice System*. Pamphlet. Harrisburg, PA.

Kalbeitzer, R. & N.E. Sevin Goldstein (2006). "Assessing the 'Evolving Standards of Decency': Perceptions of Capital Punishment for Juveniles." *Behavioral Sciences and the Law*, 24:157-178.

Kappeler, V.E. & G.W. Potter (2005). *The Mythology of Crime and Criminal Justice*, Fourth Edition. Long Grove, IL: Waveland Press.

Kappeler, V.E., M. Blumberg & G.W. Potter (2000). *The Mythology of Crime and Criminal Justice*, Third Edition. Prospect Heights, IL: Waveland Press.

Kenney, D.J. & R. McNamara (2003). "Reducing Crime and Conflict in Kentucky's Schools." *Youth Violence and Juvenile Justice*, 1(1):46-63.

Kracke, K. (2001a). *Children's Exposure to Violence: The Safe Start Initiative*. Washington, DC: U.S. Department of Justice, Office of Juvenile Justice and Delinquency Prevention.

Kracke, K. (2001b). *The "Green Book" Demonstration*. Washington, DC: U.S. Department of Justice, Office of Juvenile Justice and Delinquency Prevention.

Kupchik, A. (2007). "The Correctional Experiences of Youth in Adult and Juvenile Prisons." *Justice Quarterly*, 24(2):247-270.

Kurlychek, M.C. & B.D. Johnson (2004). "The Juvenile Penalty: A Comparison of Juvenile and Young Adult Sentencing Outcomes in Criminal Court." *Criminology*, 42:485-515.

Levick, M.L. (2000). "Zero Tolerance: Mandatory Sentencing Meets the One Room Schoolhouse." *Kentucky Children's Rights Journal*, 8:5-6.

Levin, S. (2007). "How Teens End Up Put Away for Life." *Pittsburgh Post-Gazette*, (February 18): A1, A12.

Liptak, A. (2007). "Lifers as Teenagers, Now Seeking Second Chance." *New York Times*, (October 17): A1, A24.

Magill, S. (1998). "Adolescents: Public Enemy #1." *Crime & Delinquency*, 44:121-126.

Massey, H.J. (2006). "Disposing of Children: The Eighth Amendment and Juvenile Life Without Parole after Roper." *Boston College Law Review*, 1:1-16. Available at SSRN: http://ssrn.com/abstract=926758

Menard, S. (2002). *Short-and Long-Term Consequences of Adolescent Victimization. Youth Violence and Research Bulletin*. Washington, DC: U.S. Department of Justice, Office of Juvenile Justice and Delinquency Prevention.

Merlo, A.V. (2000). "Juvenile Justice at the Crossroads: Presidential Address to the Academy of Criminal Justice Sciences." *Justice Quarterly*, 17:639-661.

Merlo, A.V. & P.J. Benekos (2003). "Defining Juvenile Justice in the 21st Century." *Youth Violence and Juvenile Justice*, 1(3):276-288.

Merlo, A.V. & P.J. Benekos (2000a). *What's Wrong with the Criminal Justice System?: Ideology, Politics, and the Media*. Cincinnati, OH: Anderson Publishing Co.

Merlo, A.V. & P.J. Benekos (2000b). "The End of Innocence: Images of Youth and Juvenile Justice Policies." Paper presented at the Annual Meeting of the American Society of Criminology in San Francisco, November 15.

Merlo, A.V., P.J. Benekos & W.J. Cook (2001). "Juvenile Justice: A Study of Student Attitudes." Paper presented at the Annual Meeting of the American Society of Criminology, Atlanta, GA, November 9.

Mihalic, S., K. Irwin, A. Fagan, D. Ballard & D. Elliott (2004). *Successful Program Implementation: Lessons from Blueprints*. Washington, DC: U.S. Department of Justice, Office of Juvenile Justice and Delinquency Prevention.

Miller, J.G. (1996). *Search and Destroy: African-American Males in the Criminal Justice System*. New York, NY: Cambridge University Press.

Moon, M.M., F.T. Cullen & J.P. Wright (2003). "It Takes a Village: Public Willingness to Help Wayward Youth." *Youth Violence and Juvenile Justice*, 1(1):32-45.

Moon, M.M., J. Sundt, F.T. Cullen & J.P. Wright (2000). "Is Child Saving Dead? Public Support for Juvenile Rehabilitation." *Crime & Delinquency*, 46:38-62.

Mumola, C.J. (2005). *Suicide and Homicide in State Prisons and Local Jails*. Washington, DC: U.S. Department of Justice, Bureau of Justice Statistics.

Nagin, D.S., A.R. Piquero, E. Scott & L. Steinberg (2006). "Public Preferences for Rehabilitation Versus Incarceration of Juvenile Offenders: Evidence from a Contingent Valuation Survey." *Criminology & Public Policy*, 5 (4):627-652.

New York Times (2002). "High School Expels Junior after Guard Finds Knife in Truck." (March 21):A23.

(The) Pennsylvania Commission on Crime and Delinquency. pccd.state.pa.us/JUVENILE/barj1.htm (7/27/02).

Platt, A.M. (1977). *The Child Savers: The Invention of Delinquency*, Second Edition. Chicago, IL: University of Chicago Press.

Powell, H. (1999). "School Violence: Statistics Reveal School Violence Declining." *The Mentor*, 1(1):4-6. Center for Justice Research and Policy, Mercyhurst College.

Puzzanchera, C.M. (2003). *Delinquency Cases Waived to Criminal Court, 1990-1999*. Washington, DC: U.S. Department of Justice, Office of Juvenile Justice and Delinquency Prevention.

Puzzanchera, C.M., B. Adams, H. Snyder & W. Hang (2006). Easy Access to FBI Arrest Statistics 1994-2004. Online. Available: http://ojjdp.ncjrs.gov/ojstatbb/ezaucr/

Repenning, K., H. Powell, A. Doane & H. Dunkle (2000). "Demystifying School Violence: A National, State, and Local Perspective on the Phenomenon of School Violence." Paper presented at the Annual Meeting of the Academy of Criminal Justice Sciences, New Orleans, LA.

Rodriguez, N. (2005). "Restorative Justice, Communities, and Delinquency: Whom Do We Reintegrate?" *Criminology & Public Policy*, 4(1):103-130.

Roper v. Simmons, 543 U.S. 551, 578 (2005).

Rothfeld, M. (2008). "Advocates Urge a Judge to Appoint a Receiver to Take Over A System They Say Remains Broken Despite Long-Standing Promises to Fix It." *Los Angeles Times*, (18 February). http://article.latimes.com/2008/02/18/metro/me-youth18. [Retrieved February 23, 2008].

Ryan, L. & J. Ziedenberg (2007). *The Consequences Aren't Minor: The Impact of Prosecuting Youth as Adults and Strategies for Reform*. Washington, DC: Campaign for Youth Justice.

Sabol, W.J., T.D. Minton & P.M. Harrison (2007). *Prison and Jail Inmates at Midyear 2006*. Washington, DC: U.S. Department of Justice, Bureau of Justice Statistics.

Schissel, B. (1997). *Blaming Children: Youth Crime, Moral Panics and the Politics of Hate*. Halifax, Nova Scotia: Fernwood Publishing.

Schwartz, H. (2002). "The Court's Terrible Two." *The Nation*, (July 22). www.thenation.com

Sickmund, M. (2006). *Juvenile Residential Facility Census, 2002: Selected Findings*. Washington, DC: U.S. Department of Justice, Office of Juvenile Justice and Delinquency Prevention.

Sickmund, M., H.N. Snyder & E. Poe-Yamagata (1997). *Juvenile Offenders and Victims: 1997 Update on Violence*. Washington, DC: U.S. Department of Justice, Office of Juvenile Justice and Delinquency Prevention.

Skiba, R. & R. Peterson (1999). "The Dark Side of Zero Tolerance: Can Punishment Lead to Safe Schools?" *Phi Delta Kappan*, 80:372-376, 381-382.

Snyder, H.N. (2008). *Juvenile Arrests 2005*. Washington, DC: U.S. Department of Justice, Office of Juvenile Justice and Delinquency Prevention.

Snyder, H.N. (2006). *Juvenile Arrests 2004*. Washington, DC: U.S. Department of Justice, Office of Juvenile Justice and Delinquency and Prevention.

Snyder, H. N. & M. Sickmund (2006). *Juvenile Offenders and Victims: 2006 National Report*. Washington, DC: U.S. Department of Justice, Office of Juvenile Justice and Delinquency Prevention.

Snyder, H.N. & M. Sickmund (1999). *Juvenile Offenders and Victims: 1999 National Report*. Pittsburgh, PA: National Center for Juvenile Justice.

Sprott, J. (1998). "Understanding Public Opposition to a Separate Youth Justice System." *Crime & Delinquency*, 44:399-411.

Stahl, A. (2008). *Drug Offense Cases in Juvenile Courts, 1985-2004*. Washington, DC: U.S. Department of Justice, Office of Juvenile Justice and Delinquency Prevention.

Stevens, T.N., K.J. Ruggiero, D.G. Kilpatrick, H.S. Resnick & B.E. Saunders (2005). "Variables Differentiating Singly and Multiply Victimized Youth: Results from the National Survey of Adolescents and Implications for Secondary Prevention." *Child Maltreatment*, 10(3):211-223.

Strom, K. (2000). *Profile of State Prisoners under Age 18, 1985-97*. Washington, DC: U.S. Department of Justice, Bureau of Justice Statistics.

Taylor, R.W., E.J. Fritsch & T.J. Caeti (2007). *Juvenile Justice: Policies, Programs, and Practices*, Second Edition. New York, NY: Glencoe/McGraw Hill.

Torbet, P. & D. Thomas (1997). "Balanced and Restorative Justice: Implementing the Philosophy." *Pennsylvania Progress*, (October):4.

Torbet, P. & L. Szymanski (1998). *State Legislative Responses to Violent Juvenile Crime: 1996-1997 Update*. Washington, DC: U.S. Department of Justice, Office of Juvenile Justice and Delinquency Prevention.

Triplett, R. (2000). "The Dramatization of Evil: Reacting to Juvenile Delinquency During The 1990s." In S.S. Simpson (ed.) *Of Crime and Criminality*, pp.121-138. Thousand Oaks, CA: Pine Forge.

Tufts, J. & J.V. Roberts (2002). "Sentencing Juvenile Offenders: Comparing Public Preferences and Judicial Practice." *Criminal Justice Policy Review*, 13(1):46-64.

Uniform Crime Reports (2007). *Crime in the United States 2006*. www.fbi.gov/ucr/cius2006/data/table_37.html [Retrieved October 12, 2007].

Urban, L.S., J.L. St. Cyr & S.H. Decker (2003). "Goal Conflict in the Juvenile Court." *Journal of Contemporary Criminal Justice*, 9(4):454-479.

Urbina, M.G. (2005). "Transferring Juveniles to Adult Court in Wisconsin: Practitioners Voice their Views." *Criminal Justice Studies*, 18(2):147-172.

Vogel, J. (1994). "Throw Away the Key: Juvenile Offenders Are the Willie Hortons of the '90s." *UTNE Reader*, (July/August):56-60.

Welsh, B., R. Loeber, B. Stevens, M. Stouthamer-Loeber, M. Cohen & D. Farrington (2008). "Costs of Juvenile Crime in Urban Areas." *Youth Violence and Juvenile Justice*, 6(1):3-27.

Widom, C.S. (1995). *Victims of Childhood Sexual Abuse-Later Criminal Consequences. Research in Brief*. Washington, DC: U.S. Department of Justice, Office of Justice Programs.

CHAPTER 2

What Causes Delinquency? Classical and Sociological Theories of Crime

Pamela Tontodonato
Frank E. Hagan

Introduction

Controversies have surrounded the functions, scope, and goals of the juvenile justice system since its inception, and the same is true of explanations of juvenile offending. It will become clear to the reader that those who explore the etiology of delinquency have a difficult task at hand. "Juvenile delinquency" encompasses a wide variety of behaviors committed by juveniles, and theories of delinquency vary in their breadth and depth. Fundamentally, Classical and Positivistic theories of delinquency fall into several paradigms that differ regarding human nature (free will versus determinism).

Discussions of theoretical material can be confusing if not overwhelming. Nonetheless, it is important to be familiar with the major theoretical perspectives in the field, since, whether explicitly or implicitly, notions about the causes of delinquency are embedded in policy decisions made about crime (For further discussion, see Paternoster & Bachman, 2001).

In this chapter, we review the major theories of juvenile delinquency. We begin with a presentation of the Classical approach, which reflects a set of underlying assumptions quite different from the theories associated with the Positivist school. The latter type, which focuses on biological and psychological correlates, is critiqued in Chapter 3. We then examine a variety of social structure, social process, and social control explanations of crime, which, together with more recent integrated and developmental theories, follow the positivistic notion of determinism. These theories assume that biological, psychological, and sociological factors cause crime and delinquency, and by following the tenets of the scientific method, these factors can be discovered. Last, we review social reaction and critical theories of delinquency, including a discussion of the major features of radical and feminist theories of crime. The policy implications of these theories and perspectives will be discussed throughout.

Correlates of Delinquency

Before exploring these theories, let us examine some of the key variables or factors associated with delinquency. These will be included as major elements in most of the theories that we will review. Most of the offenders arrested in the U.S. are young, and most delinquents mature out of crime by their mid-twenties (Snyder, 2004; Snyder & Sickmund, 2006). Gender is the best predictor of delinquency in that most offenders are male (with the exception being that females are more likely to be apprehended for running away and prostitution). The role of other demographic factors such as social class and race is the subject of debate. There is some evidence that the majority of those who are arrested for street crimes and labeled as delinquent are from the lower class. It is likely, however, that official statistics like the *Uniform Crime Reports* undercount deviance of middle- and upper-class persons. Official crime and delinquency data indicate that ethnic and racial minorities are over-represented in the criminal and juvenile justice systems (Pastore & Maguire, 2006; Snyder, 2004; Snyder & Sickmund, 2006). This difference reflects the effects of socioeconomic factors more so than inherent deviant tendencies within each group. Delinquency is higher in urban than suburban or rural areas (Hagan, 2007: 81). Crime is not randomly distributed but is concentrated in neighborhoods characterized by racial segregation, poverty, and single parent households (Sampson, 2006). Victimization data reveal similar patterns, indicating differences by age, gender, ethnicity, race, income, and residence (Pastore & Maguire, 2006).

Other key correlates of delinquency include the family, school, and peers. In an exhaustive review of the literature looking at the role of the family in delinquency, Rolf Loeber and Magda Stouthammer-Loeber (Loeber & Stouthammer-Loeber, 1986:97) found the most powerful predictors to be lack of parental supervision, parental rejection, and lack of parental involvement. Medium strength predictors included parental marital relations and parental criminality, and weaker predictors were lack of parental discipline, parental health, and parental absence. The lack of formal education has a major impact on delinquency and crime. Thus, schools, peers, and community also have a major impact on delinquency, as do economic forces such as poverty, inequality, and unemployment.

Considering the juvenile justice system, the early juvenile courts recognized the important role parents play in filling the physical, emotional, and educational needs of their children. Through the doctrine of *parens patriae* (state as parent), the court had the right to help children in cases where their parents were unable or unwilling to do so and to prevent crime by intervening with those children at risk.

This brief review also points to the fact that the causes and correlates of delinquency do not exist simply at the individual level but also at the macro level (group/community/society). We now turn to major paradigmatic approaches in the etiology of crime and delinquency.

Classical Theories

Theories of delinquency can be subsumed under a number of "schools of thought." *Classical theories* of crime and delinquency emphasize free will and rationality on the part of the offender. Prior to the articulation of the ideas expressed in the classical school, the administration of justice in Europe was cruel, uncertain, and unpredictable. Designed to control the "dangerous classes," penal policy was unfair and arbitrary. There was little connection between the severity of the act and the severity of the punishment imposed. Cesare Beccaria (1738-1794) and Jeremy Bentham (1748-1832) were the major proponents of classical ideas. "Let the punishment fit the crime" (proportionality) is a succinct way of summarizing Beccaria's thoughts. His book, *Dei Delitti e Delle Pene (On Crimes and Punishments)*, originally published in 1764, had a major impact on continental European and Anglo-American criminal justice systems (Beccaria, 1963; Bentham, 1823).

Beccaria viewed individuals as acting due to *free will* and as motivated by *hedonism* (pleasure seeking). Offenders (like non-offenders) are assumed to be rational in their decision-making process. Aiming to maximize pleasure and minimize pain, individuals choose to commit deviant acts unless the perceived punishments outweigh the anticipated pleasures. Behavior could thus be guided (deterred) by fear of punishment. In order to achieve the greatest deterrent effect, punishment should be swift, certain, and severe enough to remove any benefit that would accrue from committing the criminal act. Bentham advocated "utilitarianism" or "penal pharmacy." Utilitarianism is a practical philosophy that follows Beccaria's notion of "the greatest good for the greatest number." Both Bentham and Beccaria felt that an action is right if it produces more pleasure than pain and that a specific prescription of punishment could be assessed according to the seriousness of each crime. Although classical theory was a great improvement over the arbitrary justice that preceded it, its assumption of equality of offense and offenders ignored circumstances such as mental state, age, repeat offending, and the like. The classical school was more of a philosophy of law and justice than a theory of criminal behavior. Its philosophical principles were often viewed by its adherents as fact, rather than as theories to be analyzed by empirical evidence (Thomas & Hepburn, 1983).

Neoclassical (new classical) theories represent revisions to, and a revival of, classical theory. The neoclassical approach reflects the modifications necessary to implement classical ideas in a real world justice system. Thus, the legal system in the United States assumes free will and rationality while recognizing that there may be some mitigating circumstances to consider. In the United States, the resurgence of classical ideas in modern times has been reflected in the movement towards greater use of determinate sentencing and mandatory punishments such as "three strikes and you're out." Although admitting environmental, psychological, and other factors as mitigating influences on behavior, the emphasis is still on the free choice of the offender. Contemporary writers such as Gary Becker and James Q. Wilson (Becker, 1968; Wilson, 1983) are less concerned with treatment and rehabilitation of offenders and more concerned with establishing a punishment model based on classical ideas. Becker advocates a "cost/benefit" model of crime and delinquency in which individuals freely choose crime based on their estimates of being caught. Wilson calls for an approach that ignores criminology's overconcern with the search for basic causes of deviance and instead supports a model which emphasizes incapacitation (this is viewed as being more pragmatic and effective since criminals in jail and prison are unable to victimize outsiders).

While recognizing that social factors, individual traits, and other variables influence offending, Derek Cornish and Ronald Clarke propose a "rational choice theory" (Cornish & Clarke, 1986), in which offenders weigh opportunity costs and benefits of different crimes. Changing "opportunity structures" through target hardening and the creation of defensible space may discourage offenders. Research to this point on rational choice theory has produced mixed results. Studies show that many criminals do not carefully plan their crimes. In fact, many act impulsively and do not consider the potential consequences of their actions (Tunnell, 1991). If this is the case, then the rational choice assumption of the rational weighing of costs and benefits prior to acting is inaccurate. Thus, this is more a theory of victimization than a traditional theory of crime.

An interesting example of the policy shortcomings of the neoclassical school can be found in conservative pundits William Bennett, John DiIulio Jr., and John Walters' *Body Count: The Case for Violent Superpredators* (Bennett, DiIulio & Walters, 1996). Published in 1996, they predicted in their book that a new generation of street criminals, the "youngest, biggest and baddest generation any society had ever known" was about to descend on us. "Moral poverty" (the lack of character) rather than racism, poverty, and joblessness was viewed as the culprit. In the 1990s, however, crime declined dramatically in the very areas that they had erroneously predicted would be overrun by superpredators (Tunnell, 1991). Such conservatives are quick to call for prisons and to espouse the politics of indignant rectitude as the solution to crime and delinquency. The policy recommendations of conservative thinkers who follow classical ideas focus on deterring and incapacitating street criminals; seldom is their wrath aimed at dishonest corporate executives or elite criminals.

A related approach that has its roots in classical ideas is Lawrence Cohen and Marcus Felson's "routine activities" theory (Cohen & Felson, 1979). This theory posits that the volume of crime can be predicted by three elements: likely offenders, suitable targets, and capable guardians. An individual's life space places him or her in social settings where there exists a higher or lower likelihood of crime and delinquency. As an example, in the post-World War II period in the United States, discount department stores such as Kresge's became Kmarts, removing clerks for each department in favor of check-out stands. Goods were now openly displayed for customers and crooks to help themselves. Far greater targets were created, as was the need for greater security.

Essential contributors to what would become sociological criminology include A.M. Guerry, Adolphe Quetelet, and Emile Durkheim (See Burkhead, 2006). These thinkers were important advocates for the use of statistical data to study crime and for the idea that external variables play a role in crime causation. Guerry and Quetelet's use of statistics to draw maps of crime prevalence earned them the designation of the cartographic school (sometimes called geographic or ecological schools). Emile Durkheim's concept of "anomie" was central to many later sociological theories. He saw anomie (normlessness) as being a negative product of rapid social change and as a major cause of delinquency and social breakdown. There are numerous explanations of delinquency that fall under this model. Some of these theories have social structural elements, arguing that one's position in the social hierarchy (i.e., social class) affects one's propensity for delinquency. Others are decidedly not class-based explanations. Sociological explanations dominate criminology in the U.S., although there are also biological and psychological theories of delinquency.

Positivism

The positivist approach is quite distinct from the classical model. Generally speaking, positivist theories developed in the second half of the nineteenth century and remain popular today. Disputing the notion that people are rational and have free will, positivists saw human beings as having little free choice, with behavior determined by forces beyond their control (determinism). Biological and psychological positivism rest on three basic assumptions: the use of the scientific method, the search for pathology (sickness), and the application of therapy (treatment). Most of these theories are directed at explaining individual deviance and while haunted by simplistic theories of the past, have modern expressions that are well respected. In Chapter 3, Thomas Gamble and Amy Eisert address the biological and psychological theories of delinquency.

Mainstream Sociological Theories

Mainstream sociological theories of delinquency can be divided into a number of categories, although criminologists do not all agree on one particular typology. These include the social process (learning or subcultural) theories, anomie (strain) theories and social control theories. Social structural theories include anomie (strain) theories and social disorganization theories. Some thinkers consider cultural deviance/subcultural theories to be process theories, while others consider them social structure theories. Within the social process approach, learning and subcultural theorists see delinquency as learned behavior or as culturally transmitted. Delinquency is caused by the learning of delinquent/criminal values, rather than due to the individual pathology of the juvenile. This idea is reflected in the writings of Edwin Sutherland (1978), Walter Miller (1958), and David Matza (1964), among others.

One early important approach is found in the "Chicago School of Sociology" in the 1920s and 1930s in its theory of urban ecology. Urban ecology looked at the influences of urban place on human interactions. Natural areas emerged in cities and represented sub-communities that served specialized functions. Cities were viewed as growing in "concentric zones" or rings that influenced human behavior. Louis Wirth in "Urbanism as a Way of Life" conceived of urban life as producing social disorganization, anomie, and alienation (Wirth, 1938).

The Chicago school stressed empirical investigation of its theories. Clifford Shaw and Henry McKay (Shaw & McKay, 1942) were products of the Chicago School (the Sociology program at the University of Chicago). In the 1930s, they advocated the position that crime and delinquency were due to *social disorganization* in pathological urban environments rather than the deviant behavior of abnormal individuals. Problems such as poverty, weak social control, and migration and mobility created an environment that encouraged deviant groups and values to develop alongside conformist ones. The Chicago School made extensive use of maps and statistics from the city to examine the influence of urban areas on social pathology and deviance. Shaw and McKay plotted concentric zones against crime and delinquency data, demonstrating declines in crime as one moved further out from inner rings (i.e., away from the central business district and "transition zone"). The Chicago Area Project, initially developed by Shaw and McKay, was a long-standing crime prevention program in the city. On the negative side, such theories have been criticized for bordering on environmental determinism (the physical environment causes crime). The concentric zone theory was perhaps applicable only to Chicago in the 1920s and 1930s. However, the concept of social disorganization and community characteristics as causes of crime and delinquency experienced resurgence in popularity in criminology in the 1980s (Stark, 1987).

Contemporary ecological theorists recognize the importance of the social disorganization concept but argue that it has an indirect (rather than a direct) effect on crime. Sampson and Groves suggest that there are three neighborhood factors to be considered: the ability of a community to supervise and control teenage peer groups and gangs, the strength of local friendship networks, and the rate of local participation in formal and voluntary organizations (Sampson & Groves, 1999; Sampson et al., 2006). Sampson and colleagues defined social disorganization as the inability of community members to realize common values and goals. Sources of disorganization that indirectly affect crime include socio-economic status (poverty), residential mobility/instability, and ethnic heterogeneity. Further, Sampson and colleagues developed the notion of collective efficacy to describe "shared beliefs in a neighborhood's capability for action to achieve an intended effect, coupled with an active sense of engagement on the part of residents" (Sampon, 2006:153). Their research found that areas high in collective efficacy had lower rates of violent crime.

Other sociologists have contributed to the growing body of knowledge on the causes of crime. Robert Merton, an important advocate of the theory of anomie, wrote an influential piece (in 1938) on the role of structure in deviance and crime (See Merton, 1968). Merton suggested that, in order to understand why some groups in society had higher crime rates than others, one needed to look at the social structure (the way society is organized). Specifically, if one looks at American society, there are certain goals that the culture deems "worth striving for." For example, the U.S. places great emphasis on "making it," that is, being a success (typically defined in financial terms). At the same time, society articulates the approved (legitimate) ways that one should use to achieve this goal (e.g., getting an education and a job). Ideally, there should be a balance between the goals and the means. In a "healthy" society, where they are accessible to all, most people will conform (i.e., believe in the goal and try to achieve it using legitimate means). However, not all groups are able to achieve this goal; access to legitimate means varies depending on one's position in the class structure. Lower-class members experience the least access to legitimate means, so Merton predicted this group would be most likely to turn to crime and deviance to achieve the cultural goal of the acquisition of wealth. Such deviance is likely to occur in a society where there is imbalance between the means and goals (e.g., it is considered more important to achieve the goal (at any cost) relative to following legitimate/legal methods in the attempt to achieve the goal). Such tension, or disjuncture, between the culturally approved goals and the ability to achieve the goal using legitimate means is labeled "anomie" by Merton and is also called strain. From this perspective, then, society itself is to blame for generating crime due to the strain and pressure it places on certain groups to follow the "American Dream" in any way possible.

A recent modification of strain theory is Robert Agnew's work on a "General Strain Theory" (GST) of crime and delinquency (Agnew, 2001). Agnew notes that there are two more types of strain, in addition to the type described by Merton. Agnew argues that, for juveniles, delinquency is likely to result from negative relationships with others, more so than from blockage from achieving desired goals. Although delinquency is not the only option, it may result when a juvenile experiences negative treatment from others, or loses something positive/valuable. These experiences produce negative emotions in adolescents, such as frustration and anger. Several factors affect the juvenile's predisposition to delinquency as a coping strategy, including temperament and association with delinquent peers. GST is consistent with programs that aim to reduce delinquency by reducing the negative treatment experienced by juveniles, by reducing the probability that youth will provoke negative reactions from others, and by increasing the coping skills of and social support for juveniles (See Agnew, 2006).

Another elaboration of the anomie tradition is Steven Messner and Richard Rosenfeld's "institutional anomie theory" (Messner & Rosenfeld, 1994; 2006). Drawing on Merton's ideas, they argue that the excessive emphasis on the achievement of the American Dream, which tends to foster anomie, creates an imbalance between social institutions (e.g., the family, education), with the economy dominating. The dominance of economic goals and values makes it difficult for the other social institutions to maintain social control. Crime occurs at all levels of society (not simply the lower class) because the American Dream is applicable to all and is open-ended (one cannot be too rich or too successful). Compared to the more established theories of crime and delinquency, there have not been many empirical tests of institutional anomie theory. In general, more support has been found for the institutional dimension of the theory, compared to the cultural component (i.e., the distinctiveness of American culture) (Messner & Rosenfeld, 2006).

Perhaps the most influential sociological theory of crime and delinquency was that of Edwin Sutherland and his theory of "differential association" (Sutherland, 1978). This learning theory states that individuals become predisposed toward criminality due to an excess of contacts that advocate criminal behavior. Such contacts ("associations") will teach favorable definitions of deviance and will vary according to frequency (number of contacts), priority (time of its establishment), intensity (the meaningfulness of these contacts), and duration (length of contacts). For Sutherland, crime is learned by the same process by which conventional behavior is learned, and most of this learning takes place in intimate personal groups. Due to its general nature, differential association theory was well received and viewed as compatible with many other explanations of delinquency. One major criticism of differential association theory is that it is a pure behaviorist theory basically saying, "previous behavior causes later behavior." It concentrates solely on the transmission of crime and fails to address the issue of what causes crime and delinquency in the first place. It reveals a limited understanding of the learning of behavior. It has also been difficult to test its propositions in order to assess the empirical validity of the theory.

Ronald Akers (with Robert Burgess) incorporated Sutherland's ideas into his "differential association-reinforcement" theory (Burgess & Akers, 1966). Subsequently he developed a social learning theory of crime as well as the social structure-social learning (SSSL) theory (Akers & Jensen, 2006). Akers's work explains the mechanisms of learning, drawing on behavioral psychology (e.g., reinforcement and modeling). Several of the theoretical concepts have received a significant amount of empirical support, and findings are robust across domains of deviance as well as different societies (Akers & Jensen, 2006). Policy implications of learning theories of delinquency would involve the use of programs (based on cognitive-behavioral approaches) targeting the learning of deviant values and behaviors from significant others such as family and peers.

Albert Cohen, who had studied with Sutherland, was interested in the source of the deviant values that support crime and delinquency through his study of delinquent boys in the lower/working class urban environment (Cohen, 1955). Sometimes described as a "subcultural strain" theorist, Cohen argued that the delinquent subculture was one response to the strain experienced by lower and working-class youth in the middle-class school system. Assuming that these boys believed in middle-class values (like those articulated by Merton), the difficulties they experienced in school translated into "status frustration" and feelings of low self-esteem. Such youth would have a number of ways to respond to this strain: being a "corner boy," a "college boy," or joining a delinquent gang. Cohen argued that the response to strain is a group response, and that the nature of their delinquency revealed the retributive motive underlying the deviance, describing these acts as malicious and negativistic. Thus, gang delinquency is a response to the failure to achieve middle-class success goals and reflects counter-cultural values adhered to by the gang members. The delinquent gang substitutes its own values and sources of self-esteem for middle-class values it rejects or cannot live up to. Some examples of such middle-class values include ambition, individual responsibility, verbal skills, academic achievement, deferred gratification, middle-class manners, nonviolence, and wholesome recreation. The gang subculture becomes a means of striking back against values and expectations that the lower-class youth is unable to fulfill.

Another popular theory of the 1950s appeared in Walter Miller's article, "Lower Class Culture as a Generating Milieu of Gang Delinquency" (Miller, 1958). This theory, considered a cultural deviance/subcultural theory, is limited to explaining delinquency among adolescent male street corner gangs in lower-class, urban environments. Miller views lower-class delinquency as reflecting the "focal concerns" (dominant values) of lower-class culture. Delinquency represents a pattern of subcultural transmission of learning the values of the local environment. The gang functions to address the needs of boys raised in female-headed households. The focal concerns of the lower class include trouble, toughness, smartness, excitement, fate, and autonomy. Two values unique to gang youth are belonging and status. Getting into trouble attracts attention, while "machismo" (masculine toughness) is highly prized by lower-class males. Being quick-witted ("street-smart") demonstrates one's cleverness, while luck is perceived as controlling an unpredictable future. Independence (autonomy) is highly prized, but seldom realized by them. Miller's theory, like many others, reflects an "androcentric" (male-centered) bias, as well as bias against the lower class. The latter ignores delinquency among the middle or upper class while the former ignores female delinquency.

Like Cohen and Miller, Richard Cloward and Lloyd Ohlin (1960) had an interest in the apparent concentration of crime and delinquency in the lower class. However, they elaborated upon the delinquent subculture concept, noting that the gang subculture could take different forms: criminal, conflict, or retreatist. Like Merton, they believed that lower-class youth believed in the American Dream but often experienced lack of opportunity; however, they argued that a lower-class boy could aspire to wealth without being interested in achieving middle-class status (and vice versa). Like Sutherland, Cloward and Ohlin noted that our associations with others vary, so that the access to particular types of delinquent subcultures varied as well. That is, not only are legitimate means differentially distributed across the social structure, illegitimate opportunities are differentially distributed as well. The work of Cloward and Ohlin was quite influential in the 1960s. Their book was read by then-Attorney General Robert Kennedy, and Lloyd Ohlin helped develop what became the new federal policy of delinquency: the Juvenile Delinquency Prevention and Control Act of 1961 (Vold, Bernard & Snipes, 1998).

David Matza's *Delinquency and Drift theory* (Matza, 1964) was also well received. Like Sutherland and a number of other social process theorists, he believes that youth from any social class background have the potential to be delinquent. Matza attempts to combine the determinism of many positivistic theories with the notion of free will. Although human behavior is influenced by outside forces, he argues that individual responsibility still exists. Matza introduces three key concepts: drift theory, subterranean values, and techniques of neutralization. He sees delinquents as never entirely committed to the delinquent identity. They flirt or "drift" between deviance and conventionality.

Many delinquents are acting out subterranean values, underground values that exist alongside conventional values. Conventional society, which at times gives vent to subterranean values, supports that there is a time and place for everything. Delinquents have a bad sense of timing in expressing subterranean values such as illicit sexual behavior, slick business practices, disdain for work, substance abuse, and themes expressed in media violence. "Techniques of neutralization" are rationalizations or excuses that juveniles use to neutralize responsibility for their deviance. By pointing to subterranean values or other defenses, they attempt to explain away their responsibility. Techniques of neutralization include: denial of responsibility (due to home life or poverty), denial of harm to anyone (stealing is borrowing), denial of harm to the victim (person that was harmed is also a criminal), condemnation of the condemners (society is more corrupt than I am), and appeal to higher authority (defending one's turf). Research testing the notion of techniques of neutralization has produced mixed findings. Some studies find that some offenders do in fact rationalize their behavior away while others have a different value system (See Hindelang, 1970; Regoli & Poole, 1978; Ball, 1980).

Control theories are another important set of explanations that are considered social process models of crime and delinquency. This tradition developed in the 1950s in the U.S., although discussions of social control preceded these theories by many years. For example, Paternoster and Bachman note that Durkheim argued that people's needs must be regulated by society, and that people are moral only to the extent that they have been socialized (Paternoster & Bachman, 2001). Walter Reckless's "containment theory," one of the early important control theories, was followed by Travis Hirschi's social bond theory (Hirschi, 1969). Reckless's "containment theory" posits that individuals have various social controls (containments) that assist them in resisting the pressures that draw them to criminality (Reckless, 1967). The presence or absence of social pressures interacts with the presence or absence of containments to produce or inhibit individual delinquency and criminality. Strong families, communities, and self-concept act as containments that enable the resistance of such social pressures.

In Hirschi's view, crime is inherently appealing, and our bonds to society inhibit us from breaking the law. When these bonds are broken or weakened, individuals' personal stakes in conformity are reduced. They have less to lose by not conforming. Juveniles conform for fear of violating their group's mores and fear of ruining the personal image of them held by these groups. Hirschi postulated four elements of the bond: attachment, commitment, involvement, and belief. Time spent in conventional activities (involvement) and devotion to conformist lines of conduct (such as the desire to do well in school) are deterrents to delinquency. Attachment to significant others refers to the emotional tie to persons such as parents. A juvenile who does not care what her parents think of her (one with a weak affective link to parents) is at greater risk of delinquency. Like other social process theories, bond theory assumes that any person (regardless of social class) has the potential to be delinquent; the key factor to consider is socialization into the values and beliefs of society and the strength of social ties.

More recently, Gottfredson and Hirschi (1990) have proposed what they call a "general theory of crime," a theory of low self-control. Individuals with low self-control are the result of predisposing conditions and inadequate parenting and they are likely to engage in delinquency and other deviant behaviors. Such individuals have trouble delaying gratification and often act without thinking (impulsivity). Social and self-control theories have generated strong empirical support, and like some rival theories, demonstrate the importance of variables like family and peers (Gottfredson, 2006). Gottfredson argues that evidence for this class of theories has been found across different populations, crimes, and countries.

One recent study tested the role of parenting in delinquency as described by differential association/social learning and low self-control theories (Unnever et al., 2006). These researchers found that "bad" parenting (e.g., ineffective monitoring, coercive punishment) has both direct and indirect effects (through low self-control and antisocial or aggressive attitudes) on delinquency. Thus, social learning and low self-control theories received partial support. Based on these theories, attempts to prevent delinquency should involve improving parenting skills in several arenas, including the ability to supervise children and to avoid reinforcing deviant behaviors and attitudes.

Critical Theories

Thus far, "mainstream" theories of delinquency have been examined. Despite their strengths, these theories have been criticized for supporting a conservative, consensus-model worldview. They have an unquestioning acceptance of the existing society. They concentrate on the issue of why deviant individuals and groups are unwilling to adjust to the societal *status quo*. Issues of power and value conflict are ignored. Questions such as how delinquents can be rehabilitated and adjusted prevail, as does the positivistic orientation that stresses objectivity and empirical analysis as the basis for knowledge. Critical theories encourage an increasing variety of alternative approaches including: the labeling (social reaction) perspective, conflict theory, feminist, new critical and radical (Marxist) viewpoints. These theories view crime and delinquency as labels attached to the behavior of the less powerful by more powerful elites. The conflict model, in which competing groups struggle for power to define deviance and delinquency, is the predominant paradigm in critical theories. In this schema, delinquency may be viewed as a rational response to inequitable societal conditions. Critical theorists feel that mainstream theories ignore economic, racial, and gender inequality and their role in crime causation (Milovanovic, 1996).

Labeling (societal reaction) theory became a popular approach in the 1960s in the United States, particularly in the writings of Edwin Lemert (1967). This approach is more concerned with how behaviors come to be viewed by society as deviant, how society responds to the deviant act, and the consequences of this detection and processing on the deviant. For Lemert, deviance does not inhere in the initial act itself ("primary deviance"); it is the product of negative societal reaction (resulting in "secondary deviance"). Secondary deviance involves the psychological reorganization that takes place by the actor as a result of being caught and labeled as delinquent. The stigma produced by the process of labeling ("dramatization of evil," according to Frank Tannenbaum (1938) has a way of evoking the very traits that were the subject of complaint. Individuals perceive the meaning of their actions through the reactions of others. In this model, the machinery of social control (societal reaction) becomes as important as the act itself. Labeling is a process that may eventually produce identification with deviant images and subcultures. In other words, the delinquent may internalize the label and act in accordance with it. Lemert sees this approach as a paradigm shift in which social control leads to deviance rather than deviance leading to social control.

Frank Cullen and Robert Agnew (2006:266) give the example of changing perspectives of sexual assaults on women. In the past, rape referred to victimization by strangers in which physical injury occurred. The women's rights movement challenged this belief and broadened the label to include "acquaintance rape" or sexual assaults committed by intimates, thus creating a new definition of reality. Howard Becker (1963) used the concept of "moral entrepreneurs" to describe officials or agents who benefit from creating and labeling new categories of deviance in order to expand the social control machinery of their agency. The criminalization of drug addiction from a medical problem to a law enforcement one might serve as an example. In Becker's view, deviance, rather than being something that exists in the act itself, becomes so only by societal reaction and the subsequent stigmatization or labeling process.

Recent efforts to study labeling and its effects differentiate labeling by the "system" (juvenile or criminal justice) from labeling by significant others. Some research indicates that shaming by intimate others may produce the desired deterrent effect (Triplett & Jarjoura, 1994). An addendum to labeling theory is John Braithwaite's "shaming theory" (1989) which argues that the stigmatizing or negative shaming of offenders often makes matters worse. He calls for "reintegrative shaming" or efforts to reintegrate the offender back into the community. Current efforts at restorative or a balanced approach to justice reflect this thinking. This approach to corrections assumes that the juvenile justice system must give balanced attention to protecting the community, imposing offender accountability, and developing offender competencies to restore him or her to the community.

Critics of labeling theory point out that the theory may be overly deterministic and lends the impression that it denies individual responsibility (Akers, 1967:46). Offenders are depicted as passive robots labeled and stigmatized by "bad" society. Some critics dispute the labeling notion that no act is inherently deviant, arguing that some acts are *mala in se* (bad in themselves). Robert Bohm (1997:117) sees labeling theory not as a theory per se, but as a "sensitizing concept." In defense of the perspective, the focus on societal reaction does correct for the overly conservative, positivistic approach to theory characteristic of most mainstream theories. It also calls attention to the irony that sometimes responses to crime may, in fact, be based on inaccurate ideas and make matters worse.

Most diversion programs in juvenile justice are based on the assumption that we must avoid stigmatizing juveniles as long as possible in order to prevent "secondary deviance." In a related vein, decriminalizing the status offenses of juveniles is recommended by this approach, in order to reduce "net widening" by the juvenile justice system and more negative labeling.

Conflict theory in criminology has a long pedigree in the works of writers such as Karl Marx (1967), Georg Simmel (1908 {1955}), Willem Bonger (1969), Lewis Coser (1956), Ralf Dahrendorf (1959), and George Vold (1958). Thorsten Sellin's (1938) concept of "culture conflict" saw criminal law as originating from normative conflicts in society wherein more powerful groups have their interests served at the expense of weaker groups. Rather than society being held together by consensus, with agreement on laws and values, the coercion of the less powerful by the more powerful puts the weak at risk of greater social control. Conflict theory views this struggle as a pluralistic one in which many different groups and interests co-exist. This pluralism distinguishes the conflict perspective from the radical approach. The latter espouses an orthodox, neo-Marxian ideological view in which one variable – economics – is the paramount cause of inequality and class conflict. Austin Turk (1969) and, at one time, Richard Quinney (1970) have been major writers in this tradition. Turk views continuing conflicts as becoming routine and developing into stratification systems. This results in economic exploitation and political domination determined by the relative power of conflicting parties. Quinney saw delinquency and crime as behaviors that conflict with the interests of segments of society that have the power to shape public policy.

Writers such as W.E.B. Du Bois (1901) and Jeffery Reiman (1998) have also contributed to the conflict tradition. Du Bois, better known for his civil rights leadership, is a neglected or forgotten conflict theorist, according to Shaun Gabbidon (1999). *In The Spawn of Slavery, the Convict Lease System in the South*, Du Bois (1901) discusses the enactment of the "black codes" and convict lease system by the Southern oligarchy (rule by a few) as a means to compensate for the lost labor and profits as a result of Emancipation after the Civil War. Although this work represents one of the earliest writings on the subject of conflict criminology, the fact that it was ignored illustrates a "Eurocentric bias" in American studies of crime and delinquency. That is, there has been a dominance of writings by those of European descent and a shortage of works by those of African descent. Reiman, in *The Rich Get Richer and the Poor Get Prison* (1998), argues that acts that are criminalized are generally those of the poor and seldom are those of the powerful. In general, then, conflict theorists view the positivist quest for the causes of crime as futile and misplaced. Although some criminologists might see this goal as unrealistic, conflict theorists think that a radical restructuring of society is necessary to eliminate inequality and get at the true causes of crime. Conflict theory argues that minimally, we need a more "just" justice system, in which "crime in the suites" is treated in the same fashion as "crime in the streets."

Left realism and peacemaking perspectives demonstrate newer expressions of critical theory. Realists recognize that crime and delinquency are real problems that exist in socialist as well as capitalist societies, but insist on social justice as an important objective (Williams & McShane, 1994). Unlike Marxists, left realists accept the reality of street crime and do not view it as some revolutionary activity of the oppressed. They attempt to translate radical ideas into realistic social policy. Peacemaking theory is espoused in the later writings of Richard Quinney and Harold Pepinsky (Quinney, 1988; Pepinsky & Quinney, 1991). More of a social movement or ideology than a theory, peacemaking calls for an "expressive criminology of compassion, forgiveness, and love . . . a continuing movement for a world of peace and social justice" (Pepinsky & Quinney, 1991:ix). Peacemaking is also a nonviolent approach to justice policy and assumes that violence cannot be overcome with more violence. In the end, peacemaking is an admirable social movement, a utopian *Weltanschauung* (world view) more than it is a set of theoretical propositions to be analyzed and tested.

Radical "Marxist" criminology had its major expression before the collapse of the former Soviet Union and was reflected particularly in the writings of Richard Quinney (1977) and William Chambliss (1975). From this perspective, crime and delinquency are viewed as caused by inequalities created by the capitalist economic system. Many Marxist criminologists espouse an ideological stance that rejects the positivistic tradition of analyzing delinquency causation through objective and empirical analysis. The tenets of the radical approach are viewed as foregone conclusions requiring illustration rather than proof. Critics of Marxist criminology note that it resembles a new religion in which its "true believers" are unwilling to test, evaluate, or objectively examine their theories or beliefs.

Feminist theory represents yet another critical perspective. It argues that traditional "malestream" (male mainstream) approaches to criminology and delinquency reveal an androcentric (male-centered) bias and exclude women from analysis. Expressed particularly in topics such as rape and domestic violence, the past literature on crime assumed traditional gender roles. In feminist theory, crime and delinquency are examined as they are related to gender-based inequality (Chesney-Lind & Shelden, 1998; Simpson & Elis, 1995). Emphasizing various ideological approaches, including Marxist, interactionist, and critical theory, some feminist theorists see dominant empirical positivism as ignoring gender as a central force and as blind to its ideological bias. The victimization of women, gender differences in crime, and gendered justice (the differential treatment of females in the justice system) have received particular attention among feminist criminologists.

"Liberal feminists" were represented in early pioneering works in the 1970s such as Rita Simon's *Women and Crime* (1975) and Freda Adler's *Sisters in Crime* (1975). Both predicted an increase in female criminality as opportunities in society increased for women. Despite its appeal, little empirical support was found for this thesis. "Radical feminists" argued that liberal feminists understated the role of patriarchy and its ability to control and victimize women and believed that women should examine crime through their own experiences with sexism. Radical feminists view male aggression and control of female sexuality as the basis of patriarchy and the subordination of women. For example, they define rape as a crime of male power and the use of violence to control and dominate women.

In *Masculinities and Crime*, James Messerschmidt (1986; 1993) accuses feminists of having stereotypical views of men. Although its expression varies by age, class and race, he sees delinquency for males as a way of "doing gender" or exerting their masculinity when other means of doing so are unavailable. The different schools of feminist thought have highlighted the need for the discipline to pay greater attention to the concept of gender in criminological theorizing and research.

Integrated, Life Course, and Developmental Theories of Crime

A major problem with many of the theories that have been presented is the tendency to associate delinquency with a single cause. Critics of these theories are able to simply show circumstances in which these same conditions occurred among non-delinquents in order to discredit these single-cause explanations. This led early writers such as William Healy (1915) and Sheldon and Eleanor Glueck (1950) to propose a multifactor approach for explaining delinquency. Multiple factors such as biological, psychological, and sociological ones are combined in different variations and emphases in order to examine different types of delinquency. Although multiple factors are indeed involved in the causal explanation of delinquency, the mere identification of factors related to a process is not the same thing as a theoretical explanation. Simply identifying a list of factors associated with delinquency does not represent a scientific theory.

Integrated theories combine various theoretical approaches into one theory in an attempt to produce more powerful and sophisticated explanations. This involves more than the mere identification of factors involved in crime. Steven Messner, Marvin Krohn, and Allen Liska in *Theoretical Integration in the Study of Crime and Deviance* (Messner, Krohn & Liska, 1989) were influential in popularizing many of these theories. The most common strategy for formalizing integrated theories is their temporal ordering from end to end, appending one cause to another in sequence (Cullen & Agnew, 2006: 529). For example, a high level of strain might result in individuals joining subcultures that then lead to crime. While many theories are not viewed as possessing this integrating quality, they may in fact have that quality in linking various theories. Clifford Shaw and Henry McKay (Shaw & McKay, 1942) of the Chicago School combined elements of strain, learning, and social control theories in their social disorganization model, while Albert Cohen's lower class reaction theory combined strain and subcultural ideas (1955), and Cloward and Ohlin's differential opportunity theory combined strain and differential association theory (1960).

Numerous theories have been noted as examples of integrated theories, but the two most noteworthy have been Delbert Elliott and associates' "integrated theory of delinquency" (Elliott et al., 1979; 1985) and Terence Thornberry's "interactional theory of delinquency" (Thornberry et al., 1991; Thornberry, 2005). They argued that there are multiple causal pathways to delinquency. Using delinquency as measured by self-report surveys, Elliott and associates (Elliott et al., 1979; 1985) view delinquency as caused by a combination of strain, control, and learning variables:

1. Strain due to the gap between aspirations and achievements as well as other sources of strain such as family and school (anomie or strain theory).

2. Attachment and commitment to family and school (social control and bonding theory).

3. Exposure to, preference for, and identification with deviant peers (learning theory).

Using National Youth Survey data, Elliott et al. found that bonding and strain variables alone provided little explanation of delinquency (except as an indirect influence on peers). Social learning was most significant (Akers, 1994:189). The attempted integration of social control and social learning theory spoke favorably only of the latter. Other than prior delinquency, association with delinquent peers proved to be the best predictor of delinquency. More research, of course, is needed to confirm these results.

Thornberry and Krohn (See Thornberry, 2005) consider their interactional theory within a developmental framework. Thornberry's "interactional theory" (Thornberry et al., 1991) combines social structure, social control, and social learning approaches. For example, structural disadvantage (e.g., poverty) affects social control and learning variables; weakened bonds or lowered stakes in society predispose individuals to delinquency. Childhood temperament and parenting styles are causally interwoven. Identification and association with delinquent peers now takes place. These interrelationships are not one-way, but are reciprocal; that is, family attachment may affect school commitment, and the opposite may equally be true (Thornberry, 2006:554). He also indicated that the importance of different variables might change with the life course of the individual. School and peer relations, for example, take on more importance as a child ages. Despite shortcomings, integrated theories represent a major advance in the attempt to combine the explanatory power of a variety of independent (predictor) variables into theories of greater scope and sophistication.

Life course and developmental criminology have grown in popularity in the past two decades. Traditional theories of delinquency have neglected the early childhood years, while these approaches take a longer, dynamic view of the causes of delinquency and crime. Although there is not enough space here to cover all of the works in this area, several major efforts are summarized below.

The life course perspective stresses the age-graded nature of informal social control and the concepts of continuity and change in behavior, social ties, and human agency (See Laub, 2006). Life course theory considers the onset (beginning of delinquency commission), persistence (the trajectory of length of delinquency career) and desistance (when offenses typically cease). Laub and Sampson (2003), using the Glueck's longitudinal data, studied continuity and change over the life course, examining desistance from and persistence in offending over time. Their research indicated that, although delinquent behavior is relatively normal, there are many paths to desistance, with strong social ties reducing delinquency (and crime). Further, factors such as poor parenting and weak attachment (e.g., to school) can engender delinquency. Marriage, family, and employment are important factors to consider during the adult years.

Another dimension of theoretical analysis is the dependent (outcome) variable itself – delinquency. A major problem with many early delinquency theories had to do with the global or broad manner in which the concept delinquency was used. Hagan's concept of the "global fallacy" refers to the tendency to generalize rather specific theoretical explanations to all types of delinquency or crime (1987; 2007). Many limited, specific theories for explaining lower-class, violent, male delinquency may be inappropriate in examining middle-class, nonviolent, female delinquency. Robert Merton (1968:45) has long advocated "theories of the middle range" – explanations aimed at describing specific activity between the macroscopic (group) and microscopic (individual) levels.

Policy Implications

Acknowledged or not, public policy always contains inherent theoretical assumptions about the causes of crime. Social policy that ignores the causal roots of crime and delinquency often fails to address critical structural factors that generate the problems that the policy is attempting to resolve. Historian Arthur Schlesinger, Jr. in his *Cycles of American History* (1986) argues that history and public policy are characterized by pendular shifts in which a dominant liberal era runs its course, to be replaced by a conservative era that is in turn once again replaced by a liberal shift. Elliot Currie (1985) feels that directions in delinquency policy often reflect broader ideological trends in society more than they do new breakthroughs in research or theory.

Conservative public policy tends to adhere to the classical and neoclassical approaches to crime control. The individual and his or her personal failings are the culprit for delinquency rather than social conditions. Conservative policy concentrates on crime in the streets and is oriented toward incapacitation, deterrence, and a just-deserts doctrine (retribution). At the adult level, this emphasis, beginning in the 1980s, caused the United States to have the highest incarceration rate per capita in the free world. Many biological and psychological positivistic theories also reflect a more conservative approach to delinquency causation. From this perspective, the source of criminality is to be found in individual shortcomings and pathologies, and societal conditions are not to be blamed. The concern regarding such theories is that they (inadvertently or not) provide scientific justification for conservative ideological policies. Although many of these theories may be correct with respect to particular crimes or criminals, they ignore structural factors in crime causation and the conflict basis of criminal law. Conservatives see the choice of crime as an exercise in free will and punishment as a matter of just deserts. Such policies promote greater electronic surveillance, preventive detention, capital punishment, "no knock" searches, opposition to gun control, abolition of parole, mandatory sentencing, and restriction of community-based programs. Thus, under the classical model of behavior, efforts to control delinquency need to increase the costs and decrease the benefits of deviating from the law. To the extent that delinquents are not rational or thoughtful individuals, programs based on classical ideas are likely to be ineffective.

The liberal approach argues that, in addition to developing delinquency control measures, society must address the root causes of crime, such as inequality, racism, unemployment, lack of education, urban blight, and the like. This assumes that the government can ameliorate the social circumstances that foster crime. Crime is viewed as a symptom of these underlying problems. It is likely the case that these root causes also indirectly affect delinquency and crime through their effects on families and neighborhoods.

Each positivistic approach suggests a different focus for crime policy. Greater economic opportunity among the disadvantaged and a reduction in negative life circumstances would lessen strain (anomie theory). However, institutional anomie theory would suggest that such an approach would have limited success. Reducing the economic imperative and restoring a healthier balance between social institutions would be necessary to reduce crime in any significant way. Better environments that promote prosocial values and groups should reduce the influence of criminal "definitions" (differential association/social learning theories). Stronger families and communities would encourage a stake in conformity and make delinquency less appealing (social control theories).

Labeling and restorative justice approaches argue for the avoidance of disintegrative shaming and push for programs that bring the deviant "back into the fold." In addition, more fair enforcement of laws, including those against corporate and white-collar crime has been proposed as part of current and future social policies (conflict and radical theory).

The most effective delinquency programs tend to be multi-modal as well as being theoretically informed (Lipsey, 1992; McCord et al., 2001). Recognizing the influence of structural disadvantage and environmental factors on crime and delinquency, the National Academy of Sciences Panel on Juvenile Crime recommends providing prenatal care and programs that include components for parents, children, school, and community (McCord et al., 2001).

Sociological theories hold great promise for informing public policy at the macroscopic (societal or structural) level. Much crime is predicated on social disequilibrium rather than simply individual failures. These theories, which address the structure and institutions of society, will continue to be refined by criminologists. At the same time, given the multiple causes of delinquency and disagreement about the nature of behavior (free will versus determinism), it is easy for policymakers and the public alike to become discouraged at this seemingly insurmountable social problem. Further, these discussions occur in the context of the multiple missions of the juvenile justice system, which must balance the sometime conflicting goals of security and control with those of treatment and rehabilitation.

All too often policymakers look to politics for guidance regarding the juvenile and criminal justice systems rather than empirically verified theory. Unfortunately, there is sometimes a gap in communicating the scientific knowledge gained by researchers to practitioners and policymakers. One promising direction has been the greater receptivity to finding out "what works" and "what does not work" in policy experiments in juvenile and criminal justice (Sherman et al., 1997). A strategy of carefully testing theoretical propositions and strategies in policy field experiments, combined with rigorous evaluation of existing delinquency prevention and intervention programs, holds great promise for informing applied juvenile justice policy.

Summary and Conclusions

This chapter reveals the breadth and depth of theorizing about the causes of delinquency. Some theories fare better in terms of empirical validity than others, while others reject the positivist model completely. Mainstream delinquency theories vary in their policy implications, but explanations from a variety of perspectives stress the role of social institutions such as the family and school as important correlates of delinquency. Most recognize the importance of the peer group as a predictor of delinquency. Others emphasize structural conditions as playing a direct or an indirect role in crime causation.

Many programs aimed at delinquency prevention and control address one or more of the aforementioned variables. Ideally, treatment programs should be multifaceted and based on knowledge of "what works." Part of the difficulty lies in society's tendency to be "penny-wise and pound foolish." Although it is much cheaper in the long run to prevent crime and delinquency before it happens, most of our resources go to reactive control efforts. To illustrate this point, one study estimated that each juvenile involved in a delinquent career costs society between $83,000 and $334,000 (Cohen, 1998, cited in Snyder & Sickmund, 1999). Society at large and the youth in question would be better served by policy aimed at addressing the criminogenic circumstances outlined above and doing more to better identify high-risk youth and prevent their deviant behavior.

As criminology continues to mature as a discipline, theorizing about the causes of delinquency will become more sophisticated. Further exploration of integrated and developmental theories holds promise in explaining pathways to crime and delinquency. Using this knowledge should result in more effective treatment programs for juvenile delinquents. We are optimistic that the study of juvenile delinquency will flourish and hopeful that theory will play an important role in improving the practice of juvenile justice as well.

References

Adler, F. (1975). *Sisters in Crime*. New York, NY: McGraw-Hill.

Agnew, R. (2006). *Pressured into Crime: An Overview of General Strain Theory*. Los Angeles, CA: Roxbury Press.

Agnew, R. (2001). "An Overview of General Strain Theory." In R. Paternoster & R. Bachman (eds.) *Explaining Criminals and Crime: Essays in Contemporary Criminological Theory*, pp. 161-174. Los Angeles, CA: Roxbury Publishing.

Akers, R. (1994). *Criminological Theories: Introduction and Evaluation*. Los Angeles, CA: Roxbury Press.

Akers, R. (1967). "Problems in the Sociology of Deviance: Social Definitions and Behavior." *Social Forces*, 4(6):455-465.

Akers, R. & G. Jensen (2006). "The Empirical Status of Social Learning Theory of Crime and Deviance: The Past, Present, and Future." In F. Cullen, J.P. Wright & K. Blevins (eds.) *Taking Stock: The Status of Criminological Theory*, pp. 37-76. New Brunswick, NJ: Transaction Publishers.

Ball, R. (1980). "An Empirical Evaluation of Neutralization Theory." *Criminologica*, 4, 22-32.

Beccaria, C. (1963). *On Crimes and Punishments*. Translated by Henry Paolucci. Indianapolis, IN: Bobbs-Merrill.

Becker, G. (1968). "Crime and Punishment: An Economic Approach." *Journal of Political Economy*, 76:169-217.

Becker, H. (1963). *Outsiders: Studies in the Sociology of Deviance*. New York, NY: The Free Press.

Bennett, W., J. Dilulio & J. Walters (1996). *Body Count: Moral Poverty and How to Win America's War against Crime and Drugs*. New York, NY: Simon and Schuster.

Bentham, J. (1823). *Introduction to the Principles of Morals and Legislation*. Oxford: Oxford University Press, originally published in 1789.

Bohm, R. (1997). *A Primer on Crime and Delinquency*. Belmont CA: Wadsworth.

Bonger, W. (1969). *Criminality and Economic Conditions*. Bloomington IN: Indiana University Press.

Braithwaite, J. (1989). *Crime, Shame and Reintegration*. Cambridge, UK: Cambridge University Press.

Burgess, R. & R. Akers (1966). "A Differential Association-Reinforcement Theory of Criminal Behavior." *Social Problems*, 14:128-147.

Burkhead, M.D. (2006). *The Search for the Causes of Crime*. Jefferson, NC: McFarland and Co.

Chambliss, W. (1975). "Toward a Political Economy of Crime." *Theory and Society*, 2:152-153.

Chesney-Lind, M. & R. Shelden (1998). *Girls, Delinquency and Juvenile Justice*, Second Edition. Belmont, CA: Wadsworth.

Cloward, R.A. & L.E. Ohlin (1960). *Delinquency and Opportunity: A Theory of Delinquent Gangs*. New York, NY: The Free Press.

Cohen, A. (1955). *Delinquent Boys: The Culture of the Gang*. New York, NY: The Free Press.

Cohen, L. & M. Felson (1979). "Social Change and Crime Rate Trends: A Routine Activities Approach." *American Sociological Review*, 44:588-608.

Cohen, M. (1998). "The Monetary Value of Saving a High-Risk Youth." *Journal of Quantitative Criminology*, 14(1):5-33.

Cornish, D. & R. Clarke (eds.) (1986). *The Reasoning Criminal: Rational Choice Perspectives on Offending*. New York, NY: Springer-Verlag.

Coser, L. (1956). *The Functions of Social Conflict*. New York, NY: The Free Press.

Cullen, F.T. & R. Agnew (eds.) (2006). *Criminological Theory: Past to Present (Essential Readings)*, Third Edition. Los Angeles, CA: Roxbury Press.

Currie, E. (1985). *Confronting Crime*. New York, NY: Pantheon Press.

Dahrendorf, R. (1959). *Class and Class Conflict in Industrial Society*. Stanford, CA: Stanford University Press.

Dannefer, D. & R.K. Schutt (1982). "Race and Juvenile Justice Processing in Court and Police Agencies." *American Journal of Sociology*, 87:1113-1132.

Du Bois, W.E.B. (1901). "The Spawn of Slavery: The Convict-Lease System in the South." *The Missionary View of the World*, 14:737-745.

Elliott, D.S., S.S. Ageton & R.J. Canter (1979). "An Integrated Theoretical Perspective on Delinquent Behavior." *Journal of Research in Crime and Delinquency*, 16:3-27.

Elliott, D.S., D. Huizinga & S.S. Ageton (1985). *Explaining Delinquency and Drug Use*. Beverly Hills, CA: Sage Publishing Company.

Gabbidon, S. (1999). "W.E.B. Du Bois on Crime: American Conflict Criminologist." *The Criminologist*, 24(1):1, 3, 20.

Glueck, S. & E. Glueck (1950). *Unraveling Juvenile Delinquency*. Cambridge, MA: Harvard University Press.

Gottfredson, M.R. (2006). "The Empirical Status of Control Theory in Criminology." In F. Cullen, J.P. Wright & K. Blevins (eds.) *Taking Stock: The Status of Criminological Theory*, pp. 77-100. New Brunswick, NJ: Transaction Publishers.

Gottfredson, M.R. & T. Hirschi (1990). *A General Theory of Crime*. Stanford, CA: Stanford University Press.

Hagan, F. (2007). *Introduction to Criminology: Theories, Methods and Criminal Behavior*, Sixth Edition. Thousand Oaks, CA: Sage Publishing Company.

Hagan, F. (1987). "The Global Fallacy and Theoretical Range in Criminological Theory." *Journal of Justice Issues*, 2:19-31.

Healy, W. (1915). *The Individual Delinquent*. Boston, MA: Little, Brown.

Hindelang, M. (1970). "The Commitment of Delinquents to Their Misdeeds: Do Delinquents Drift?" *Social Problems*, 17:509-519.

Hirschi, T. (1969). *Causes of Delinquency*. Berkeley, CA: University of California Press.

Laub, J. (2006). "Edwin H. Sutherland and the Michael-Adler Report: Searching for the Soul of Criminology Seventy Years Later." *Criminology*, 44(2):235-257.

Laub, J. & R. Sampson (2003). *Shared Beginnings, Divergent Lives: Delinquent Boys to Age 70.* Cambridge, MA: Harvard University Press.

Lemert, E. (1967). *Human Deviance, Social Problems and Social Control.* New York, NY: Prentice-Hall.

Lipsey, M.W. (1992). "Juvenile Delinquency Treatment: A Meta-Analytic Inquiry into the Variability of Effects." In T. Cook, H. Cooper, D.S. Cordray et al. (eds.) *Meta-Analysis for Explanation: A Casebook*, pp. 83–26. New York, NY: Russell Sage Foundation.

Loeber, R. & M. Stouthammer-Loeber (1986). "Models and Meta-Analysis of the Relationship between Family Variables and Juvenile Conduct Problems and Delinquency." In N. Morris & M. Tonry (eds.) *Crime and Justice: An Annual Review of Research, volume 7*, pp. 29-149. Chicago, IL: University of Chicago Press.

Marx, K. (1967). *Capital.* Vol. 1. New York, NY: International.

Matza, D. (1964). *Delinquency and Drift.* New York, NY: Wiley.

McCord, J., C. Spatz Widom & N. Crowell (eds.) (2001). *Juvenile Crime, Juvenile Justice.* National Research Council and Institute of Medicine. Panel on Juvenile Crime: Prevention, Treatment, and Control. Committee on Law and Justice and Board on Children, Youth, and Families. Washington, DC: National Academy Press.

Merton, R. (1968). *Social Theory and Social Structure.* New York, NY: The Free Press.

Messerschmidt, J. (1993). *Masculinities and Crime.* Lanham, MD: Rowman and Littlefield.

Messerschmidt, J. (1986). *Capitalism, Patriarchy and Crime: Toward a Socialist, Feminist Criminology.* Totowa, NJ: Rowman and Littlefield.

Messner, S. & R. Rosenfeld (2006). "The Present and Future of Institutional-Anomie Theory." In F.T. Cullen, J.P. Wright & K. Blevins (eds.) *Taking Stock: The Status of Criminological Theory*, pp. 127-148. New Brunswick, NJ: Transaction Publishers.

Messner, S. & R. Rosenfeld (1994). *Crime and the American Dream*, Second Edition. Belmont, CA: Wadsworth.

Messner, S., M. Krohn & A. Liska (eds.) (1989). *Theoretical Integration in the Study of Deviance and Crime: Problems and Prospects.* Albany, NY: State University of New York Press.

Miller, W. (1958). "Lower-Class Culture as a Generating Milieu of Gang Delinquency." *Journal of Social Issues*, 14(3):141-173.

Milovanovic, D. (1996). "Postmodern Criminology." *Justice Quarterly*, 13:567-610.

Pastore, A.L. & K. Maguire (eds.) (2006). *Sourcebook of Criminal Justice Statistics* [Online]. Available: http://www.albany.edu/sourcebook/ [Retrieved November 12, 2007.]

Paternoster, R. & R. Bachman (2001). "The Structure and Relevance of Theory in Criminology." In R. Paternoster & R. Bachman (eds.) *Explaining Criminals and Crime: Essays in Contemporary Criminological Theory*, Chapter 1, pp. 1-10. Los Angeles, CA: Roxbury Publishing.

Pepinsky, H. & R. Quinney (eds.) (1991). *Criminology as Peacemaking.* Bloomington, IN: Indiana University Press.

Quinney, R. (1988). "Crime, Suffering, Service: Toward Criminology of Peacemaking." *The Quest*, Winter: 102-116.

Quinney, R. (1977). *Class, State and Crime*. New York, NY: David McKay.

Quinney, R. (1970). *The Social Reality of Crime*. Boston, MA: Little, Brown.

Reckless, W. (1967). *The Crime Problem*. New York, NY: Appleton-Century-Crofts.

Regoli, R. & E. Poole (1978). "The Commitment of Delinquents to Their Misdeeds: A Reexamination." *Journal of Criminal Justice*, 6: 261-269.

Reiman, J. (1998). *The Rich Get Richer and the Poor Get Prison*, Fifth Edition. Boston, MA: Allyn and Bacon.

Sampson, R.J. (2006). "Collective Efficacy Theory: Lessons Learned and Directions for Future Inquiry." In F.T. Cullen, J.P. Wright & K. Blevins (eds.) *Taking Stock: The Status of Criminological Theory*, pp. 149-167. New Brunswick, NJ: Transaction Publishers.

Sampson, R.J. & W.B. Groves (1999). "Community Social Disorganization and Crime." In F.T. Cullen & R. Agnew (eds.) *Criminological Theory: Past to Present*, Chapter 7, pp. 71-76. Los Angeles, CA: Roxbury Publishing.

Sampson, R.J., S. Raudenbush & F. Earls (2006). "Collective Efficacy and Crime." In F.T. Cullen & R. Agnew (eds.) *Criminological Theory: Past to Present* (Essential Readings), Third Edition, pp. 109-114. Los Angeles, CA: Roxbury Publishing.

Schlesinger, A., Jr. (1986). *The Cycles of American History*. Boston, MA: Houghton Mifflin.

Sellin , T. (1938). "Culture Conflict and Crime." *Social Science Research Council Bulletin*, 41:1-7.

Shaw, C.R. & H.D. McKay (1942). *Juvenile Delinquency and Urban Areas*. Chicago, IL: University of Chicago Press.

Sherman, L., D. Gottfredson, D. MacKenzie, J. Eck, P. Reuter & S. Bushway (1997). *Preventing Crime: What Works, What Doesn't, What's Promising: A Report to the United States Congress*. Washington, DC: National Institute of Justice, February.

Simmel, G. (1955 {1908}). *Conflict and the Web of Group Affiliations*. Translated by Kurt H. Wolff & Reinhard Bendix. New York, NY: The Free Press.

Simon, R. (1975). *Women and Crime*. Lexington, MA: Lexington Books.

Simpson, S. & L. Elis (1995). "Doing Gender: Sorting out the Caste and Crime Conundrum." *Criminology*, 33:47-81.

Snyder, H.N. (2004). *Juvenile Arrests 2002*. OJJDP Juvenile Justice Bulletin. Washington, DC: U.S. Department of Justice, Office of Justice Programs, Office of Juvenile Justice and Delinquency Prevention.

Snyder, H.N. & M. Sickmund (2006). *Juvenile Offenders and Victims: 2006 National Report*. Washington, DC: U.S. Department of Justice, Office of Justice Programs, Office of Juvenile Justice and Delinquency Prevention. Available online at http://ojjdp.ncjrs.gov/ojstatbb/nr2006/. [Retrieved November 12, 2007].

Snyder, H.N. & M. Sickmund (1999). *Juvenile Offenders and Victims: 1999 National Report*. Pittsburgh, PA: National Center for Juvenile Justice. Available online at http://www.ncjrs.org/html/ojjdp/nationalreport99/chapter3.pdf.[Retrieved December 10, 2007].

Stark, R. (1987). "Deviant Places: A Theory of the Ecology of Crime." *Criminology*, 25:893-909.

Sutherland, E. (1978). *Criminology*, Tenth Edition. Philadelphia, PA: Lippincott.

Tannenbaum, F. (1938). *Crime and the Community*. Boston, MA: Ginn.

Thomas, C. & J. Hepburn (1983). *Crime, Criminal Law and Criminology*. Dubuque, IA: William C. Brown.

Thornberry, T. (2006). "Toward an Interactional Theory of Delinquency." In F.T. Cullen & R. Agnew (eds.) *Criminological Theory: Past to Present (Essential Readings)*, Third Edition, pp. 551-562. Los Angeles, CA: Roxbury Publishing.

Thornberry, T. (2005). "Explaining Multiple Patterns of Offending across the Life Course and across Generations." *Annals of the American Academy of Political and Social Science*, 602:156-195.

Thornberry, T., A. Lizotte, M. Krohn, M. Farnworth & S. Jang (1991). "Testing Interactional Theory: An Examination of Reciprocal Causal Relationships among Family, School, and Delinquency." *Journal of Criminal Law and Criminology*, 82:3-35.

Triplett, R. & R. Jarjoura (1994). "Theoretical and Empirical Specification of Informal Labeling." *Journal of Quantitative Criminology*, 10:241-276.

Tunnell, K. (1991). *Choosing Crime: The Criminal Calculus of Property Offenders*. Chicago, IL: Nelson-Hall.

Turk, A. (1969). *Criminality and the Legal Order*. Chicago, IL: Rand, McNally.

Unnever, J., F. Cullen & R. Agnew (2006). "Why Is 'Bad' Parenting Criminogenic? Implications from Rival Theories." *Youth Violence and Juvenile Justice*, 4(1): 3-33.

Vold, G. (1958). *Theoretical Criminology*. New York, NY: Oxford University Press.

Vold, G., T. Bernard & J. Snipes (1998). *Theoretical Criminology*, Fourth Edition. New York, NY: Oxford University Press.

Williams, F. & M. McShane (1994). *Criminological Theory*, Second Edition. Englewood Cliffs, NJ: Prentice-Hall.

Wilson, J.Q. (1983). *Thinking about Crime*. New York, NY: Basic Books.

Wirth, L. (1938). "Urbanism as a Way of Life." *American Journal of Sociology*, 44(4):8-20.

CHAPTER 3

Delinquency Theory: Examining Delinquency and Aggression through a Biopsychosocial Approach

Thomas J. Gamble
Amy C. Eisert

Introduction

This chapter examines the emerging explanations of delinquency occurring at the interface between psychology and biology in the most general sense. Approaches based on social learning will not be reviewed here because they are essentially continuous with the sociological approach covered in Chapter 2 (Akers, 1985; Patterson, 1986).

This is a book about controversies, but what can be controversial about applying biological and psychological science to delinquency? It is obvious that all human behavior, including that behavior defined as delinquent, has a biological basis. Without our sensory surfaces, the environment could not affect us. Without motor neurons, we could not engage in any behavior. Without the cortex, we could not plan, scheme, or conspire. It is evident that understanding complex human behavior is the very purpose of psychology. How could it be that psychology, the science of behavior and mental processes – how people learn, behave, and think – is not relevant to understanding delinquency? What is the source of controversy about applying biological and psychological explanations to crime and delinquency?

There are really two foundations for the controversy. The first is the acknowledgment that biological and psychological factors play an important role in all human behavior while denying that they play an important role in individual differences among people in their propensity to commit criminal or delinquent acts. A main focus of criminology is to understand why some people offend and others do not. If delinquent and nondelinquent youth are essentially the same biologically and psychologically, and differ primarily in the environments to which they are exposed, there is little reason to apply biopsychological approaches in attempts to explain causes of delinquency. The extent to which biological and psychological factors help explain individual differences in criminal or delinquent conduct is the main topic of this chapter and will be reviewed in detail below.

The second fundamental reason why psychological and biological factors are controversial in some circles is that they focus attention on the individual rather than on the social environment. This can be seen as setting the stage for regressive social policy. Why bother to correct horrendous social conditions if the important causes of social deviance are within the individual rather than the environment? At first glance, this concern might seem alarmist. To demonstrate otherwise, it is instructive to review how biological and psychological explanations for deviance played a role in the eugenics movement within the United States.

The Unsavory and Unscientific

Early Biological and Psychological Contributions to Eugenics

Francis Galton, a cousin of Charles Darwin and known to social science students as an inventor of the correlation coefficient, was also the individual who coined the term "eugenics" in 1883 (Kevles, 1985). Eugenics comes from the Greek word meaning "noble in heredity," and Galton saw eugenics as the "science" of improving human stock by giving "the more suitable races or strains of blood a better chance of prevailing speedily over the less suitable" (Kevles, 1985:iv). Eugenics presented itself as solid science derived from Darwin's theory of evolution, but it was based on a misreading of how natural selection operates.

The eugenics movement understood natural selection (the mechanism by which Darwinian evolution operates) as leading to progressive development in species. Especially in the hands of Herbert Spencer and the "Social Darwinists," they imagined that evolution was a progressive force leading to increased complexity and the advancement of civilization. Western Europe, especially northern or Nordic regions, was seen as the current pinnacle of evolutionary progress, and by selective breeding, it was believed this peak could be advanced. As a consequence of their theorizing, they believed that ameliorative social programs were dangerous because they interfered with the progress of evolution by not allowing the genetically weak and inferior to perish before reproducing their kind (Kevles, 1985).

In fact, Darwinian evolutionary theory does not conceptualize evolution as a necessarily progressive force. It might just as easily lead to reductions in complexity if less complex organisms (viruses, for example) are better able to survive and reproduce. In addition, Darwinian forces can easily lead to an evolutionary dead end. Evolutionary design and change are based entirely on current environmental circumstances. If these circumstances change, a feature that was helpful could quickly become useless or worse.

There is no prescience or teleology in natural selection. It is not aiming toward increased complexity and has no insight into what the future circumstances will require. Nonetheless, this misreading of evolutionary theory as essentially progressive, aided by some biologists and psychologists, led to a variety of perverse social policies in Nazi Germany, as is well known, but also in the progressive-era United States (Bauer, 2001). In particular, the IQ test movement, as represented by psychologists Henry Goddard and Carl Brigham, fueled fears that high reproductive rates by recent immigrants (especially those from the Mediterranean region) and by the feebleminded would seriously undermine the genetic stock of the United States (Goddard, 1914:4; Brigham, 1923:xx, 197).[1] Positive eugenics arose to attempt to increase birth rates among the "fit," and negative eugenics arose to sponsor policies that would decrease child bearing among the "unfit."

The Eugenics Movement in the United States

In the United States, the eugenics movement led to restrictions on immigration from certain countries and regions, as well as to the forced sterilization of the "feebleminded." In 1917, Goddard reported that two out of five of those who arrived in steerage at Ellis Island were "feebleminded." The term "feebleminded" was a catchall for a variety of undesirable traits, such as delinquency and criminality, excessive sexual promiscuity (leading presumably to even more breeding), dependence on social programs, and low intelligence. In April 1927, in the case of *Buck v. Bell*, the U.S. Supreme Court (by an 8 to 1 vote) declared that forced sterilization on eugenic grounds did not violate the Constitution. The Court's opinion was written by Justice Oliver Wendell Holmes and read in part: "The principle that sustains compulsory vaccination is broad enough to cover cutting the Fallopian tubes . . . Three generations of imbeciles are enough" (*Buck v. Bell*, 274 U.S. 436 (1927)). By 1930, sterilization laws were on the books of 24 states, and by the mid 1930s, some 20,000 forced sterilizations had been legally performed in the United States. It was the even more barbarous use of eugenics in Nazi Germany that finally led to the waning of its influence in the United States.

Given just this one example of eugenics, it is no wonder that skepticism, controversy, and caution accompany any attempts to import biological and psychological theorizing into criminology. While not all biologists or psychologists signed onto the eugenics approach, this poor showing by biologically and psychologically based theory quite understandably helped give impetus to the strong sociological approach in American criminology.

All that being said, this chapter will present evidence that biological and psychological approaches, if properly integrated with sociological theorizing, are worth exploring, and that concepts and findings from those disciplines will enrich our understanding of delinquency. If there are, as this chapter will argue, useful insights and relevant empirical findings from biology and psychology, we ignore them to the detriment of our science. However, the danger of regressive policies emerging from the use of these approaches still lingers and vigilance remains necessary.

A General Introduction to the Biopsychosocial Model

The Standard Social Science Model

Subsequent to the misuses of evolutionary theory in the eugenics movement, the resultant excesses of biopsychological theorizing, the emergence of behaviorism with its emphasis on environment, and due to interesting sociological findings from the Chicago School and advances in Boasian anthropology, there arose what Tooby and Cosmides refer to as the Standard Social Science Model (SSSM) (Tooby & Cosmides, 1992). This model holds that there is no fixed human nature and that all important differences among individuals arise from forces within the social and cultural environment. This view held sway in delinquency theory, as well as in social science more generally, until relatively recently when a variety of findings from the biopsychological perspective could no longer be ignored (Tooby & Cosmides, 1992; Bjorklund & Pellegrini, 2002).

The Nature–Nurture Controversy

While the SSSM held sway in criminology, in psychology and psychiatry, the futility of the nature-nurture controversy gave rise to the biopsychosocial model, which was becoming the default orientation. The nature-nurture controversy refers to the attempts to determine whether any particular psychological trait (IQ for example) is the result of biological forces (nature) or social environmental forces (nurture). As research progressed, it became clear that this distinction was not tenable. The biopsychosocial model holds that all human behavior arises from the combination of biological, psychological, and social forces and that attempts to untangle them in a simple orthogonal way would lead to empirical or theoretical stagnation. For example, in research on schizophrenia (a disorder once attributed to a particular form of mothering), it became clear that genetic factors play a significant role. If one member of a pair of monozygotic (identical) twins is diagnosed with schizophrenia, the probability of the other receiving a similar diagnosis is approximately 50 percent. In other words, an identical twin of an individual suffering from schizophrenia is 50 times more likely to suffer from the disease than is an individual chosen at random. This finding holds even if the twins were reared apart (Rowe, 2002).

Two inferences from this research are evident. One is that there is a strong genetic component of schizophrenia, and the other is that genetics alone cannot account for the disorder. If genes were the only player, identical twins, who share 100 percent of their genes in common, would have 100 percent concordance for schizophrenia rather than the observed 50 percent. Hence, some non-genetic factor must be at work as well. Similar kinds of findings arose from research on a wide variety of psychological traits, including other mental disorders, personality characteristics, IQ, and some forms of criminality. The operative question shifted from whether a particular trait was a result of nature or nurture, to trying to understand how biological, psychological, and social factors interact to produce human behavior. This model has become so well entrenched that it is endorsed in the Diagnostic and Statistical Manual of the American Psychiatric Association and is a staple in introductory psychology textbooks (American Psychiatric Association (APA), 1994).

Diathesis-Stress Model

One important framework from the biopsychosocial approach is the "diathesis-stress" model (Wicks-Nelson & Israel, 2000). This refers to the view that individuals differ in their underlying vulnerability to any particular disorder (referred to as their diathesis), but whether the individual actually exhibits the disorder will depend upon the environmental stresses to which he or she is exposed. In addition to abnormal psychology and psychiatry, this model is common in the public health approach to disease. Individuals may vary in their underlying vulnerability to heart disease or lung cancer or addiction, but whether they manifest the disorder will depend on environmental factors, such as exposure to smoking or stress.

Researchers who take this approach argue that certain kinds of delinquent or criminal behavior may also be understood in a similar manner. Individuals may vary in their underlying (biological) vulnerability or propensity to criminal or delinquent conduct, but whether they exhibit that behavior will depend on environmental factors. From this perspective, individuals who have a very low diathesis, say for aggression, can grow up in very difficult environments without becoming aggressively delinquent, while individuals who have a high diathesis for aggression will become aggressive even without a great deal of environmental stress. Each individual, except identical twins, will vary in his or her underlying vulnerability, and the combination of this diathesis with environmental forces will influence his or her developmental outcomes. It is easy to see how this approach is applicable to one of the vexing problems of purely sociological approaches; that individuals who grow up in very similar circumstances often do not show similar conduct.

To estimate the likelihood that an individual will exhibit delinquency, one needs to know something about their underlying vulnerability and something about their environment. Perhaps individuals with very high vulnerability for delinquency will exhibit the conduct even in the best of environmental circumstances, while individuals low in vulnerability will not exhibit the conduct even in the worst of circumstances, with the majority of individuals falling somewhere between these extremes.

The underlying inherited structure of an individual is referred to as the genotype. The way in which that genotype is manifested in an individual is the phenotype. Any given genotype is compatible with a range of phenotypic manifestations. For example, each individual is born with a genotype that influences height, but that genotype is compatible with a range of heights based upon nutrition and other factors. Therefore genotype matters and is very influential, but in the contemporary view, genotype is not destiny. When the trait in question is not a purely physical trait (e.g., height) but is a complex behavioral pattern (e.g., aggression) the relationship between genotype and phenotype can get even more complex.

An individual familiar with delinquency research will immediately see a potential problem with this approach. The problem is that some forms of delinquent conduct are essentially normative (Elliot, Ageton, Huizinga, Knowles & Canter, 1983; Moffitt, Silva, Lynam & Henry, 1994). On self-report measures, very large proportions of youth admit to engaging in some delinquent behavior. One might ask where the individual differences are that the diathesis-stress approach is designed to explain. A diathesis-stress approach is particularly good at explaining individual differences, especially in view of similar environmental conditions. However, if almost all youth exhibit some delinquency, then the approach may seem gratuitous. Of course, the same criticism can be applied to sociological explanations. If essentially everybody is delinquent, then it cannot very well vary by circumstances in the social environment.

The Dependent Variable in Delinquency Research

This leads us to the "dependent variable" issue in delinquency research. In research, the dependent variable is what one is trying to explain. If "engaging in any form of delinquent behavior" is the dependent variable, then one certainly does not need to utilize diathesis-stress explanations. The approach most take is to distinguish between serious recidivist delinquency and the more common forms of delinquency (Loeber & Farrington, 1998). As the self-report research makes clear, minor delinquency is so common that it will not be significantly affected by any variable whether social or biopsychological. However, serious, recidivist delinquency is another matter. It is much less common, engaged in by fewer than 10 percent of youth, starts earlier, is more violent and prolific, and is far less likely to desist in adulthood (Moffitt, 1993). It is this form of delinquency that is of particular interest to the biopsychosocial model.

Nature–Nurture and Delinquency

Age of Onset and Delinquency

The research on the serious, recidivist form of delinquency has provided some important impetus to the biopsychosocial approach because it does show the pattern one would expect. According to Farrington and associates, age of onset is among the best predictors of the severity and course of delinquency (1990). Several studies have, therefore, attempted to determine a biological or environmental basis that is potentially linked to the age of delinquency onset. In a review of the behavioral genetic research on delinquency, DiLalla and Gottesman (1989) distinguished between a "continuous" subtype of delinquent and the "transitory" subtype, and suggested that the continuous subtype had a stronger genetic influence on delinquent offending. Moffitt (1993) proposed a distinction between adolescent-limited and life-course persistent offenders. Moffitt noted that as many as 80 percent of adolescents exhibit some antisocial behavior, but serious and persistent antisociality is present in only about 5 percent of the population (Taylor, Iacono & McGue, 2000). Taylor, Iacono, and McGue examined whether "early starters" have an underlying genetic influence on their offending, while the delinquency of "late starters" is more environmentally mediated (This is consistent with the works of DiLalla & Gottesman, 1989 and Moffitt, 1993).

Patterson also reported the distinction between early starters and late starters, but interpreted it from a social learning perspective (1986). According to Patterson, early starters acquire their antisocial behavior essentially through coercive cycles of interaction with their parents, which is followed by school failure and affiliation with antisocial peers. Taylor et al. suggest that Patterson's theory fails to account for the full range of behavioral problems expressed by early starters (Taylor et al., 2000). The coercive interchanges with parents and their consequences have difficulty explaining why early starters also show impulsivity, inattention, overactivity, negative emotional arousal, and decreased autonomic arousal. Taylor et al. proposed that it is an underlying genetic liability that gives rise to early starters' antisociality and tested their proposal on a group of 36 early starters, 86 late starters and 25 nondelinquent controls from a sample of 11-year-old twins. According to Taylor et al. (2000:641):

> The hypotheses in this study were largely supported by the data. Briefly, as compared to late starters and nondelinquent controls, early starters had lower verbal and spatial memory functioning, more problems related to psychological, emotional, and behavioral inhibition,

higher negative emotionality, earlier and more persistent association with antisocial peers, and higher familial transmission of antisocial behavior and greater genetic influence on their phenotype.

From this perspective it not correct to say that delinquency is genetic or environmental. Some forms of delinquency have a stronger genetic basis than do others, but it is never the case that a particular portion of DNA is directly responsible for socially defined behavior, such as delinquency.

Gene-Environment Correlations: Nature versus Nurture or Nature and Nurture

As we are seeing, much of psychology has given up on the nature-nurture controversy. Another insight from the bio-psycho-social approach that led to this move away from conceptualizing behavior as the result of either nature or nurture is the realization that genes (nature) and environment (nurture) interact in very complex ways (Scarr & McCarthy, 1983). The nature-versus-nurture approach assumes that environment and biology are independent of each other (uncorrelated) so that the variance in any particular conduct can be broken down into environmental and biological components. However, if environment and biology are correlated, untangling environmental and biological influences becomes much more difficult. The example of "sensation seeking" may help make this point clear.

Individuals vary in terms of sensation-seeking-behavior (Raine, 1993). Some individuals seek out excitement and risk, while others are sufficiently aroused with very low levels of stimulation. Each person has an optimum level of stimulation, and this varies from individual to individual. When an individual is understimulated, he or she seeks out excitement; when overstimulated he or she seeks stability and quiet. Individuals with a high need for sensation will naturally seek out stimulating environments, while individuals with a low need for stimulation will avoid such environments. As a result, the environment that each is exposed to will differ dramatically, but the environment itself is, at least partially, a function of its underlying biological characteristics. So, while the environment may have an effect on them, this effect may be due as much to their biology – which led them to the environment – as to the environment itself. If the stimulus seeker seeks out and falls in with other stimulus seekers engaged in high-risk activities, can the consequences of their conduct really be attributed solely to the environmental influences?

Shared and Non-shared Environmental Influence

Recognizing the complex relationship between genetics and the environment, some researchers have focused on the study of families who theoretically share similar genetics and environment. There had been a tradition of attributing similarities in sibling behavior to the shared environment of the family. However, families provide genes as well as environments, so it is possible that sibling similarity may result from the contribution of genes rather than a shared family environment. In an influential article, Plomin and Daniels (1987) argued that once the commonality among siblings that is accounted for by genes is considered, siblings are no more alike than individuals selected at random from the population. In other words, there appeared to be no effect reflecting the shared environmental influence of growing up in the same family. This finding, while still puzzling to many, is widely accepted in psychology and behavior genetics (Turkheimer & Waldron, 2000). To be sure, Plomin and Daniels did not assert that there is no environmental influence on behavioral outcomes, but only that the shared environment of the family could not account for them. They noted, "What runs in families is DNA. Not experiences shared in the home. However, environmental factors are very important even though experiences shared by siblings are not" (Plomin, Manke & Pike, 1996:85-86). This issue is, of course, related to the genotype-environment interaction issue just discussed.

It is not only the case that genetic factors influence which environments individuals choose, it is also the case that genetic factors may influence how different individuals evoke different environmental influences (O'Connor, Deater-Deckard, Fulker, Rutter & Plomin, 1998). Genetically influenced behavioral differences will elicit different parental behavior causing children in the same family to live in somewhat different parenting environments (Bell, 1968), and environmental-gene correlations may also promote psychosocial risks for behavioral difficulties across the life span (Caspi & Moffitt, 1995). This would be referred to as nonshared environment, that is, environments unique to each family member, rather than the shared environmental influence affecting all children within the same family.

Heritability

Heritability is a term that expresses the strength of genetic influence on a trait in a given population. It is normally presented as a heritability coefficient. This coefficient ranges in value from 0.0 to 1.0. It represents the proportion of individual differences in a trait accounted for by genetic differences among the individuals. The heritability of eye color is 1, and the heritability of height is about .9, (that is, 90 percent of the variation in height is due to genetic differences) (Rowe, 2002). In interpreting heritability coefficients, there are a couple of issues that must be kept in mind. One is that a heritability estimate is based upon a particular population in particular circumstances, and generalization to other populations and circumstances is not straightforward. The problem is that any estimate of how much of a trait is a function of genetics is not only a function of how the genes operate, but also of similarity in the environment. If environments are held constant (i.e. very similar), then the only source of variation left is genetics. If environments vary considerably, then percent of variance accounted for by genetics can be expected to decline (Scarr & Weinberg, 1976). As a result, heritability estimates must be treated with caution.

The other issue has to do with the relationship between correlational statistics and the statistical analysis of mean differences. Behavioral geneticists tend to focus on correlational analysis, such as heritability, while other researchers are often interested in mean, or average, differences between groups (Bjorklund & Pellegrini, 2002). It is possible to reach different conclusions from the same data set depending on which form of statistical analysis is used.

These two phenomena (amount of variance in the environment and the use of correlations rather than means) can occur together, and if not sensitively analyzed, can lead researchers to miss very important findings. Scarr and Weinberg (1976) made this clear in their study of transracial adoption. In this study, the subjects were white parents, all from middle-class homes, who had adopted low-income black children. When a correlational analysis was conducted, it was found that the correlation between the IQ levels of the black children and their biological parents (.43) was significantly higher than the correlation between the black child's IQ and that of his or her adoptive parents (.29). However, when comparing means, the average IQ of the black children placed in the middle-class homes was 110, or 20 points higher than the mean IQ of comparable black infants reared in the lower-class black community. Twenty points of IQ is over a standard deviation and marks the difference between low average intelligence and high average intelligence. This is a huge difference attributable to environment, but if the analysis of means was not conducted or reported, the Scarr and Weinberg study would be just one more study demonstrating stronger genetic than environmental effects on IQ. The reason for this is the restriction in range of environmental variation in the middle-class homes. Because the environmental conditions in these homes were relatively homogeneous, the only variable left in terms of predicting the rank order of the children's measured intelligence was genetics. An interesting implication is that if educational opportunity is improved for all children, heritability estimates should rise (Scarr, 1992; Bronfenbrenner & Ceci, 1994). Such methodological caveats must be kept in mind in interpreting the following research.

Genetics and Crime

As noted above, it is difficult and futile to try to determine whether any complex human behavior is due to biological factors (nature) or due to environmental factors (nurture). As noted in the diathesis-stress approach outlined above, an individual with a genetic disposition toward aggression or delinquency will actually exhibit the behavior when faced with particular kinds of environmental stress (Wicks-Nelson & Israel, 2000). All behavior is the result of the interaction of biological and environmental forces. Clearly, in order for human behavior to be at all adaptive to changing social conditions, it must be responsive to environmental conditions. No one doubts that human behavior, including delinquency and crime, is affected by environmental circumstances. There is doubt, however, about the extent to which nonenvironmental factors, such as genetic inheritance, affects the likelihood of delinquent behavior. The weight of the evidence (mostly from behavior genetics) seems to be in the direction of some effect of genetics.

Brain Development, Neurochemistry, and Delinquency

It is widely held that the human prefrontal cortex is involved in the inhibition of behavior, in planning, and the maintenance of attention. In somewhat oversimplified language, when brain systems (for example, the motivational and emotional areas of the limbic system) suggest an impulsive action that promises immediate gratification, it is the prefrontal cortical areas including the medial frontal and the orbito-frontal cortex that examine the longer-term implications of the conduct and, when necessary, appropriately inhibit it. If the prefrontal cortex is not sufficiently active, the ill-considered impulsive action may occur (Rowe, 2002).

Individuals differ in the strength of prefrontal inhibitory activity and such differences are sometimes genetically influenced. It is well established that serious attention deficits are much more common in the offspring of individuals with attention deficits, and a leading theory of Attention Deficit Hyperactivity Disorder (ADHD) strongly implicates deficits in the prefrontal cortex (Barkley, 1997). Additional support for a possible role for the prefrontal cortex in uninhibited and impulsive behavior comes from a model proposed by Gray (1976, 1987).

Gray suggests two significant processes at work in the brain. One is focused on activation (the behavioral activation system or BAS) and the other is focused on inhibition (the behavioral inhibition system or BIS). The BAS activates behavior in pursuit of reward or pleasure and is hypothetically related to the neurotransmitter dopamine (Raine, 1993; Moeller, 2001). The BIS inhibits pleasure-motivated behavior based on cues that the behavior might be followed by punishment and is hypothetically related to the neurotransmitters serotonin and norepinephrine (Newman, 1997). Aggression or delinquency may arise from an overactive BAS and/or an underactive BIS. Gray (1976, 1987) suggested that the prefrontal cortex plays an important role in the BIS. Deficiencies in prefrontal activation of the BIS might lead to uninhibited conduct (Moffitt et al., 1998; Moeller, 2001).

In adolescence in particular, there are also important developmental aspects of brain structure and function that affect behavior. Early in the twentieth century the psychologist, G. Stanley Hall described adolescence as a time of 'storm and stress'. By the beginning of the twenty-first century that view had moderated considerably due to work by Arnett (1999) and others who demonstrated that most adolescents navigate the period with apparently little difficulty. More recently the view has shifted back with many behavioral scientists again emphasizing adolescent vulnerabilities, but now with a healthy realization of individual differences in adolescent development.

Ronald Dahl has been instrumental in defining the contemporary neurobehavioral view of adolescence. As Dahl (2004) points out, adolescence presents two puzzles: (1) how to understand high rates of morbidity and mortality despite robust physical health and (2) increasing rates of reckless behavior despite improved capacity for decisionmaking. Shouldn't the increases in physical health and decision-making capacity evident in adolescence have the opposite effect? Dahl (2004) argues that among the neurobehavioral effects of puberty are a variety of biologically based changes in emotion and motivation which lead to a natural increase in risk taking, sensation seeking, and emotional intensity. This leads many adolescents into a relatively long period of highly charged emotionality without a cortical circuitry well-enough developed to effectively deal with it. While it is true that frontally supported decisionmaking continues to improve through adolescence, the mechanisms and processes are still sufficiently fragile that they break down under the very conditions of high arousal that puberty presents. Dahl summarizes some of the recent research in this area as follows (2004:17).

> Taken together this pattern of findings suggests that the primary puberty-specific changes are related to activation of the strong drives, appetites, emotional intensity, and sensation seeking that occurs at puberty... In contrast, most aspects of cognitive development – including reasoning, logic and capacities for self-regulation of emotions and drives – are still developing slowly and continue long after puberty is over.

Further complicating the matter is the fact that puberty arrives earlier in industrial societies while the acceptance of adult roles and responsibilities, which marks the end of adolescence, is occurring later. This combination has had the effect of prolonging the period of adolescent vulnerability in industrial societies by 6- or 7-fold over what is found in traditional societies, (i.e., from 2 to 4 years to 14 or more years) (Schlegel & Barry, 1991). Taking liberty with Dahl's metaphor, one can think of the period of adolescence for many youth as undertaking a relatively long drive in a turbo-charged vehicle with yet undeveloped driving skills.

If it is the case that adolescence contains both some endogenous vulnerability resulting from biologically based stimulus-seeking, coupled with a delay in the development of cortical cognitive control mechanisms, then an explanation of the age distribution of delinquency presents itself. The age distribution generally shows a rise in delinquency beginning in early adolescence (perhaps under the influence of endogenous pubertal changes) and then a decline in later adolescence and early adulthood (perhaps under the influence of increasing cognitive control).

Interacting with these developmental changes in brain structure are fluctuating levels of neurotransmitters such as serotonin, dopamine, and norepinephrine that may also be relevant to antisocial behavior. These molecules are an important part of the way in which neurons (nerve cells) activate or modulate behavior. The availability of neurotransmitters and neurotransmitter receptors is related to psychiatric symptomology, and most of the psychiatric medications for major mental illnesses affect the availability of neurotransmitters. If the production of neurotransmitters and neurotransmitter receptors are influenced by genetic factors (as is suggested by the heritability of many mental illnesses), and if the nervous system's use of neurotransmitters is related to aggression or antisociality, then this presents another possible mechanism for how genes might affect criminal behavior.

In a general population study by Moffitt and associates (1998), serotonin levels were found to be associated with violence and criminal convictions. This study also controlled for drug use, social class, as well as other competing explanations. It is also noteworthy that serotonin levels have been found to modulate aggression in a variety of nonhuman animals (Moeller, 2001; Meyer-Lindenberg et al., 2006). Caspi et al. (2002) studied the genetics of aggression more directly. In this landmark developmental study, convincing evidence is presented for one mechanism by which genetics (albeit in interaction with environment) can affect aggression. The study found that a genetic variant of the MAO-A gene, a gene which helps metabolize serotonin as well as dopamine and norepinephrine, is associated with heightened aggression, but only in males who had been maltreated. Some readers may be aware that the Caspi et al. finding is somewhat counterintuitive because the genetic variant that they found to be positively correlated with aggression would have the presumed effect of increasing the availability of serotonin in the synapse. Because serotonin is positively correlated with impulse control, the finding is puzzling. Gridley and Hoff (2007) present ways to reconcile the apparently discrepant findings.

The neurotransmitter norepinephrine has also been found to be associated with aggression in children in Raine's 1993 meta-analysis and in studies by Olweus (1987) and Magnusson (1988). Thus, it appears that molecules created by the genetic instructions are related to aggressive and delinquent behavior, creating a plausible scenario for how genes may affect the propensity for antisocial conduct. In any case, the very influential study by Caspi et al. and the work by Raine, Olweus, and Magnusson demonstrate the principle themes of this chapter; first that biological factors including genetics are relevant in the study of aggression, and second, that complex human behavior always involves interactions between biological and experiential factors.

Twin and Adoption Studies

The research bearing on whether genetics affects delinquency or crime is usually based upon studies comparing delinquency rates among individuals with similar genes but different environments and those with different genes and similar environments. This is most easily examined in studies of twins. One research method examines the similarity in delinquency or aggression among identical (monozygotic) twins and same-sex fraternal (dizygotic) twins. The logic is that if same-sex fraternal twins raised together by the same parents, in the same home and the same neighborhood, and who attend the same schools, are less alike in terms of delinquent or aggressive conduct than are identical twins raised together, then that provides evidence that genetics plays some role in the behavior. Environment differs little between either set of twins, but the identical twins share 100 percent of their genes in common, and the fraternal twins share only (on average) 50 percent of their genes in common. Hence, if identical twins are more similar (concordant) for delinquency than are fraternal twins, the difference is (at least in part) attributed to genetics (Plomin et al., 1997).

Adoption studies provide another methodology used to examine genetic influences on behavior, including aggression and delinquency. Adoption studies typically examine children separated from their biological parents at birth and reared by adoptive parents. In such a case, one set of parents provides the genetic contribution but not the child's environment. If children are more similar in aggression or crime to the biological parent (who they never met) than to the adoptive parent who reared them, the implication is that the genetic contribution of the biological parents played an important role in the development of delinquency (Papalia, Olds & Feldman, 1999).

A final method combines the two and examines fraternal and identical twins separated at birth and reared by different families. If the identical twins are more similar in concordance for aggression or delinquency than are the fraternal twins, it suggests the effect of their fully shared genetic makeup.

Evidence from both twin and adoption studies support some genetic contribution for antisocial behavior in adults (Moeller, 2001). For example, Raine reviewed 13 studies using the twin methodology and found an average concordance rate of 51.5 percent for monozygotic twins and 20.6 percent for dizygotic twins (1993). More recent studies have shown significant heritability for both aggression and antisocial personality disorder (Moeller, 2001).

With regard to studies of youth, virtually all the research supports a statistically significant genetic contribution to "externalizing" (e.g., aggressive, delinquent, antisocial) behavior (Moeller, 2001). In these studies, it is typical for the genetic component to account for about 50 percent of the variance in externalizing behavior. It is important to note, however, that most of the studies also find a role for environmental factors. For example, Rowe (1983) found that mathematical models that include both genetic and environmental components are necessary to fit the data collected. In genetic behavioral research, the environment is separated into shared and nonshared environment as explained above. Most of the behavioral genetic studies find some effect for both but generally a greater effect for nonshared environmental factors, as one would expect from the Plomin research presented previously in this chapter (Moeller, 2001).

Adoption and twin studies are not unambiguous. They make assumptions about the similarities and differences of environments that are difficult to verify, yet the number and consistency of the findings are hard to ignore. Nonetheless, it may seem preposterous to some that genes, (i.e., portions of DNA which essentially only code for the production of proteins) can affect whether a 17-year-old decides to steal a car, take drugs, or assault someone. To make the picture more convincing, one has to indicate some plausible mechanisms about how genetic factors may influence antisocial behavior. If it can be shown that brain structures or neurochemical processes are implicated in aggressive conduct, the case for genetic components becomes much more plausible.

Attachment and Delinquency

As noted, early-onset delinquency is of particular interest to psycho-biological theorists. We presented evidence that genetic transmission may be part of the explanation for early-onset antisociality. An alternative approach is based upon the theory of attachment proposed by John Bowlby (1969, 1973, 1980, 1988). One source of attachment theory is evolutionary ethology. Infants are seen as biologically predisposed to seek optimal levels of proximity to their earliest caregivers because such proximity protects them from predators and accidents. Because, over evolutionary time, the primary caregivers were also likely to be the biological parents, behavior that promoted the survival of the offspring benefited the evolutionary fitness of the biological parent as well as the offspring. In attachment theory, the caregiver is seen as providing a secure base that comforts the infant when fear or anxiety rises and provides a zone of security or safe haven from which the infant can explore the environment.

When the infant signals a need for greater (or lesser) proximity, perhaps through crying or holding up her arms or squirming, and the caregiver responds appropriately, the infant starts establishing primordial schemas for social relations (internal working models of the social world). In particular, the infant establishes two basic schemas that form the basis for social relationships: first, that the caregiver, and by extension others, are reliable and benevolent, and second, that the child herself is worthy of nurturance and care. This fits very clearly in the biopsychosocial model. The evolutionary ethology aspect is biological, the solicitous care by the caregiver is social, and the internal representations are psychological factors. If all goes well, the child forms a secure attachment and is ready to meet the challenges of social development in positive ways. If the caregiver is careless, angry, abusive, or unresponsive, nonsecure attachment results, and the child is at risk for a variety of negative social and psychological outcomes (Cicchetti & Greenberg, 1991; Sroufe, 1990; Sroufe, Carlson, Levy & Egeland, 1999).

Research supports a statistically significant association between the presence of nonsecure attachment and psychosocial risk for negative developmental outcomes, including aggression and delinquency (Rosenstein and Horowitz, 1996; Lyons-Ruth, 1996; Allen, Hauser & Borman-Spurrell, 1996; Renken, Egeland, Marvinney, Mangelsdorf & Sroufe, 1989). There is also research support for secure attachment playing a "protective" role; that is, the presence of a secure attachment makes negative developmental outcomes less likely (Loeber, 1990).

A controversy in the attachment literature has to do with causal direction. The classical attachment orientation is that improperly responsive parental behavior causes the insecure attachment and the associated developmental risk. One alternative explanation is that largely genetic temperamental factors lead to the insecure attachment. Yet another is that coercive cycles between babies and parents lead to non-optimal parenting and to the attachment difficulties. In her review, Karlen Lyons-Ruth suggests that hostile maternal behaviors are observable prior to the initiation of coercive cycles between parents and young children (1996). She also notes that interventions directed at enhancing parental behavior have positive influences on the quality of attachment, suggesting that the direction of causality is (at least partially) from parent behavior to quality of attachment rather than exclusively from genetic factors to quality of attachment.

Mental Disorders and Crime

Relationship between Serious Mental Disorder and Crime

As previously noted, researchers have attempted to define the relationship between biological and psychological factors and their impact on one's propensity to commit crimes. One such area of study is that of mental disorders and their relationship with crime and violence. Past research regarding serious mental disorders and crime has primarily been conducted on institutionalized populations and has found no significant relationship between mental disorder and crime (Monahan and Steadman, 1983; Rabkin, 1979). However, recent studies that have included the general population have found a statistically significant relationship between mental disorder and crime. A re-analysis of the Epidemiologic Catchment Area study by Swanson et al. (1990) concluded that individuals with major mental disorders had significantly higher rates of violence; roughly 11 to 13 percent compared to 2 percent of the general population. Link et al. (1992) identified that mental patients who were actively experiencing psychotic symptoms (delusions and hallucinations) were at an elevated risk of violence, while those patients who were not actively experiencing psychosis were not at an appreciably higher risk for violence than other members of the general community who had never been treated for psychiatric conditions. The connection, therefore, between serious mental disorders and crime, is more likely related to current psychotic symptoms of the individual rather than to the diagnosis of a mental health disorder (Monahan, 1996; Appelbaum, Robbins & Monahan, 2000). Longitudinal studies, however, have not demonstrated that increases in psychiatric symptoms lead to a greater likelihood of violence (Kraemer, Kazdin, Offord & Kessler, 1997). In addition, some studies suggest that the likelihood of violence among those with mental disorders is increased when co-occuring with substance abuse disorders (Monahan, Steadman et al., 2001; Swanson, Holzer, Ganju & Jono, 1990). Therefore, the relationship between mental disorders and crime and violence has yet to be clearly understood.

Although some evidence exists pertaining to a link between serious mental health disorders and crime and violence, it is important to note that research has identified that the proportion of violence in society attributable to that group is small, clearly below 10 percent and possibly as low as 3 percent (Walsh, Buchanan & Fahy, 2001; Norko & Baranoski, 2005; Monahan, 1996). Much of the research pertaining to mental disorders and crime are in relation to delinquency which will be explored in the following section.

Childhood Mental Disorders: Their Relationships to Crime and Delinquency

While in general there is little relationship between the diagnosis of a mental disorder and criminal or delinquent offending, there are some mental disorders for which the link to delinquency and crime is well established. In childhood, three disorders are significantly associated with delinquency: attention deficit hyperactivity disorder (ADHD), oppositional defiant disorder (ODD), and conduct disorder. Antisocial personality disorder is also strongly related to criminal conduct, and while it is not normally diagnosed in childhood, its diagnosis in adulthood requires the presence of conduct disorder symptoms in childhood (APA, 1994). The prominent symptoms of ADHD include developmentally inappropriate inattention, hyperactivity, and impulsiveness. Oppositional defiant disorder is characterized by a "recurrent pattern of defiant, disobedient, and hostile behavior which is directed toward authority figures and which causes significant impairment in everyday functioning" (APA, 1994:91). Conduct disorder is defined as "a repetitive and persistent pattern of behavior in which the basic rights of others or major age-appropriate societal norms or rules are violated" (APA, 1994:85).

The relationship among these disorders, and between the disorders and delinquency, has been the subject of much research and theoretical disagreement. One issue is whether these are in fact different disorders. The co-morbidity among these disorders is high. Between 84 percent and 96 percent of youth with conduct disorders also meet the criteria for oppositional defiant disorders (Wicks-Nelson & Israel, 2000). However, most children with oppositional defiant disorder do not receive a diagnosis of conduct disorder. According to Hinshaw, Lahey, and Hart (1993), about 50 percent of oppositional defiant youth retain their ODD diagnosis, 25 percent remit, and the other 25 percent progress to a conduct disorder diagnosis. This leads some to believe that ODD is a precursor of conduct disorder, while others disagree (Frick et al., 1991). As many as 65 percent of ADHD children are co-morbid for ODD, and up to 30 percent are co-morbid for conduct disorder (Barkley, 1997). However, the current evidence is that ADHD is a distinct disorder from both ODD and conduct disorder (Schachar & Wachsmuth, 1991). Tremblay (1992) found that ADHD youth without aggression are no more likely to receive diagnoses of conduct disorder or be adjudicated delinquent than are non-ADHD youth, also supporting the distinctive nature of ADHD. However, the prognosis for youth co-morbid for ADHD and conduct disorder is especially poor. According to Forehand, Wierson, Frame, Kempton, and Armistead (1991), children in a combined ADHD-conduct disorder group experienced more arrests, and their first arrest was at an earlier age. In addition, Andersson, Magnusson, and Wennberg (1997) found that children with ADHD plus aggression at age 13 were much more likely to develop alcoholism and criminality before the age of 25 compared to a control group. Finally, Vitelli (1996) reviewed childhood records of 100 maximum-security inmates and not only found significant co-morbidity between conduct disorder and ADHD in their backgrounds but also found that only the presence of conduct disorder was a significant predictor of adult criminality.

A reasonable interpretation of the research on these childhood mental disorders and delinquency is that ODD and conduct disorder represent a developmental progression toward antisociality where a majority of ODD youth remit or stay oppositional and a minority of about 25 percent progress to conduct disorders (Loeber, Lahey & Thomas, 1991). It is also possible that conduct disorder is a developmental precursor of antisocial personality disorder, with a majority remitting but a substantial minority progressing to antisocial personality disorder.

Childhood Psychopathy

An interesting recent development is the attempt to unravel the childhood roots of psychopathy. The Diagnostic and Statistical Manual of the American Psychiatric Association contains no specific diagnosis for psychopathy. In the current taxonomy, the closest diagnosis is antisocial personality disorder, but it is clear to many researchers that psychopathy represents a distinct syndrome from antisocial personality disorder. The syndrome was described by Cleckley (1976) and elaborated through a significant program of research by Hare (1970, 1981, 1984, 1991; Hare, Hart & Harpur, 1991).

Psychopathic offenders are particularly chronic and prolific in their offense history. They commit more crimes, more serious crimes, and a wider variety of crimes (Hare, 1981; Hare, McPherson & Forth, 1988; Harris, Rice & Cormier, 1989). Psychopathic individuals are also distinct in terms of personality characteristics. They are callous, impulsive, deceitful, manipulative and have shallow social commitments. They show distinct neurophysiological correlates, especially related to the executive functions mediated by the frontal lobes (Newman, 1987; Newman & Wallace, 1993). Finally, they are unique in their response to treatment. While empathy-building treatments reduce recidivism among nonpsychopaths, they increase recidivism among psychopaths (Rice & Harris, 1995). While psychopaths engage in copious antisocial "externalizing" behaviors (such as aggression, theft, and substance abuse), they are not especially prone to internalizing disorders (such as anxiety and depression) (Lynam, 1997).

The heterogeneity of childhood behavior problems is a major impediment to effective prediction of future behavior and to the treatment and prevention of serious delinquency. The need to distinguish among subgroups is well recognized (Lynam, 1997; Hinshaw, Lahey & Hart, 1993). Given that psychopathy represents a distinct subgroup among adults, it is reasonable to explore whether a similar subgroup exists among juveniles. Lynam has explored this possibility and found evidence for the existence of childhood psychopathy (1997).

Lynam made use of data from the Pittsburgh Youth Study, a longitudinal study of randomly selected high-risk sample of fourth-grade boys enrolled in Pittsburgh public schools (Van Kammen, Loeber & Stouthamer-Loeber, 1991). His research utilized a measure of childhood psychopathy, referred to as the CPS, which is based on Hare's Psychopathy Check List (PCL), as well as neuropsychological measures and measures of internalizing and externalizing behavior, personality, self-reported delinquency, and social class (1991). According to Lynam, "The results suggest that psychopathy has a childhood manifestation and that this manifestation can be measured reliably. Psychopathic children, like their adult counterparts, were the most frequent, severe, aggressive, and temporally stable offenders" (1997:435). Lynam also reported that scores on the CPS predicted delinquency "above other known robust predictors of delinquency, such as previous delinquency, SES, impulsivity and IQ" (1997:435).

IQ and Delinquency

The relationship between IQ and delinquency has been the subject of research and analysis for many years. One of the most often replicated findings in research on delinquency is the 8 to 12 point (one-half standard deviation) mean difference in IQ between delinquents and nondelinquents (Hirschi & Hindelang, 1977; Henry & Moffitt, 1997; Kazdin, 1995; West & Farrington, 1973; Loeber, Farrington, Stouthamer-Loeber, Moffitt, Caspi, White, Wei & Beyers, 2003). The inverse relationship between IQ and delinquency demonstrates a "dose-response" effect. In the Loeber et al. study based on the Pittsburgh Youth Study, the eight-point IQ difference rose to an 11-point difference for the most serious delinquents (2003). However, the research has been much more informative about what this association does not mean than about what it does mean. The research strongly indicates that it is not an artifact of socioeconomic status or race (Henry & Moffitt, 1997; Loeber et al., 2003). It has been suggested that the inverse correlation between IQ and delinquency is the result of a greater likelihood of less intelligent youth being apprehended or charged, but since the finding holds on self-report data as well as in the official data, that explanation is not supported.

Motivational factors have also been studied on the assumption that delinquent youth are not as interested in performing well on IQ tests. However, in the Loeber et al. research, when research assistants, blind to the nature of the study, rated videotapes of boys taking the IQ test, they found only small differences between the delinquent and nondelinquent youth on behavioral indicators of motivation, accounting for only about two IQ points. Loeber et al. also found similar IQ differences in youth from advantaged and disadvantaged neighborhoods and, when controls for impulsiveness and executive dysfunction are included, the correlation is reduced but remains statistically significant (Lynam, Moffitt & Stouthamer-Loeber, 1993; Loeber et al., 2003).

Perhaps the best explanation for the IQ-delinquency association is one postulated by Lynam et al. (1993) and Loeber et al. (2003). They argue that low IQ leads to school failure and resulting frustration and humiliation. This alienates youth from the school and its prosocial influences and leads to delinquency. There is some evidence for this in the Lynam et al. (1993) path analysis, which found that 75 percent of the relationship between IQ and delinquency was mediated through lack of school achievement. The implication of this finding is that steps must be taken to make school as rewarding an experience for youth with lower IQs as it is for youth with higher IQs. This strategy conflicts with the current emphasis on school performance and testing, which can be expected to further alienate low-IQ youth from the school setting.

Hostile Attributional Bias

Kenneth Dodge has explored how the tendency to attribute hostile intent to others is related to aggression (1980, 1986, 1991). In ambiguous social situations, it is often difficult to correctly attribute intent to another actor, and individuals differ in the extent to which they conclude that an ambiguous social behavior is aggressive. For example, if someone bumps into you in the hall, they may have done so because they are clumsy or preoccupied, or they may have intended to harm or embarrass you. Naturally, those youth who make hostile attributions in such circumstances are more likely to respond aggressively than are others, and those youth who have a disposition to make hostile attributions generally will be more aggressive than other youth. Dodge has distinguished between early-stage processing of social information and later-stage processing. Early-stage processing involves failure to attend to relevant social cues (the process of interpreting intentions) and the tendency to access aggressive responses. Later-stage processing includes the assessment of the likely outcome of aggressive behavior. Early-stage processing problems are hypothesized to be related to reactive aggression while proactive aggression would result from later-stage processing. It is likely that proactive aggression is the result of learning that aggression often brings about desired results, while reactive aggression, which is related to deficits in social information processing, may be more endogenous. Dodge and Coie reported that reactively aggressive boys demonstrate cognitive problems in early-stage processing, but such problems are absent in proactively aggressive youth (1987). Dodge, Price, Bachorowski, and Newman (1990) found that early stage processing difficulties are associated with undersocialized aggression. The emergence of reactive aggression is also related to early physical abuse and harsh punishment. Dodge, Lochman, Harnish, Bates, and Pettit (1997) found that 41 percent of abused children in their sample met the criteria for reactive aggression, while the criteria was met by only 15 percent of the nonabused children.

Self-Esteem

Another common belief is that that delinquency, antisocial conduct, and poor mental health are associated with low self-esteem (Taylor, 1989; Taylor & Brown, 1988). Some have proposed that boosting self-concept will reduce levels of depression and aggression (Cairns & Cairns, 1988; Harter, 1983). However, more recently, this perspective has been called into question. Baumeister, Smart, and Boden have proposed that individuals with high levels of self-esteem are more likely to be aggressive (1996). In their view, raising self-esteem may actually increase, rather than decrease, aggression. From Baumeister's perspective, the aggression related to high self-esteem derives from the fact that individuals with very high self-concepts are threatened by any feedback that challenges their self-views.

Research on children's self-perceptions has generally supported the link between positively biased self-perceptions and aggressive behavior (David & Kistner, 2000). David and Kistner report a study by Garrison, Earls and Kindlon (1983) that found that children with positively biased self-evaluations were rated by clinicians and teachers as more aggressive than were children with accurate or negatively biased self views. David and Kistner (2000) studied 859 children in third through fifth grades from 61 classrooms, representing males and females, as well as white and black youth. They reported a link between positively biased self-perceptions and aggression based on peer nominations of aggression. This effect held even after controlling for the effects of gender and ethnicity (David & Kistner, 2000). Moreover, contrary to Baumeister's notion that there is an optimal range of bias, (i.e. that a small amount of positive self-perception bias is healthy, but too much is problematic) David and Kistner found a linear relationship between positive bias and peer-nominated aggression.

An Evolutionary Psychological Approach to Gender Differences in Delinquency

The trait that most strongly distinguishes between violent and nonviolent individuals is gender, with male gender as the strongest single predictor of violence. Despite the fact that delinquency by girls has been increasing as a proportion of all delinquency, violent delinquency is still essentially a male phenomenon (Cook & Laub, 1998). More than 90 percent of all juvenile murders are committed by males (Snyder & Sickmund, 1999). A similar gender ratio is present for adults, and when one examines stranger homicide alone, the ratio increases from 9:1 to 30:1. The question naturally arises as to what accounts for these differences.

Because roughly the same proportion of females as males live in poverty, live in very poor neighborhoods, come from disorganized families, attend troubled schools, and have a low IQ, these variables do not provide promising leads for the explanation of this striking difference. Perhaps the most common explanation appeals to socialization differences based on cultural expectations and definitions of appropriate behavior for males versus females. This may provide an explanation, but it is difficult to sort out whether parents and other socializing agents are responding to gender-based preferences or are responsible for creating them.

Another potential challenge facing the socialization hypothesis is the cross-cultural and cross-temporal ubiquity of the gender differences in aggression and crimes of violence. For example, Coie and Dodge (1998) found that gender differences in aggression held across socioeconomic groups in the United States and are also apparent in Mexico, Britain, Ethiopia, Kenya, India, and the Philippines, among others.

The analysis of gender differences presented in this chapter is based primarily on work by David Bjorklund and colleagues (Bjorklund & Harnishfeger, 1995; Bjorklund & Kipp, 1996; Bjorklund & Pellegrini, 2002). We noted above that differences in the inhibitory capacity of the prefrontal cortex might be related to delinquency. Bjorklund has explored whether, over evolutionary time, domain-specific gender differences in inhibition may have arisen. In Bjorklund's reasoning, if human females have evolved superior inhibitory capacity in certain aggression-relevant domains, this may account for the dramatic and ubiquitous gender differences in aggression.

According to Bjorklund, the evolutionary origin of the postulated female superiority in inhibitory capacity stems from gender differences in parental investment in offspring. From the Darwinian perspective, both males and females are designed to maximize fitness through reproduction. However, over the bulk of evolutionary time, males and females have been in very different circumstances in regard to reproduction. Males can achieve reproductive success by impregnating as many women as possible. The biologically essential male investment in mating and reproduction is limited to the contribution of replenishable sperm. Females on the other hand, have a much more significant biologically essential investment, including the nine month commitment related to gestation. In addition, caring for the uniquely immature human infant after birth has disproportionately fallen to women across cultures and time. Trivers (1972) introduced the notion that these differences in investment would lead to differences between men and women in reproductive strategies.

As we have seen, females must make a far greater investment in reproduction than do males. Because of this, a woman maximizes her reproductive interests by mating with a man who will not only provide good genes but will also stay around to provide resources for her during pregnancy and for her offspring after pregnancy. From the evolutionary perspective, that should lead to a more cautious reproductive strategy, with women being more selective in their mating than men. Oliver and Hyde (1993) provide evidence that women are more selective and men are more indiscriminate in engaging in sex.

Bjorklund and colleagues speculate that these gender differences in reproductive and parenting strategies may have led to evolutionary selection pressure toward enhanced inhibitory capacity among females. In their 1996 article, Bjorklund and Kipp reviewed the evidence for enhanced inhibitory capacity among females in those domains (sexual, social, and behavioral) where parental investment theory would predict it. The evidence reviewed generally supported the predictions derived from parental investment theory. Women appear to be better able to deploy inhibitory strategies in social situations, especially in concealing facial and bodily expressions and in control of emotions. Women are better able to delay gratification and resist temptation and there is a suggestion, though the number of studies is very small, that women are better able to control sexual arousal.

The order of magnitude difference in crimes of violence has defied convincing explanation for decades. Socialization practices may account for the difference, but if socialization were that powerful, there would be far less social deviance and delinquency than there is. It may still be the case that socialization is at the heart of the difference, but a socialization-only case has not yet been convincingly made. In the meantime, evolutionary psychology has proposed that, based on Darwinian approaches to differential reproductive strategies between males and females, women have evolved greater inhibitory capacity in those very domains (social, sexual, and behavioral) that would affect aggressive behavior.

Summary and Discussion

At the beginning of this chapter we discussed that biopsychological explanations of delinquent and criminal behavior are often seen as more politically or socially regressive than social explanations. It is now time to revisit that issue briefly. If the use of such approaches leads social policy away from improving those social conditions that make delinquent and criminal conduct more likely (i.e. those social conditions that increase the stress portion of the diathesis-stress equation), then the approaches are being inappropriately used for regressive ends. Biopsychological explanations, however, can also have positive social consequences.

First of all, it is not the case that simply because a disorder has biological roots that it is more difficult to alter than behavior that has social roots. There are many examples of biologically based disabilities that are readily corrected. Nearsightedness is a clear example of a biologically based disability that is easily corrected. Most mental disorders are much more likely to be treated effectively once the biological factors giving rise to them are better understood. If, for example, it is determined that reactive aggression is the result of diminished neurotransmitter uptake in the prefrontal cortex, we may have better capacity to improve it in a humane fashion than we currently do. Moreover, while it is the case that in crime and delinquency, biologically based explanations are seen as politically less progressive, the opposite is the case for mental illnesses. Most advocates for the mentally ill stress that mental disorders are brain-based illnesses and are not the fault of the affected individual or his or her family. This is seen as reducing the stigma associated with such problems and making rehabilitation more likely while strengthening the argument against incarceration of mentally ill offenders. Similarly in substance abuse circles, a commitment to the view that addiction is a biologically based disease makes effective and humane treatment more likely. In regards to sexual preference, it is generally more liberal to see homosexual preferences as based in biology rather than caused by having particular experiences in childhood or as the result of a "lifestyle" choice. We have not only seen that biological factors are relevant to any thorough discussion of delinquency, but have also seen how delinquency often arises during a transitional period, where endogenous factors make adolescents particularly vulnerable. Such mitigating factors should certainly affect justice system options for delinquent youth.

Scientific theories are, in the final analysis, just tools. What is most important in terms of enhancing human dignity is how they are deployed and what policy implications are derived from them. In any case, if we have convinced you that biopsychological approaches hold important information, then it is incumbent on all social scientists to be receptive to what they have to offer. It is perfectly clear that these approaches will never replace social etiology. If human behavior is to be adaptive, it must be open to environmental influences and the diathesis-stress approach explicitly recognizes social factors as relevant. Looking into the next century, the question that remains is not whether biological or psychological or sociological approaches will be most successful in understanding crime and delinquency, but rather how successful will we be in describing how biological, psychological, and sociological factors interact to produce delinquent behavior.

Endnotes

[1] Brigham reported that the Alpine and Mediterranean "races" were "intellectually inferior to the Nordic "race."

References

Akers, R.L. (1985). *Deviant Behavior: A Social Learning Approach*, Third Edition. Upper Saddle River, NJ: Prentice Hall.

Allen, J.P., S.T. Hauser & E. Borman-Spurrell (1996). "Attachment Theory as a Framework for Understanding Sequelae of Severe Adolescent Psychopathology: An 11-Year Follow-up Study." *Journal of Consulting and Clinical Psychology*, 64:254-263.

American Psychiatric Association (1994). *Diagnostic and Statistical Manual of Mental Disorders*, Fourth Edition. Washington, DC: Author.

Andersson, T., D. Magnusson & P. Wennberg (1997). "Early Aggressiveness and Hyperactivity as Indicators of Adult Alcohol Problems and Criminality: A Prospective Longitudinal Study of Male Subjects." *Studies on Crime and Crime Prevention*, 6:7-20.

Appelbaum, P., P. Robbins & J. Monahan (2000). "Violence and Delusions: Data from the MacArthur Risk Assessment Study." *American Journal of Psychiatry*, 157:566-572.

Arnett, J.J. (1999). Adolescent Storm and Stress, Reconsidered. *American Psychologist*, 54: 317-326.

Barkley, R.A. (1997). "Behavioral Inhibition, Sustained Attention, and Executive Functions: Constructing a Unifying Theory of ADHD." *Psychological Bulletin*, 121(1):65-94.

Bauer, G. (2001). "Shrouded Legacy: The History of the American Eugenics Movement." *Health Generations Supplement*, 1(3).

Baumeister, R.F., L. Smart & J.M. Boden (1996). "Relation of Threatened Egotism to Violence and Aggression: The Dark Side of High Self-esteem." *Psychological Review*, 103:5-33.

Bell, R.Q. (1968). "A Reinterpretation of the Direction of Effects in Studies of Socialization." *Psychological Review*, 75:81-95.

Bjorklund, D.F. & A.D. Pellegrini (2002). *The Origins of Human Nature*. Washington, DC: American Psychological Association.

Bjorklund, D.F. & K.K. Harnishfeger (1995). "The Role of Inhibition Mechanisms in the Evolution of Human Cognition." In F.N. Dempster & C.J. Brainerd (eds.) *New Perspectives on Interference and Inhibition in Cognition*, pp. 141-173. New York, NY: Academic Press.

Bjorklund, D.F. & K. Kipp (1996). "Parental Investment Theory and Gender Differences in the Evolution of Inhibition Mechanisms." *Psychological Bulletin*, 120:163-188.

Bowlby, J. (1988). *A Secure Base: Clinical Implication of Attachment Theory*. London: Routledge and Kegan Paul.

Bowlby, J. (1980). *Attachment and Loss: Vol. III: Loss*. New York, NY: Basic Books.

Bowlby, J. (1973). *Attachment and Loss: Vol. II: Separation: Anxiety and Anger*. New York, NY: Basic Books.

Bowlby, J. (1969). *Attachment and Loss: Vol. I: Attachment*. New York, NY: Basic Books.

Brigham, C.C. (1923). *A Study of American Intelligence*. Princeton, NJ: Princeton University Press, pp. xx, 197.

Bronfenbrenner, U. & S.J. Ceci (1994). "Nature-Nurture Reconceptualized in Developmental Perspective: A Bioecological Model." *Psychological Review*, 101:568-586.

Buck v. Bell, 274 U.S. 436 (1927).

Cairns, R.B. & B.D. Cairns (1988). "The Sociogenesis of Self Concepts." In N. Bolger, A. Caspi, G. Downey & M. Morehouse (eds.) *Persons in Context: Developmental Processes*, pp. 181-202. New York, NY: Cambridge University Press.

Caspi, A., J. McClay, T.E. Moffitt, J. Mill, J. Martin & I.W. Craig (2002). "Role of Genotype in the Cycle of Violence in Maltreated Children." *Science*, 297, August 2, 851-854.

Caspi, A. & T.E. Moffitt (1995). "The Continuity of Maladaptive Behavior: From Description to Understanding in the Study of Antisocial Behavior." In D. Cicchetti & D. Cohen (eds.) *Developmental Psychopathology*, 2:472-511. New York, NY: Wiley.

Cicchetti, D. & M.T. Greenberg (eds.) (1991). "Special Issue: Attachment and Developmental Psychopathology." *Development and Psychopathology*, 3:347-531.

Cleckley, H. (1976). *The Mask of Sanity*. St. Louis, MO: Mosby.

Coie, J.D. & K.A. Dodge (1998). "Aggression and Antisocial Behavior." In N. Eisenberg & W. Damon (eds.) *Handbook of Child Psychology*, 3(5):779-862. New York, NY: Wiley.

Cook, P.J. & J.H. Laub (1998). "The Epidemic of Youth Violence." In M. Tonry & M.H. Moore (eds.) *Youth Violence: Crime and Justice*, 24:27-64. Chicago, IL: University of Chicago Press.

Dahl, R.E. (2004). *Adolescent Brain Development: Vulnerabilities and Opportunities*. New York, NY: Academy of Science, 1021: 1– 22.

David, C.F. & J.A. Kistner (2000). "Do Positive Self-Perceptions Have a 'Dark Side'? Examination of the Link between Perceptual Bias and Aggression." *Journal of Abnormal Child Psychology*, 28(4):327-337.

DiLalla, L.F. & I.I. Gottesman (1989). "Heterogeneity of Causes of Delinquency and Criminality: Lifespan Perspectives." *Development and Psychopathology*, 1:339-349.

Dodge, K.A. (1991). "The Structure and Function of Reactive and Proactive Aggression." In D.J. Pepler & K.H. Rubin (eds.) *The Development and Treatment of Childhood Aggression*, pp. 201-218. Hillsdale, NJ: Lawrence Erlbaum Associates.

Dodge, K.A. (1986). "A Social Information Processing Model of Social Competence in Children." In M. Perlmutter (ed.) *Eighteenth Annual Minnesota Symposium on Child Psychology*, 18:77-125. Hillsdale, NJ: Lawrence Erlbaum Associates.

Dodge, K.A. (1980). "Social Cognition and Children's Aggressive Behavior." *Child Development*, 51:162-170.

Dodge, K.A. & J.D. Coie (1987). "Social Information Processing Factors in Reactive and Proactive Aggression in Children's Peer Groups." *Journal of Personality and Social Psychology*, 53:1146-1158.

Dodge, K.A., J.E. Lochman, J.D. Harnish, J.E. Bates & G.S. Pettit (1997). "Reactive and Proactive Aggression in School Children and Psychiatrically Impaired: Chronically Assaultive Youth." *Journal of Abnormal Psychology*, 106(1):37-51.

Dodge, K.A., J.M. Price, J. Bachorowski & J.P. Newman (1990). "Hostile Attributional Biases in Severely Aggressive Adolescents." *Journal of Abnormal Psychology*, 99:385-392.

Elliot, D.S., S. Ageton, D. Huizinga, B.A. Knowles & R.J. Canter (1983). "The Prevalence and Incidence of Delinquent Behavior: 1976-1980." *The National Youth Survey Report No.26*. Boulder, CO: Behavioral Research Institute.

Farrington, D.P., R. Loeber, R. Elliot, J.D. Hawkins, D.B. Kandel, M.W. Klein, J. McCord, D.C. Rowe & R.E. Tremblay (1990). "Advancing Knowledge about the Onset of Delinquency and Crime. In B. Lahey & A. Kazdin (eds.) *Advances in Clinical Child Psychology*, 13:283-342. New York, NY: Plenum.

Forehand, R., M. Wierson, C. Frame, T. Kempton & L. Armistead (1991). "Juvenile Delinquency Entry and Persistence: Do Attention Problems Contribute to Conduct Problems?" *Journal of Behavior Therapy and Experimental Psychiatry*, 22:261-264.

Frick, P.J., B.B. Lahey, R. Loeber, M. Stouthamer-Loeber, S. Green, E.L. Hart & M.A.G. Christ (1991). "Oppositional Defiant Disorder and Conduct Disorder in Boys: Patterns of Behavioral Covariation." *Journal of Clinical Child Psychology*, 20:202-208.

Garrison, W., F. Earls & D. Kindlon (1983). "An Application of the Pictorial Scale of Perceived Competence and Acceptance within an Epidemiological Survey." *Journal of Abnormal Child Psychology*, 11:367-377.

Goddard, H.H. (1914). *Feeble-mindedness: Its Causes and Consequences*. New York, NY: Macmillan.

Gray, J.A. (1987). "Perspectives on Anxiety and Impulsivity: A Commentary." *Journal of Research in Personality*, 21:493-509.

Gray, J.A. (1976). "The Neuropsychology of Anxiety." In I.G. Sarason & C.D. Spielberger (eds.) *Stress and Anxiety*, 3:3-26. Washington, DC: Hemisphere.

Gridley, M.C. & R. Hoff (2007). "The MAO-A Gene's Seemingly Paradoxical Effect on Aggression." *Psychology Journal*, 4(2):72-76.

Hare, R.D. (1991). *Manual for the Hare Psychopathy Checklist-Revised*. North Tonawanda, NY: Multi-Health Systems.

Hare, R.D. (1984). "Performance of Psychopaths on Cognitive Tasks Related to Frontal Lobe Function." *Journal of Abnormal Psychology*, 93:113-140.

Hare, R.D. (1981). "Psychopathy and Violence." In J.R. Hayes, T.K. Roberts & K.S. Solway (eds.) *Violence and the Violent Individual*, pp. 53-74. Jamaica, NY: Spectrum.

Hare, R.D. (1970). *Psychopathy: Theory and Practice*. New York, NY: Wiley.

Hare, R.D., L.M. McPherson & A.E. Forth (1988). "Male Psychopaths and Their Criminal Careers." *Journal of Consulting and Clinical Psychology*, 56:710-714.

Hare, R.D., S.D. Hart & T.J. Harpur (1991). "Psychopathy and the DSM–IV Criteria for Antisocial Personality Disorder." *Journal of Abnormal Psychology*, 100:391-398.

Harris, G.T., M.E. Rice & C.A. Cormier (1989). "Violent Recidivism among Psychopaths and Nonpsychopaths Treated in a Therapeutic Community." *Penetanguishene Mental Health Center Research Report*, 6:181.

Harter, S. (1983). "Developmental Perspectives on the Self-system." In E.M. Hetherington & P.H. Mussen (eds.) *Handbook of Child Psychology. Vol. 4: Socialization, Personality, and Social Development*. New York, NY: Wiley.

Henry, B. & T.E. Moffitt (1997). "Neuropsychological and Neuroimaging Studies of Juvenile Delinquency and Adult Criminal Behavior." In D.M. Stoff, J. Breiling & J.D. Maser (eds.) *Handbook of Antisocial Behavior*, pp. 280-288. New York, NY: Wiley.

Hinshaw, S.P., B.B. Lahey & E.L. Hart (1993). "Issues of Taxonomy and Comorbidity in the Development of Conduct Disorder." *Development and Psychopathology*, 5:31-49.

Hirschi, T. & M.J. Hindelang (1977). "Intelligence and Delinquency: A Revisionist Review." *American Sociological Review*, 42:571-587.

Kazdin, A.E. (1995). *Conduct Disorders in Childhood and Adolescence*, Second Edition. Thousand Oaks, CA: Sage.

Kevles, D.J. (1985). *In the Name of Eugenics*. New York, NY: Alfred A. Knopf, Inc.

Kraemer, H.C., A.E. Kazdin, D.R. Offord & R.C. Kessler (1997). "Coming to Terms with the Terms of Risk." *Archives of General Psychiatry*, 54:337–343.

Link, B.G., H. Andrews & F.T. Cullen (1992). "The Violent and Illegal Behavior of Mental Patients Reconsidered." *American Sociological Review*, 57(3):275-292.

Loeber, R. (1990). "Development and Risk Factors of Juvenile Antisocial Behavior and Delinquency." *Clinical Psychology Review*, 10:1-41.

Loeber, R., B.B. Lahey & C. Thomas (1991). "Diagnostic Conundrum of Oppositional Defiant Disorder and Conduct Disorder." *Journal of Abnormal Psychology*, 100:379-390;

Loeber, R. & D.P. Farrington (eds.) (1998). *Serious and Violent Juvenile Offenders: Risk Factors and Successful Interventions*. Thousand Oaks, CA: Sage Publications, Inc.

Loeber, R., D.P. Farrington, M. Stouthamer-Loeber, T.E. Moffitt, A. Caspi, H.R. White, E.H. Wei & J.M. Beyers (2003). "The Development of Male Offending: Key Findings from 14 Years of the Pittsburgh Youth Study." In T. Thornberry & M. Krohn (eds.) *Longitudinal Research in the Social and Behavioral Sciences*, pp. 93-136. New York, NY: Kluwer/Plenum.

Lynam, D.R. (1997). "Pursuing the Psychopath: Capturing the Fledgling Psychopath in a Nomological Net." *Journal of Abnormal Psychology*, 106(3):425-438.

Lynam, D., T. Moffitt & M. Stouthamer-Loeber (1993). "Explaining the Relation between IQ and Delinquency: Class, Race, Test Motivation, School Failure, or Self-Control?" *Journal of Abnormal Psychology*, 102:187-196.

Lyons-Ruth, K. (1996). "Attachment Relationships among Children with Aggressive Behavior Problems: The Role of Disorganized Early Attachment Patterns." *Journal of Consulting and Clinical Psychology*, 64(1):64-73.

Magnusson, D. (1988). "Aggressiveness, Hyperactivity, and Autonomic Activity/Reactivity in the Development of Social Maladjustment." In D. Magnusson (ed.) *Individual Development From an Interactional Perspective: A Longitudinal Study*, pp. 153-172. Hillsdale, NJ: Lawrence Erlbaum Associates.

Meyer-Lindenberg, A., J.W. Buckholtz, K. Bhaskar, A.R. Hariri, L. Pezawas, G. Blasi, A. Wabnitz, R. Honea, B. Verchinski, J. Callicott, M. Egan, V. Mattay & D.R. Weinberger (2006). "Neural Mechanisms of Genetic Risk for Impulsivity and Violence in Humans." Proceedings of the National Academy of Sciences, 103 (16): 6269-6274.

Moeller, T.G. (2001). *Youth Aggression and Violence*. Mahwah, NJ: Lawrence Erlbaum Associates.

Moffitt, T.E. (1993). "Adolescence-Limited and Life-Course-Persistent Anti-Social Behavior: A Developmental Taxonomy." *Psychological Review*, 100:674-701.

Moffitt, T.E., G.L. Brammer, A. Caspi, J.P. Fawcett, M. Raleigh, A. Yuwiler & T. Silva (1998). "Whole Blood Serotonin Relates to Violence in an Epidemiological Study." *Biological Psychiatry*, 43:446-457.

Moffitt, T.E., P.A. Silva, D.R. Lynam & B. Henry (1994). "Self-reported Delinquency at Age 18: New Zealand's Dunedin Multidisciplinary Health and Developmental Study." In J. Junger-Tas, G.J. Terlouw & M.W. Klein (eds.) *Delinquent Behavior Among Youth People in the Western World: First Results of the International Self-report Delinquency Study*, pp. 354-369. Amsterdam: Kugler.

Monahan, J. (1996). "Violence Prediction: The Past Twenty and the Next Twenty Years." *Criminal Justice and Behavior*, 23:107-120.

Monahan, J. & H. Steadman (1983). "Crime and Mental Disorder: An Epidemiological Approach." In M. Tonry & N. Morris (eds.) *Crime and Justice: An Annual Review of Research*, 4:145-189. Chicago, IL: University of Chicago Press.

Monahan, J., H. Steadman, E. Silver, P. Appelbaum, P. Robbins, E. Mulvey et al. (2001). *Rethinking Violence Risk Assessment: The MacArthur Study of Mental Disorder and Violence*. New York, NY: Oxford University Press.

Newman, J.P. (1997). "Conceptual Models of the Nervous System: Implication for Antisocial Behavior." In D.M. Stoff, J. Breiling & J.D. Maser (eds.) *Handbook of Antisocial Behavior*, pp. 324-335. New York, NY: Wiley.

Newman, J.P. (1987). "Reaction to Punishment in Extraverts and Psychopaths: Implications for the Impulsive Behavior of Disinhibited Individuals." *Journal of Research Personality*, 21:464-480.

Newman, J.P. & J.F. Wallace (1993). "Diverse Pathways to Deficient Self-regulation: Implications for Disinhibitory Psychopathology in Children." *Clinical Psychology Review*, 13:699-720.

Norko, M. & M.V. Baranoski (2005). "The State of Contemporary Risk Assessment Research." *Canadian Journal of Psychiatry*, 50:18-26.

O'Connor, T.G., K. Deater-Deckard, D. Fulker, M. Rutter & R. Plomin (1998). "Genotype-Environment Correlations in Late Childhood and Early Adolescence: Antisocial Behavioral Problems in Coercive Parenting." *Developmental Psychology*, 34(5):970-981.

Oliver, M.B. & J.S. Hyde (1993). "Gender Differences in Sexuality: A Meta-Analysis." *Psychological Bulletin*, 114(1):29-51.

Olweus, D. (1987). "Testosterone and Adrenaline: Aggressive Antisocial Behavior in Normal Adolescent Males." In S.A. Mednick, T.E. Moffitt & S.A. Stack (eds.) *The Causes of Crime: New Biological Approaches*, pp. 263-282. Cambridge, UK: Cambridge University Press.

Papalia, D.E., S.W. Olds & R.D. Feldman (1999). *A Child's World: Infancy through Adolescence*, Eighth Edition. Boston, MA: McGraw-Hill.

Patterson, G.R. (1986). "Performance Models for Antisocial Boys." *American Psychologist*, 41:432-444.

Plomin, R. & D. Daniels (1987). "Why Are Children in the Same Family So Different from One Another?" *Behavioral and Brain Science*, 10:1-60.

Plomin, R., J.C. DeFries, G.E. McClearn & M. Rutter (1997). *Behavior Genetics*, Third Edition. New York, NY: Freeman.

Plomin, R., B. Manke & A. Pike (1996). "Siblings, Behavioral Genetics, and Competence." In G. Brody (ed.) *Sibling Relationships: Their Causes and Consequences*, pp. 85-86. Norwood, NJ: Ablex Publishing.

Raine, A. (1993). *The Psychopathology of Crime*. San Diego, CA: Academic Press.

Rabkin, J.G. (1979). "Criminal Behavior of Discharged Mental Patients: A Critical Appraisal of the Research." *Psychological Bulletin*, 86:1-27.

Renken, B., B. Egeland, D. Marvinney, S. Mangelsdorf & L.A. Sroufe (1989). "Early Childhood Antecedents of Aggression and Passive-Withdrawal in Early Elementary School." *Journal of Personality*, 57:257-281.

Rice, M.E. & G.T. Harris (1995). "Violent Recidivism: Assessing Predictive Validity." *Journal of Consulting*, 63:737-748.

Rosenstein, D.S. & H.A. Horowitz (1996). "Adolescent Attachment and Psychopathology." *Journal of Consulting and Clinical Psychology*, 64(2):244-253.

Rowe, D.C. (2002). *Biology and Crime*. Los Angeles, CA: Roxbury Publishing Company.

Rowe, D.C. (1983). "Biometrical Genetic Models of Self-Reported Delinquent Behavior: A Twin Study." *Behavior Genetics*, 13:473-489.

Scarr, S. (1992). "Developmental Theories for the 1990s: Development and Individual Differences." *Child Development*, 63:1-19.

Scarr, S. & K. McCarthy (1983). "How People Make Their Own Environments: A Theory of Genotype a Environment Effects." *Child Development*, 54:424-435.

Scarr, S. & R.A. Weinberg (1976). "IQ Test Performance of Black Children Adopted by White Families." *American Psychologist*, 31:726-739.

Schachar, R.J. & R. Wachsmuth (1991). "Family Dysfunction and Psychosocial Adversity: Comparison of Attention Deficit Disorder, Conduct Disorder, Normal and Clinical Controls. Special Issue: Childhood Disorders in the Context of the Family." *Canadian Journal of Behavioural Science*, 23:332-348.

Schlegel, A. & H. Barry (1991). *Adolescence: An Anthropological Inquiry*. New York, NY: The Free Press.

Snyder, H.N. & M. Sickmund (1999). *Juvenile Offenders and Victims: 1999 National Report*. Washington, DC: Office of Juvenile Justice and Delinquency Prevention.

Sroufe, L.A. (1990). "Considering the Normal and Abnormal Together: The Essence of Developmental Psychopathology." *Development and Psychopathology*, 2:335-347.

Sroufe, L.A., E.A. Carlson, A.K. Levy & B. Egeland (1999). "Implications of Attachment Theory for Developmental Psychopathology." *Development and Psychopathology*, 11:1-13.

Swanson, J., C. Holzer, V. Ganju & R. Jono (1990). "Violence and Psychiatric Disorder in the Community: Evidence from the Epidemiologic Catchment Surveys." *Hospital and Community Psychiatry*, 41:761-770.

Taylor, J., W.G. Iacono & M. McGue (2000). "Evidence for a Genetic Etiology of Early-Onset Delinquency." *Journal of Abnormal Psychology*, 109(4):634-643.

Taylor, S.E. (1989). *Positive Illusion: Creative Self-deception and the Healthy Mind*. New York, NY: Basic Books.

Taylor, S.E. & J.D. Brown (1988). "Illusion and Well-being: A Social Psychological Perspective on Mental Health." *Psychological Bulletin*, 103:193-210.

Tooby, J. & L. Cosmides (1992). "The Psychological Foundation of Culture." In J. Barkow, L. Cosmides & J. Tooby (eds.) *The Adapted Mind*, pp. 19-136. New York, NY: Oxford University Press.

Tremblay, R.E. (1992). "The Prediction of Delinquent Behavior from Childhood Behavior: Personality Theory Revisited." In J. McCord (ed.) *Facts, Frameworks, and Forecasts: Advances in Criminological Theory*, pp. 193-230. New Brunswick, NJ: Transaction.

Trivers. R.L. (1972). "Parental Investment and Sexual Selection." In B. Campbell (ed.) *Sexual Selection and the Descent of Man*, pp. 136-179. Chicago, IL: Aldine.

Turkheimer, E. & M. Waldron (2000). "Nonshared Environment: A Theoretical, Methodological, and Quantitative Review." *Psychological Bulletin*, 126(1):78-108.

Van Kammen, W.B., R. Loeber & M. Stouthamer-Loeber (1991). "Substance Use and Its Relationship to Conduct Problems and Delinquency in Young Boys." *Journal of Youth and Adolescence*, 20:399-414.

Vitelli, R. (1996). "Prevalence of Childhood Conduct and Attention-Deficit Hyperactivity Disorders in Adult Maximum-Security Inmates." International Journal of Offender Therapy and Comparative Criminology, 40:263-271.

Walsh, E., A. Buchanan & T. Fahy (2001). "Violence and Schizophrenia: Examining the Evidence." *British Journal of Psychiatry*, 180:490-495.

West, D.J. & D.P. Farrington (1973). *Who Becomes Delinquency?* London: Heinemann.

Wicks-Nelson, R. & A.C. Israel (2000). *Behavior Disorders of Childhood*, Fourth Edition. Upper Saddle River, NJ: Prentice Hall.

CHAPTER 4

Youth, Drugs, and Delinquency

Frank P. Williams III
Marilyn McShane

Introduction

By its very definition, illicit drug use by young people would automatically constitute a crime; therefore, all illicit drug use is delinquency. Consequently, it would be impossible to be an illicit drug user without being a delinquent. Also, because it is illegal for youth to consume alcohol, health professionals, policymakers, and others often refer to any alcohol use by youngsters as "abuse." Thus, the connection between drug use, abuse, and delinquency is not as clear as it would seem. People, particularly those with a vested interest in the drug/delinquency connection, frequently treat drug use, drug abuse, and delinquency as if they were separate behaviors. This approach obviously yields a high correlation among the three issues because of the fact that each is a potential version of the others (like measuring the same behavior three different ways and calling each measurement result a different behavior). As a result, drug use and delinquency appear to be highly correlated and many have assumed that there is a real causal connection: drugs cause delinquency. Evidence is needed to make this determination.

One of the problems has been the difficulty in assessing the use of drugs across the entire United States youth population. Because those entering the juvenile justice system (delinquents) have been readily available to test and question, it is easy to believe that the drug problem lies with them. According to the FBI's *Uniform Crime Reports*, in 2005 more than 141,000 juveniles were arrested on state and local drug charges nationwide (Federal Bureau of Investigation, 2006). Of those arrested in 2002, the Arrestee Drug Abuse Monitoring (ADAM) Program found that close to 60 percent of the juvenile males and 46 percent of the females tested positive for drug use at arrest (National Institute of Justice, 2004). Although it is more difficult to survey children in schools, government studies of 12th graders find that almost 50 percent have tried an illicit drug, 27 percent have used some form of illicit drug, other than marijuana and almost 20 percent did so in the year of the survey (Johnson, O'Malley, Bachman & Schulenberg, 2007). Thus, if one takes this literally, there seems to be at least some evidence that drug use is in epidemic proportions.

As with most concerns, there are problems in accepting information at face value. Take, for example, the way we determine the existence of drug use. It is not uncommon to find reports that 75 percent (or more) of juveniles (or delinquents) use drugs or have used drugs. The matter of what "use" refers to is a critical one. Again, those with a vested interest (for instance, drug treatment staff or law enforcement personnel) treat this information, and talk about it, as if we are a nation of drug-addicted juveniles. Many of those juveniles reporting use are simply saying they have tried some drug, frequently in a minute quantity at some point in their lives, like taking one puff of a marijuana cigarette. Certainly, something more than this is suggested by statements that most of our children have "used drugs." Before one gets concerned about the rampant nature of juvenile drug use in our society, it makes sense to find out more about it. This means asking detailed questions, not a simplistic few questions about "what drugs have you used?" Researchers doing surveys usually make distinctions between experimentation, periodic or episodic use and more regular or daily use of a variety of prohibited substances. Researchers also ask about the quantity of use, because that can be a different issue than the frequency of use. When this more complex approach is taken, the results can paint a different picture from the highly touted epidemic of juvenile drug use.

The question that concerns many is whether other forms of delinquency occur before, during, or after involvement with illegal substances. The reason this is important is that establishing cause and effect relationships between delinquency and drugs has been notoriously difficult. As we noted earlier, it is possible that there is no cause and effect relationship because of the interplay of definitions (drug use and delinquency being the same thing). In addition, there is some evidence that initial cigarette, alcohol, and drug use all occur at about the same time (Williams & Dull, 1981). There are those who see experimentation with drugs as a normal part of adolescence. If this is so, something like an "age of experimentation" may be responsible for most of drug use and, possibly, delinquency as well. Under this circumstance, there would be no "causal connection" between drugs and delinquency. Moreover, most research seems to indicate that some involvement with cigarettes, alcohol, and drugs, as well as some forms of delinquency are quite normal for teens (Elliott, Huizinga & Menard, 1989). Given this, important issues for social scientists are why some juveniles get further and more negatively involved in substance use than others, why some begin much earlier than their peers and why some also commit other, more serious, criminal offenses and continue in these behaviors longer in life.

Finally, one of the key debates is whether the use of illegal drugs is more prevalent today than in the past. Such information tends to be difficult to come by, primarily because there is no one data set that has been collected over a long period of time so that a true basis for comparison does not exist. This does not mean, however, that there is no past information on drug use and abuse by juveniles. The problem is that in order to compare research findings, the same survey questions, definitions of drug use and abuse, and even the same juvenile population have to be used across time. That simply doesn't exist. As a result, estimates of juvenile drug use and abuse from the past are quite suspect and often depend on how those estimates fit into the estimator's ideology.

History and Nature of the Issues

Forming Public Perceptions of Drug Use

Perceptions of youth involvement with drugs seem to be propelled by the amount of information we receive daily about this issue. It is hardly surprising that people feel bombarded with facts on teen substance abuse from television, school curricula, and political advertisements so that it seems much worse than years ago, even though youth involvement with high risk behaviors, such as smoking and drinking is probably no more prevalent than in the past.

What is different today is the vast number of support groups, research organizations, and national, state, and local agencies involved in the tracking and treating of social problems. These all have a vested interest in certain issues and their studies, programs, websites, and press releases are designed to keep the issue in the forefront of the public's mind and on the political agenda. For instance, the Center for Substance Abuse Treatment, the National Parents' Resource Institute for Drug Education, and the National Inhalant Prevention Coalition have all received money from the National Centers for Disease Control and the Office of Juvenile Justice and Delinquency Prevention to sponsor a National Youth Drug Survey with the results published in the *Journal of Drug Issues*. Because these federal agencies are the equivalent of political interest groups, there is some likelihood that the results of their sponsored surveys could be biased. Indeed, if these were pharmaceutical or medical studies, the authors would be assumed to be biased because of the sponsorship.

Was there a Drug Epidemic?

Much of the literature from the mid 1980s to the early 1990s refers to a drug epidemic in the United States. While it is true that some new types of drugs emerged and became popular, and some old drugs saw an increase in their usage, the overall picture of drug use from the 1970s to the 1990s leads one to question the conventional wisdom. Indeed, overall drug use was already declining by the time the war on drugs was declared. For high school seniors, the juvenile group with the highest drug use rates, the prevalence of monthly illicit drug use other than marijuana declined after reaching a high in 1981 of 21.7 percent (Johnston, O'Malley, Bachman & Schulenberg, 2006). This decline continued until it reached a low of 6.3 percent in 1992, and then increased to a relatively stable 10 percent from 1995 to the present (Figure 4.1). Marijuana use among twelfth graders followed the same trends, with a high of 37 percent in 1978 to a low of 11.9 percent in 1992, and then an increase stabilizing at about 20 percent. Moreover, the downward trend line from *before* the drug war began is about the same as that during the period of 1984 to 1992. Because marijuana accounts for such a large portion of illicit drug use, trends of "all illicit drugs" primarily track marijuana use, therefore it is important to remember that other drug use is substantially lower. For instance, the two lines in Figure 4.1 representing any illicit drug use and marijuana use are approximately the same. Alcohol use reflects the same trend, although the percentage is twice as high. The facts indicate that an overall drug epidemic may never have happened and allegations of a rise in delinquency driven by drug use may be questionable.

Figure 4.1. **Yearly Percentage of 30-day Drug Use Prevalence for High School Seniors**

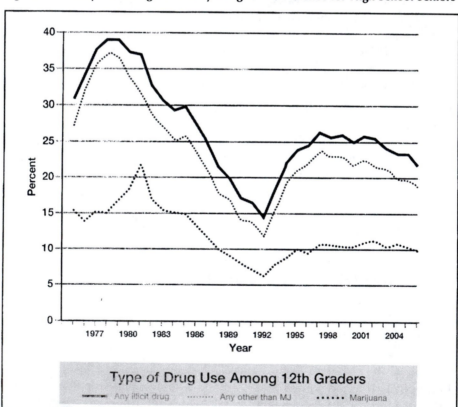

Table created by authors. Data source: Johnston, L.D., P.M O'Malley, J.G. Bachman & J.E. Schulenberg (December 21, 2006).

While delinquency appears to have maintained constant or decreasing rates over time, the prevalence of drug use appears to have decreased between the late 1970s and the early 1990s (Browning & Huizinga, 1999). In fact, arrests for drug offenses seem to be the primary cause of the 35 percent increase in the number of youth held in detention in the 1990s (*Juvenile Justice Digest*, 2000). Throughout the past decade, juveniles appear to consistently represent about 11 percent of all arrests for drug abuse violations (Federal Bureau of Investigation, 2006). It also appears that while fewer of the more serious delinquents are using hard drugs, those youth who are identified as hard drug users are committing more serious criminal offenses (Browning & Huizinga, 1999). Rather than a causal connection from drugs to serious delinquency, the relationship may simply be a product of two decades of get-tough drug policy – those juveniles with the greatest drug problems have gotten tough.

How then did the alleged drug epidemic begin? One reasonable answer is that it was the product of a political campaign. Beginning in the early 1980s, the Reagan administration, operating as promised on its conservative agenda, saw illicit drug use as an undesirable and dangerous behavior and, equally important, a holdover from the old liberal days of the late 1960s. They were convinced that drugs led to crime and so the drug agenda meshed nicely with their "get-tough-on-crime" approach. Messages and press releases began to circulate decrying the danger of illicit drug use. In short, the Reagan administration began to manipulate public opinion. Gallup Polls during the first years of the 1980s asked about the "most important problems facing our nation;" illicit drug use was nowhere in sight on the polls' list of respondents' items. After two years of administration messages concerning the problem of drugs, the Spring 1984 Gallup Poll finally scored a hit – drug use appeared for the first time in the top 10 national problems. President Reagan promptly declared that the public was effectively demanding that he do something about a drug epidemic. Then he announced a war on drugs and installed the new position of "drug czar." It can be argued that the drug epidemic began at that point as a product of the manipulation of public opinion to further a political and ideological agenda.

Media and Drug Use Reporting

The newspapers, television news, and other media sources of public information on drug use and delinquency are also implicated in the rise of the drug problem. Because the media are driven by what sells, the greatest play is given to sensationalistic information. Illicit drugs easily satisfy that criteria and stories about juveniles and drug use are even more sensational. As a result, a substantial amount of news coverage has discussed the issue. Unfortunately, the number of media reports on a subject does not reflect its actual frequency or its seriousness. Yet the public, in hearing or reading about sensational stories of drugs and delinquency, has come to a reasonable conclusion that a serious problem exists, if not an epidemic. For instance, while those most likely to use drugs clearly fall within the older age groups, media reports will highlight the most controversial events involving the youngest children. The headlines trumpet catchy phrases, like "Many kids start huffing before age 12, some as early as age 7" (Fackelmann, 2002:D8) without ever telling you "how many" before age 12 and "how many" as early as age 7. The real truth is that delinquency and drug use, while common, are not frequently of the sensational type. Most of what occurs is mundane, minor, and not really newsworthy.

Another source of public information about drugs and delinquency is found in television crime shows and movies. The images conveyed by these shows reflect stereotypes driven by sensationalist reportage. However, if they are repeated time and time again, the public comes to accept these stereotypes as accurately reflecting the connections between drug use and delinquency. Juvenile drug users invariably get into trouble and, ultimately, end up both addicted and involved in serious crime. The addiction image is an integral part of this stereotype, created decades ago by governmental moral entrepreneurs. If a youth tries drugs experimentally, invariably he or she ends up addicted to stronger and stronger drugs and is forced into a life of crime to pay for the addiction. Of course, the reported 75 to 80 percent of juveniles who have tried drugs (viewed as evidence of an epidemic by some) shows us that the stereotype is just that – if it were true then some three-quarters of our youth would be serious delinquents (Wolfgang, Figlio & Sellin, 1972)[1]. Media images, then, present another important but false impression of the drug/delinquency connection.

Surveys and Other Evidence of Drug Use

Today, most of what we know about drug use comes from self-report studies. Self-reports ask youth to report on their behaviors and attitudes. Since the mid-1980s, researchers have routinely asked youth about various forms of drug use, including cigarettes and alcohol, and it is probably true that almost all types of drugs have been included on a survey at some time or another. More commonly, however, these surveys only ask about use of certain types of drugs: marijuana, cocaine, ecstasy, and other common and popular drugs of the day. Thus, there are some drugs about which we have little adequate evidence of their use.

The amount of drug use among today's juveniles is about the same as it has been for the past 5 to 7 years. Table 4.1 shows the percentage of various types of drugs used by high school seniors during the "last 12 months" and the "last month," as reported in the *Monitoring the Future* survey (Johnston, O'Malley, Bachman & Schulenberg, 2006). As can be seen, about 3 of 4 high school seniors have had an alcoholic drink, even if only a sip, during the past year and about one-half during the past month. That is far and away the most prevalent drug used by youth. Ironically, however, older individuals whose experiences date as far back as the 1920s, recall imbibing at about the same rate as their counterparts throughout the twentieth century, including today's youth. The most prevalent illicit drug used by seniors is marijuana, with about one-third using during the past year and about 1 in 5 using during the past month. From that amount, the past-year usage for other drugs declines to somewhere between 1 in 10 to 1 in 100 seniors having used a drug. The past-month figures for "harder" drugs range from 1 in 20 to 1 in 250 having used a drug. While these data present a drug problem of sorts, it is also clear that high school seniors are not engaged in an "epidemic" of illicit drug use. We also reflect that the two most commonly used drugs, alcohol and marijuana, are perhaps of least concern. Finally, a press release by John P. Walters, the national drug czar in 2007, highlighted a recent survey[2] which showed that substance use among school youth "has dropped to the lowest level since the early 1990s" (Infobeat, 2002).

Table 4.1 **Illicit Drug and Alcohol Use by High School Seniors, 2001**

	Used within the last:	
Drugs	12 Months	30 Days
Alcohol	73.3	49.8
Marijuana	37.0	22.4
Stimulants	10.9	5.6
Hallucinogens	8.4	3.2
Other Opiates	6.7	3.0
Sedatives	5.7	2.8
Inhalants	4.5	1.7
Tranquilizers	6.5	3.0
Cocaine	4.8	2.1
Steroids	2.4	1.3
Heroin	0.9	0.4

Source: *Monitoring the Future, National Results on Adolescent Drug Use.* (University of Michigan, 2002).

Issues of Accuracy

Because most drug use data are derived from surveys, there are typical survey problems. For instance, there are no good independent assessments of whether a respondent who says he or she uses drugs really is engaged in the behavior. Juveniles have been known to overstate drug use – it might be seen as "cool" to brag about drug use when, in fact, there has been very little use – or, out of fear of reprisal, understate frequent drug use. Similar issues have arisen in delinquency surveys. On the whole, independent assessments have agreed with the survey responses. Whether this is also true for juvenile drug use and abuse is not yet known.

Other problems come from the use of different questions and wording on surveys. For instance, one survey may ask whether a youth has used a particular drug within the past week, another may ask if the drug has "ever" been used, and yet another may ask about use during the past year. Assuming the wording is the same in all questions, except for the frequency of use, it is obvious that the results cannot be compared. This problem is particularly important over time. Self-report surveys conducted over the past 20 years are unlikely to have the same terminology and response types. Perhaps even more critical is the method of determining the degree of drug use and abuse. If the surveys have not been comparable in their language, they have been even less comparable in their methods of assessing degree of use. In spite of this, however, there are a few ongoing surveys, such as the National Longitudinal Youth Survey, the Monitoring the Future survey, and the National Survey on Drug Use and Health (formerly called the National Household Survey on Drug Abuse), where the methodology is consistent enough to suggest some answers. Much of juvenile drug use evidence and trends reported here are derived from those sources (Johnston et al., 1998a, 1998b).

An additional source of information is found in our juvenile justice system. From that source we know that juveniles who have been detained and/ or adjudicated for delinquent acts are also likely to be involved with drugs. Even here, though, the quantity and frequency of drug use is not well known. There are also survey studies that show a correlation between reported drug use and reported delinquent acts. One must be cautious in interpreting these correlations as evidence that drug use and abuse cause delinquency. A simple explanation for such a correlation is that drug use and delinquent acts are both forms of exciting, dangerous, and risky behaviors that fulfill some adolescent need or urge. A juvenile who engages in delinquency may also engage in drug use for the same or similar reasons. One should also remember our earlier caution: Drug use is itself an illegal and delinquent act, therefore drug use and delinquency are not independent behaviors. In sum, most of the public's information on juvenile drug use tends to come from a large number of questionable surveys of youth and from detained and adjudicated delinquents.

Error Rates

As a wider range of interest groups are involved in analyzing drug use, the types of youth who are being studied, and the various youth issues being examined increases. Changes in whom and how we survey, the questions we ask and what we include alters not only the size of the problem but the definition of the problem itself. For example, an Atlanta-based organization that works with parents and schools to provide drug education began to survey students in grades four to six, something not normally done. Consequently, its results drew widespread attention ending up in the *New York Times* as "Risk of Drug Use Rises in Middle Schools" (Wren, 1999). The article reported "sharp jumps" and "dramatic increases" but, ironically, almost all of the levels noted for use of drugs, alcohol, or cigarettes were under 3 percent with most under one percent. Many students do not view these surveys seriously and we could conservatively estimate that at least 1 percent of the students would be unreliable respondents. Consequently, it is easy to see that the margins of error in research would negate any significant "changes" in these data. The bottom line is that more than 97 percent of these elementary school students are not using any type of prohibited substance – a finding that should be quite welcome.[3]

Perspectives and Research on Drug Use and Delinquency

Theories about Drug Use

There are many theories of drug use and abuse; each discipline interested in the subject seems to have several. In general, the theories range from those created by general public opinion to highly technical biochemical versions. We will examine some of the more popular versions here.

Public Opinion-Oriented Theory

Theories of this variety are partially based in scientific, discipline-based perspectives but stretch the evidence and connect various threads of thought to create common-sense explanations. Such approaches are not uncommon in law enforcement and governmental circles and are politically attractive during drug wars. One of the more frequently-heard theories is called the "escalation or progression" hypothesis. This theory argues that some substances, such as marijuana, act as gateway drugs or beginner drugs which inevitably lead to the use of stronger and more addictive substances. The perspective also posits that there is an almost predictive path to addiction and that the average user will progress in both the type of drugs they use, and the doses of those substances that they use. According to escalation theory, the life of the abuser will gradually become more disruptive and dysfunctional as drug abuse becomes the center of existence. The theory essentially depicts users as becoming progressively more serious abusers and, finally, addicts who steal to support their habits and who probably live on the streets. Obviously, the policy implications of this theory involve the elimination of drug use, particularly among the young who are likely to experiment and get involved with gateway drugs. Thus, programs teaching drug abstinence (former First Lady Nancy Reagan's "Just Say No" campaign and the DARE program are examples) are foremost among proponents of this approach. The major problem with this theory is that it is driven by media images and is at odds with much of the existing evidence on drug use and abuse.

Biochemical Theories

Theories oriented toward the biochemical and neurological makeup of humans are among the most complex perspectives on drug use and are based almost entirely on research findings. While there are several varieties, there are major commonalities among them. First, there is little concern with outside factors, either social or psychological. The issue is essentially that of addiction and the way the body reacts to drugs. The human neurochemical system is made up of hormones and enzymes that affect how information is transmitted to the major neurological component, the brain. The nervous system, including the brain, contains a series of receptors in which various chemical compounds are designed to fit. Drugs are among the chemicals that fit into these receptors; in fact, the human body naturally produces a variant of almost all known drugs – and that is why the receptors exist. The second ingredient in a biochemical theory, then, is that drugs are virtually natural to the body.

The third ingredient is that an excess or dearth of certain chemicals or enzymes can cause changes in cellular function, especially the brain. Drugs can either be transmuted into or serve to create these compounds. Therefore, cellular change is the basis of addiction. Finally, there may be genetic predispositions (higher or lower levels of production of these hormones and enzymes) to certain drugs and, ultimately, addiction. Policy implications of such approaches are the treatment of drug abuse as a disease. Much of the juvenile and criminal justice system's involvement in fighting illicit drugs, in particular the application of punitive laws, would be eliminated in favor of a medical model.

Sociological Theories

Most sociological approaches look at personal and environmental risk factors that may predispose a youth toward engaging in deviant activity. These include: values and attitudes that support antisocial activities; peers and family members' attitudes and experiences with these risk-taking behaviors; poor attachment to school and prosocial community activities; and exposure to environments with high rates of deviant activity and lower levels of neighborhood investment. Many of these concepts serve as the basis for the popular criminological approaches of social control (See Travis Hirschi, 1969, as the leading exponent of social control theories) and differential association theories (Sutherland, 1947). Overall, approaches that consider the effects of drug-using friends seem to be the strongest predictors of juvenile drug use (Hawkins, Jensen, Catalano & Lishner, 1988; Kandel, 1980; Thornberry & Krohn, 1997). The preceding chapters of this book contain detailed descriptions of these theories so we will not belabor the point here. The commonality is that they all treat drug use and abuse as just another form of deviance.

Drug prevention efforts under sociological theories would involve changing the beliefs and attitudes associated with drug and alcohol use. Social norming programs across the country today attempt to involve the youth themselves in spreading the message that the most popular youth are not using drugs, that one does not have to give in to peer pressures to be popular, and that responsible behavior is valued. The idea behind these programs is that young people misperceive the frequency and depth of drug use and that misconception in itself generates some use that could be curtailed with more accurate information about the extent of drug and alcohol use. Other policies would call for closer relations with parents, more attention to school performance, after-school activities, and stressing conventional goals.

Psychological Theories

Psychological theories tend toward two different approaches: those that are psychoanalytic and those that are behavioristic. Psychoanalytic theories tend to assume that the unconscious mind controls behavior and cognition. This mind goes through stages of development and problems at any one stage can result in problem behaviors. Freud's classic construction of id, ego, and superego serve to explain drug abuse. If the ego and superego are relatively undeveloped, the impulsive id gains the upper hand and an individual might be more likely to experiment with and abuse drugs in a search for pleasurable experiences. Other psychoanalytic perspectives assume the conscious and unconscious mind must be in balance. If one develops poorly, this balance is thrown off and the personality develops internal conflicts. Under this approach, a juvenile with internal conflicts created by earlier emotional trauma may begin to act out, drug use being one of the several behavioral options. Drug prevention policies derived from psychoanalytic theories would create programs of treatment designed to resolve underlying issues. Juvenile drug courts are one form of such policies, attempting to provide individualized treatment to overcome negative peer and family issues.

Like sociological theories, learning theories are rooted in the influence of significant or influential others on a youth's behavior. More specifically, these theories address the process of copying or modelling the behavior of those we respect. They focus on how a person responds to cues in the environment which may provide reinforcement or rewards and punishments which serve to establish certain patterns of behavior in those who seek positive feedback and acceptance among others. According to learning theorists, youth learn deviant or delinquent responses the same way they learn socially acceptable skills. Drug prevention policies based on these theories would encourage educating children about the dangers of drugs using programs such as DARE.

Unraveling a Complex Relationship

Although research seems to consistently indicate a substance abuse and delinquency correlation, the complexity of the relationship between the two, and other high risk behaviors, makes it difficult to determine which, if any, may be an antecedent and which may be consequences.[4] In fact, Dembo et al. (2007) suggest that each one seems to enhance the risk of the other. There are no simple answers. More realistically, troubled youth seem to face multiple overlapping challenges including child abuse and neglect, mental health problems, poverty, illicit drug use, poor school performance, learning disabilities, and family instability including frequent residential moves, unemployment and parental involvement in crime and substance abuse. In addition, neighborhoods with higher levels of disorder and decline have also been linked to higher levels of adolescent drug use (Hawkins et al., 1988; Jang & Johnson, 2001).

Studies have indicated various correlations among negative involvement with drugs, delinquent and antisocial behavior, and mental health and school problems. In fact, the specific nature of these relationships in terms of temporal sequencing and mitigating influences are still not well explained though often studied. However, those factors that seem best able to predict delinquency are typically not the same as those factors predicting adolescent drug use.

To give the reader a sense of the type of research and typical findings, we present a summary of some recent research findings on delinquency and drug use in Table 4.2. It should be clear that most research locates a correlation between delinquency and drug use. At the same time, this relationship refers to virtually all drugs, from alcohol to cigarettes to marijuana to the hardest of drugs. Thus, there is nothing particularly special about the connection of certain drugs, such as crack cocaine, with delinquency. In addition, there is substantial evidence that the drug-delinquency correlation can be mediated by parents, peers, educational attainment, and so forth. Does drug use cause delinquency, or does delinquency cause drug use? At present, there is no compelling evidence that either causes the other.

Gangs, Guns, Media, and Drugs

Complicating the search for answers about drug use and delinquency are the possible intervening effects of other factors such as gangs, the lethality of weapons, and the popular criticisms of violent movies and music. Concerned about these possible relationships, the U.S. Department of Health and Human Services (1999) spent $400,000 on a Stanford University study of both movies and songs, particularly rap music. While the findings simply quantified the "appearance of" or "reference to" alcohol, tobacco and illegal drugs, many critics concluded that the entertainment industry was treating substance abuse too lightly. Comments ranged from accusing the media of

Table 4.2 **Recent Research on the Relationship between Drugs Abuse and Delinquency**

Study	Sample	Relationship between drugs & delinquency	Other variables analyzed
Bui, Ellickson & Bell (2000)	3000 West Coast 10th & 12th graders	Early delinquent behavior more likely to predict later drug use	Emotional distress did not appear to predict either delinquency or drug use
Dembo, Wareham & Schmeidler (2007)	278 youth in justice system in National Institute on Drug Abuse study	Delinquency decreased over time but delinquency seemed to exacerbate substance use which increased over time	Increasing substance use with age may be related to easier access
Garnier & Stein (2002)	198 Northern California youths followed 18 years	Teen drug use & delinquency related to peers with similar behaviors	SES indirectly related to delinquency, maternal drug use indirectly related to teen drug use
Whiteford (2007)	2001 National Household Survey on Drug Abuse (17,429 youths 12-17 yrs)	Adolescents who used substances more likely to commit crime, be arrested for crime & be more versatile in offending, more use increased crime relationship	Girls more likely to be dabbler or casual user & boys more often abstain or heavy use
Welte et al. (2005)	625 Buffalo NY males age 16-19	Substance use & consequences co-occur with rise in delinquent career, those who use more substances also commit more crime	Alcohol had more effect in early delinquency; drug use delays maturing out of delinquency
Slesnick & Prestopnik (2005)	226 treatment-engaged substance abusing youth (13-17 years of age) from a runaway shelter	Dual diagnoses are common, substance abusing runaways had higher levels of anxiety also conduct & affect disorders, few gender differences & few differences between Anglo & Hispanic youth	Less than 15% ever received substance abuse treatment from shelters
Nation & Heflinger (2006)	214 youth 12-18 yrs in public funded substance abuse treatment study in one southern state (70% were inpatient)	Antisocial peers & delinquent acts strongest predictors of substance abuse	Alcohol use, binge drinking & marijuana use most common substances used
Tubman, Gil & Wagner (2004)	Over 5,000 middle school students & families in South Florida over 3 yrs (6th to 9th graders)	Those reporting both substance use & delinquency had higher mean levels of both than those youth only reporting only one or other	With age, alcohol, & delinquency more normative as was illicit substance use, though drug use was common in only small portion of sample

Source: Compiled by authors.

"glorifying" drug use to simply being too casual about its presence (Lichtblau, 1999). Ironically, a study of what factors youth identify as influencing them toward delinquency or drug use found that media imitation was not significant (Teevan & Dryburgh, 2000). The 56 teen boys interviewed cited having fun, alleviating tensions, emotional release, thrill seeking and peer pressure as major reasons for using illicit substances.

Gangs

The gang factor has also been researched to assess its links with delinquency and drug use. While studies seem to indicate that gang membership is correlated with both drug use and delinquency, it is also clear that gang activity varies between cities and regions and it is difficult to make generalizations about which behaviors occur first. The connection, and evidence, between gangs and drugs is also complicated by political and funding maneuvers by law enforcement and federal agencies. For instance, a federal agency announced in the late 1980s that it was interested in funding police intervention programs to resolve an obvious gang-drug connection. A gang unit in the Los Angeles police department saw a major funding opportunity and provided data showing that gangs were selling drugs in sufficient quantities to be one of Los Angeles' major drug sources. Federal funding came almost automatically. Years later, however, the original data were exposed as fraudulent – there was very little evidence that, at that time, Los Angeles gangs were engaged in the drug trade. In fact, the federal agency (National Institute of Justice) asked for a portion of its money back. Thus, while there is no question that some gangs sell drugs and some focus exclusively on drug selling, the gang-drug connection is not as clear as law enforcement and allied government agencies would have us think.

Some theories argue that the same type of youth who is attracted to gangs is also attracted to drug use and delinquency. Others argue that the pressures of gang membership increase the risk of youth engaging in drug use or crime. While some find that the gang is the explanation for higher levels of both drug use and delinquent activity (Thornberry et al., 1991) a more in-depth look found that youth who were previously involved with drug use and delinquency did not escalate those activities with gang membership while those who did not have previous drug and crime histories began them with gang membership (Zhang, Welte & Wieczorek, 1999).

Policy Responses: Drug Prevention and Treatment

Prevention

Drug and alcohol abuse prevention programs most often take the form of education and awareness programming. The focus is on teaching about the negative physical, emotional, economic, and social consequences of drug use and abuse. These programs also assist young people in developing the personal and interpersonal skills necessary to resist peer pressures to try tobacco, alcohol, and other illicit drugs and to have healthy and productive alternatives to activities that center around substance abuse. One, the Life Skills Training Program which is school-based, involves homework that is assigned to be done with parents (*Juvenile Justice*, 1998). Other forms of prevention programming include environmental approaches and alternative activities but we will discuss two major types here: DARE and drug testing programs.

DARE Programs

The oldest of today's drug prevention programs is Drug Abuse Resistance Education (DARE), dating to 1983. DARE is designed as a cooperative effort between law enforcement and public schools and, as a result, has a great deal of support from several constituencies. It is also the most popular drug prevention program, as it is in most schools in the U.S. DARE is actually a collection of programs focused on school children from kindergarten through high school, although most schools only use the core curriculum designed for the 5th and 6th grades.

The original core grade 5-6 curriculum has a trained police officer delivering 17 weeks of once-a-week, 45-minute, classroom lessons. The curriculum has three main thrusts: psychological inoculation, resistance skills training, and personal and social skills training. The first two are expressly oriented toward drugs, the latter is more generic in its orientation and seeks to improve general life skills. There is also an attempt to improve knowledge of drug effects and produce negative attitudes towards drugs. A new curriculum is under development and testing, in part in response to criticisms of the original DARE program. Borrowing from cognitive and life-skills programs that have been somewhat successful in preventing drug use, the new curriculum will be aimed at seventh and ninth graders rather than the usual fifth grade audience. In addition, the DARE officer will serve more as a facilitator rather than as the sole instructor. The focus of the curriculum is now problem-solving activities and an examination of the complex reasoning behind real-life decisionmaking, all in the context of refusing to use drugs.

How well does DARE work? If one listens to its supporters, DARE is extremely effective.[5] Evidence abounds that police officers, parents, school teachers, governmental agencies and politicians all have positive attitudes toward the program and, furthermore, they think it works. There is also evidence that children exposed to DARE are less likely to find drugs attractive, at least in the short term. However, the basic question is whether DARE affects drug-taking behavior, not attitudes. The rigorous research on this crucial issue is almost unanimous: There is no evidence of behavioral change except for a few very small and very short-term effects. Two major longitudinal studies of DARE over 6 and 10 years show no effect (Rosenbaum & Hanson, 1998). Because of its popularity, DARE still exists in most middle schools. A revised curriculum, based on cognitive skills training developed by another anti-drug program and designed in concert with researchers, is supposed to resolve previous issues. However, it is also true that DARE is a large non-profit corporation taking in substantial amounts of money. Moreover, as Schram (2007) notes, the program messages and orientation match the political climate of the past decade and thus is symbolically important. Thus, DARE is unlikely to disappear even if the new curriculum proves unsuccessful in reducing drug-taking behavior.

Drug Testing

Drug screening and random testing are also possible, but are among the more invasive prevention methods available today. Parents can purchase kits for testing their children at home. The Supreme Court decision in *Board of Education of Pottowatomie County v. Earls* (2002) determined that public middle and high schools can mandate drug tests for students who participate in extracurricular activities. This decision broadened the scope of a previous decision that had allowed drug screening for athletes. Although costs and controversy have resulted in few schools actually conducting drug testing, many student activists and civil libertarians are concerned about the possible abuses of such policies. Still, 70 percent of the more than 1,000 people polled by *USA Today/CNN* (Henry, 2002) supported the school district's testing of students who participate in non-athletic activities.

Treatment Issues

Treatment methods are as varied as the different theories of substance abuse. One's view of what causes drug use will also suggest how to prevent drug abuse. Still, the problems of designing and implementing successful drug treatment programs are not as simple as matching the right person to the right approach. Research tends to indicate that youth differ from adults in their patterns of drug use, the developmental and social factors that underlie drug use as well as the way drugs affect the brain (Currie, 1985; Winters et al., 2000) so that program interventions should not just be reproductions of adult substance abuse treatments. In addition, agencies must make decisions about the role of drug abuse in the etiology of each delinquent usually during assessment. What should be treated treat first, the primary need or the symptoms? Finally, concerns are also raised about various ethical issues of treatment – does one have to admit one has a problem? Should treatment be reserved for those most ready and willing to undergo – should treatment be mandatory? Should society be concerned about the invasiveness of drug testing, the continued screening of one's blood or urine after probation terms are completed or fines paid?

Treatment Programs

Self-help methods are usually independent support groups that meet regularly (daily) to share experiences and build the skills necessary to achieve and maintain abstinence and to assist each other as they learn how to cope with the challenges of leading a drug-free lifestyle. Early experiments with treatment communities for youth such as the Silverlake Experiment and the Provo Experiment relied on the principles of symbolic interaction and the power of group dynamics with anti-delinquent norms to bring about change in the group as well as in each individual participant. This principle that Don Cressey (1964) referred to as "retroflexive reformation" has been the underlying theme of anti-drug programming such as Alcoholics Anonymous and Narcotics Anonymous. Although there is much debate in the professional arena about the use of paraprofessionals or reformed addicts to treat clients, many therapeutic communities use both licensed and "experienced" staff support as well as group counseling strategies.

Culturally specific programming has also been suggested for the treatment of addictions and substance abuse. Most of the programs in this area have been in the early intervention stage at which drug behavior is not yet involved. Culturally specific programs strive to connect the ethnic identity of the youngsters to their behaviors. Where African-Americans are concerned, a few drug programs have reported positive results in producing negative attitudes toward drugs (Emshoff, Avery, Raduka & Anderson, 1996). Ohio has even designated two culturally specific programs (the Youngstown Urban Minority Alcoholism and Drug Abuse Outreach Program and Project Impact) as exemplary projects. Similarly, a program for Native Americans has produced lower rates of substance abuse among participants (Baca & Koss-Chioino, 1997). If the results hold up over time, the concept of targeting ethnic identity for drug prevention may have merit.

Drug Courts

The final treatment and prevention program we will examine is one that is applied after the fact: drug courts. Such courts spread rapidly during the 1990s with more than 260 juvenile drug courts across U.S. jurisdictions by the end of the year 2003 (Huddleston, Freeman-Wilson & Boone, 2004). Juvenile drug courts are patterned after the original adult courts but require adaptation for the juveniles. Such courts take most of the drug cases from other juvenile courts (assuming certain criteria are met) and judges work together with probation officers and prosecutors. This specialization and the court's dual focus on accountability and treatment make this different from the normal juvenile court.[6] An assumption is that specialized treatment, intensive supervision and the judge's personalized case management will eliminate juvenile drug use and abuse. On the whole, drug courts work toward reducing negative influences in the juvenile's life, addressing family problems related to drug use, and providing motivation to change behaviors. These three foci are primarily expressed in preventing further drug experimentation and targeting social and psychological factors facilitating drug use. Juveniles are given incentives to improve their behaviors and it is assumed they will have a few failures. Given a judge's greater control over the case, the failures can be dealt with on a personalized basis.

Research on the effectiveness of drug courts is still in its infancy. While some positive results exist, most of those studies are not rigorously

Butler County, Pennsylvania: Dispositional Hearing

designed and fail to account for other factors that might explain the results.[7] For instance, one Southern California drug court proclaimed itself successful in reducing drug use but used acceptance criteria that created a "cream of the crop" group for itself while comparing results to a much more hard-core probation group. Fortunately, the Drug Abuse Education, Prevention and Treatment Act of 2001 provided federal funds for research on drug courts. Since then, a study by Henggeler et al. (2006) found that while rates of delinquency and drug use decreased in juveniles in drug court, it was not enough to significantly differentiate recidivism rates for youth in family court and those in drug court or drug court combined with therapeutic treatment.

Future Directions

The connection between juvenile delinquency and drug use is an undisputed but causally obscure one. Much of the concern over juvenile drug use is the product of moral entrepreneurs (people who crusade for a just cause and attempt to define the problem for others), media sensationalism and political agendas. The combination of a war on crime and a war on drugs during the 1980s and 1990s created a public frenzy and the assumption of an out-of-control drug epidemic. The solution was to criminalize everything associated with drugs and punish as severely as possible. Thus, the major initiatives were the creation of criminal law, law enforcement, and application of the law. The fact is that none of this worked.

The question before us now is where do we go from here? The previous generation of prevention and treatment programs either took a back seat to the punitive approach or were themselves part of the juvenile and criminal justice systems. These programs were also primarily based in political ideology and their "successes" were more likely to be based on popularity rather than rigorous scientific evidence. It would appear that we are now headed into an era of greater emphasis on prevention and treatment. Policy initiatives at present are exploring ways to handle juvenile drug use without the thoroughly punitive nature of the past. It is unlikely that this break with punitiveness will be complete – there are too many politicians attuned to the value of being tough on crime and delinquency.

What is needed is an understanding that much of juvenile drug use is a common episode in a period of adolescent experimentation. At this point, abuse and addiction are rarely the issues. Thus, we need drug policies that are more honest with children – not the "brain in the frying pan" propaganda that has been popular. Nonpunitive treatment must come to the forefront with children who are beyond experimentation. And, not least of all, we need funding for rigorous research on those strategies and programs that currently seem promising. When the research says a program works, we should put it into place and not be concerned with its political popularity. How much of this will take place? Very likely little of it will occur. The truth of the matter is that our policy initiatives are rarely based on research and evidence; rather, they are predicated on political expediency.

Endnotes

[1] The estimates of the number of serious delinquents are rather uniform at around 6 to 8 percent of youth. See Wolfgang, Figlio & Sellin, 1972.

[2] The National Parents Research Institute for Drug Education (PRIDE) surveys school children from grades 6 through 12. The 2001–2002 survey, released on July 17, 2002, reported substance use down across almost all measures.

[3] One interesting feature is that youth, and indeed all citizens, in the 1800s and early 1900s had a much greater exposure to drugs, cigarettes, and alcohol. In fact, it is likely that the period after the Civil War was an all-time high for drug addiction and most of those addicted were in the middle classes.

[4] See, for instance, a recent NHSDA brief (Office of Applied Studies, 2001) which reports a correlation between violence (most of which was fighting) and alcohol and illicit drug use within the past month and refers to it as a "close link." The implication is that drug use causes violence.

[5] Perhaps because the amount of information demonstrating DARE's lack of success threatened federal funding, its founder and president finally agreed that DARE was not effective. See Miller, 2001.

[6] For further explanation of Drug Court philosophy and emphases see Roberts, Brophy, and Cooper, 1997.

[7] There are some reasonable evaluations of drug courts but even these have difficulty accounting for some important conditions affecting the results. See Vito and Tewksbury, 1998; Perters and Murrin, 2000.

References

Baca, L. & J. Koss-Chioino (1997). "Development of a Culturally Responsive Group Counseling Model for Mexican American Adolescents." *Journal of Multicultural Counseling and Development*, 25(2):130-141.

Board of Education of Pottowatomie County v. Earls, 122 S. Ct. 2559, (2002).

Browning, K. & D. Huizinga (1999). *Highlights of Findings from the Denver Youth Survey*. Washington, DC: U.S. Department of Justice, Office of Juvenile Justice and Delinquency Prevention.

Bui, K., T. Van, P. Ellickson & R. Bell (2000). "Cross-lagged Relationships among Adolescent Problem Drug Use, Delinquent Behavior, and Emotional Distress." *Journal of Drug Issues*, 30(2):283-304.

Cressey, D.R. (1964). *Delinquency, Crime and Differential Association*. The Hague: M. Nijhoff.

Currie, E. (1985). *Confronting Crime*. New York, NY: Pantheon Press.

Dembo, R., J. Wareham & J. Schmeidler (2007). "Drug Use and Delinquent Behavior." *Criminal Justice and Behavior*, 34(5):680-696.

Elliott, D.S., D. Huizinga & S. Menard (1989). *Multiple Problem Youth, Delinquency, Substance Use, and Mental Health Problems*. New York, NY: Springer Verlag.

Emshoff, J., E. Avery, G. Raduka & D. Anderson (1996). "Findings from SUPERSTARS: A Health Promotion Program for Families to Enhance Multiple Protective Factors." *Journal of Adolescent Research*, 11:68-96.

Fackelmann, K. (2002). "Millions of U.S. Kids Have Tried Huffing." *U.S.A. Today*, (Thursday, March 14):D8.

Federal Bureau of Investigation (2006). *Crime in the United States 2005*. Washington, DC: U.S. Department of Justice.

Garnier, H. & J.A. Stein (2002). "An 18-year Model of Family and Peer Effects on Adolescent Drug Use and Delinquency." *Journal of Youth and Adolescence*, 31(1):45-56.

Hawkins, J.D., J.M. Jensen, R.F. Catalano & D. Lishner (1988). "Delinquency and Drug Abuse: Implications for Social Service." *Social Service Review*, 62:258-284.

Henggeler, S., C. Halliday-Boykins, P. Cunningham, J. Randall, S. Shapiro & J.E. Chapman (2006). "Juvenile Drug Court: Enhancing Outcomes by Integrating Evidence-Based Treatments." *Journal of Consulting & Clinical Psychology*, 74:42-54.

Henry, T. (2002). "Some Say Drug-Test Ruling Will Make Schools Safer." *USA Today*, (Friday, June 28):9A.

Hirschi, T. (1969). *Causes of Delinquency*. Berkeley, CA: University of California Press.

Huddleston, C., K. Freeman-Wilson & D. Boone (2004). *Painting the Current Picture: A National Report card on Drug Courts and Other Problem Solving Programs in the U.S.* Alexandria, VA: National Drug Court Institute.

Infobeat (2002). "Survey Finds Drops in Drug, Alcohol Use Among Students." *Infobeat* (July 18) www.infobeat.com [Retrieved July 18, 2002].

Jang, S.J. & B.R. Johnson (2001). "Neighborhood Disorder, Individual Religiosity, and Adolescent Use of Illicit Drugs: A Test of Multilevel Hypotheses." *Criminology*, 39(1):109-143.

Johnston, L.D., P.M. O'Malley, J.G. Bachman & J.E. Schulenberg (2007). *Monitoring the Future: National Results on Adolescent Drug Use: Overview of Key Findings, 2006.* Washington, DC: U.S. Department of Health and Human Services, National Institute on Drug Abuse.

Johnston, L.D., P.M. O'Malley, J.G. Bachman & J.E. Schulenberg (December 21, 2006). *Teen Drug Use Continues Down in 2006, Particularly among Older Teens; But Use of Prescription-type Drugs Remains High.* University of Michigan News and Information Services: Ann Arbor, MI. www.monitoringthefuture.org [Retrieved November 1, 2007.]

Johnston, L.D., P.M. O'Malley & J.G. Bachman (1998a). *National Survey Results on Drug Use from the Monitoring the Future Study, 1975-1997*, Volume 1, Secondary School Students. Washington, DC: U.S. Department of Health and Human Services, National Institute on Drug Abuse.

Johnston, L.D., P.M. O'Malley & J.G. Bachman (1998b). *National Survey Results on Drug Use from the Monitoring the Future Study, 1975-1998.* Washington, DC: National Institutes of Health.

Juvenile Justice (1998). "Prevention Works: On the Front Lines with CSAP Director Karol Kumpfer." 5(2):3-10.

Juvenile Justice Digest (2000). "Drug Crimes Lead to Detention Surge." 28(23):3.

Kandel, D.B. (1980). "Drug and Drinking Behavior among Youth." *Annual Review of Sociology*, 6:235-285.

Lichtblau, E. (1999). "Drug Use in Movies, Music Cited." *Houston Chronicle*, (Thursday, April 29):A6.

McBride, D.C., C.J. Vander Waal, Y.M. Terry & H. Van Buren (1999). *Breaking the Cycle of Drug Use among Juvenile Offenders.* Washington, DC: National Institute of Justice.

Miller, D.W. (2001). "DARE Reinvents Itself – With Help from Its Social-Scientist Critics: Change Spurred by Threat to Cut Federal Financing of Popular Drug-Prevention Program." *The Chronicle of Higher Education*, (Oct 19):A12-A14.

Monitoring the Future, National Results on Adolescent Drug Use (2002). University of Michigan.

Nation, J.H. & C. Heflinger (2006). "Risk Factors for Serious Alcohol and Drug Use: The Role of Psychosocial Variables in Predicting the Frequency of Substance Use among Adolescents." *The American Journal of Drug and Alcohol Abuse*, 32:415-433.

National Institute of Justice (2004). *Arrestee Drug Abuse Monitoring (ADAM) Program in the United States, 2003.* Washington, DC: U.S. Department of Justice.

Office of Applied Studies (2001). *Youth Violence Linked to Substance Use.* NHSDA Report (November 9). Washington, DC: Substance Abuse and Mental Health Services Administration.

Perters, R.H. & M.R. Murrin (2000). "Effectiveness of Treatment-based Drug Courts in Reducing Criminal Recidivism." *Criminal Justice and Behavior*, 27:72-97.

Roberts, M., J. Brophy & C. Cooper (1997). *The Juvenile Drug Court Movement.* OJJDP Fact Sheet # 59, March. Washington, DC: U.S. Department of Justice, Office of Juvenile Justice and Delinquency Prevention.

Rosenbaum, D.P. & G.S. Hanson (1998). "Assessing the Effects of School-Based Drug Education: A Six-Year Multilevel Analysis of Project DARE." *Journal of Research in Crime and Delinquency*, 35:381-412.

Schram, P.J. (2007). "Delinquency Programs that Failed." In M.D. McShane & F.P. Williams III (eds.) *Youth Violence and Delinquency: Juvenile Treatment and Crime Prevention*, pp. 18-35. Westport, CT: Praeger.

Slesnick, N. & J. Prestopnik (2005). "Dual and Multiple Diagnosis among Substance Using Runaway Youth." *The American Journal of Drug and Alcohol Abuse*, 31:179-201.

Sutherland, E.H. (1947). *Criminology*, Fourth Edition. Philadelphia, PA: Lippincott.

Teevan, J.J. & H.B. Dryburgh (2000). "First Person Accounts and Sociological Explanations of Delinquency." *The Canadian Review of Sociology and Anthropology*, 37(1):77-93.

Thornberry, T.P., A.J. Lizotte, M.V. Krohn, M. Farnsworth & S.J. Jang (1991). "Testing Interactional Theory: An Examination of Reciprocal Causal Relationship among Family, School and Delinquency." *Journal of Criminal Law and Criminology*, 82:3-35.

Thornberry, T. & M. Krohn (1997). "Peers, Drug Use, and Delinquency." In D.M. Stoff, J.Breiling & J.D. Maser (eds.) *Handbook of Antisocial Behavior*. New York, NY: Wiley.

Tubman, J., A. Gil & E. Wagner (2004). "Co-Occuring Substance Use and Delinquent Behavior during Early Adolescence." *Criminal Justice and Behavior*, 31:463-488.

University of Michigan (2002). *Monitoring the Future, National Results on Adolescent Drug Use: Overview of Key Findings 2001*. Ann Arbor, MI: University of Michigan.

U.S. Department of Health and Human Services, Substance Abuse and Mental Health Services Administration (1999). *Summary of Findings from the 1998 National Household Survey on Drug Abuse*. Rockville, MD: U.S. Department of Health and Human Services.

Vito, G. & R.A. Tewksbury (1998). "The Impact of Treatment: The Jefferson County (Kentucky) Drug Court Program." *Federal Probation*, 62(2):46-53.

Welte, J.W., G. Barnes, J. Hoffman, W. Wieczorek & L. Zhang (2005). "Substance Involvement and the Trajectory of Criminal Offending in Young Males." *The American Journal of Drug and Alcohol Abuse*, 31:267-284.

Whiteford, S.W. (2007). *The Adolescent Drug-Crime Relationship: Desistence and Gateway Theories across User Levels*. New York, NY: Lfb Scholarly Pub Lic

Williams, F.P. III & R.T. Dull (1981). "Marijuana, Alcohol and Tobacco: Reassessment of a Presumed Relationship." *Journal of Drug Education*, 11(2):129-139.

Winters, K., R. Stinchfield, E. Opland, C. Weller & W. Latimer (2000). "The Effectiveness of the Minnesota Model Approach in the Treatment of Adolescent Drug Abusers." *Addiction*, 95:601-612.

Wolfgang, M., R.M. Figlio & T. Sellin (1972). *Delinquency in a Birth Cohort*. Chicago, IL: University of Chicago Press.

Wren, C. (1999). "Survey: Risk of Drug Use Rises in Middle Schools." Reprinted from *New York Times* in *Houston Chronicle*, (Thursday, April 8):4A.

Zhang, L., J.W. Welte & W.F. Wieczorek (1999). "Youth Gangs, Drug Use, and Delinquency." *Journal of Crime and Justice*, 27(2):101-109.

CHAPTER 5

Violence and Schools: The Problem, Prevention, and Policies

Richard Lawrence

Introduction

Approaching the end of the school year in April, 1999, it appeared as if the year would end with an all-time low number of student deaths. The tragic incident at Columbine High School in Littleton, Colorado, on April 20, changed that. Eric Harris and Dylan Klebold brought an arsenal of weapons to the school, walked down the hallways into the cafeteria and the library, shooting students in a hail of gunfire. At least 20 students were injured and 13 killed before they turned their guns on themselves. The 15 deaths at Columbine brought the total number of students killed in that school year to 26. The fact that the total number of school-associated deaths in 1998-1999 was still smaller than most previous years was no source of comfort.

Columbine was the worst school shooting incident in the history of the United States. Scenes of the tragedy were graphically played and replayed on television news shows for months following the incident. The shocking nature of the Columbine High School incident and the extensive media attention it received made an impact on students and parents throughout the nation. In a Gallup Poll conducted one year after the Columbine shootings, two-thirds (66%) of Americans stated that they believed it is likely that a similar attack could occur in their own community (Gillespie, 2000). The shocking nature of Columbine and other school shooting incidents, combined with the extensive news media coverage they receive, make it difficult to view the relatively small number of school shooting deaths in perspective. Compared with the approximately 2,000 juvenile homicides in the nation each year, school-associated deaths are relatively rare. Nevertheless, few persons are likely to take comfort in the fact that schools are still safer than most other places, including students' own homes. Society expects schools to be safe places, and even a small number of students killed at school each year is shocking and unacceptable.

This chapter examines the trends in school violence, lessons learned from school shooting incidents, the problem of bullying, and school violence prevention programs. The chapter also addresses the implications and potential effectiveness of policies such as "zero tolerance" and other violence-prevention strategies.

The Problem of School Crime and Violence

Crime and violent behavior in schools are problems that continue to demand the attention of educators, school administrators, and juvenile justice officials. School crime is not a new problem, but one which criminologists and policymakers have for many decades attempted to understand and prevent (Lawrence, 2007). The fear of victimization among students interferes with a safe learning environment and requires considerable time and effort from school staff that could otherwise be devoted to normal school activities. Responses of police and school staff have been varied.

Reactions to school violence are often focused more on reactive law enforcement and punitive measures than on preventive initiatives. In the wake of the highly publicized school shootings, school administrators have initiated "zero-tolerance" policies and increased the number of suspensions and expulsions of students making threats or carrying weapons onto school property. More police and security officers are being hired to patrol school hallways, and many schools have installed security cameras and metal detectors. Juvenile courts have responded by certifying as adults the students involved in school shootings, and transferring their cases to adult criminal court.

There is no clear research that added security, enforcement, and punitive measures alone will prevent school violence. As long as some students feel unsafe in and around schools and perceive that authorities cannot protect them, some weapons will continue to find their way in, especially given the ready availability of handguns. School violence prevention requires a more comprehensive, balanced, and preventive approach, in addition to punitive sanctions.

Trends in School Violence

The amount of crime committed in the nation's schools continues to be a concern. In 1999-2000, an estimated 1.5 million violent incidents occurred in public schools (K-12). One or more violent crimes were reported to police in 36 percent of all public schools; and 71 percent of school officials reported one or more violent incidents (DeVoe et al., 2003:24). Twenty percent of schools experienced one or more serious violent crimes (rape or other sexual assault, physical attack, fight, threat of attack with a weapon, robbery, and aggravated assault). One or more thefts were reported in 46 percent of schools (DeVoe et al., 2003:24). These statistics depict a serious crime problem in schools, but likely do not portray the true extent of the problem. School crimes are underreported because not all crimes are reported to principals and the crimes reported to principals are not always reported to police. Many crimes in schools are instead handled as disciplinary matters with the schools (Addington et al., 2002). Official reports of school crimes also reflect the policies and practices of teachers, principals, and school districts (Welsh, 2001).

Fear of being victimized at school affects students and their ability to learn and focus on their education. They respond in a variety of ways, ranging from avoiding school to carrying weapons for self-defense. Findings of the School Crime Supplement (SCS) to the National Crime Victimization Survey (NCVS) show that five percent or more of students avoid places in school because of fear of being attacked or bullied (DeVoe et al., 2003:38). Most common places avoided are hallways or stairs, parts of the cafeteria, restrooms, or locker rooms. Levels of fear and avoidance behaviors are not equal among students. Black and Hispanic students (7% and 6%, respectively) reported avoiding places more than white students (4%); sixth-grade students (7%) were more likely to avoid certain areas than twelfth-graders (3%); and students in urban areas (6 percent) avoid areas more than suburban or rural students (4%) (DeVoe et al., 2003:38). Some avoid school altogether. A significant portion of absenteeism and school truancy may be blamed on bullying and school violence. Some students carry weapons for self-defense or retaliation. Six percent of ninth- through twelfth-grade students reported they carried a weapon to school at least once in the 30 days before the survey (DeVoe et al., 2003:38). Circumstances and precipitating factors surrounding many of the school shootings indicate that the shooters had experienced bullying and harassment in the weeks and months prior to the incident. The potential for such tragic events exists whenever bullying, harassment, and threats are allowed to go unchecked.

"Everyday school violence" involving bullying, threats, pushing, hitting, and fights create an atmosphere of fear in schools. When teenagers were asked by the *New York Times* and CBS News poll what are the biggest problems where they go to school, they listed "violence" (16%) and "drugs" (14%) as their biggest concerns (Maguire & Pastore, 1999:98). Parents and adults express similar concerns. The 1998 Phi Delta Kappa/Gallup Poll of the public's attitudes toward the public schools found that the biggest concerns were drugs, discipline, control problems, fighting, violence, and gangs (Maguire & Pastore, 1999:99).

In summary, research clearly indicates that violence is a problem that affects virtually all schools. The extent of the problem varies according to school size, location, and racial/ethnic background as well as the age of the students. Regardless of size and location of the schools, however, a majority of school officials report some crimes occurring every year. Some teachers report being victims of personal and property crimes, but the majority of crimes in schools involve students as victims and perpetrators. The most recent available measures of school crime and violence in the United States indicate that the problems have *not* increased significantly in the past several years and, in fact, school shooting incidents, assaults involving injuries, and weapon possession have actually decreased. Increased sensitivity to and concern about school violence have resulted in more extensive and frequent measures to assess students' reported victimizations. Continuing the practice of annual measures and reports on school safety will help to determine whether the frequency of reported victimization occurs simply because more students are sensitized to the problem, and therefore reporting more, or because the problems are in fact increasingly common in too many schools.

Lessons Learned from School Shootings

Violent shooting incidents at school involving multiple fatalities have garnered more media coverage and public attention than most other types of violent crimes in the United States.[1] School shootings that result in deaths and serious injuries are shocking for at least two reasons: first, they occur relatively infrequently, and second, we expect schools to be safe places, free of the dangers of street crime. Since school shooting incidents are rare and shocking events, they are newsworthy and therefore draw extensive media coverage. Such coverage of scattered incidents of school violence occurring over several years and separated by wide geographical locations has had the effect of distorting the actual incidence and probability of similar tragedies occurring in other schools. Research shows that school shootings are rare events in which fatalities represent only a fraction of the number of young people who are victims of homicide each year (Lawrence & Mueller, 2003). The Federal Bureau of Investigation (FBI) reports the number of homicides involving juveniles but does not report homicides according to the location of the crime. "School-associated deaths" are reported annually by the National School Safety Center (NSSC) (2007). A sample of school shootings involving multiple fatalities in the United States from 1974 to 2007 is shown in Table 5.1.

The immediate response to most school shooting incidents has been shock and surprise, particularly because they involved middle-class white boys from small city or suburban schools in communities that had not been characterized by violence or high crime. Media stories focused on the shooters, their families, friends, and personal background and most persons who knew them expressed surprise and remarked that they had not been involved in any serious delinquent or violent behavior before the shooting. These incidents have received considerable attention and have resulted in responses ranging from violence prevention programs in the school curriculum to physical security devices such as metal detectors and surveillance cameras. Initial reports of the shootings seemed to suggest that the young shooters just "snapped" with little warning, and that most school shootings were very unpredictable events.

Table 5.1 **School Shooting Incidents Involving Multiple Fatalities in the U.S., 1974 – 2007***

Date	Location	Alleged Perpetrator (Age)	Victims
Dec. 1974	Olean, NY	Anthony Barbaro (18)	3
May 1992	Olivehurst, CA	Eric Houston (20)	3
Jan. 1993	Grayson, KY	Scott Pennington (17)	2
Oct. 1995	Blackville, SC	Toby Sincino (16)	3
Feb. 1996	Moses Lake, WA	Barry Loukaitis (14)	3
Feb. 1997	Bethel, AK	Evan Ramsey (16)	2
Oct. 1997	Pearl, MS	Luke Woodham (16)	3
Dec. 1997	W. Paducah, KY	Michael Carneal (14)	3
Mar. 1998	Jonesboro, AR	Andrew Golden (11) Mitchell Johnson (13)	5
Apr. 1998	Pomona, CA	Unknown gang member(s)	2
May 1998	Springfield, OR	Kip Kinkel (15)	4
Apr. 1999	Littleton, CO	Eric Harris (18) Dylan Klebold (17)	15
Mar. 2001	Santee, CA	Charles Andrew Williams (15)	2
Apr. 2002	Red Lion, PA	James Sheets (14)	2
Sept. 2003	San Diego, CA	William Hoffine (58) (Killed son, Evan Nash, 14)	2
Sept. 2003	Cold Spring, MN	Jason McLaughlin (15)	2
Mar. 2005	Red Lake, MN	Jeff Weiss (17)	8
Oct. 2006	Nickel Mines, PA	Charles Roberts (32)	6

* The listed cases are those involving multiple fatalities in "school-associated violent deaths" including suicides that occurred in or around schools, on the way to or from school, or at school events. Victims may include students, teachers, other school staff, and passers-by.

[Sources: Adapted from National School Safety Center, 2007; Newman, 2004.]

"Warning Signs" of School Violence

The attention and widespread concern generated by school shootings prompted public officials and school administrators to find ways to prevent similar tragedies. The question that immediately came to mind was whether school shootings could have been predicted and prevented. Were there some warning signs that should have been apparent to those close to the shooters days or weeks before the shootings? Newspaper and television stories following shooting incidents identified the shooters as troubled individuals who were often isolated from the main student population and sometimes showed signs of being troubled. Some had even made verbal threats or similar indications that hinted at the potential for violence. In hindsight, following the shootings, these signs seemed obvious to the casual viewers. Most students and teachers, however, did not expect those verbal threats to actually be carried out. Many students make threats, but few act on them.

The various strategies for identifying potential violent offenders vary, ranging from "profiling" to "risk assessment," "threat assessment," and "warning signs." The terms are often used interchangeably by various writers without a clear definition of the meaning, the methods used, or the accuracy and limitations of any given strategy. Among the earliest attempts to identify potentially violent students were a checklist of the "characteristics" of youth involved in school-associated violent deaths (National School Safety Center, 1998) and a list of "warning signs" distributed by the U.S. Department of Education that could describe students at risk of serious violent behavior in schools (Dwyer, Osher & Warger, 1998). These were soon followed by publications of professional organizations such as the International Association of Chiefs of Police (Kramen, Massey & Timm, 1999); the American Psychological Association (2000); the FBI (O'Toole, 1999); and the Secret Service (Reddy et al., 2000). In efforts to identify important variables, social scientists have conducted detailed, comprehensive case studies of the family backgrounds of the shooters (Newman, 2004). The methods have varied, but the goal of these studies has been an attempt to produce "profiles" or common characteristics of students likely to engage in school violence.

Criminal profiling is multidisciplinary, drawing from the studies of criminal behavior (criminology), mental illness (psychology and psychiatry), and physical evidence (biology and chemistry). Profiling relies on inductive and deductive reasoning for developing a profile of a criminal that is based on evidence (Holmes & Holmes, 1996; and Turvey, 1999). Nonetheless, profiling is highly probabilistic and conclusions and predictions can never be made with 100 percent confidence. The fact that there are relatively few school shootings means that attempting to develop an accurate profile of a school shooter is nearly impossible (Lawrence, 2007:150-153). This holds true whether we are attempting to develop a profile, common characteristics, or "warning signs" that may help identify potentially violent students. The "warning signs" were established on the premise that: (1) students involved in school violence did not just "snap"; (2) the incidents did not just happen without prior warning; (3) the students and the incidents do share several characteristics in common; and (4) violent incidents can be prevented when administrators, teachers and other students are attentive to the warning signs.

There are, however, a number of problems with the warning signs. Despite a cautionary note against labeling and stigmatizing some students and overreacting based on a few warning signs, there is a danger that some students may be incorrectly identified as violence risks. It is very difficult to predict violent behavior. Many students have several of the warning signs, including school problems, being loners with few friends, engaging in fights, property damage, alcohol and drug use, carrying weapons, and making threats. Few, if any of them, however, will ever act out with lethal violence in school.

The warning signs are likely to produce many "false positives," meaning that many non-violent students will be incorrectly identified as likely to engage in violence. Attempts to single out potentially violent students also can do more harm than good by stigmatizing and marginalizing already troubled youth. Youth who feel ostracized by other students may exemplify some of the warning signs and then be labeled by teachers and administrators, thereby exacerbating the tendency to act out violently.

The warning signs have also been criticized for focusing almost exclusively on individual characteristics and psychological problems of troubled students (Fox & Levin, 2001.) The blame is therefore located outside the school setting, with the assumption that it is the students who must change, not the schools. School administrators who view problem students as victims of poor parenting, family conflict, excessive exposure to media violence, and parental abuse and neglect tend to believe that school violence prevention programs would have little effect and are a waste of scarce resources (Fox & Levin, 2001). Focusing on the individual student also ignores a number of other situational and environmental problems that should be addressed in order to prevent school violence. There is evidence that some students carry weapons to school for protection after they have been bullied and threatened by other students. They claim that school administrators have done little to protect them or to intervene to stop bullying and harassment. Research has established the importance of school structure as well as institutional and community factors in explaining disorder, misconduct and weapon possession in schools (Welsh, Greene & Jenkins, 1999; Wilcox & Clayton, 2001).

Threat Assessment

A threat assessment approach goes beyond simple warning signs and accounts for multiple factors to assess the potential for school violence. The FBI developed a threat assessment perspective that recognizes four types of threats (direct, indirect, veiled, and conditional) proffered and a four-pronged threat assessment model. The first, student personality traits and behavior, includes most of the same individual "warning signs" discussed above. The FBI includes three other environmental influences in assessing the threat of school violence: (1) family dynamics: turbulent parent-child relations, access to weapons in the home, lack of parental discipline and control, and no limits or monitoring of TV viewing; (2) school dynamics: tolerance for disrespectful behavior, inequitable discipline, inflexible culture, pecking order among students, and a code of silence; and (3) social dynamics: media and entertainment influences, peer groups, drugs and alcohol, and the copycat effect (O'Toole, 1999:21-23).

The U.S. Secret Service studied 37 school shooting incidents involving 41 attackers, applying the same strategy used in identifying persons who pose a threat to the President of the United States (Vossekuil, Reddy & Fein, 2000). They found that incidents of targeted violence at school are rarely impulsive. The shooters had planned the attack for days and even weeks before the incident, often as revenge for previous threats, bullying, or other personal reasons. Many of the attackers were known to hold a grievance at the time of the attack, and had told peers about these prior to the attack. Because information about the school shooters' intents and planning was potentially knowable before the incidents, some of the attacks might have been preventable.

The Secret Service emphasizes that it is helpful to distinguish between *making* a threat (telling people they intend to harm someone) and *posing* a threat (engaging in behaviors that indicate an intent, planning, or preparation for an attack). Adults should focus their concerns on someone who actually poses a threat. The Secret Service threat assessment approach recommends conducting an inquiry to gather information and answering key questions to determine whether a person making a threat actually poses a threat. The questions focus on: (1) motivation for the behavior of the person making the threat; (2) the ideas and intentions communicated; (3) an unusual interest in targeted violence; (4) evidence of attack-related behaviors and plans; (5) mental condition; (6) level of mental sophistication or organization to carry out the plan; (7) recent personal losses; (8) consistency between communication and behaviors; (9) concern by peers and others about the person's potential for harm; and (10) factors in the individual's life, environment, or situation that might affect the likelihood of an attack (Reddy, Borum, Berglund, Vossekuil, Fein & Modzeleski, 2001:169).

Assessing Risk Assessment

Profiles, warning signs, and risk-assessment tools for identifying and predicting school violence may be helpful in alerting students and teachers to possible indicators of a potentially violent student. It is important to recognize, however, that these have not been tested for reliability or validity. As a result, there are questions about the usefulness or accuracy of warning signs or violence indicators. Some may be harmful when predictions result in false positives. A closer examination of profiling, risk and threat assessment, and warning signs is necessary to assess their relative strengths and limitations. Table 5.2 presents a list of 26 characteristics, profiles, or warning signs from five of the organizations and sources noted above. The characteristics or warning signs in the Table were included on at least two or more of the agencies' lists. The characteristics or warning signs which were more frequently listed (they were included by four of the agencies) were: uncontrolled anger; drug/alcohol use or abuse; member of a gang, cult, or antisocial group; and feelings of rejection. Twelve characteristics, including those related to bullying, were included on three of the lists. Only five of the original 20 characteristics of the FBI offender profile matched or were sufficiently similar

Table 5.2. **Comparison of Characteristics, Profiles, or Warning Signs of School Violence Risk**

Characteristics, "Profile," or "Warning Signs" of Violence Potential or Risk	"Characteristic," "Profile", or "Warning Sign" Included in the List = X[a]				
APA: American Psychological Association; FBI: Federal Bureau of Investigation; IACP: International Association of Chiefs of Police; NSSC: National School Safety Center; USDOE: U.S. Department of Education.	APA	FBI	IACP	NSSC	USDOE
Anger - uncontrolled	X		X	X	X
Animal Cruelty/Abuse	X		X		
Bullying / Aggressive Behavior - Verbal Abuse of Others	X		X	X	
Bullying / Aggressive Behavior – Threatens others (general)	X		X	X	
Bullying – Victim	X		X	X	
Domestic Violence (exposure to, witnessed)			X	X	
Drug/Alcohol Use and/or Abuse	X		X	X	X
Depression and Mood Swings			X	X	
Empathy (lack of empathy skills)	X		X		
Expresses violence in writings, artwork, etc.			X	X	X
History of Discipline Problems (general)	X			X	X
History of Violent or Aggressive Behavior	X		X		X
Intolerance (Prejudice or Dislike of those who are different)		X	X		X
Member of Gang, Cult, Antisocial group (incl. delinquent peer group)	X	X	X	X	
Parental Involvement / Monitoring (low)			X	X	
Precipitating event (psychological trauma that may or did trigger violence)		X	X		
Rejection (perceived or real rejection by peers/family; or no close friends; loner)	X		X	X	X
School Failure (poor academic performance)	X		X		X
Social Isolation (feelings of loneliness; lack of friends)		X	X	X	
Suspended / Expelled / Truant in the past (history of school discipline problems)		X	X	X	
Threats (previous) – Suicide (threat or attempt)			X	X	
Threats (previous) – Violence or Terrorist threat	X		X		X
TV/Entertainment (preferences for violent themes)			X	X	
Weapons – Brought weapon to school	X		X	X	
Weapons – Access to, general ("inappropriate access to")	X				X
Weapons – Talks about / Preoccupied with	X		X	X	

[a] The list of characteristics, profile factors, or warning signs includes those that were included on 2 or more of the lists of agencies.

[Sources: American Psychological Association, 2000; Aultmann-Bettridge et al., 2000; Band & Harpold, 1999; Dwyer et al., 1998; Kramen et al., 1999; Lawrence, 2007; National School Safety Center, 1998.]

with those identified by other agencies. The FBI profiles were developed by law enforcement officers at a regional meeting in Arkansas and were based on six shooting cases. The other three lists (APA, IACP, and U.S. Dept. of Education) were developed by multidisciplinary groups of experts including educators and mental health professionals; the NSSC list is based on more than 200 school-associated deaths from 1992 to 1998.

A study assessing the reliability and validity of the school violence indicators found that 28 percent of future offenders might be correctly identified with a 4 percent false-positive rate. An analysis using the upper 10 percent of risk (those scoring high on six or more factors) found that 43 percent of future offenders would be correctly identified but there would be a 22 percent false-positive rate (Aultmann-Bettridge, Elliott & Huizinga, 2000). Profiles and warning signs can help identify potentially violent students in schools, but the false positive rate is unacceptably high. As a result, the school violence risk and threat assessment tools currently available are not sufficiently reliable or valid nor are they strongly supported by empirical evidence (Lawrence, 2007).

Bullying

One of the most common victimization experiences reported by students is bullying. Most persons have witnessed or been a victim of bullying at some time during their school experience. Bullying has been defined as the repeated oppression, either physical or psychological, of a less powerful person by a more powerful one; or as students being picked on or made to do things they did not want to do (Farrington, 1993:381; Kaufmann et al., 2000). Bullying has not been recognized as a serious problem in the United States until fairly recently. It has often been downplayed as simply teasing or minor harassment that is an unpleasant but "normal" part of going to school. The problem of bullying has been taken more seriously in Scandinavian countries where research on bullying has been ongoing for many years (Olweus, 1978).

Surveys of more than 150,000 Norwegian students indicated that 15 percent of students in grades 1 through 9 have been involved in bullying incidents, either as bullies (about 7%) or as victims (about 9%) (Olweus, 1978; 1993). Research on bullying among school children has attracted attention in other countries, including Great Britain, Canada, and the United States only in the past 10-15 years (Farrington, 1993). Data from other countries indicate that the bullying problem is at least comparable to or greater than that in Norwegian schools. School officials in the United States and the U.S. Department of Education now recognize that bullying is a major problem in schools, and one that may precipitate more serious assaults and violence.

Statistics on bullying were finally added to the "Indicators of School Crime and Safety, 2000" with 5 percent of students ages 12 through 18 reporting that they had been bullied at school in the past 6 months (Kaufman et al., 2000). Students in lower grades were more likely to be bullied than students in higher grades. About 10 percent of students in grades 6 and 7 reported being bullied, compared to about 5 percent of students in grades 8 and 9 and about 2 percent in grades 10 through 12. Boys were more likely to be bullied in grades 6 and 7 than were girls (12% versus 7%), but there was little difference in the percentage of boys and girls being bullied in the other grade levels. More boys than girls bully other students. A large percentage of girls report that they are mainly bullied by boys. Bullying is a greater problem among boys but girls are also involved in bullying. Bullying among boys tends to be more physical; girls typically use more subtle forms of harassment, such as slandering, spreading rumors, exclusion from a group, and manipulating friendship relations (Olweus, 1978; 1993).

Contrary to what many believe, bullying is not a consequence of large schools or class sizes nor is it explained as a reaction to school failure or frustration. Research suggests that bullying is more closely related to personality characteristics of bullies and victims. Victims of bullying tend to be more anxious and insecure than students in general. They are often cautious, sensitive, quiet, have low self-esteem, are often lonely, and have few close friends at school. Bullies have a greater acceptance of violence than other students, are often characterized by impulsivity, have a need to dominate others, and express little empathy for victims. They are usually physically stronger, and they use violence and aggression more than most students. Contrary to the belief that bullying is a reaction to underlying insecurity, research indicates that bullies have little anxiety or insecurity, and do not suffer from poor self-esteem (Olweus, 1993; 1994).

Studies suggest that there are short- and long-term consequences for both the perpetrators and the victims of bullying. Victims of repeated bullying may experience more physical and psychological problems, and they tend not to grow out of the role of victim. Results of longitudinal studies show that persons who were bullied in early grades also report being bullied several years later. Students who were bullied may suffer as adults with depression, poor self-esteem, and other mental health problems (Olweus, 1993). Bullies also have a higher likelihood of further problems as adults. Elementary students who were bullies had higher rates of school absenteeism and were more likely to drop out than other students. Bullying may also be a factor in later delinquent and violent behavior. Research conducted in Scandinavia found that bullies were much more likely than their non-bullying peers to commit antisocial acts, including drunkenness, vandalism, fighting, theft, and to have been arrested in early adulthood (Olweus, 1993).

Preventing Bullying at School

Bullying is not something that can be ignored or treated as simply normal adolescent behavior. Many children suffer greatly from bullying. Some respond by withdrawing and staying home from school. Others become more aggressive themselves. There are even documented cases of suicide among victims of bullying. A school program to prevent bullying should consider the following:

- Increase awareness of the bully/victim problem. Assess the extent of the problem in each school through an anonymous survey of students.

- Present an in-service training session for school personnel on the bullying problem; present results of the survey; compare with national and international data on bullying; and explain the characteristics of victims and bullies.

- Organize a parent-teacher meeting to inform parents about bullying and what the school is doing to prevent it. Provide parents with the information presented to teachers. Show a video on bullying (available from the National School Safety Center), and solicit parents' input on preventing bullying.

- Develop clear rules against bullying, including a definition of bullying and the various oppressive and harassing behaviors that are forbidden. Enforce the rules with appropriate sanctions that are agreed upon by school personnel, parents, and students.

- School personnel should provide adequate supervision on school grounds during recess; in school hallways, stairways, restrooms and areas where students are most vulnerable to bullying. Provide support and protection for the victims, and help them develop friendships.

- Teachers should discuss bullying with students in class, and use role-playing exercises and video presentations. Teachers should talk to identified bullies, their victims, and their parents (See Olweus, 1993; 1994; and Farrington, 1993).

Responses to School Violence

As noted earlier, schools are expected to be safe places where students can learn in a protected environment that is free of drugs and violence that occur in other parts of the community. School shooting incidents are shocking tragedies that run counter to these expectations. That is a major reason for the widespread media and public attention that accompanies the random incidents of threats and shootings in American schools each year (Lawrence & Mueller, 2003). Every incident invariably raises questions about what causes some students to react violently. The public's view of the causes of violence in schools places most of the blame on parents, the easy availability of guns, violent themes in entertainment and music, school discipline practices, news media coverage, and bullying and teasing by students at school.

A Gallup poll asked respondents what they thought were the most important factors causing school shootings. Most (92%) attributed the causes of school shootings to students' home life and relationship with their parents; 77 percent blamed the availability and ease of obtaining guns; 68 percent stated that violence in entertainment and music was a cause; 67 percent said the way schools discipline students was a factor; 64 percent blamed the news media for its widespread coverage of shootings; and 62 percent stated that bullying and teasing of students at school was a major cause of shootings (Moore, 2001). When asked to describe what would be the single most important thing that could be done to prevent another incidence of school shootings, Americans (31%) are most likely to mention greater parental involvement and responsibility. The other responses most frequently mentioned were "more security at schools" and "stricter gun control" but these were noted by only 14 and 11 percent of the respondents, respectively (Moore, 2001). School principals also identified lack of parental supervision most frequently as the cause of school violence, and their second most frequent cause was the lack of parent involvement with the schools (Price & Everett, 1997).

School Practices and Policies

The perception of widespread school violence and the fear that such incidents could happen in any school has influenced the way principals manage, how teachers teach, and how students learn and relate to each other. According to a national survey of school principals, most public schools now have zero-tolerance policies toward serious student offenses (Kaufman et al., 2000:133). A "zero-tolerance policy" was defined as a school or district policy that mandates predetermined consequences or punishments for specific offenses. At least 9 out of 10 schools reported zero-tolerance policies for firearms (94%) and weapons other than firearms (91%). Most schools also had policies of zero tolerance for alcohol (87%), other drugs (88%), and tobacco (79%) (Kaufman et al., 2000:133).

Security measures were also implemented in schools. Visitors are required to sign in before entering most school buildings (96%); 80 percent of public schools reported having a closed campus policy that prohibited most students from leaving the campus for lunch; and 53 percent of public schools controlled access to their school grounds. Drug sweeps are conducted regularly in 36 percent of public middle schools and 45 percent of public high schools (Kaufman et al., 2000:134). Metal detectors are rarely used, with only 4 percent of public schools reporting random metal detector checks on students, and only one percent using metal detectors on a daily basis. School resource officers have been claimed by many as an important tool for reducing school crime, but only about one-third (34%) of principals reported having law enforcement officers stationed in their schools. A majority of public schools (78%) reported having some type of formal school violence prevention or reduction program (Kaufman et al., 2000:134).

Unintended Consequences of Interventions

The United States is not alone in facing problems of school violence. It is truly an international problem, and we can learn much from the interventions practiced in other countries. Excluding students from school for violence and drug use has been a common approach in the United States and other countries. The problems with expulsions and suspensions are that they increase the likelihood that those students will become even more involved in delinquency, drugs, and violence. Expulsions are therefore only a short-term fix, because the increasing levels of delinquency and drug use by the problem students in the community continue to affect the schools. Tougher policies such as "zero tolerance" and the threat of suspension and expulsion are some of the most publicized and visible efforts toward school violence prevention.

There is confusion, however, about exactly what these policies mean. Usually they refer to tough, uniform, and mandatory punishments for serious school rule violations that result in automatic and immediate expulsion. Many school boards in Canada say that they have zero-tolerance policies, but in practice their policy has a range of consequences, from curfews and extra work to suspensions and exclusion (Shaw, 2001). Principals and school boards in the United States are often faced with the dilemma of having to expel a student when an alternative consequence may have seemed preferable. Since the passage of the 1994 Federal Gun-Free Schools Act requiring schools to expel students carrying firearms, the number of expelled students doubled in some states, but has now declined somewhat (U.S. Departments of Education and Justice, 2000). Zero-tolerance policies and expulsions are being critically examined, and many question whether such policies make schools safer in the long run and whether the overall costs justify the practice. The community, and therefore also the school, may be at continued risk from expelled students who do not re-enter school, fall farther behind academically, and are at risk of more serious criminal activity (Kingery, 2001). Intervention projects offering alternatives to school suspension and expulsion are being funded and developed by the U.S. Department of Education and studied by the Hamilton Fish Institute.

Toward Effective School Violence Prevention

State Departments of Education and local school districts have developed policies and strategies for violence prevention, but research evidence of their effectiveness is mixed. Policies that focus on tighter security, crime control, and disciplinary sanctions have not proven to be effective, and may in fact contribute to student misbehavior (Hyman & Perone, 1998). Most of the violence prevention programs currently being employed in the schools, such as conflict resolution, peer mediation, metal detectors, and locker searches and sweeps, have either not been thoroughly evaluated or have been evaluated and found to be ineffective (Elliott, Hamburg & Williams, 1998; Gottfredson, 1997). An effective school violence prevention program must begin with the premise that school violence is *not* separate from violence that occurs in the community, on the streets, or in the home. Violent behavior in school is an extension of students' experiences in the community and in their homes.

Effective violence prevention efforts therefore require the active involvement of the students and their parents, the community and social agencies, law enforcement, juvenile authorities, and school personnel. Effective crime prevention must be comprehensive and link several community agencies and social institutions in cooperative ventures. Isolated and independent crime prevention efforts will not work. If positive results in crime reduction are expected, then it makes more sense to focus on "what works" than to focus on symbolic messages such as "zero tolerance." Tougher laws and the threat of punishment will be largely ineffective in preventing crime and violence unless they are accompanied by, and reinforced by, the informal social controls in the community. Youth are less likely to be deterred by legal sanctions when they are receiving inconsistent and contradictory messages from their families, their peers, the community, and the media. Attempting to reduce crime through reactive and retributive legal sanctions has taught us that broader interdisciplinary and interagency approaches are necessary to address the social and personal problems underlying criminal behavior.

School-Based Violence Prevention

Schools are perhaps the single most effective resources for delinquency prevention. They are the most direct link between families and communities. More than any other government agency, they provide access to virtually all students throughout their developmental years, and can help to counter the adverse influences to which young people are exposed in the community. School staff are well-equipped to help students develop prosocial values, and positive thinking and communication skills. Research supports the importance of education and school involvement in helping youth avoid delinquent behavior. Programs that have shown positive results are those aimed at clarifying acceptable behavioral norms, establishing and consistently enforcing school rules, and school-wide campaigns to reduce bullying and drugs in schools. The most effective school programs are comprehensive instructional programs that focus on social competency skills (self-control, responsible decisionmaking, problem solving, and communication skills) and that are delivered over a period of time to continually reinforce those skills (Gottfredson, 1997:5-55).

Educators will continue to be under pressure to react to school violence with highly visible law enforcement and security strategies. Parents and the public are demanding that they "do something." School administrators will continue to hire police and security officers and consider security technologies in order to improve school safety, reduce fears, protect their own liability, and to show that they *are* "doing something." After zero-tolerance policies came under attack for being too rigid, educators encouraged more interaction between adults and students and encouraged students to take more responsibility for school safety through awareness and reporting of potential violence

(Newcomb, 2001). This new emphasis on student responsibility for reporting suspicions or threats from other students is successful, and some potentially violent incidents have been prevented. Experts are encouraged by the broad range of strategies used in schools that includes a mix of law enforcement, high standards, after-school programs, and family involvement (Newcomb, 2001).

Federal Initiatives for Safe Schools

Following a number of tragic shooting incidents, President Clinton directed the U.S. Departments of Education and Justice in December 1997 to prepare for the first time an annual report on school safety. In addition to providing an overview of the nature and scope of school crime, the first report (for 1998) described actions that schools and communities can take to address this critical issue. Steps for developing and implementing a comprehensive school safety plan include:

- Establish school-community partnerships;
- Identify and measure the problem;
- Set measurable goals and objectives;
- Identify appropriate research-based programs and strategies;
- Implement the comprehensive plan;
- Evaluate the plan; and
- Revise the plan on the basis of the evaluation (U.S. Departments of Education and Justice, 1999).

The first annual report on school safety describes what can be done to develop and implement a school safety plan and to ensure its success. The plan recommends that communities work together, overcome barriers, monitor progress, and regularly evaluate the effectiveness of the selected strategies. Table 5.3 summarizes what communities, schools, students, parents, police and juvenile justice authorities, businesses, and elected officials and government agencies can do in a collaborative strategy to prevent school violence.

International developments in school safety programs reveal a number of emerging trends. Among these trends are the following:

- Framing the issues more on school safety and less on school violence.
- Linking school safety with the needs of victims and victimizers and to healthy behaviors.
- Changing emphasis from a reactive or punitive focus on perpetrators of school violence to proactive approaches.
- Shifting from physical, situational prevention, or school expulsion to comprehensive approaches that use a range of policies and programs.

Table 5.3 **Recommendations for School Violence Prevention**

Schools

- Provide admin. support, assess & enhance school safety
- Redesign school facility, eliminate dark, secluded, unsupervised spaces
- Report, analyze violent and non-criminal events
- Design effective discipline policy
- Build partnerships with local L.E.
- School security professionals design, maintain school security system
- Train school staff in viol. prevention
- Provide students access to school psychologists & counselors
- Provide crisis response services
- Implement schoolwide education & training to avoid & prevent violence
- Use alt. schools to educate violent & weapon-carrying students
- Create a climate of tolerance
- Provide appropriate educational services to all students
- Reach out to community, business to improve student safety
- Involve students in decision making on policies & programs
- Prepare an annual report on school crime and safety

Students

- Behave responsibly
- Report crimes and threats to school officials
- Get involved in anti-crime programs
- Learn how to avoid becoming a victim
- Seek help, express fears to school staff

Communities

- Establish school-comm. partnerships
- Identify & measure the problem
- Set measurable goals and objectives
- Identify appropriate programs, strategies
- Implement a comprehensive plan
- Evaluate and revise the plan
- Elected Officials/Gov. Agencies
- Provide leadership for school crime prevent.
- Support school crime prevention research
- Encourage schools to monitor & report crime
- Discuss legislation for school viol. prevention
- Collaborate with local, State, Fed. agencies

Table 5.3 *(continued)*
Parents
• Actively communicate with children • Be clear & consistent in disciplining children • Model prosocial behavior; take part in family management. training • Get involved with school & community organizations • Keep guns, weapons out of reach of children • Limit children's exposure to crime and violence
Police/Juvenile Authorities
• Establish working relationship with the schools • Respond to reports of criminal activities in the school • Consult with school authorities and parents re: security • Work with youth to maintain constructive relationship
Business
• Adopt a local school • Provide training in basic job skills • Provide internships and employment opportunities • Provide scholarships to deserving students • Offer resources to local schools • Provide release time to parents and volunteers

- Using programs geared both to problem students and to the entire school population, teachers, and families.

- Developing school-community partnerships.

- Targeting at-risk schools using evaluated model programs.

- Involving young people in the assessment of problems and project design (Shaw, 2001:21).

The emphasis on moving from school violence to school safety perhaps best illustrates the need for a proactive approach rather than the traditional reactive responses to school violence. Although the extent and types of problems experienced by schools vary in different schools and communities, some common strategies and intervention methods have begun to emerge. The approaches emphasize four major issues: (1) perceiving the school within its community setting by opening school buildings to local residents and students after school hours, inviting citizens to participate in school activities and creating links with local businesses and other professional groups; (2) focusing on the school atmosphere, not just physical security or individual students; (3) using a partnership problem-solving model; and (4) employing multiple strategies, not single programs (Shaw, 2001:23).

The most successful violence prevention programs address the entire school population, have designed special projects to target at-risk groups and individuals, and solicit teacher support. The 1999 *Annual Report on School Safety* provides examples of model prevention programs that use well-designed projects, have demonstrated effectiveness, have been adapted to local school and community needs, and can be implemented as part of a comprehensive school safety plan. A key point is that a safe school is the result of careful planning and a thorough understanding of the school's physical, social, and cultural environment. An important part of increasing school safety is choosing programs that can be readily integrated with other activities to effectively address local needs. Schools should select programs and strategies based on the results of a thorough needs assessment. Parents, citizens, and community leaders must be actively involved in developing and implementing the comprehensive school safety plan. The model violence prevention programs summarized in the 1999 *Annual Report on School Safety* include clearly publicized codes of conduct and school regulations, policies to deal with daily events and situations, safety plans to deal with serious incidents, support for students with particular problems, and curricula and other learning tools for teachers to improve conflict resolution and mediation skills (U.S. Departments of Education and Justice, 1999).

The Real Controversies about School Violence

No discussion of school violence would be complete without addressing the real controversies behind this problem, which are two-fold: the news media coverage of school violence and the issue of race in news media portrayals of crime perpetrators and victims. These issues are important for consideration in order to maintain a proper perspective of the problem of school violence in relation to the total amount of crime throughout communities. Extensive resources are being allocated to respond to school violence, so it is doubly important to implement violence prevention programs and resources equitably to all victims and segments of communities; and to ensure that our responses are consistent for all individuals, schools, and communities. As with the history of criminal justice in America, this has not always been practiced.

News Media Coverage of School Violence

School violence, particularly school shootings, has been reported in the news media way out of proportion to their actual occurrence (Lawrence & Mueller, 2003). In 1998, for example, there were 1,960 total reported murder victims under the age of 18, and only 43 of those (2 percent) were school-associated deaths in the 1997-98 school year (Snyder & Sickmund, 1999; Lawrence & Mueller, 2003). Most homicides involving juveniles receive no more media attention than other tragic violent crimes and accidents. School-associated homicides, on the other hand, become national news events that are repeated for days, weeks, and even months after the incident. For months following the Columbine High School shootings (Littleton, Colorado) ABC ran 93 stories on the evening news, CBS did 106, and NBC, 97 (Lawrence, 2007; Stossel, 1999). School shooting incidents tend to garner an inordinate amount of coverage because they are relatively rare and dramatic events (Surette, 1998). The problem is that disproportionate news media coverage tends to exaggerate the nature and extent of the crime, and incites widespread and irrational fears about the true potential for victimization (Chiricos et al., 2000). News media reports of crime are the sole or primary sources of information about crime and the criminal justice system for most Americans (Surette, 1998). Thus, as previously noted, it should not be surprising that in a Gallup Poll conducted one year after the Columbine shootings, two-thirds (66%) of Americans stated that they believed it is likely that a similar attack could occur in their own community (Gillespie, 2000). Exaggerated fears of school shootings, often fueled by distorted news media coverage, may be prompting violence prevention policies that are more harmful than helpful to students.

Race and School Violence

The news media, and particularly television news, disproportionately connect race and crime, especially violent crime (Dorfman & Schiraldi, 2001). Studies have found that African-Americans were over-represented as perpetrators of crime and that more television and newspaper coverage was given to crime incidents involving white victims than those involving black victims (Romer, Jamieson & DeCoteau, 1998; Weiss & Chermak, 1998). Sorenson et al. (1998) noted the news media's preference for stories of white homicide victims over Black victims, and coined the term "worthy victim" to describe who gets attention in newspaper stories about homicide. Mike Males compared a number of juvenile shooting incidents and came to the conclusion that those receiving the most news media coverage were the ones involving white victims in schools (Males, 2001). The school shootings that received little media attention were those involving minority victims. Disproportionate news media coverage of school shootings involving white student victims is another facet of the distorted coverage of crime documented by Romer and his associates (1998) and by Weiss and Chermak (1998).

Two paradoxical issues are raised by such disproportionate and distorted coverage of school shootings. First, it appears that school violence was not viewed as much of a problem and not given so much attention as long as the incidents were fights and assaults with weapons involving minority students in urban, inner-city schools. Fights and assaults are not new problems for schools, and have occurred with some frequency for years. It appears that when school violence was primarily a problem in urban inner-city schools, little attention was paid to it, and few state or federal resources or funds were made available. School violence, particularly shooting incidents, have received news media coverage and national attention primarily when they have occurred in suburban and small city schools and when the shooters and victims are primarily white middle-class students. The frequency of juvenile homicides has not increased over the past several years, but the nature and location of juvenile homicides has changed somewhat.

The second and related part of the paradox is that the distorted and disproportionate news media coverage of school violence involving white victims has generated more attention and concern, along with more resources, more funding, and a multitude of state and federal programs for school violence prevention to be implemented in local schools and communities. The important issue now is that these resources, funds, and programs be allocated with equity, without regard to the race, ethnicity, or social class of the students who are most at risk of school violence. Just as proper balance and context in news reporting is important, so also is the equitable implementation of school violence prevention programs throughout all schools and communities. Research on crime prevention and planning has found that policies that lack collaboration and comprehensiveness are doomed to fail. The goal of safe and healthy schools is too important to not apply best efforts and practices based on sound research evidence of their effectiveness.

Endnotes

[1] A school-associated violent death is any homicide, suicide, or weapons-related violent death in the United States in which the fatal injury occurred: on the property of a public, private, or parochial elementary or secondary school, Kindergarten through grade 12, (including alternative schools); on the way to or from regular sessions at a school; while person was attending or was on the way to or from an official school-sponsored event; as a direct result of school incidents, functions or activities, whether on or off a school bus/vehicle or school property (National School Safety Center, 2007).

References

Addington, L., S.A. Ruddy, A.K. Miller, J.F. DeVoe & K.A. Chandler (2002). *Are America's Schools Safe? Students Speak Out: 1999 School Crime Supplement*. Washington, DC: National Center for Education Statistics.

American Psychological Association (2000). "Warning Signs." Washington, DC: American Psychological Association. http://apahelpcenter.org/ [Retrieved November 29, 2007].

Aultmann-Bettridge, T., D.S. Elliott & D. Huizinga (2000). "Predicting School Violence: Analyzing the Validity and Reliability of Violent Student 'Profiles'." Paper presented at the American Society of Criminology, San Francisco.

Band, S.R. & J.A. Harpold (1999). "School Violence: Lessons Learned." *FBI Law Enforcement Bulletin*, 68(9): 9-15.

Chiricos, T., K. Padgett & M. Gertz (2000). "Fear, TV News, and the Reality of Crime." *Criminology*, 38(3):755-785.

DeVoe, J.F., K. Peter, P. Kaufman, S.A. Ruddy, A.K. Miller, M. Planty, T.D. Snyder & M.R. Rand (2003). *Indicators of School and Safety: 2003*. Washington, DC: U.S. Departments of Education and Justice.

Dorfman, L. & V. Schiraldi (2001). *Off Balance: Youth, Race & Crime in the News*. Washington, DC: Youth Law Center, Building Blocks for Youth.

Dwyer, K., D. Osher & C. Warger (1998). *Early Warning, Timely Response: A Guide to Safe Schools*. Washington, DC: U.S. Department of Education.

Elliott, D.S., B. Hamburg & K.R. Williams (1998). "Violence in American Schools: An Overview." In D.S. Elliott, B. Hamburg & K.R. Williams (eds.) *Violence in American Schools*, pp. 3-28. Cambridge, UK: Cambridge University Press.

Farrington, D.P. (1993). "Understanding and Preventing Bullying." In M. Tonry (ed.) *Crime and Justice: A Review of Research*, Vol. 17, pp. 381-458. Chicago, IL: University of Chicago Press.

Fox, J. & J. Levin (2001). *The Will to Kill: Making Sense of Senseless Murder*. Boston, MA: Allyn and Bacon.

Gillespie, M. (2000). "One in Three Say It Is Very Likely that Columbine-Type Shootings Could Happen in Their Community." *The Gallup Poll Monthly*, 415(April):47-50.

Gottfredson, D. (1997). "School-Based Crime Prevention." In L. Sherman, D. Gottfredson, D. MacKenzie, J. Eck, P. Reuter & S. Bushway (eds.) *Preventing Crime: What Works, What Doesn't, What's Promising*, pp. 5-1 – 5-74. Washington, DC: U.S. Department of Justice.

Holmes, R.M. & S.T. Holmes (1996). *Profiling Violent Crimes: An Investigative Tool*, Second Edition. Thousand Oaks, CA: Sage Publications.

Hyman, I. & D. Perone (1998). "The Other Side of School Violence: Educator Policies and Practices that May Contribute to Student Misbehavior." *Journal of School Psychology*, 36(1):7-27.

Kaufman, P., X. Chen, S.P. Choy, S.A. Ruddy, A.K. Miller, J.K. Fleury, K.A. Chandler, M.R. Rand, P. Klaus & M.G. Planty (2000). *Indicators of School Crime and Safety, 2000*. Washington, DC: U.S. Departments of Education and Justice.

Kingery, P. (2001). *Zero Tolerance: The Alternative Is Education*. Washington, DC: Hamilton Fish Institute.

Kramen, A.J., K.R. Massey & H.W. Timm (1999). *Guide for Preventing and Responding to School Violence*. Alexandria, VA: International Association of Chiefs of Police.

Lawrence, R. (2007). *School Crime and Juvenile Justice*, Second Edition. New York, NY: Oxford University Press.

Lawrence, R. & D. Mueller (2003). "School Shootings and the Man-Bites-Dog Criterion of Newsworthiness." *Youth Violence and Juvenile Justice*, 1(4):330-345.

Maguire, K. & A.L. Pastore. (1999). *Bureau of Justice Statistics Sourcebook of Criminal Justice Statistics—1998*. Washington, DC: U.S. Department of Justice.

Males, M. (2001). "The Real Story Left Untold: It's Time to Junk the Cliches about Kids and Guns." *Los Angeles Times*, (March 11):M1, M6.

Moore, D.W. (2001). "Americans Look to Parents to Stop School Shootings." *The Gallup Poll Monthly*, No. 427(April):33-35.

National School Safety Center (2007). "School-Associated Violent Deaths Report." Westlake Village, CA: National School Safety Center. www.nssc1.org [Retrieved November 21, 2007].

National School Safety Center (1998). *Checklist of Characteristics of Youth Who Have Caused School-Associated Violent Deaths*. Westlake Village, CA: National School Safety Center.

Newcomb, A. (2001). "Schools Derailing Violence." *The Christian Science Monitor*, 93 (February 3):1,4.

Newman, K. (2004). *Rampage: The Social Roots of School Shootings*. New York, NY: Basic Books.

Olweus, D. (1994). "Bullying: Too Little Love, Too Much Freedom." *School Safety Update*, (May):1-4.

Olweus, D. (1993). "Victimization by Peers: Antecedents and Long-Term Outcomes." In K.H. Rubin & J.B. Asendorf (eds.). *Social Withdrawal, Inhibitions, and Shyness*, pp. 315-341. Hillsdale, NJ: Erlbaum.

Olweus, D. (1978). *Aggression in the Schools*. London: Hemisphere Publishing Corporation.

O'Toole, M.E. (1999). *The School Shooter: A Threat Assessment Perspective*. Quantico, VA: FBI Academy.

Price, J.H. & S.A. Everett (1997). "A National Assessment of Secondary School Principals' Perceptions of Violence in the Schools." *Health Education and Behavior*, 24(2):218-229.

Reddy, M., R. Borum, J. Berglund, B. Vossekuil, R. Fein & W. Modzeleski (2001). "Evaluating Risk for Targeted Violence in Schools: Comparing Risk Assessment, Threat Assessment, and Other Approaches." *Psychology in the Schools*, 38(2):157-172.

Romer, D., K. Jamieson & N. DeCoteau (1998). "The Treatment of Persons of Color in Local Television News: Ethnic Blame Discourse or Realistic Group Conflict?" *Communication Research*, 25(3):286-305.

Shaw, M. (2001). *Promoting Safety in Schools: International Experience and Action*. Washington, DC: U.S. Department of Justice.

Snyder, H.N. & M. Sickmund (1999). *Juvenile Offenders and Victims: 1999 National Report*. Pittsburgh, PA: National Center for Juvenile Justice.

Sorenson, S., G. Manz & R. Berk (1998). "News Media Coverage and the Epidemiology of Homicide." *American Journal of Public Health*, 88:1510-1514.

Stossel, J. (1999). "20/20." (October 22). Canton, MI: ABC News Transcripts.

Surette, R. (1998). *Media, Crime, and Criminal Justice: Images and Realities*, Second Edition. Pacific Grove, CA: Brooks/Cole.

Turvey, B. (1999). *Criminal Profiling: An Introduction to Behavioral Evidence Analysis*. San Diego, CA: Academic Press.

U.S. Departments of Education and Justice (2000). *2000 Annual Report on School Safety*. Washington, DC: U.S. Departments of Education and Justice.

U.S. Departments of Education and Justice (1999). *1999 Annual Report on School Safety*. Washington, DC: U.S. Departments of Education and Justice.

Vossekuil, B., M. Reddy & R. Fein (2000). "Safe School Initiative: An Interim Report on the Prevention of Targeted Violence in Schools." Washington, DC: U.S. Secret Service.

Weiss, A. & S.M. Chermak (1998). "The News Value of African-American Victims: An Examination of the Media's Presentation of Homicide." *Journal of Crime and Justice*, 21(2):71-88.

Welsh, W.N. (2001). "Effects of Student and School Factors on Five Measures of School Disorder." *Justice Quarterly*, 18(4):911-947.

Welsh, W.N., J.R. Greene & P.H. Jenkins (1999). "School Disorder: The Influence of Individual, Institutional, and Community Factors." *Criminology*, 37(1):73-115.

Wilcox, P. & R.R. Clayton (2001). "A Multilevel Analysis of School-Based Weapon Possession." *Justice Quarterly*, 18(3):509-539.

CHAPTER 6

A World of Risk:
Victimized Children in the Juvenile Justice System – An Ecological Explanation, a Holistic Solution

John H. Lemmon
P.J. Verrecchia

In this chapter, the relationship between dependency (child maltreatment and status offending) and delinquency will be examined from a social ecology perspective. Initially, dependency would appear to be exclusively a family problem. Children are maltreated within their immediate environment as victims of violence (i.e., physical abuse), exploitation (i.e., sexual abuse), or neglect (i.e., lack of parental supervision). Children become status offenders as a consequence of other parent-child relationship problems (e.g., ungovernability and truancy). Dependent children tend to come from dysfunctional families, and dysfunctional families tend to bring about maltreated and incorrigible children who are at risk for delinquent behaviors. The connection appears logical enough to attract the interest of juvenile justice policymakers and practitioners. However, what has eluded policymakers and practitioners is the dynamic of this relationship. To provide a context for better understanding how dependency and delinquency are interrelated, basic concepts and the scope of status offending and maltreatment are reviewed.

Definitions and Scope of the Problems

Status Offending

Status offenders are children under the jurisdiction of the juvenile court because they have engaged in behaviors that, although not illegal if they were adults, violate the values and expectations of childhood. Some types of status behaviors include truancy, running away from home, being incorrigible (which means habitually disobeying one's parents), violating curfew, under-age drinking, and promiscuity. However, this list of behaviors is not exhaustive. Because adult expectations of childhood are so value-driven, there are substantial variations in how status offenses are defined. For example, pro-scribed activities under South Dakota's status offender statute have included patronizing pool halls, habitually wandering around railroad yards, smoking cigarettes, writing or using obscene or vulgar language, or being guilty of immoral sexual conduct (Murray, 1983).

While "status offender" is the most commonly used term to describe these children, they are also referred to as unruly or incorrigible, or described by acronyms such as PINS (persons in need of supervision) or CHINS (children in need of supervision), depending on the jurisdiction providing supervision (Whitehead & Lab, 2006). Status offenders are essentially a legal category of children. The juvenile court has extended its supervision through the applica-tion of *parens patriae*. Because *parens patriae* authorized jurisdiction over delinquency and child maltreatment matters, the court eventually extended its legal authority over children who have disturbed relationships with parents and school authorities (Murray, 1983). John Murray (1983) describes five categories of behaviors that offer a useful definition of status characteristics. One category includes curfew violations and incorrigibility (also referred to as ungovernability). The second category includes running away from home and sexual promiscuity. The third category includes children who are out of control at home (e.g., violent, disruptive, or in need of supervision). The fourth category includes the use of tobacco, alcohol, and other drugs and is generally associated with involvement with delinquent peers. The final cat-egory is truancy, which involves habitual illegal absences from school.

According to a U.S. Department of Justice report prepared by the Nation-al Center for Juvenile Justice (NCJJ), in 1997, the nation's juvenile justice system formally disposed of an estimated 158,500 status offender cases (Puzzanchera, Stahl, Finnegan, Snyder, Poole & Tierney, 2000). In 2004, the number of formally processed status offense cases increased to 159,400 (Stahl, 2008). This and subsequent NCJJ reports are based on formally handled cases only. Critics argue that results based on official records should be interpreted with caution since results vary based on self-reporting versus official data. For example, Murray (1983) cited studies that report gender differences found in official data studies that reflect differential processing of male and female status offenders (e.g., Chesney-Lind, 1977), racial and ethnic differences due to differential patterns of law enforcement (e.g., Erick-son, 1972), or a greater propensity of some ethnic groups to use the court to support parental authority (e.g., Weisbrod, 1981) as well as differences in family structure that prompt judicial authorities to be more willing to inter-vene with low-income and single-parent families (Murray, 1983). Because officially reported data underestimate the true extent of the problem, and also because reporting bias distorts the true measure of gender, race, and social class effects, the following NCJJ data present disturbing evidence concerning the nature and scope of status offending among at-risk children.

The number of petitioned status offender cases handled in 1997 was 101 percent higher than the number of cases handled in 1988 (Puzzanchera et al., 2000). Likewise, the number of petitioned truancy cases increased by 96 percent, runaway cases by 93 percent, incorrigibility cases by 65 percent, and state liquor offense cases by 56 percent. In 1997, the nation's juvenile courts processed 5.5 petitioned status offender cases for every 1,000 juveniles in the population (Puzzanchera et al., 2000). The 1997 case rate was 78 percent higher than the 1988 case rate with truancy increasing by 74 percent, runaway cases by 71 percent, incorrigibility by 46 percent, and liquor law violations by 38 percent.

The trend toward increased offending also underscores key demographic variations. Girls, for example, accounted for a larger increase in the number of referrals (105% versus 98% for boys) (Puzzanchera et al., 2000). Among boys, the largest increase was for runaway offenses (a 105 percent increase) while among girls the largest increase was for liquor law violations (a 108% increase). Secondly, a trend toward minority over-representation was clearly emerging. Between 1988 and 1997, the number of petitioned status offender cases increased 96 percent for white youths, but 122 percent for African-Americans, and 104 percent for other minorities (Puzzanchera et al., 2000). Moreover, case rate estimates indicated that for children ages 15 and younger, African-Americans had the highest rates of reported truancy, ungovernability, and runaway offenses.

A follow up study by NCJJ using data from 1990 to 1999 found more evidence concerning variations in demographic trends (Puzzanchera, Stahl, Finnegan, Tierney & Snyder, 2003). The researchers used a sample of 102,231 status offenders from 2,030 jurisdictions in 35 states representing 68 percent of the United States juvenile population. They identified, for example, that juveniles ages 15 and younger comprised two-thirds of all runaway cases while three-fourths of all liquor law violations were committed by juveniles 16 years of age or older (Puzzanchera et al., 2003).

Girls represented 61 percent of the runaway offenses, slightly less than half of the truancy cases (46 percent), 45 percent of the incorrigibility cases, and only 30 percent of the liquor law violations. White youth accounted for most of the status offenses, including 74 percent of the runaways, 71 percent of the truants, 72 percent of the incorrigibles, and 90 percent of the liquor law violators (Puzzanchera et al., 2003). Nevertheless, the trend toward increased minority offending continued to be evident. African-American youth were substantially overrepresented in the percent of runaway, truant, and incorrigible offenders. For example, Stahl (2008) reported that of petitioned status offenses in 2004, 36 percent of Black youth were petitioned for truancy (compared to 35% for whites), 25 percent for ungovernability (compared to 13% for whites), and 19 percent for runaway (compared to 11% for whites).

Reporting on case processing trends from 1985-2002, Snyder and Sickmund (2006) found that adjudication rates for truancy, incorrigibility, and liquor law violations were equivalent (between 625 to 630 per 1,000 cases) while the rate for runaway offenses (459 per 1,000) was substantially lower. Although the typical disposition for all status offenses was probation, a higher proportion of runaway (12%) and incorrigible (16%) youth went into placement.

The NCJJ reports suggest two disturbing trends. First, the frequency and the rate of status offenses are increasing, and, for some categories, including runaways and truancies, these increases have nearly doubled. More children are experiencing problems at home and in school. Secondly, certain groups of children, namely girls and minorities, are becoming increasingly more at-risk.

Child Maltreatment

Child maltreatment can be classified into four general categories. These include physical abuse, sexual abuse, psychological abuse, and neglect. Maltreatment involves acts of commission by parents, guardians, or caretakers such as physically assaulting and injuring their children. Maltreatment also involves acts of omission as in cases of neglect where parents fail to provide their children with adequate care or protection. Physical abuse can be defined as the physical injury of a child resulting in severe pain or impairment or accompanied by physical evidence of a continuous pattern of separate, unexplained injuries to children, (The Pennsylvania Child Protective Services Law, Act 124 of 1975, 11 P.S. Section 2201 *et seq.*). Sexual abuse includes the acts of forcible or statutory rape or incest, involuntary deviant sexual intercourse, sexual assault, promoting prostitution, or engaging children to participate in pornography (The Pennsylvania Child Protective Services Law).

While the definitions of physical and sexual abuse have been generally accepted among professionals and the public, there has been substantially less consensus over how psychological abuse and neglect should be defined. The development of an adequate definition of psychological abuse has been restricted by complicated philosophical, scientific, legal, political, and cultural issues. Despite these challenges, considerable progress has been made in the past 20 years to create a rationally defensible definition that appears to have substantial professional and public support (Hart, Brassard, Binggeli & Davidson, 2002). According to guidelines recently established by the American Professional Society on the Abuse of Children (APSAC):

> Psychological abuse means a repeated pattern of caretaker behavior or extreme incidents that convey to children that they are worthless, flawed, unloved, unwanted, or only of value in meeting another's needs (American Professional Society on the Abuse of Children, 1995:2; Hart et al., 2002:81).

Figure 6.1 **Types of Maltreatment**

Child Maltreatment

Q: **What are the different types of child maltreatment?**

A: **Child maltreatment occurs when a caretaker is responsible for, or permits, the abuse or neglect of a child. There are several different types of child maltreatment.**

- **Physical abuse** includes physical acts that caused or could have caused physical injury to the child.

- **Sexual abuse** is involvement of the child in sexual activity to provide sexual gratification or financial benefit to the perpetrator, including contacts for sexual purposes, prostitution, pornography, or other sexually exploitative activities.

- **Emotional abuse** is defined as acts or omissions that caused or could have caused conduct, cognitive, affective, or other mental disorders.

- **Physical neglect** includes abandonment, expulsion from the home, failure to seek remedial health care or delay in seeking care, inadequate supervision, disregard for hazards in the home, or inadequate food, clothing, or shelter.

- **Emotional neglect** includes inadequate nurturance or affection, permitting maladaptive behavior, and other inattention to emotional/development needs.

- **Educational neglect** permitting chronic truancy or other inattention to educational needs.

Source: *OJJDP Statistical Briefing Book*. Online. Available: http://ojjdp.ncjrs.gov/ojstatbb/victims/qa02101. asp?qaDate=19990930. Released on September 30, 1999. Adapted from Snyder, H. & M. Sickmund (1999). *Juvenile Offenders and Victims: 1999 National Report*, p. 40. Washington, DC: Office of Juvenile Justice and Delinquency Prevention.

The APSAC guidelines define six categories of psychological abuse that involve: (1) spurning, which involves the hostile rejection, belittling, and humiliation of children; (2) terrorizing, which involves behaviors that threaten children with death, injury, or abandonment; (3) isolating, which involves acts that consistently deny children the opportunities to interact with peers and adults inside and outside their home; (4) exploiting and corrupting, which involves acts that encourage children to develop self-destructive, criminal, deviant, or other maladaptive behaviors; (5) denying emotional responsiveness, which involves acts that ignore children's attempts toward, and need for, parental interaction; and (6) mental health, medical, and educational neglect, which involves acts that ignore or fail to provide children with necessary treatment for mental health, medical, or educational needs (American Professional Society on the Abuse of Children, 1995:74; Hart et al., 2002:82).

Neglect is the most common and most ambiguously defined form of child maltreatment and clearly reflects the normative nature of child welfare services. According to *Child Maltreatment 2004*, more than 60 percent of all child maltreatment cases involved neglect (Snyder & Sickmund, 2006; U.S. Department of Health and Human Services, 2006). Fundamentally, neglect involves acts of omission that may be intentional or unintentional. There has been ample debate over how to accurately define the intentionality of parental neglect, particularly when considering cultural differences (Erikson

& Egeland, 2002). This is particularly problematic when legal definitions of neglect are employed. For instance, it is a fairly common and reasonable practice among low-income families to send their children to live with friends or relatives when income and resources become scarce. In many jurisdictions this is considered shuttling, which is a form of neglect (Erikson & Egeland, 2002). Neglect varies greatly in terms of level of severity.

Figure 6.2: **Most Common Forms of Maltreatment**
Percent of victims by maltreatment type, 2003

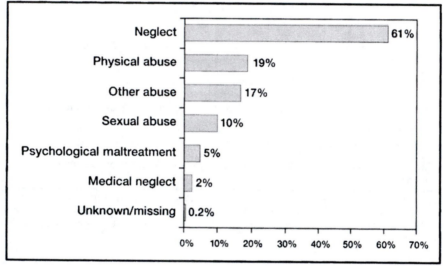

Source: *OJJDP Statistical Briefing Book.* Online. Available: http://ojjdp.ncjrs.gov/ojstatbb/victims/qa02108. asp?qaDate=2003. Released on March 27, 2006. Adapted from Snyder, H. & M. Sickmund (2006). *Juvenile Offenders and Victims: 2006 National Report*, Chapter 2. Washington, D.C.: Office of Juvenile Justice and Delinquency Prevention.

Neglect can be fatal, due to inadequate physical protection, nutrition, or health care. Neglect is also the cause of "failure to thrive" syndrome, a condition in which infants can die from a lack of human contact (Erickson & Egeland, 2002:3). While the damaging effects of neglect can be evident at the time of occurrence (e.g., unattended life-threatening dangers in the home or children suffering from poor physical hygiene), neglect also produces long-term damage that presents no apparent harm at the time of the incident. This calls into question the long-term consequences of neglect. Neglect is associated with a variety of educational, psychological, and social problems, including reduced intellectual ability, academic achievement, attachment to others, and delinquency and criminality (Garbarino, 1999; Crittenden & Ainsworth, 1989; Widom, 1989d; Lemmon, 1999; 2006).

In 2004, the National Child Abuse and Neglect Data System (NCANDS) estimated that 3.5 million American children received an investigation through child protective services (CPS). Based on a victim rate of 11.9 per 1,000 children, NCANDS estimated that between 872,000 and 906,000 children were victims of child abuse and neglect (U.S. Department of Health and Human Services, 2006). Of the substantiated victims, 62.4 percent experienced neglect, 17.5 percent were physically abused, 9.7 percent were sexually abused, 7 percent were psychologically maltreated, and 2.1 percent were medically neglected. NCANDS data for 2005 indicated that state and local child protective services (CPS) units investigated 3.6 million children who were reported to be abused or neglected. Of these, 899,000 or 12.1 per 1,000 children were classified as victims of maltreatment, 63 percent as victims of neglect, 17 percent as victims of physical abuse, 9 percent as victims of sexual abuse, and 7 percent as victims of psychological abuse (U.S. Department of Health and Human Services, 2007).

The rate of all children receiving an investigation increased 32 percent from 36.1 per 1,000 children in 1990 to 47.8 per 1,000 children in 2004. However, the rate of victimization decreased slightly from 13.4 per 1,000 in 1990 to 11.9 per 1,000 in 2004 (U.S. Department of Health and Human Services, 2006). Trends in the national referral and victimization rates suggest that more at-risk children are being identified but that the victimization rate has held constant.

The NCANDS data also provide clarification concerning variations in maltreatment victimization based on gender, age, race, and ethnicity. The risk of maltreatment victimization was roughly the same for boys and girls. For 2004, roughly 48 percent of the victims were boys and 52 percent were girls (U.S. Department of Health and Human Services, 2006). However, age was inversely related to victimization rate. The youngest children had the highest victimization rate with rates decreasing with each older age group. The rate of victimization for the age group birth to three years was 16.1 per 1,000 children; for the 4- to 7-year-old age group the rate was 13.4 per 1,000; for the 8- to 11-year-old age group the rate was 10.9 per 1,000, for the 12- to 15-year-old age group the rate was 9.3 per 1,000, and for the 16- to 17-year-old age group, the rate was 6.1 per 1,000 (U.S. Department of Health and Human Services, 2006).

More than one-half of all victims (53.8%) were White, 25 percent were African-American, and 17 percent were Hispanic (U.S. Department of Health and Human Services, 2006). The over-representation of African-American children was reflected in their victimization rate of 19.9 per 1,000 children followed by Pacific Islanders at 17.6 per 1,000, and Native-Americans and Alaska Natives at 15.5 per 1,000. White and Hispanic children had substantially lower victimization rates of 10.7 and 10.4 per 1,000, respectively. Asian children had the lowest victimization rate at 2.9 per 1,000 (U.S. Department of Health and Human Services, 2006).

In 2005, 1,460 children died as the result of child abuse and neglect, a mortality rate of approximately two per 100,000 which was 21 percent higher than the 1999 rate (U.S. Department of Health and Human Services, 2007). Age and race appear to be risk factors in maltreatment mortality. Seventy-seven percent of the deaths occurred among children younger than four years of age, while 26 percent of the deaths occurred among African-American children, which is twice the expected rate.

The recent NCANDS data (U.S. Department of Health and Human Services, 2006; 2007) have also identified a number of maltreatment related risk factors. For example, children with allegations of multiple types of maltreatment (i.e., abuse and neglect) were nearly three times more likely to be maltreated than those who had experienced a singular type (i.e., neglect only). Sexual abuse allegations were 71 percent more likely to be substantiated than physical abuse allegations. Children with disabilities were 68 percent more likely to be victims of maltreatment than children without disabilities and children who had been prior victims of maltreatment were 84 percent more likely to experience recurrence than those who were not prior victims (U.S. Department of Health and Human Services, 2006).

The data on maltreatment recurrence are particularly disturbing. A 20-state analysis of the 1999 NCANDS data reported that 7.5 percent of all victims suffered a subsequent incident of abuse or neglect within six months of their initial substantiation (U.S. Department of Health and Human Services, 2001:31-32). Moreover, research that examined maltreatment recurrence over longer periods of time (e.g., 5 to 10 years), reports recurrence rates of 50 percent or more (DePanfilis 1995; DePanfilis & Zuravin 1992, 1998; Herrenkohl, Herrenkohl, Egolf & Seech, 1979). According to analyses by the U.S. Department of Health and Human Services, children who have been victims of maltreatment are over 2.7 times more likely to be revictimized than non-victims (2001:31-32). The NCANDS findings reflect the general consensus that the strongest predictor of future victimization is past victimization.

Compounding what is already a significant problem is the fact that the archival data represent only a fraction of the total amount of maltreatment that is actually occurring in the United States. Like crime or drug usage, state and federal data consistently underestimate the actual extent of child abuse and neglect. In 1981, Richard Gelles, one of the leading researchers on family violence, lamented that "we don't know a *damn* thing about whether child maltreatment is increasing, decreasing, or staying the same" (Ashby, 1997:4). Gelles's comments reflected the confusion and concerns of the time. Today, we still encounter this problem but we have a better grasp on the nature of maltreatment, its connection to other risk factors, and its effect on adverse outcomes, such as delinquency. The next section considers some of the research on the maltreatment/delinquency link.

Examination of the Maltreatment Delinquency Link

Early on, the idea that violence breeds violence served as a guiding paradigm to explain the maltreatment-delinquency connection. However, later reviews of the evidence (Garbarino & Gilliam, 1980; Widom, 1989b, 1989c; Howing, Wodarski, Kurtz & Gaudin, 1993) suggested that the relationship was more apparent than real. If a relationship actually exists, the causal *sequelae* are far more complex than originally thought. Garbarino and Gilliam's conclusion that the alleged relationship had not passed scientific muster was a realistic appraisal of the state of empirical evidence through the late 1980s.

Many of the earlier studies were limited to one type of maltreatment, mostly abuse, (Bolton, Reich & Gutierres, 1977; Gutierres & Reich, 1981; Mouzakitis, 1981) or failed to distinguish abused from neglected children (Alfaro, 1981; Wick, 1981; Kratcoski, 1982) in their analyses. Much of the earlier evidence was based on retrospective self-reports (Mouzakitis, 1981; Rhoades & Parker, 1981) that indicated high rates of maltreatment among samples of incarcerated offenders. These findings contrasted with results from prospective studies (Silver, Dublin & Lourie, 1969; Bolton et al., 1977) that reported much lower rates of offending among samples of maltreated children.

When dimensions of maltreatment were examined, the results have indicated variations in effects. For instance, McCord (1979, 1983a, 1983b) reported the highest incidence of delinquency among rejected children (29%), with lower rates observed among neglected (15%) and abused (10%) children, and the lowest incidence occurring among non-maltreated children (7%). Though the earlier studies were informative, methodological problems related to retrospective and cross-sectional designs, non-probability samples, inadequate conceptualization, and control of extraneous variables limited understanding of whether maltreatment actually affected delinquency and how variations in types or the level of maltreatment affected subsequent offending. Clearly, there was enough evidence to continue with both lines of research, as McCord's findings suggested.

Subsequent research employing prospective, comparison groups (Widom 1989a, 1989d, 1991; Zingraff, Leiter, Johnsen & Myers, 1993; Leiter, Meyers & Zingraff, 1994; Smith & Thornberry, 1995) and cohort designs (Widom & Ames, 1994; Lemmon, 1999; 2006) reports that the presence of maltreatment is a significant contributor to later delinquency and criminality. Prospective studies appear to be a better way to examine the maltreatment-delinquency relationship because they have fewer validity-related problems than retrospective studies. Recent studies have also provided more information about dimensions of the maltreatment-delinquency relationship.

In Widom's initial examinations (1989a, 1989d) she employed a prospective, matched comparison group design that controlled for gender, race, age, and socioeconomic status. She found that the presence of maltreatment significantly increased the probability of juvenile and adult arrests, particularly arrests for violent crimes. In a later analysis, Widom and Ames (1994) reported that sexual abuse did not increase one's risk for criminal behavior, while neglect proved to be a significant risk factor. Still later, Weeks and Widom (1998), in a retrospective study of incarcerated male offenders reversed these findings by reporting that sex offenders were more likely to report sexual victimization. The study also reported that neglect was associated with later violence while physical abuse was not.

Later research on the maltreatment-delinquency link (Zingraff et al., 1993; Leiter et al., 1994; Smith & Thornberry, 1995; Lemmon, 1999, 2006; Johnson-Reid & Barth, 2000; Lemmon, Verrecchia & Austin, 2008) further illustrates how complicated the relationship seems to be. Zingraff's comparison of groups of maltreated, general school population, and low-income children indicated that the overall arrest rate was highest among the maltreated children (13.7%), followed by the low-income group (9%), and lowest among the general school population (5.3%). The arrest rates on specific complaints including property crimes, violence, and status offenses followed the same pattern. These arrest rates varied by type of maltreatment and were highest among neglected children (16%) and lowest among the sexually abused (8.3%). However, multivariate models controlling for demographic factors reduced the maltreatment effect, forcing Zingraff and colleagues (1993) to conclude that the relationship may be exaggerated. A subsequent study led by Leiter et al. (1994) examining school achievement and delinquency produced other ambiguous results. Leiter et al.'s findings indicated that most school and delinquency outcomes of children with substantiated maltreatment reports did not differ from those whose maltreated reports were unsubstantiated. One implication is that seriousness of maltreatment may affect school achievement and delinquency but the substantiation process is not accurately measuring it.

Lemmon (1999) found that the presence of maltreatment was a significant factor affecting the initiation, continuation, and severity of delinquency. Lemmon's results are consistent with the findings of other researchers (Widom, 1989a, 1989d; Zingraff et al., 1993; Smith & Thornberry, 1995) concerning official measures of delinquency. Additional analyses on types of maltreatment indicated that the presence of neglect as well as the joint occurrence of abuse and neglect increased the likelihood of delinquent behavior. On the other hand, the presence of abuse only was not associated with delinquency. Similar results were found regarding chronic delinquency. In fact, neglect was reported to be a strong indicator of violent offending. Lemmon's results are consistent with Widom's findings regarding the apparent criminogenic impact of neglect on violence (See Widom & Ames, 1994; Weeks & Widom, 1998).

Smith and Thornberry (1995) examined two questions concerning the relationship between maltreatment and delinquency. Does the relationship exist in the presence of other delinquency-related risk factors? Are the various dimensions of maltreatment, (e.g., frequency, severity, and duration) risk factors for official and self-reported delinquency? They found that a history of maltreatment was significantly related to the prevalence and frequency of officially reported delinquency. Apart from increasing the risk of being arrested one or more times, a history of maltreatment was also related to more serious forms of self-reported delinquency including violent crimes. Maltreatment continued to be a significant predictor of the prevalence and frequency of official and self-reported violent crimes even when race, ethnicity, gender, social class, family structure, and mobility were held constant.

Examining the Effect of the Dimensions of Maltreatment

Tests examining the effects of dimensions of maltreatment, including duration, frequency, and severity, produced mixed results. For example, the frequency of maltreatment was positively associated with officially reported delinquency as well as self-reported serious and violent offending but not with moderate offending. Subjects in the top third of the maltreatment recurrence distribution had the highest delinquency scores on all measures and were significantly higher than non-maltreatment group scores. However, the differences between the top one-third and the lower two-thirds maltreatment groups were not large enough to be statistically significant. Their findings also demonstrated that a majority of maltreated children were not delinquent. This finding suggests the presence of protective factors that might insulate these children from risk. In conclusion, Smith and Thornberry suggest that extensive maltreatment is somehow associated with higher rates of chronic and violent delinquency in a relationship that is not clearly understood at present.

Important as these findings are, methods that employ between-group comparisons (maltreated versus non-maltreated children) fail to take into account that maltreatment varies along different dimensions (See Smith & Thornberry, 1995). Although some work has been started, research is still needed on how different dimensions of maltreatment, including stage of development, subtypes, frequency, and severity, affect a variety of behavioral consequences.

Based on a retrospective study of incarcerated youth offenders in England, Hamilton and her colleagues (2002) reported an interaction between recurrent maltreatment and type of perpetrator on measures of delinquency. Youth who had experienced maltreatment revictimization (more than one incident committed by different perpetrators) were more likely to have committed violent and/or sex offenses compared to youth who had experienced intrafamilial repeat victimization (more than one incident committed by the same perpetrator(s)), or youth with no maltreatment histories. In addition, those who had experienced both revictimization and repeated victimization were the most likely to have committed violent and/or sex offenses. The study suggests that each subsequent perpetrator exacerbates the effect of previous incidents of maltreatment which might explain the pattern between revictimization by different perpetrators and more serious forms of offending. Though Hamilton's findings broaden our understanding of the nature of victim-perpetrator relationship in maltreatment recurrence, caution is advised in drawing any firm conclusions due to the nature of the design and the small and specialized sample from which their data were drawn. Still, the evidence suggests that children exposed to increased recurrence of maltreatment are more likely to commit serious crimes.

Lemmon (2006) examined the relationship between maltreatment recurrence and various dimensions of delinquency among a cohort of at-risk youth. The results indicated that maltreatment recurrence is a significant predictor of early onset, chronic, and violent youth offending. The relationship continued to exist in the presence of other delinquency risk factors. Within the maltreatment subgroup, a curvilinear pattern was observed. This pattern suggested that child welfare placement services reduce the effects of maltreatment recurrence on chronic and violent youth offending. The maltreatment recurrence-delinquency relationship followed a linear pattern among youth receiving in-home services and a curvilinear pattern among those receiving placement services.

A subsequent study (Lemmon, Verrecchia & Austin, 2008) further reported that recurrence produced direct effects on all dimensions of youth offending, independent of individual and environmental risk factors. On the other hand, maltreatment severity produced no effects on youth offending. However, an inverse relationship was discovered indicating that children who are high in recurrence are low in severity. These findings indicate that the maltreated children most at risk for later offending are those that experience chronic, but less severe maltreatment. Child welfare services, however, mediated the maltreatment and other environmental risks. For instance, length of services delayed the onset of offending, while child welfare placement services decreased chronic and violent offending. Ongoing research by Lemmon and his colleagues employing structural equation modeling has confirmed that maltreatment recurrence produces both direct and indirect effects on chronic and violent offending.

Maltreatment and Youth Incarceration

Johnson-Reid and Barth's research (2000) on risk and mediating factors on youth incarceration rates in California reported similar results. They found that neglect and multiple recurrence of maltreatment were significant predictors of youth incarceration. Furthermore, Johnson-Reid and Barth reported that maltreated youth who experienced less severe maltreatment were less likely to receive adequate services. The implication of these findings is that chronic but less severely maltreated children were not receiving adequate services in the child welfare system. On the other hand, while the provision of in-home and foster placement services did not change the risk of incarceration among Caucasian children, African-American and Hispanic children who received services beyond investigation were significantly less likely to be incarcerated in California's juvenile justice system. These findings are encouraging in light of the fact that minority children encounter more environmental risks (e.g., poverty, discrimination, and social disorganization) than children from the dominant culture likely would experience.

Because much of the research has been derived from officially reported maltreatment, consideration should be given to the type of services provided to these children and their families to determine how these factors might affect the maltreatment-delinquency relationship. A number of studies indicate that out-of-home services, particularly foster care, may be harmful to maltreated children (Palmer, 1979), increase the risk of delinquency (Ryan & Testa, 2005), or be of little therapeutic benefit (Runyan & Gould, 1985) in preventing delinquency. However, much of the research indicates that placement services are seldom done well. Recent studies on improved foster-care models (Chamberlain, 1998) suggest that specialized programs like multidimensional foster care significantly reduce serious and chronic delinquent behavior. The major element in providing clinical services is the building of a caring and trusting relationship. The improved models of placement services emphasize attachment building while providing continuous care and standards of discipline consistent with a social learning approach to treatment. Loeber and Farrington (2001) illustrate this idea by pointing out that each developmental pathway is merely a different manifestation of the same underlying deviancy. Whether or not a child advances on a criminal trajectory is due, in part, to the treatment he or she receives at home. Repeated maltreatment might not necessarily condemn a child to a life of crime if he or she receives the necessary protective and clinical services.

In conclusion, the research clearly indicates that the presence of maltreatment is a risk factor in later delinquency and criminality. In prospective studies employing equivalent groups of children, those with maltreatment histories were significantly more likely to participate in subsequent delinquent and criminal offending compared to those with no histories of maltreatment. The research on various types of maltreatment suggests that child neglect is a highly criminogenic risk factor, particularly in violent offending. Finally, current research on the interactions of maltreatment recurrence and severity indicate that chronically but less severely maltreated children are at highest risk for subsequent youth offending. Evidence also indicates that child welfare service can mediate the combined effects of individual characteristics, maltreatment, and other environmental risk factors. The study of these effects – the inner workings of individual characteristics, risk factors within in the immediate environment (including maltreatment), and cultural values and beliefs that produce effects on delinquent offending – is known as the Social Ecology Perspective. A review of this model is presented in Appendix A, at the end of this chapter.

The Social Developmental Model

Another model that has generated favorable research as well as development of innovative programs is the Social Developmental Model (SDM). The principal authors of the model are David Hawkins and Richard Catalano (See Hawkins & Catalano, 1992; Hawkins, Catalano & Miller, 1992; Hawkins & Catalano, 1993; Brewer, Hawkins, Catalano & Neckerman, 1995; Hawkins, Catalano & Brewer, 1995; Catalano & Hawkins, 1996; Herrenkohl, Hawkins, Ick-Joong, Hill & Battin-Pearson, 2001). Their model is premised on the assumption that children live in a world of risks. These risks are embedded within two ecological domains. One set exists within the child (at the ontogenic level). The other set exists within four specific micro-systems that comprise the child's immediate environment. These include the family, the peer group, the school, and the community. As children are exposed to increasing numbers of risks, their chances of becoming chronic and violent offenders increase as well. Hawkins and Catalano (1993) identified a variety of risk factors associated with delinquency and violence, along with other forms of deviance including drug abuse, teenage pregnancy, and dropping out of school.

Risk factors associated with violence within the individual (ontogenic) domain include perinatal difficulties including low birth weight, early aggressiveness, risk-taking behaviors, hyperactivity, low intelligence, and incorrigibility. Family risk factors include poverty, lack of parental supervision, marital and family conflict, and child maltreatment. Some of the community and peer-group risk factors include communities that are disorganized, afford few opportunities for attachment, and have extreme economic deprivation. School risk factors include truancy, low academic aspirations and performance, along with weak attachments to the school (Brewer et al., 1995; Hawkins et al., 1995; Herrenkohl et al., 2001).

How risks are translated into delinquent outcomes is a function of the specific characteristics of the child that are molded through interactions within the immediate environment. The social developmental model (Catalano & Hawkins, 1996; Herrenkohl et al., 2001) hypothesizes a specific socialization process that leads either to conformity or deviancy. Hawkins and Catalano (1992) argue that the socialization process is the same regardless of whether it produces pro-social or anti-social behaviors. The process involves four concepts derived from differential opportunity (Cloward & Ohlin, 1960), differential association (Sutherland & Cressey, 1974), operant and social learning (Bandura, 1969; Akers, 1985), and the social bond (Hirschi, 1969).

All children have inherent characteristics (e.g., the ability to run fast or the potential to understand math concepts) that if developed can lead to conformity (i.e., winning a track scholarship to college) or deviancy (i.e., using math skills to run a profitable drug sales operation). Whether the child becomes a track star or an efficient drug distributor depends on the opportunities and degree of involvement that are provided, the skills that are developed, and the recognition received for displaying those skills. The child will develop a bond with the person or groups who provide him with these opportunities, skills, and recognition. Once established, the social bond has the power to affect the child's values and behaviors independent of these other processes. In other words, the child will learn and incorporate the values and beliefs of the attachment figures and behave in a similar manner. If the social bond is developed with pro-social groups, like the football team or the church youth group, the bond will enhance conformity and inhibit deviancy. On the other hand, if the bond is developed with a delinquent gang it will enhance deviancy and inhibit conformity.

The social developmental model assumes that children learn patterns of pro-social and anti-social behaviors in different socializing groups through-out the maturation process (Herrenkohl et al., 2001). During the pre and elementary schools years, the family and school are the primary socializing groups. During the middle- and early-high school years it is the peers and community groups. By late-adolescence and early-adulthood, living partners, marriage, work, and community relationships become the major influences on beliefs and behaviors.

Informal Supervision meeting between youth and probation officer.

Additional Evidence

Hawkins and Catalano's research indicates that maltreated, incorrigible, and truant children are at serious risk of becoming habitual and violent offenders. There is good deal of support for their claim. The notion that risk factors place children on pathways to deviance is the basic assumption that underscores Rolf Loeber and David Farrington's work in the area of developmental criminology (Farrington, 1986; Loeber, 1990; Loeber, Wei, Stouthamer-Loeber, Huizinga & Thornberry, 1999; Loeber & Farrington, 2001). Through their research, Loeber and Farrington identified an array of individual characteristics, including impulsivity, aggression, and low intelligence, along with risks within the immediate environment including disorganized communities, associations with delinquent peers, poor aca-demic performance, child maltreatment, lack of parental supervision, and parent-child attachment disorders which are strongly associated with serious and violent youth offending. Developmental criminology is built around the concept of a "stepping stones model" to chronic and violent offending (See Farrington, 1986). Loeber (1990) described a similar process referring to it as the 'stacking of problem behaviors.' The idea is that sets of individual char-acteristics (e.g., neurological impairment, aggressive behaviors) and micro-level risks (e.g., lack of parental supervision, academic problems, delinquent peers) emerge early in life and the interactions of these characteristics and environmental risks place children on a trajectory to ever-increasing deviant behaviors. Through their work in the Pittsburgh Youth Study, Loeber and his colleagues (Loeber & Hay, 1994) identified three specific deviant pathways. These include a pathway to status offending, referred to as the authority-avoidance pathway, a covert pathway that begins with minor property crimes and culminates with serious offenses such as burglaries, and an overt pathway which begins with minor aggression like bullying and culminates with felony-level violence such as robberies.

Environmental factors also weigh heavily in Garbarino's (1999) studies on maltreatment and resiliency. Garbarino argued that maltreatment affects a child's cognitive beliefs and these beliefs can generate criminal thinking and behavior. He reported that maltreated children are hypersensitive to negative social cues and oblivious to positive ones. Maltreated children perceive their world as one full of danger and humiliation. Consequently, they are prone to draw the erroneous conclusion that aggression is their only effective coping strategy.

While acknowledging that maltreatment is a robust predictor of delinquency, Garbarino (1999) also noted that there are a variety of resiliency factors including characteristics of the child, along with support systems within the community and the culture, that can mediate the adverse effects of maltreatment. He reported that children who hold religious beliefs grounded in spirituality, who have higher intelligence and higher tolerance for frustration are able to effectively cope with their maltreatment experiences. Children who have stable and positive relationships with at least one caring and competent adult are more likely to overcome their abuse and/or neglect experience. Children who can rely on networks of community supporters such as teachers, coaches, counselors, and clergy are more resilient. Children who reside in stable and safe communities are better able to cope with their maltreatment experience. Garbarino (1999) also highlighted macro-level factors that enhance a child's resiliency. Cultures that value economic equality, democratic principles, and a commitment to human rights provide environments in which children can cope more effectively with their traumatic experiences.

The implication is that these risk factors, though highly predictive of crime, are not absolute. Though dependent children live in a world of risk, risk does not have a complete monopoly over their lives. Dependent children also have characteristics that can be developed and support mechanisms that can be mobilized to help them become resilient. Loeber and Farrington's choice of the term "pathway" is an appropriate description of the process. While there are certainly pathways that lead to deviance there are alternative pathways that lead to healthy development. The next section presents three initiatives that offer alternative pathways.

Programs that Help

Communities That Care

Communities That Care (CTC) is an operating system based on the social developmental model (See Hawkins & Catalano, 1992; Catalano & Hawkins, 1996) that provides research-based tools to help communities promote the positive development of children and youth, and prevent adolescent substance abuse, delinquency, teen pregnancy, school dropout, and violence. It is unique in that it is (1) inclusive – engaging all areas of the community in promoting healthy development, (2) proactive--identifying and addressing priority areas *before* young people become involved in problem behaviors; targeting early predictors of problems rather than waiting until problems have become entrenched in young people's lives, (3) based on rigorous research – from a variety of fields-sociology, psychology, education, public health, criminology, medicine, and organizational development, and (4) community specific – each community uses its own data-based profile to craft a comprehensive long-range plan for strengthening existing resources and filling identified gaps.

The CTC model helps communities mobilize and engage members of the community in healthy futures for children and youth. They establish shared vision, common language, and a collaborative planning structure to integrate community efforts to address youth and family issues, establish priorities for action which are based on community strengths and challenges, define clear and measurable outcomes that can be tracked over time to show progress and ensure accountability, identify gaps in the current response to priorities, and select programs and strategies that have demonstrated effectiveness in filling identified gaps and evaluate progress toward desired outcomes.

Communities That Care has four primary areas that comprise a research foundation. The first is the social development strategy – the research framework that guides communities toward their vision of positive futures for young people. The social developmental strategy begins with the goal of healthy, positive behaviors for young people. In order to develop healthy behaviors, young people must be immersed in environments that consistently communicate healthy beliefs and clear standards for behavior. Research indicates that young people who have strong bonds to their families, schools, and communities are more invested in following the beliefs and standards held by these groups. These bonds are created by providing opportunities for young people to be involved in meaningful ways, skills for successful involvement, and recognition for their involvement.

The second area is a comprehensive, community-wide approach to public health issues. Heart disease, breast cancer, and drunk driving are all issues that have been addressed by mobilizing all segments of the community to educate and promote behavior change. Communities That Care engages all areas of the community in promoting the positive development of young people, including youth, parents, service providers, local government, law enforcement, education, faith community, business community, recreation, health, mental health, and social services.

The use of data-based predictors and protective factors is the third component of the foundation. Research has identified 19 risk factors that are reliable predictors of adolescent substance abuse, delinquency, school dropout, teen pregnancy, and violence. Understanding the risk factors helps communities understand what they should do to prevent problem behavior. Protective factors hold the key to understanding how to reduce those risks and how to encourage positive behavior and social development.

These protective factors include gender (i.e., girls are less likely to develop behavior problems in adolescence than boys); resilient temperament – children who adjust to change or recover from disruption easily are more protected from risk; outgoing temperament – children who are outgoing enjoy being with people and engage easily with others are more protected; intelligence – bright children appear to be more protected from risk; healthy beliefs and clear standards – parents, teachers, and community members who hold clearly stated expectations regarding children and adolescent behaviors are helping to protect young people from risk. Parents who develop and reinforce clear family rules about drug use, school attendance and performance, sexual behavior, and behavior in the family and community are creating a buffer for their children as they move into the high-risk adolescent years. When family rules and expectations are consistent with, and supported by, other key influences on young people (e.g., school, peers, the media, the larger community), it is as though a protective shield is erected around the young person that buffers him/her from risk.

Research on bonding demonstrates that children living in high-risk environments can be protected from behavior problems by a strong, affectionate relationship with an adult who cares about, and is committed to, their healthy development. The caring adult can be a parent, teacher, extended family member, coach, employer, or an adult from the child's faith community. The most critical aspect of this relationship is that the youth has a long-term investment in the relationship, and that he or she believes the relationship is worth protecting. This investment is what motivates young people to abide by the healthy beliefs and clear standards held by these important adults in their lives. The fourth area of the research foundation is the Blueprints for Violence Prevention Programs which is discussed below.

Blueprints for Violence Prevention

In 1996, the Center for the Study and Prevention of Violence, with funding received from the Colorado Division of Criminal Justice, the Centers for Disease Control and Prevention, and the Pennsylvania Commission on Crime and Delinquency, launched a national violence prevention initiative to identify and replicate violence prevention programs that are effective. The project, led by Delbert Elliott, is known as the "Blueprints for Violence Prevention" (Elliott, 1997, 1998).

Elliott gathered a team of nationally recognized researchers and established a set of rigorous standards to evaluate delinquency prevention programs claiming to be effective. Hundreds of programs applied for selection. To be chosen as a Blueprint Program, applications had to meet four research criteria. First, the programs had to be evaluated based on a strong research design that included experimental design with random assignment, evidence of low subject attrition, and adequate construct validity. Second, based on the research design, programs had to illustrate significant deterrent effects. Third, the programs had to prove to be effective in multiple settings. Finally, the programs had to illustrate sustained effects lasting at least one year or more beyond the conclusion of services. Programs were also evaluated on their cost-effectiveness.

Thus far, 11 programs have been selected as Blueprint Models. (For more details about the Blueprint for Violence Prevention Programs visit the Center for the Study and Prevention of Violence website at: http://www.colorado.edu/cspv/blueprints/. The following discussion outlines three of these. The first, the Nurse-Family Partnership, is a maltreatment prevention program. The other two, Functional Family Therapy and Multisystemic Therapy, are delinquency prevention initiatives.

Nurse-Family Partnership

The Nurse-Family Partnership (NFP) (formerly Prenatal and Infancy Home Visitation by Nurses), evolved from two decades of work by David Olds and his colleagues in developing and testing of child health and development initiatives and maltreatment prevention programs with low income, first-time mothers (Olds, Henderson, Chamberlin & Tatelbaum, 1986; Olds, Hill & Mihalic 1998a; Olds, Hill & Rumsey, 1998b).

Nurse home visitation is a program that sends nurses to the homes of pregnant women who are predisposed to infant health and developmental problems, (e.g., at-risk of preterm delivery and low birth weight children). Home visiting promotes the physical, cognitive, and social-emotional development of children, and provides general support as well instructive parenting skills to parents. Treatment begins during pregnancy and continues to 24 months postpartum. Screening and transportation are also offered as part of the treatment. Nurse home visitation significantly increased obstetric health, parent-child relationships, and reduced child maltreatment in controlled studies (Daro & Donnelly, 2002:xxvii).

Functional Family Therapy

Functional Family Therapy (FFT), developed by James Alexander and Bruce Parsons (1982; see also Sexton & Alexander, 2000), is a short-term family systems approach that has been quite effective in dealing with unmotivated youth offenders and their families who have few resources to support them. Functional Family Therapy is derived from systems theory, cybernetics, and cognitive-behavioralism. According to this approach, all behavior is adaptive in that it serves a function of regulating relationships within the family. Alexander and Parsons (1982) have identified three different behavioral functions: (1) merging, which means seeking closeness; (2) separating, which means seeking independence; and (3) mid-pointing, which involves seeking both simultaneously. Conflict generally arises when family members have incompatible functions. For instance, a mother attempts to merge with her 15-year-old son while he is trying to separate from her. In order to understand the relationship and complexity of these functions, therapy is built around assisting family members to communicate more effectively with each other.

The therapy process can be divided into four phases. Phase 1 is the engagement phase where the therapist develops an alliance with the family. In Phase 2, the therapist and family work together to identify the various functions and behaviors within the home. Emphasis is placed upon incompatible functions and the unacceptable behaviors that stem from them. Behaviors that are either too muted or too intense (e.g., the 15-year-old son's attempt to separate from his mother by staying out all night) are identified and modified. Phase 3 is the therapy phase and emphasizes the development of communication skills and cognitive-behavioral strategies that modify family member expectations and behaviors. Incongruent communication (e.g., saying one thing, but meaning something else) is central to problematic interactions. Therapy focuses on teaching families to be more congruent in their communication with each other.

The final phase involves education. Families are taught specific communication skills that will improve parent-child relationships and maintain the changes that have occurred in therapy. Controlled comparison studies with follow-up periods of one, three, and even five years have demonstrated significant and long-term reductions in youth re-offending, while comparative cost figures have indicated very large reductions in program costs compared to other treatment approaches (Daro & Donnelly, 2002).

Multisystemic Therapy

Multisystemic Therapy (MST), developed by Scott Henggeler and his colleagues (1998), is based on a social-ecological approach to delinquent behavior. Henggeler's basic assumption is that youth deviancy is multi-determined and involves the interplay of individual characteristics along with family, school, community, and peer group risk factors. Theoretically, it is an eclectic model principally derived from the fields of social ecology (Bronfenbrenner, 1977, 1979), systems theory, and cognitive-behavioral therapy, although there are also other lesser contributors as well.

MST views individuals as living within a complex social network. Behavioral problems can stem from problematic interactions within any of the youth's social networks. Consequently, MST targets the risk factors that contribute to the youth's anti-social behavior. MST uses the strengths and resources in each youth's social network to promote positive behavior change. MST employs a family preservation model of service delivery that features low caseloads; goals that are set primarily by the family; a team treatment approach that might employ various clinicians, caseworkers, community organizers, supervisors, and consultants; and an emphasis upon community-based interventions (Mihalic, Irwin, Elliott, Fagan & Hansen, 2001). Family intervention plans can include strategic family therapy, structural family therapy, behavioral parent training, and/or cognitive behavior therapies. The family interventions seek to improve parents' abilities to monitor and discipline their children. Peer interventions seek to remove youth from deviant peers and help develop pro-social friends while educational and vocational interventions seek to improve youth functioning in school and at work. MST is reported to be effective in long-term reduction in re-arrests and out-of-home placements of young offenders. Families receiving MST also report improvement in parent-child interactions and a reduction in family mental health problems. Despite the intensity of services, MST has also been demonstrated to be cost-effective (Mihalic et al., 2001:10).

The Blueprint Programs illustrate how scientific study, coupled with governmental support, have the potential to improve the lives of at-risk children. However, it is not a simple formula. Scientific inquiry oftentimes produces more questions than it answers. At best, it is an uneven process full of apparent successes and failures. Programs that seem to make logical sense oftentimes do not meet science's standards for achievement. Changes in public policy, insufficient funding, and inadequate implementation can produce programs that are compromised and flawed. Moreover, a host of social and economic conditions can confound the best efforts of science and government. As a result, we will continue to struggle to create the ideal society for our children. The discussion below suggests another strategy in this direction.

Future Directions: Restorative Justice

The debate over the future of the criminal justice system has historically revolved around issues of rehabilitation and punishment. However, a relatively new ideology is being tried (mostly in juvenile justice) that takes into consideration the needs of the offender, the community, and the victim. This philosophy is Restorative Justice.

Restorative justice requires that criminal justice professionals devote attention to (1) enabling offenders to take responsibility for their actions, (2) increasing offender competencies, and (3) protecting the public. In 1995, the Commonwealth of Pennsylvania introduced Restorative Justice into its Juve-

Source: Pennsylvania Juvenile Court Judges' Commission, 1997.

nile Court legislation. With the passage of an amendment to the Pennsylvania Juvenile Act, Act 33, Pennsylvania's juvenile justice system became guided by the following purpose:

> Consistent with the protection of the public interest, to provide for children committing delinquent acts programs of supervision, care and rehabilitation which provide balanced attention to the protection of the community, the imposition of accountability for offenses committed and the development of competencies to enable children to become responsible and productive members of the community (Pennsylvania Juvenile Court Judges' Commission, 1997:3).

This model of justice is based on the belief that crime is against not only the government but also the victim and the community. This is an ancient idea common to tribal and religious traditions of many cultures. Crime is seen as an injury that hurts not only victims and the community but the offender as well. As such, all parties should be a part of the response to the crime, with an emphasis on the obligation of the offender to make things right.

Restorative justice requires offenders to face their victims and victimized communities, and to repair the harms that their actions have caused (Armstrong, Maloney & Romig, 1990; Zehr, 1990; Umbreit, 1994; Bazemore & Umbreit, 1995, 2001). Instead of defining offenders in terms of deficits, restorative justice defines them in terms of their capacity to make reparations. "Obligations under a restorative justice model call for full admission of wrongdoing, full admission of who was damaged by the behavior, commitment to right the wrong by doing reparation, making apology or delivering restitution, and being willing to be held accountable and willing not to reoffend" (Carter, 2005:5).

As this chapter has demonstrated, youthful offenders are sometimes themselves victims of abuse, neglect, and maltreatment. In contrast to retributive justice which seeks punishment, the restorative approach recognizes that delinquents are also victims and are harmed by their offending behaviors. As a means to holding offenders accountable while protecting the public, restorative justice also promotes therapeutic interventions to prevent cycles of delinquency and criminality. The values inherent in this model reflect a more balanced and reintegrative juvenile justice system.

References

Akers, R.L. (1985). *Deviant Behavior: A Social Learning Approach*, Third Edition. Belmont, CA: Wadsworth.

Alexander, J.F & B.V. Parsons (1982). *Functional Family Therapy*. Monterey, CA: Brooks/ Cole Publishing.

Alexander, J.F., C. Pugh, B.V. Parsons & T.L. Sexton (2000). "Functional Family Therapy." In D.S. Elliott (ed.) *Blueprints for Violence Prevention, Book 3*, Second Edition. Boulder, CO: Center for the Study of Violence, Institute of Behavior Science, University of Colorado.

Alfaro, J.D. (1981). "Report on the Relationship between Child Abuse and Neglect and Later Socially Deviant Behavior." In R.J. Hunner & Y.E. Walker (eds.) *Exploring the Relationship Between Child Abuse and Delinquency*, pp. 175-219. Montclair, NJ: Allanheld, Osmun & Co.

American Professional Society on the Abuse of Children (APSAC) (1995). *Guidelines for the Psychosocial Evaluation of Suspected Psychological Maltreatment of Children and Adolescents*. Chicago, IL: APSAC.

Armstrong, T., D. Maloney & D. Romig (1990). "The Balanced Approach in Juvenile Probation: Principles, Issues, and Applications." *Perspectives*, (Winter):8-13.

Ashby, L. (1997). *Endangered Children: Dependency, Neglect, and Abuse in American History*. New York, NY: Twayne Publishers.

Bandura, A. (1969). "Social Learning of Moral Judgments." *Journal of Personality and Social Psychology*, 11:275-279.

Bandura, A. & R.H. Walters (1963). *Social Learning and Personality Development*. New York, NY: Holt, Rinehart, and Winston.

Bazemore, G. & M.S. Umbreit (2001). *A Comparison of Four Restorative Conferencing Models*. Washington, DC: U.S. Department of Justice, Office of Juvenile Justice and Delinquency Prevention.

Bazemore, G. & M.S. Umbreit (1995). "Rethinking the Sanctioning Function in Juvenile Court: Restrictive or Restorative Responses to Youth Crime." *Crime & Delinquency*, 41(3):296-316.

Beck, J.S. (1995). *Cognitive Therapy: Basics and Beyond*. New York, NY: Guilford Press.

Becker, H.S. (1973). *Outsiders*. New York, NY: Free Press.

Becvar, R. & D. Becvar (1998). *Systems Theory and Family Therapy: A Primer*, Second Edition. Lanham, MD: University Press of America.

Belsky, J. (1980). "Child Maltreatment: An Ecological Integration." *American Psychologist*, 35:320-355.

Belsky, J. & J. Vondra (1989). "Lessons from Child Abuse: The Determinants of Parenting." In C.D. Carlson & V. Carlson (eds.) *Child Maltreatment: Theory and Research on the Causes and Consequences of Abuse and Neglect*, pp. 153-202. New York, NY: Cambridge University Press.

Bolen, R.M. (2000). "Validity of Attachment Theory." *Trauma, Violence, & Abuse*, 1:128-153.

Bolton, F.G., J. Reich & S.E. Gutierres (1977). "Delinquency Patterns in Maltreated Children and Siblings." *Victimology*, 2:26-38.

Bowlby, J. (1969). *Attachment*. New York, NY: Basic Books.

Brennan, P.A., S.A. Mednick & J. Volavka (1995). "Biomedical Factors in Crime." In J.Q. Wilson & J. Petersilia (eds.) *Crime*, pp. 65-90. San Francisco, CA: ICS Press.

Brewer, D.D., J.D. Hawkins, R.F. Catalano & H.J. Neckerman (1995). "Preventing Serious, Violent, and Chronic Juvenile Offending: A Review of Selected Strategies in Childhood, Adolescence, and the Community." In J.C. Howell, B. Krisberg, J.D. Hawkins & J.J. Wilson (eds.) *A Sourcebook: Serious, Violent, and Chronic Juvenile Offenders*, pp. 61-141. Thousand Oaks, CA: Sage Publications.

Bronfenbrenner, U. (1979). *The Ecology of Human Development: Experiments by Nature and Design*. Cambridge, MA: Harvard University Press.

Bronfenbrenner, U. (1977). "Toward an Experimental Ecology of Human Development." *American Psychologist*, 32:513-531.

Burgess, R.L. (2005). "Evolutionary Theory of Human Development." In R.L. Burgess & K. MacDonald (eds.) *Evolutionary Perspectives on Human Development*, pp. 1-19. Thousand Oaks, CA: Sage Publications.

Burgess, R.L. (1997). "Behavior Genetics and Evolutionary Psychology: A New Look at the Transmission of Maltreatment across Generations." Paper presented at the Annual Meeting of the Behavior Genetics Association, Toronto, Canada.

Burgess, R.L. (1979). "Child Abuse: A Social Interactional Analysis." In B.B. Lahey & A. Kazdin (eds.) *Advances in Clinical Child Psychology*, (Volume 2) pp. 141-172. New York, NY: Plenum Press.

Burgess, R.L. & R.D. Conger (1978). "Family Interaction in Abusing, Neglectful, and Normal Families." *Child Development*, 49:1163-1173.

Burgess, R.L. & A. Drais-Parrillo (2005). "An Analysis of Child Maltreatment: From Behavioral Psychology to Behavioral Ecology." In R.L. Burgess & K. MacDonald (eds.) *Evolutionary Perspectives on Human Development*, pp. 305-330. Thousand Oaks, CA: Sage Publications.

Carter, R. (2005). "Restorative Justice: Working toward Healing, Peace and Forgiveness." *Restorative Directions Journal*, 1(1):4-9.

Catalano, R.F. & J.D. Hawkins (1996). "The Social Developmental Model: A Theory of Anti-Social Behavior." In J.D. Hawkins (ed.) *Delinquency and Crime: Current Theories*, pp. 149-197. New York, NY: Cambridge University Press.

Chamberlain, P. (1998). *Blueprints for Violence Prevention, Book 8: Multidimensional Treatment Foster Care*. Boulder, CO: Center for the Study and Prevention of Violence.

Chesney-Lind, M. (1977). "Judicial Paternalism and the Female Status Offender: Training Women to Know Their Place." *Crime & Delinquency*, 23:121-130.

Cloward, R.A. & L.B. Ohlin (1960). *Delinquency and Opportunity: A Theory of Delinquent Gangs*. New York, NY: Free Press.

Cohen, A.K. (1955). *Delinquent Boys: The Culture of the Gang*. Glencoe, IL: Free Press.

Corey, G. (2005). *Theory and Practice of Counseling and Psychotherapy*, Seventh Edition. Pacific Grove, CA: Thomson/Wadsworth Publishers.

Crittenden, P.M. & M.D.S. Ainsworth (1989). "Child Maltreatment and Attachment Theory." In D. Cicchetti & V. Carlson (eds.) *Child Maltreatment: Theory and Research on the Causes and Consequences of Child Abuse and Neglect*, pp. 432-463. New York, NY: Cambridge University Press.

Daro, D. & A.C. Donnelly (2002). "Child Abuse Prevention: Accomplishments and Challenges." In J.E.B. Myers, L. Berliner, J. Briere, C.T. Hendrix, C. Jenny & T.A. Reid (eds.) *The APSAC Handbook on Child Maltreatment*, Second Edition, pp. 431-448. Thousand Oaks, CA: Sage Publications.

DePanfilis, D. (1995). "Epidemiology of Child Maltreatment Reccurences." Unpublished Doctoral Dissertation, University of Maryland at Baltimore, School of Social Work, Baltimore, MD.

DePanfilis, D. & S.J. Zuravin (1998). "Rates, Patterns, and Frequency of Child Maltreatment Recurrences Among Families Known to CPS." *Child Maltreatment*, 3:27-42.

DePanfilis, D. & S.J. Zuravin (1992). "Predicting the Recurrence of Child Maltreatment." Paper presented at the Ninth International Congress of Child Abuse and Neglect, Chicago, IL.

Elliott, D.S. (Series Editor) (1998). *Blueprints for Violence Prevention, Books 3-8*. Boulder, CO: Institute of Behavioral Science, Regents of the University of Colorado.

Elliott, D.S. (Series Editor) (1997). *Blueprints for Violence Prevention, Books 1-2*. Boulder, CO: Institute of Behavioral Science, Regents of the University of Colorado.

Erickson, M.F. & B. Egeland (2002). "Child Neglect." In J.E.B. Myers, L. Berliner, J. Briere, C.T. Hendrix, C. Jenny & T.A. Reid (eds.) *The APSAC Handbook on Child Maltreatment*, Second Edition, pp. 3-20. Thousand Oaks, CA: Sage Publications.

Erickson, M.F., B. Egeland & R. Pianta (1989). "The Effects of Maltreatment on the Development of Young Children." In D. Cicchetti & V. Carlson (eds.) *Child Maltreatment: Theory and Research on the Causes and Consequences of Child Abuse and Neglect*, pp. 647-684. New York, NY: Cambridge University Press.

Erickson, M.L. (1972). "The Changing Relation between Official and Self-Reported Measures of Delinquency: An Exploratory Descriptive Study." *Journal of Criminal Law, Criminology and Police Science*, 62:388-395.

Erikson, E.H. (1968). *Identity, Youth and Crisis*. New York, NY: Norton.

Fahlberg, V.I. (1970). *A Child's Journey through Placement*. Indianapolis, IN: Perspective Press.

Fantuzzo, J.W. (1990). "Behavioral Treatment of the Victims of Child Abuse and Neglect." *Behavior Modification*, 14:316-339.

Farrington, D.P. (1986). "Stepping Stones to Adult Criminal Careers." In D. Olweus, J. Block & M.R. Yarrow (eds.) *Development of Antisocial and Prosocial Behavior*, pp. 359-384. New York, NY: Academic Press.

Garbarino, J. (1999). *Lost Boys: Why Our Sons Turn Violent and How We Can Save Them*. New York, NY: Anchor Books.

Garbarino, J. & G. Gilliam (1980). *Understanding Abusive Families*. Lexington, MA: Lexington Books.

Garbarino, J. & K. Kostelny (1991). "Child Maltreatment as a Community Problem." *Child Abuse and Neglect*, 16:455-464.

Gelles, R. (1975). "The Social Construction of Child Abuse." *American Journal of Orthopsychiatry*, 45:363-371.

Gelles, R. (1973). "Child Abuse as Psychopathology: A Sociological Critique and Reformation." *American Journal of Orthopsychiatry*, 43:611-621.

Gil, D. (1971). "Violence against Children." *Journal of Marriage and the Family*, 33:639-648.

Gil, D. (1970). *Violence against Children: Physical Abuse in the United States*. Cambridge, MA: Harvard University Press.

Goldenberg, I. & H. Goldenberg (1985). *Family Therapy: An Overview*, Second Edition. Monterrey, CA: Brooks/Cole.

Gottfredson, M.R. & T. Hirschi (1990). *A General Theory of Crime*. Stanford, CA: Stanford University Press.

Gutierres, S. & J.A. Reich (1981). "A Developmental Perspective on Runaway Behavior: Its Relationship to Child Abuse." *Child Welfare*, 60:89-94.

Hamilton, C.E., L. Falshaw & K.D. Browne (2002). "The Link between Recurrent Maltreatment and Offending Behaviour." *International Journal of Offender Therapy and Comparative Criminology*, 46:75-94.

Hart, S.N., M.R. Brassard, N.J., Binggeli & H.A. Davidson (2002). "Psychological Maltreatment." In J.E.B. Myers, L. Berliner, J. Briere, C.T. Hendrix, C. Jenny & T.A. Reid (eds.) *The APSAC Handbook on Child Maltreatment*, Second Edition, pp. 79-103. Thousand Oaks, CA: Sage Publication.

Hawkins, J.D. & R.F. Catalano (1993). *Risk-Focused Prevention Using the Social Developmental Strategy*. Seattle, WA: Developmental Research and Programs.

Hawkins, J.D. & R.F. Catalano (1992). *Communities That Care: Action for Drug Abuse Prevention*. San Francisco, CA: Jossey-Bass.

Hawkins, J.D., R.F. Catalano & D.D. Brewer (1995). "Preventing Serious, Violent, and Chronic Juvenile Offending: Effective Strategies From Conception to Age." In J.C. Howell, B. Krisberg, J.D. Hawkins & J.J. Wilson (eds.) *A Sourcebook: Serious, Violent, and Chronic Juvenile Offenders*, pp. 47-60. Thousand Oaks, CA: Sage Publications.

Hawkins, J.D., R.F. Catalano & J.Y. Miller (1992). "Risk and Protective Factors for Alcohol and Other Drug Problems in Adolescence and Early Adulthood: Implications for Substance Abuse Prevention." *Psychological Bulletin*, 112:64-105.

Heide, K.M. & E.P. Solomon (2004). "Parental Neglect in Cases of Kids who Kill Parents." Paper presented at the 2004 Annual Meeting of the Academy of Criminal Justice Sciences, Las Vegas, Nevada.

Henggeler, S.W., S.J. Schoenwald, C.M. Borduin, M.D. Rowland & P.B. Cunningham (1998). *Multisystemic Treatment of Antisocial Behavior in Children and Adolescents: Treatment Manuals for Practitioners*. New York, NY: Guilford Press.

Herrenkohl, R.C., E.C. Herrenkohl & B.P. Egolf (1983). "Circumstances Surrounding the Occurrence of Child Maltreatment." *Journal of Consulting and Clinical Psychology*, 51:424-431.

Herrenkohl, R.C., E.C. Herrenkohl, B.P. Egolf & M. Seech (1979). "The Repetition of Child Abuse: How Frequently Does It Happen?" *Child Abuse and Neglect*, 3:67-72.

Herrenkohl, T.I., J.D. Hawkins, C. Ick-Joong, K.G. Hill & S. Battin-Pearson (2001). "School and Community Risk Factors and Interventions." In R. Loeber & D.P. Farrington (eds.) *Child Delinquents: Development, Intervention, and Service Needs*, pp. 211-246. Thousand Oaks, CA: Sage Publications.

Hirschi, T. (1969). *Causes of Delinquency*. Berkeley, CA: University of California Press.

Howing, P.T., J.S. Wodarski, P.D. Kurtz & J.M. Gaudin (eds.) (1993). *Maltreatment and the School-Age Child: Developmental Outcomes and System Issues*. New York, NY: Haworth.

Johnson-Reid, M. & R.P. Barth (2000). "From Maltreatment Report to Juvenile Incarceration: The Role of Child Welfare Services." *Child Abuse and Neglect*, 24:505-520.

Kandel, E.R. (2006). *In Search of Memory: The Emergence of a New Science of Mind*. New York, NY: Norton Books.

Kempe, C.H. (1973). "A Practical Approach to the Protection of the Abused Child and Rehabilitation of the Abusing Parent." *Pediatrics*, 51:804-812.

Krohn, M.D., T.P. Thornberry, C. Rivera & M. LeBlanc (2001). "Later Delinquency Careers." In R. Loeber & D.P. Farrington (eds.) *Child Delinquents: Development, Intervention, and Service Needs*, pp. 67-93. Thousand Oaks, CA: Sage Publications.

Kratcoski, P.C. (1982). "Child Abuse and Violence against the Family." *Child Welfare*, 61:435-444.

Kuhn, T. (1970). *The Structure of Scientific Revolution*, Third Edition. Chicago, IL: University of Chicago Press.

Leiter, J., K.A. Myers & M.T. Zingraff (1994). "Substantiated and Unsubstantiated Cases of Child Maltreatment: Do Their Consequences Differ?" *Social Work Research*, 18:67-82.

Lemert, E.M. (1951). *Social Pathology: A Systematic Approach to the Theory of Sociopathic Behavior*. New York, NY: McGraw-Hill.

Lemmon, J.H., P.J. Verrecchia & T.L. Austin (2008). "Developing and Validating a Measure of Maltreatment Severity: An Examination of the Relationship of Maltreatment Dimensions on Youth Offending in the Context of Individual, Other Environmental Risks, and Mediating Factors." Unpublished manuscript.

Lemmon, J.H. (2006). "The Effects of Maltreatment Recurrence and Child Welfare Services on Dimensions of Delinquency." *Criminal Justice Review*, 31(3):1-28.

Lemmon, J.H. (1999). "How Child Maltreatment Affects Dimensions of Juvenile Delinquency in a Cohort of Low-Income Urban Males." *Justice Quarterly*, 16:357-376.

Lewin, K. (1936). *Problems of Topological Psychology*. New York, NY: McGraw-Hill.

Lightcap, J.L., J.A. Kurland & R.L. Burgess (1982). "Child Abuse: A Test of Some Predictions from Evolutionary Theory." *Ethology and Sociobiology*, 3:61-67.

Loeber, R. (1990). "Development and Risk Factors of Juvenile Antisocial Behavior and Delinquency." *Clinical Psychology Review*, 10:1-41.

Loeber, R. & D.P. Farrington (2001). "The Significance of Child Delinquency." In R. Loeber & D.P. Farrington (eds.) *Child Delinquents: Development, Intervention, and Service Needs*, pp. 1-22. Thousand Oaks, CA: Sage Publications.

Loeber, R. & D.P. Farrington (1998). *Serious and Violent Juvenile Offenders: Risk Factors and Successful Interventions*. Thousand Oaks, CA: Sage Publications.

Loeber, R. & D.F. Hay (1994). "Developmental Approaches to Aggression and Conduct Problems." In M. Rutter & D.F. Hay (eds.) *Development through Life: A Handbook for Clinicians*, pp. 488-516. Oxford, UK: Blackwell Science.

Loeber, R., E. Wei, M.Stouthamer-Loeber, D. Huizinga & T. Thornberry (1999). "Behavioral Antecedents to Serious and Violent Juvenile Offending: Joint Analyses from the Denver Youth Survey, the Pittsburgh Youth Study, and the Rochester Developmental Study." *Studies in Crime and Crime Prevention*, 8:245-263.

McCord, J. (1983a). "A Forty Year Perspective on Effects of Child Abuse and Neglect." *Child Abuse and Neglect*, 7:265-270.

McCord, J. (1983b). "A Longitudinal Study of Aggression and Antisocial Behavior in Adult Men." In K.T. Van Dusen & S.A. Mednick (eds.) *Prospective Studies of Crime and Delinquency*, pp. 269-275. Boston, MA: Kluwer-Nijhoff.

McCord, J. (1979). "Some Child-Rearing Antecedents of Criminal Behavior in Adult Men." *Journal of Personality and Social Psychology*, 8:1477-1486.

McMullin, R.E. (2000). *The New Handbook of Cognitive Therapy Techniques*. New York, NY: W.W. Norton & Company, Inc.

Merton, R.K. (1938). "Social Structure and Anomie." *American Sociological Review*, 3:672-682.

Mihalic, S., K. Irwin, D. Elliott, A. Fagan & D. Hansen (2001). *Blueprints for Violence Prevention*. Juvenile Justice Bulletin. Washington, DC: U.S. Department of Justice, Office of Juvenile Justice and Delinquency Prevention.

Miller, W.B. (1958). "Lower Class Culture as a Generating Milieu of Gang Delinquency." *Journal of Social Issues*, 15:5-19.

Mouzakitis, C.M. (1981). "An Inquiry into the Problem of Child Abuse and Juvenile Delinquency." In R.J. Hunner & Y.E. Walker (eds.) *Exploring the Relationship between Child Abuse and Delinquency*, pp. 220-232. Montclair, NJ: Allanheld, Osmun & Co.

Murray, J.P. (1983). *Status Offenders: A Sourcebook*. Boys Town, NE: The Boys Town Center.

Olds, D., C. Henderson, R. Chamberlin & R. Tatelbaum (1986). "Preventing Child Abuse and Neglect: A Randomized Trial of Nurse Home Visitation." *Pediatrics*, 78:65-78.

Olds, D., P. Hill & S.F. Mihalic (1998a). *Blueprints for Violence Prevention, Book 7: Prenatal and Early Childhood Nurse Home Visitation*. Boulder, CO: Center for the Study and Prevention of Violence.

Olds, D., P. Hill & E. Rumsey (1998b). *Prenatal and Early Childhood Nurse Home Visitation*. Juvenile Justice Bulletin. Washington, DC: U.S. Department of Justice, Office of Juvenile Justice and Delinquency Prevention.

Palmer, S.E. (1979). "Predicting Outcome in Long-Term Foster Care." *Journal of Social Service Research*, 3:201-214.

Patterson, G.R. (1976). "The Aggressive Child: Victim and Architect of a Coercive System." In L.A. Hamerlynck, L.C. Handy & E.J. Mash (eds.) *Behavioral Modification and Families: Volume I Theory and Research*. New York, NY: Brunner/Mazel.

Patterson, G.R., D.M. Capaldi & L. Bank (1991). "An Early Starter Model for Predicting Delinquency. "In D.J. Pepler & K.H. Rubin (eds.) *The Development and Treatment of Childhood Aggression*, pp. 139-168. Hillsdale, NJ: Lawrence Erlbaum.

Pennsylvania Child Protective Services Law, Act 124 of 1975, 11 P.S. Section 2201.

Pennsylvania Juvenile Court Judges' Commission (1997). *Balanced and Restorative Justice in Pennsylvania: A New Mission and Changing Roles within the Juvenile Justice System*. Harrisburg, PA: Pennsylvania Juvenile Court Judges' Commission.

Pianka, E.R. (1970). "On r- and K-Selection." *American Naturalist*, 104:592-597.

Puzzanchera, C., A.L. Stahl, T.A. Finnegan, H.N. Snyder, R.W. Poole & N. Tierney (2000). *Juvenile Court Statistics 1997*. Washington, DC: U.S. Department of Justice, Office of Juvenile Justice and Delinquency Prevention.

Puzzanchera, C., A.L. Stahl, T.A. Finnegan, N. Tierney & H.N. Snyder (2003). *Juvenile Court Statistics 1999*. Pittsburgh, PA: National Center for Juvenile Justice.

Quinney, R.A. (1970). *The Social Reality of Crime*. Boston, MA: Little-Brown.

Rhoades, P.W. & S.L. Parker (1981). *The Connection between Youth Problems and Violence in the Home*. Portland, OR: Oregon Coalition against Domestic and Sexual Violence.

Runyan, D.K. & C.L. Gould (1985). "Foster Care for Child Maltreatment: Impact on Delinquent Behavior." *Pediatrics*, 75:562-568.

Ryan, J.P. & M.F. Testa (2005). "Child Maltreatment and Juvenile Delinquency: Investigating the Role of Placement and Placement Instability." *Children and Youth Services Review,* 27:227-249.

Satir, V.M. (1967). *Conjoint Family Therapy*, Revised Edition. Palo Alto, CA: Science and Behavior Books.

Sexton, T.L. & J.F. Alexander (2000). *Functional Family Therapy.* Juvenile Justice Bulletin. Washington, DC: U.S. Department of Justice, Office of Juvenile Justice and Delinquency Prevention.

Shaw, C.R. & H.D. McKay (1942). *Juvenile Delinquency and Urban Areas.* Chicago, IL: University of Chicago Press.

Silver, L.B., C.C. Dublin & R.S. Lourie (1969). "Does Violence Breed Violence? Contributions From a Study of the Child Abuse Syndrome." *American Journal of Psychiatry,* 126:404-407.

Simons, R.L., L.B. Whitbeck, R.D. Conger & W. Chyi-In (1991). "Intergenerational Transmission of Harsh Parenting." *Developmental Psychology,* 27:159-171.

Simons, R.L., L.G. Simons & L.E. Wallace (2004). *Families, Delinquency, and Crime: Linking Society's Most Fundamental Social Institution to Anti-Social Behavior.* Los Angeles, CA: Roxbury Press.

Smith, C. & T.P. Thornberry (1995). "The Relationship between Childhood Maltreatment and Adolescent Involvement in Delinquency." *Criminology,* 33:451-481.

Snyder, H.N. & M. Sickmund (2006). *Juvenile Offenders and Victims: 2006 National Report.* Washington, DC: U.S. Department of Justice, Office of Juvenile Justice and Delinquency Prevention.

Stahl, A. (2008). *Petitioned Status Offense Cases in Juvenile Courts, 2004.* Washington, DC: U.S. Department of Justice, Office of Juvenile Justice and Delinquency Prevention.

Stearns, S. (1992). *The Evolution of Life Histories.* New York, NY: Oxford University Press.

Straus, M.A. (1994). *Beating the Devil Out of Them: Corporal Punishment in American Families.* Lexington, MA: Lexington Books.

Sutherland, E.H. & D.R. Cressey (1974). *Criminology*, Ninth Edition. Philadelphia, PA: Lippincott.

Tannebaum, F. (1938). *Crime and the Community.* New York, NY: Columbia University Press.

Tinbergen, N. (1951). *The Study of Instinct.* London, UK: Oxford University Press.

Umbreit, M.S. (1994). *Victim Meets Offender: The Impact of Restorative Justice and Mediation.* Monsey, NY: Criminal Justice Press.

U.S. Department of Health and Human Services (2007). *Child Maltreatment 2005.* Washington, DC: U.S. Government Printing Office.

U.S. Department of Health and Human Services (2006). *Child Maltreatment 2004.* Washington, DC: U.S. Government Printing Office.

U.S. Department of Health and Human Services (2001). *Child Maltreatment 1999: Reports from the States to the Child Abuse and Neglect Data System.* Washington, DC: U.S. Government Printing Office.

Weeks, R. & C.S. Widom (1998). *Early Childhood Victimization Among Incarcerated Adult Male Felons*. Research Preview. Washington, DC: U.S. Department of Justice, National Institute of Justice.

Weisbrod, J.A. (1981). *Family Court Disposition Study*. New York, NY: Vera Institute of Justice.

Whipple, E.E. & C. Webster-Stratton (1991). "The Role of Parental Stress in Physically Abusive Families." *Child Abuse & Neglect*, 15:279-291.

Whitehead, J.T. & S.P. Lab (2006). *Juvenile Justice: An Introduction*, Fifth Edition. Newark, NJ: LexisNexis/Matthew Bender & Co., Inc.

Wick, S.C. (1981). "Child Abuse as Causation of Juvenile Delinquency in Central Texas." In R.J. Hunner & Y.E. Walker (eds.) *Exploring the Relationship between Child Abuse and Delinquency*, pp. 233-239. Montclair, NJ: Allanheld, Osmun & Co.

Widom, C.S. (1991). "The Role of Placement Experiences in Mediating the Criminal Consequences of Early Childhood Victimization." *American Journal of Orthopsychiatry*, 61:195-209.

Widom, C.S. (1989a). "Child Abuse, Neglect, and Violent Criminal Behavior." *Criminology*, 27:251-271.

Widom, C.S. (1989b). "Does Violence Beget Violence? A Critical Examination of the Literature." *Psychological Bulletin*, 106:3-28.

Widom, C.S. (1989c). "The Intergenerational Transmission of Violence." In N.A. Weiner & M.E. Wolfgang (eds.) *Pathways to Criminal Violence*, pp. 137-201. Newbury Park, CA: Sage Publications.

Widom, C.S. (1989d). "The Cycle of Violence." *Science*, 244:160-166.

Widom, C.S. & M.A. Ames (1994). "Criminal Consequences of Childhood Sexual Victimization." *Child Abuse & Neglect*, 18:303-318.

Wilson, W.J. (1987). *The Truly Disadvantaged: The Inner-City, the Underclass, and Public Policy*. Chicago, IL: The University of Chicago Press.

Zehr, H. (1990). *Changing Lenses: A New Focus for Crime and Justice*. Scottsdale, PA: Herald Press.

Zingraff, M.T., J. Leiter, M.C. Johnsen & K.A. Myers (1993). "The Mediating Effect of Good School Performance on the Maltreatment-Delinquency Relationship." *Journal of Research in Crime and Delinquency*, 31:62-91.

Appendix A

A Social Ecology Explanation of the Dependency-Delinquency Link

Historically, the juvenile court has directed considerable efforts and resources toward remedying family-related problems in the hope of eliminating or at least reducing delinquency. The *parens patriae* model was based on the assumption that the juvenile court could serve as the surrogate parent for wayward children. In the meantime, criminological explanations of delinquency have covered the gamut of theories from global approaches that feature a class conflict perspective (Tannebaum, 1938; Lemert, 1951; Quinney, 1970) to ones that emphasize overriding cultural issues like strain (Merton, 1938) or cultural conflict (Cohen, 1955; Miller, 1958) to causes embedded in the child's immediate environment such as social disorganization (Shaw & McKay, 1942) or relationships within the family (Hirschi, 1969; Gottfredson & Hirschi, 1990) to ones that consider individual characteristics ranging from learned behaviors (Bandura & Walters, 1963; Sutherland & Cressey, 1974) to psychodynamic conflict (Erikson, 1968) to the physiology of the brain (Brennan, Mednick & Volavka, 1995). Theory development in the field of maltreatment studies has followed a similar pattern.

Explanations of maltreatment etiology have ranged from global theories that feature social stress (Gelles, 1973, 1975) or cultural beliefs (Gil, 1971) to the genre of theories that emphasize family system characteristics including coercive interactions (Fantuzzo, 1990), attachment issues (Bowlby, 1969; Crittenden & Ainsworth, 1989), and other stress-inducing factors within the family's immediate environment (e.g., unemployment, family size, and single parenthood) (Belsky & Vondra, 1989). Other theories emphasize child characteristics like temperament (Herrenkohl, Herrenkohl & Egolf, 1983) or parent characteristics including childhood histories of maltreatment (Straus, 1994), cognitive styles (Simons, Whitbeck, Conger & Chyi-In, 1991), and psychiatric disturbances (Whipple & Webster-Stratton, 1991). Today, policymakers and theorists recognize the need for an integrated and comprehensive approach to the understanding and treatment of at-risk youth offenders.

Although the sequence and interplay of dependency-delinquency relationships are complicated, they can now be better understood by considering the work of academics and practitioners outside the field of juvenile justice. In particular, this includes systems theorists and psychologists (particularly child development specialists) who have examined the social ecology model or have applied it in their practices. The social ecology model was originally developed by mathematicians examining how feedback mechanisms operate in controlling both simple and complex systems, and by natural scientists in biological studies of the effects of environmental changes on ecosystems (Becvar & Becvar, 1998). These ideas attracted the attention of family systems theorists such as Gregory Bateson, Murray Bowen, and John Weakland who recognized the potential of an ecological approach in treating dysfunctional families. Systems theorists recognized that living systems exist in a hierarchy of levels and that each level (ranging from the cells within the body to international organizations) is made up of subsystems intra-connected with other components of its system and inter-connected with systems external to it (Goldenberg & Goldenberg, 1985). The idea that families are psychosocial systems is now a guiding principle in understanding how family structure and communication patterns affect family dysfunction.

Child development theory has made a substantial contribution in informing juvenile justice practice. In fact, current understanding of social ecology and its application for practice has largely been influenced by work of child development specialists like Urie Bronfenbrenner who referred to his theory as the "ecology of human development." From a developmental perspective, social ecology features the interaction of factors that exist on three levels; the global environment, the individual's immediate environment, and characteristics of the individual himself.

Although he is widely recognized as the most prominent contributor to the social ecology movement, Bronfenbrenner (1977:515) credits his ideas to Kurt Lewin's pioneering efforts in the field of social psychology. Lewin (1936) was the first to recognize that behavior was a function of the interaction of person and environment. Based on Lewin's ideas, Bronfrenbrenner (1977, 1979) broke with conventional theories of child development by arguing that personality develops through a series of progressive, mutual accommodations throughout the lifespan of the ever-developing human and his/her ever-changing environment. Bronfenbrenner questioned the depth of understanding offered by conventional theories such as Freud's id-centered Psychodynamic Model which saw personality development as a function of individual resolution of psychosexual conflicts, or Skinner's environmental model which claimed that personality developed passively through processes of operant conditioning.

Bronfrenbrenner (1977, 1979) asserted that personality developed in the context of two distinct multi-person systems. One system involves the individual in direct interaction with his/her environment (e.g., a child abused by his parents, or a teenager who participates in a burglary as the result of peer pressure). The other involves cultural forces beyond the individual's immediate environment (i.e., various ideologies and belief systems that shape a person's perceptions of the world). Bronfrenbrenner's model outlined three domains within the immediate environment, which he referred to as the micro, meso and exo-systems. The micro-system is the complex of relations between the child and his/her immediate environment, such as parent-child relationships within the home. The meso-system is a system of micro-systems that comprises face-to-face interactions in settings at particular points in a person's life span. For example, the meso-system of a 12-year-old boy might include his parents, grandparents, uncles and aunts, siblings, cousins, peers, teachers, coaches and/or clergy. The boy's meso-system will change as he gets older and moves from home to college, or joins the armed forces, or takes his first job, or gets married. The exo-system is an extension of the meso-system embracing other specified social structures, both formal and informal, which does not involve face-to-face interactions but still impinge upon the person's immediate environment. An illustration of exo-system effects might involve the chain of events that begins with an economic recession in the nation's housing industry that results in a father, employed as a carpenter, losing his job, which in turn reduces the life chances of his son who is forced to quit school to support the family.

Whereas the effects of micro-systems will vary from environment to environment, (e.g., whereas one child grows up to be an emotionally healthy and competent adult, due in part to being raised in a secure, loving family, another child becomes a chronic offender, due in part to the ongoing neglect he has experienced in his family), macro-system forces impact on all persons in society in a generally static manner. Bronfenbrenner referred to macro-systems as the ideological blueprints for a society. They are manifestly and latently articulated through laws, rules, values, and beliefs and are instilled into the personality through the socialization process. The macro-system includes the overarching beliefs and values of a culture and encompasses its economic, social, legal, political, educational, religious, and family institutions. The key conceptual point in Bronfenbrenner's theoretical scheme is that these systems are not only inter-connected; they are embedded within each other. The micro, meso, and exo-systems are concrete manifestations of the macro-system. Micro-systems are embedded in meso-systems which, in turn, are embedded in exo-systems, which, in turn, are embedded in macro-systems. The result is that personality is shaped in the context of these micro (i.e., a child's maltreatment experience) to macro-level (e.g., cultural values related to aggression and material success) forces.

One implication of Bronfenbrenner's ideas about macro-systems is that these forces have the potential to generate resiliency (i.e., moral development and competency) for some and produce risk (i.e., deviancy) for others. To illustrate this point, consider two cultural values held by Americans. Americans value freedom and competition. Freedom and competition foster creativity and responsibility as well as propensity for self-absorption and deceit. An American culture based on economic, intellectual, and political freedoms generates benefits for many but also produces consequences for some. This conservative social model fosters the competition of ideas, and creates wealth, equity, and reciprocity. It advances individual freedom, the development of knowledge, and features an open political forum driven by the rule of law. However, the conservative model is not conducive to social justice. When one considers the fact that dependent children are the most disadvantaged in society, the absence of social justice norms in our economic, social, and political formulas generate more risk and fewer resiliency factors for maltreated children and status offenders. Whether a particular factor (i.e., freedom of expression) at one level of the social eco-system produces contributions for society or crimes largely depends upon the factors within the immediate environment as well as the characteristics of the individual. All of these conditions are nested within each other and need to be sorted out.

Theorists and practitioners from other areas of psychology quickly grasped the significance of Bronfenbrenner's ideas. Since social ecology provided a useful scheme to incorporate divergent explanations of normal development, it might also be useful in understanding the dynamics of abnormal development. In 1980, Jay Belsky published an essay in *American Psychologist* in which he applied Bronfenbrenner's ecological concepts in developing an integrated etiology of child maltreatment. While acknowledging the importance of exo- and macro-level factors, Belsky pointed out that Bronfenbrenner had overlooked the individual differences that parents bring with them to the family micro-system, and how these characteristics affect parent-child interactions that result in maltreatment.

Belsky incorporated ideas from Tinbergen (1951) and Burgess (1979) to identify a third level of risk, which Tinbergen referred to as ontogenic development. Ontogenic development includes physiological and psychological characteristics that predispose parents to maltreating their children. These characteristics might include psychiatric disturbances like depression; impairment as the result of drug or alcohol abuse; personality defects including antisocial, borderline, and narcissistic disorders; immature coping skills, lower levels of intelligence, or histories of physical injury or emotional trauma. These characteristics, singularly or in combination with other factors, would affect the parents' thoughts, emotions, and behaviors that would contribute to maltreatment.

Belsky's efforts at integrating the three levels of risk, the macro (cultural values and institutional forces), the exo- and micro-levels (risks within the immediate environment), and the ontogenic (individual) characteristics incorporated disparate psychological (Kempe, 1973) and sociological explanations (Gil, 1970; Gelles, 1973) of maltreatment. While each approach was useful, both were incomplete. Moreover, the disparate perspectives have tended to fracture the field of study into one camp or the other. Social ecology reconciled both points of view at least in regard to a general agreement over the key correlates of maltreatment (e.g., cultural norms that legitimize physical punishment of children, poverty, and psychiatric conditions of parents such as depression or drug abuse).

However, identification of correlates offered only a partial understanding of the causal pathways to maltreatment. According to Burgess and

Drais-Parillo (2005), what was missing from the ecological model was an understanding of the actual processes that connected the physical punishment norms or the poverty or the maternal depression to the maltreatment, and subsequently, to delinquency. Consideration of this question gave rise to investigations of negative parent-child interactions, referred to as the social interactional approach (Burgess & Drais-Parrillo, 2005). This laid the foundation for Burgess's life history theory of maltreatment. Beginning with Burgess, we will now present some of the key theories of maltreatment and delinquency derived from the social ecology perspective.

Ecological Theories of Maltreatment and Delinquency

The Life History Theory of Maltreatment

Early in his career, Burgess became interested in examining the patterns of communication that distinguished abusive and neglectful families. Trained in the social sciences, he initially developed his ideas from behavioral and social psychology, sociology, and anthropology. Later, Burgess adopted a genuine social ecology perspective by incorporating behavioral biology (behavioral ecology, behavior genetics, and evolutionary psychology) into his studies of maltreatment.

Burgess observed that even in the presence of risk factors highly correlated with maltreatment, like unemployment (Gil, 1971) or social isolation (Erickson, Egeland & Pianta, 1989), maltreatment was not invariant (Burgess & Drais-Parrillo, 2005). Most parents exposed to these types of environmental stressors or who carry these individual risks do not maltreat their children. Burgess and others (See Patterson, 1976) reasoned that some type of triggering mechanism had to be in place to actually generate the maltreatment. Further study that examined behavioral sequences within families (See Burgess & Conger, 1978; Burgess, 1979) indicated that communication patterns among maltreatment families over-emphasized aversive cues and under-emphasized positive ones. Abusive and neglectful parents and their children reciprocated each other's negative behaviors while overlooking their positive behaviors. For example, if the parents resorted to violence when frustrated their children were more likely to resort to violence when they became frustrated. However, if the parents employed good table manners, their children were less likely to use good table manners. Family members paid attention to and learned more about the negative behaviors and fewer of the positive ones. Burgess and his colleagues further reported that members of maltreatment families were more demanding of each other and less willing to meet those demands (Burgess & Drais-Parrillo, 2005).

Based on these results, Burgess concluded that the triggering mechanism for maltreatment was the family's style of interaction. The pattern of family interaction consisted of learned negative cues presented by both parents and children and reciprocated by each of them. Burgess's assertion is supported by a variety of family therapy approaches, including Virginia Satir's Conjoint Model as well as Functional Family Therapy (Alexander & Parsons, 1982; Alexander, Pugh, Parsons & Sexton, 2000). Satir (1967) observed in her clinical practice that dysfunctional families communicate in a closed manner which impairs opportunities for input. In dysfunctional families, rules are rigid and members are incapable of genuine intimacy. Satir's treatment approach featured the modeling of congruent communication that allowed members to articulate their needs and respond to the needs of others. Functional family therapists also maintain that dysfunction is a product of incongruent communication and they pay particular attention to meta-communication patterns. Meta-communication contains the metaphors and non-verbal cues that signal the real meanings that underscore the message (e.g., anger and resentment). From a Functional Family Therapy perspective, meta-communication is the triggering mechanism for the conflict, or in Burgess's case, the maltreatment. There is abundant clinical and empirical support for Burgess's assertion about social interaction. He extended his line of inquiry to ask, why do these destructive interactions develop?

To answer this question, Burgess presented an evolutionary model of human development which referenced the original theory of ecology, Charles Darwin's Theory of Natural Selection (See Burgess, 2005:305-323). The ecological premise is based on the idea that all living organisms, no matter how primitive or sophisticated, have two commonalities. The molecular structure of all living cells is the same and has remained unchanged throughout the course of evolution. The common strand connecting man to the most primitive "surviving" single-celled organisms and to all other ancestors now extinct is that they all share the same molecules. Whether it is single-celled bacteria, or a simple multi-cellular organism (e.g., a fly or a worm) these creatures use the same molecules to organize their maneuvering through their environment that human beings use to think, feel, and respond to ours (Kandel, 2006).

The second commonality is that the living cell is resilient. The survival of organisms depends on the ability of cells to make adaptations to the environment. From Kandel's (2006) perspective, evolution is a never-ending process in which living cells combine into ever-increasing sophisticated structures to meet the demands of the environment (i.e., it is estimated that the human brain contains a million-trillion neural connections alone). Whether it involves cell adaptations to improve the night vision of predators, to improve the speed of the hunted, or to improve the reasoning abilities of the human brain, the history of life is the history of cellular adaptations to environments.

This is the central idea that underscores life history theory. Any evolutionary successful organism must balance its allocation of time, energy, risk, and resources to meet its own survival and reproduction needs, and that these reproduction efforts are strategic (Burgess & Drais-Parrillo, 2005; See also

Pianka, 1970; Stearns, 1992). Regarding reproduction efforts, parents will employ one of two strategies, which Pianka (1970) referred to as *r* (mating) and *K* (parenting) strategies, based on the environmental conditions they face. When faced with transient and unpredictable environments, parents will pursue *r* (mating) strategies that permit them to reproduce prolifically with low levels of investment in the care of their offspring. *K* (parenting) strategies display evolved traits of higher investment in the care of their offspring in response to competition with other members of their species for limited resources. From the evolutionary perspective, both are rational (cost-benefit) strategies in response to the ecological constraints placed upon the parent.

Burgess and Drais-Parrillo (2005) point out that parents will pursue *r* (mating) strategies in environments where they have, or perceive they have, little ability to increase their life chances or the life chances of their children. Under these conditions, low-parental investment increases the risk of maltreatment. They illustrate their point by citing some of the maltreatment literature concerning the variety of parental traits, like aggressiveness and impulsivity (Burgess, 1997), child traits like physical health problems and step-child status (Lightcap, Kurland & Burgess, 1982), ecological risks like poverty (Wilson, 1987), and social isolation (Garbarino & Kostelny, 1991) affecting low-parental investment strategies.

Although the combination of these traits with certain ecological factors will affect varying levels of parental care, Burgess (2005) further asserts that natural selection has led to the evolution of psychological mechanisms that enable humans to decide on the degree of investment they will make in the care of their children. This investment is based on a cost-benefit analysis. Parental altruism and relatedness to their children, factors essential for the care of children, are driven by the benefits expected from each child weighed against the costs incurred that will result in a reduction of the parent's own chance for survival. Note that Burgess's model pivots on the idea of balancing genetically driven survival and reproductive needs. A parent who experiences social and economic impoverishment, who has poor problem-solving skills, and has a disruptive and aggressive child, will perceive few benefits in providing high quality care.

On the other hand, high parental investment not only ensures reproductive success but also addresses survival needs as well. Parents who employ high investment strategies will raise children who are physically fit, emotionally stable, and intellectually competent. These characteristics improve the parent's own survival chances but also produce benefits for society. Illustrating this point, Burgess (2005:326-327) cites Capaldi and Patterson's (1989) work on the effects of parent management styles on delinquency. Capaldi and Patterson identified four components of high-investment parenting that contribute to pro-social behavior of children: positive reinforcement for pro-social behavior, rational and humane discipline, close supervision, and modeling of effective problem-solving skills.

In summary, Burgess maintains that the causes of maltreatment and its connection to delinquency are an inter-disciplinary task that requires a synthesis of different levels of analysis incorporating biological, psychological, and sociological variables. A similar approach was taken by John Bowlby (1969) who argued that an infant's genetically imprinted drives set off a chain of events leading to maltreatment and psychological disorders. It was Bowlby's ideas that generated the attachment theory movement which is currently the most widely recognized approach in maltreatment studies and provides the clearest understanding of how family dynamics affect delinquency.

Attachment Theory

In his research on displaced children of the Second World War, Bowlby (1969) produced evidence documenting the adverse effects on personality development due to inadequate maternal care, particularly during infancy. He called attention to the acute distress experienced by young children when separated from their loved ones. Although trained as a psychoanalyst, Bowlby disagreed with Freud over several conceptual, clinical, and methodological issues that his attachment approach can aptly be described as an authentic "paradigm shift" (Kuhn, 1970). Psychoanalytic theory assumes that there are only two sources of human motivation: food and sex (Corey, 2005). Bowlby argued that there is a third fundamental drive, attachment, which he defined as any behavior that results in a person attaining and maintaining proximity to some other clearly identified person who is able to provide protection, comfort, and support. This propensity to develop intimate attachments is inherent in human nature. Moreover, it is neither subordinate to, nor derivative from, the drives for food and sex.

Bowlby believed that attachment behavior was organized by means of a control system within the autonomic (involuntary) nervous system (ANS). The ANS is part of the peripheral nervous system responsible for physiological functioning including heart rate, respiration, and digestion (Kandel, 2006:45). Although the ANS can function in tandem with the conscious mind (i.e., regulating sexual arousal), most of the actions are involuntary (i.e., regulating heart rate) without conscious control or sensation and are designed to keep the human alive. The implication is that attachment behavior is a physiological process (much like regulating heart rate) which is essential for sustaining life.

Attachment behavior operates like other processes within the ANS as a regulating system. Bowlby referred to this as environmental homeostasis, a process which maintains a person's relationship to attachment figures, within certain limits of distance and accessibility, using increasingly sophisticated methods of communication. The development of attachment behaviors begins in the neonatal state and continues throughout life and is sustained by reciprocating behaviors between parents and children. Survival of humans, particularly infants, is best insured when proximity to mothers, fathers, and other responsible caregivers is maintained. Threats to infant survival, such as loud noises, feelings of discomfort, exposure to strange persons or objects, or being left alone, trigger these survival-seeking behaviors. Infant signals such as crying universally tend to attract mothers. Once close bodily contact is attained, the aversive signals are terminated and replaced with positive ones such as smiling and clinging.

The desired outcome of infant attachment behavior is the close proximity to the parent figure. However, it is subjectively translated as a sense of security on a cognitive level which is essential for personality growth. Although tolerable lengths of time and physical distance increase with age, older children and adults feel lonely and anxious when separated from their loved ones for any lengthy period of time and will seek out attachment figures during times of stress. To account for the tendency of attachment to become internalized, attachment theorists (Bowlby, 1969; Fahlberg, 1970; Crittenden and Ainsworth, 1989; Bolen, 2000) have articulated the notion of the "representational models of self" in delineating pathways to personality development. During the first year of life, infants develop a set of core beliefs about themselves, their parents, and the world in general based on the way parents communicate and behave toward them (Beck, 1995; McMullin, 2000). Once established, these cognitive models govern how infants feel and think about their parents and themselves, how they expect to be treated by others, and how they plan to behave toward them.

Crittenden and Ainsworth (1989) profiled three principal patterns of attachment and described the family interactions which promote each pattern. The first pattern involves secure attachment. In families with secure parent-child attachment, the child is confident that his/her parents will be available and responsive if he/she would encounter a stressful situation. With this guarantee, the child readily explores his/her environment which facilitates intellectual, emotional, and moral development. The secure relationship is promoted by parents, particularly mothers during the early years of life, who are constantly available, sensitive to the child's signals, and respond in a caring and competent manner. Patterns of communication between securely attached parents and children are characterized by congruent communications and honest expressions of feelings.

The other two patterns described by Crittenden and Ainsworth, anxious-ambivalent and anxious-avoidant, are characteristic of dysfunctional parent-child relationships that can result in child abuse and neglect. The sequence of maltreatment begins with parental insensitivity and unresponsiveness to the infant's genetically imprinted survival drive for attachment to the parents, especially the mother. The subsequent interactions result in the emergence of insecure (or anxious) attachment.

In cases of anxious-ambivalent attachment, the child's bid for proximity is frustrated by the parents' inconsistent responses. The anxious-ambivalent relationships are marked by a lack of stability which increases the persistence and intensity of the attachment behaviors which include feelings of anger. When the mothers respond, they are ambivalent and the child reacts with more distress when separated. Because of the child's uncertainty about whether or not the parent will respond, the child is prone to separation anxiety, tends to cling, and is unwilling to explore the environment. When the parent responds to the child, the experience is unrewarding to both. The anxious-ambivalent relationship is marked by conflict that is promoted by a parent who is available and helpful on some occasions but not others. Threats of abandonment are used as a means of control. Lack of parental supervision is a common symptom of anxious-ambivalent relationships and is a strong predictor of delinquency. Most often, these children are the victims of chronic but less severe maltreatment. Recent evidence uncovered by Lemmon, Verrecchia & Austin (2008) indicates that the high recurrence/low severity male maltreatment victim has the highest risk for subsequent youth offending.

Crittenden and Ainsworth labeled the second pattern of dysfunctional attachment the anxious/avoidant disorder. Of the two, this is the most pathological pattern of attachment disorder. Under these conditions, the child displays little stress when separated from parents and upon reunion avoids rather than seeks proximity with them. In this case, the child has no confidence that he will be cared for or protected. On the contrary, he or she expects to be rejected. In extreme cases, children suffering from anxious/avoidant disorders can develop sociopathic tendencies along with deeply embedded feelings of rage. Bowlby (1969) observed that in some cases of severe avoidant attachment disorders, the signals triggering attachment behaviors were blocked, immobilizing the attachment behavioral system. He called this immobilized response "defensive exclusion" and suggested that part of the autonomic nervous system controlling attachment can be temporarily or permanently deactivated. As a result of these pathological conditions, the signals that would allow the child to experience and share empathy and love are excluded.

Heide and Solomon's (2004) research on the biology of neglect provides further evidence for Bowlby's assertions. Heide and Solomon reported that severe neglect, particularly in infancy, creates traumatic stress that compromises development of the right hemisphere of the brain. The damaged neural circuits in the right hemisphere have significant psychological consequences. Severely neglected children do not function well under stress and do not develop the ability to regulate the intensity and duration of their emotions. These children stay angrier and frightened longer than normal because their ability to reason through these emotions has been impaired. Consequently their behaviors tend to be impulsive and are driven by anger and fear. Moreover, they have difficulty understanding emotions expressed by other people and, as a result, they fail to develop empathy which is a capacity necessary for making moral judgments.

Although some of the earlier criminological theories (Hirschi, 1969) recognized a maltreatment-delinquency connection, the idea that maltreatment was a risk factor for youthful offending was not given serious attention until comparative models were developed in the late 1980s. The following discussion identifies some of the ecological models of youthful offending that feature the maltreatment-delinquency link.

Coercion Theory

Patterson, Capaldi & Bank (1991) articulated a coercion theory of delinquency which illustrates the social interactional approach developed by Burgess and his colleagues (Burgess & Conger, 1978; Burgess, 1979; Burgess & Drais-Parrillo, 2005). Patterson et al. identified two distinct groups of youthful offenders: early starters, who begin their offending in childhood and tend to become chronic criminals, and late starters, who begin their offending in adolescence and continue for only a brief period of time (Patterson et al., 1991; Krohn, Thornberry, Rivera & LeBlanc, 2001). The distinction between early starters and chronic offenders is that their anti-social behavior is caused by poor parental management.

Coercion theory is built on the principles of operant conditioning. The process generally begins with irritable but incompetent parents who negatively scan the child's behaviors so that even neutral actions evoke criticism and verbal assaults (Simons, Simons & Wallace, 2004). These verbal assaults often produce angry and defiant responses from the child who feels unfairly attacked and maltreated (Simons et al., 2004). The result is an escalation of aversive exchanges which reinforces the child's anti-social behaviors as well as the parents' inept parenting (Simons et al., 2004). After the parents have escalated the confrontation and realize that the situation has gotten out of control, they tend to deescalate the threats of punishment. Their inconsistent actions negatively reinforce the child's anti-social responses. Consequently, the child learns that when confronted by authority figures such as teachers or police officers, if he or she escalates the confrontation by becoming more aggressive, the adults will relent. This sequence of negative reinforcements promotes the belief that aggression and violence are effective coping strategies. Unfortunately, this style of social interaction limits the child's life chances. Patterson et al. (1991) reports that coercive youth are more likely to fail in school and be rejected by their peers. As a result, this increases the likelihood of depression and increases the likelihood that youth will associate with other delinquent peers who model and reinforce the same coping strategies.

CHAPTER 7

Prosecuting Juvenile Offenders in Criminal Court

Joseph Sanborn

Introduction

The decision to prosecute juvenile offenders in criminal court is arguably the most important decision made regarding youth who are charged with committing crimes.[1] Without a doubt, this issue is among the most controversial in the field of juvenile justice due primarily to the severity of the stakes involved. If adjudicated in juvenile court, the youth can expect mostly rehabilitation-oriented, relatively brief sanctions, preferably and often even presumptively served in the community or at worst in an institution that more often resembles a school than a prison; moreover, the delinquent record earned in this forum expires when the youth reaches adulthood, assuming there are no additional arrests for criminal behavior. If convicted in criminal court, however, the youth can expect mostly punitive-oriented, long-lasting sanctions, most likely to be served in the same facilities as hard-core, career adult criminals; moreover, the criminal record earned in that forum results in a debilitating and permanent stain on the offender's character, as well as the loss of significant civil liberties, with or without any reoccurrence of crime. It should not be surprising, then, that this topical area attracts individuals driven by serious passions and strong ideology. It hasn't helped matters that many, if not most, of the observations and analyses of the issue have utilized language that is confusing and, at times, downright inaccurate. This chapter hopes to provide a clear and objective explanation of this most important subject, while also discussing the very important implications behind subjecting young defendants to trial in the criminal court.

The Founding of Juvenile Court as an Alternative to Criminal Court

Not that long ago the prosecution of *all* juveniles charged with *any* crime had to occur in criminal court. The reason is that before 1899 there were no juvenile courts. In that year a group of individuals secured permission to open the first juvenile court in the city of Chicago. In a short time every state had a juvenile court system. Juvenile court reformers were concerned about the plight of juvenile offenders being processed en masse in criminal court. This concern ranged from youth whose low-level criminal behavior was ignored due to paling in comparison to the serious crimes of adults, to youth who committed serious crimes themselves and were then subjected to the rigors of criminal courts and prisons. The founding of juvenile court offered an alternative to the extreme results of criminal court. The juvenile court would be a forum dedicated to improving the life-situation of virtually all juvenile offenders, while also trying not to destroy the life-chances of offending youth. Bolstering the optimism of the juvenile court founders was the recent emergence of the field of psychology. Psychology offered the possibility that juvenile offenders actually could be cured instead of merely punished and possibly intimidated into law-abiding behavior. Although the founders of juvenile court opened its doors with profound idealism and hopes for success, they were not blind to the prospect that some juvenile offenders, perhaps the older, more chronic and violent among them, might be beyond the rehabilitative capacities of the juvenile justice system. Consequently, even the first statutes that granted the authority to begin the juvenile court experiment provided an escape clause for the most problematic juvenile criminals: transfer to, or direct prosecution in, criminal court. In other words, even from the very first days of its existence the understanding was that juvenile court was not an all-or-nothing proposition. There would be an opportunity to prosecute some, albeit relatively few, juvenile offenders in criminal court if absolutely necessary.

From the start, what is very critical to realize is that, although all states quickly adopted the idea of juvenile court, not all legislatures were on the same page as to exactly who is a juvenile. The selection of age limits is somewhat arbitrary. According to common law, adult responsibility started at the age of 14. Even youth below that age (and above the age of seven) could be convicted in criminal court if the prosecutor could overcome the presumption that the offender was incapable of forming the intent (or *mens rea*) necessary to be held liable for a crime. In modern times, the vast majority of states settled on the notion that adult responsibility for crime should begin at the age of eighteen. Thus, when the term juvenile is employed today most people are thinking of youth below or at the age of 17. However, from the beginning days, some states elected to end the juvenile court experiment by the time offenders had reached the age of 16 or 17. Not surprisingly, the "juveniles" in the states that have reduced the minimum criminal court age to 16 or 17 historically have accounted for, and today still account for, the majority of "juveniles" prosecuted in criminal court. This is simply because all of the youth of those ages have to be tried in criminal court regardless of their criminal record or severity of the crime at hand.

Another preliminary matter that needs to be addressed is that the legislature is the source of power in determining which juveniles are eligible for prosecution in criminal court. Actually, it is the legislature that determines whether there will be a juvenile court in the first place and what its jurisdiction will and will not include. One of the first items that the legislature must resolve is the age boundary of the juvenile court, or what is the maximum age of its jurisdiction. As explained above, some states have elected to guarantee the prosecution of at least some juveniles in criminal court by adopting 16 or 17 as the maximum age of juvenile court. There are other ways in which the legislature can mandate the criminal prosecution of certain categories of juveniles, which will be examined below. Otherwise, the legislature is powerless to isolate and select a specific juvenile for criminal prosecution. In other words, if, at the time of the crime, a juvenile who is eligible for juvenile court jurisdiction commits a particularly heinous offense that seems to warrant prosecution in criminal court, there is no way for the legislature to personally and directly bring about that result. Instead, the legislature must have granted this authority to a judge or a prosecutor. Judges and/or prosecutors have been empowered by legislatures in all states to transfer some youth to criminal court. Unfortunately some writers in this field use the term legislative transfer to refer to one or more transfer situations. This is inappropriate in that transfer is a decision made regarding a particular juvenile offender. As a term, transfer should be limited to situations in which a youth could have gone to juvenile court, but someone decided this youth should be transferred instead to criminal court. This type of individualized decision is impossible for a legislature to accomplish, and thus there is no such thing as legislative transfer. Instead, there are only judicial and prosecutorial transfers since it is these officials who have been empowered by the legislature to make this individualized decision. Moreover, inasmuch as all of the power to bring about the criminal prosecution of juveniles has been delegated by a legislature, all transfer is legislative in origin. Consequently, it is uninformative and even misleading to identify any particular type of transfer as legislative.

How Juveniles End up Being Prosecuted in Criminal Court

Before discussing the criminal prosecution of juveniles, it is necessary to agree what is a juvenile. Most jurisdictions (i.e., 37 states, the federal jurisdiction, and the District of Columbia) identify 18 years of age as the commencement of adulthood, at least for purposes of criminal prosecution. Thus, from a national perspective, it seems fair to say that any time an offender younger than 18 years of age has been prosecuted in criminal court, this represents a juvenile defendant. From this perspective there are two basic ways for a juvenile to be forced to face prosecution in criminal court. Another way of expressing this outcome is to say that the juvenile has been *excluded* from juvenile court. There are some people who will refer to this issue as *transfer* (as in transfer to criminal court), but the topic is much broader than mere transfer. In other words, while transfer accounts for the presence of some juveniles in criminal court, it does not explain the presence of all youth there; exclusion does. Exclusion occurs when a prosecutor or judge decides to transfer a youth to criminal court (or *discretionary exclusion*), and exclusion occurs when a juvenile has been defined as an adult prior to the commission of the current offense, which means the offender's trial must occur in criminal court (or *mandatory exclusion*). We will consider these in reverse order.

Mandatory Exclusion (or conferring adult legal status on juveniles)

In mandatory exclusion the "youth" was actually an adult, legally speaking, before the offense was committed. This youth left home already legally recognized as an adult despite being at an age below 18, perhaps even considerably below this threshold. In other words, adult status already had been conferred upon this young person *before* the crime, which is why the case must be prosecuted, if at all, in adult court. The legislature can define these categories of youth and can bring about their exclusion from juvenile court without the current and direct assistance of judges or prosecutors. Any juveniles who satisfy the requirements of the category's definition legally transform themselves into adults. To date, there are three categories of juveniles who have been redefined as adults.

The first category has already been discussed. It involves those states that have adopted a minimum criminal court age below 18 years of age. Thirteen states have elected to initiate adult status for prosecution of crimes at the ages of 16 or 17.[2] These states have adopted the mandatory exclusion of "juveniles" from juvenile court jurisdiction by conferring adult status on youth who would be regarded as juveniles throughout most of the country; 16- and 17-year-olds in these states simply are adults when they commit their offenses, and must go, if anywhere, to criminal court.

The second category includes states that regard a juvenile who has been transferred to criminal court in the past as no longer juveniles in actuality, especially (and perhaps only) if the youth has been convicted in criminal court. This category represents a kind of "you can't go home again" approach to crime control. Thirty states consider a juvenile who has been convicted in criminal court to be an adult.[3] Some states require the conviction to be a felony or an offense that qualified for transfer in the first place.

The third and final category allows a youth to "strike out" of juvenile court. So far, this is possible in only one state. Florida law provides that youth who have accumulated three separate felony adjudications that result in three separate commitment dispositions are adults with regard to prosecution for crimes.

Youth in handcuffs and leg irons is escorted by two officers.

All juveniles who have passed the thresholds required in these categories have positioned themselves for mandatory prosecution in criminal court if they commit a crime. As adults, these juveniles cannot face prosecution in juvenile court due to that court's lack of jurisdiction over them (i.e., they are adults). There is no discretion available to court officials; there is no decision to be made, which is why the term mandatory is appropriate. This is the only type of exclusion that is guaranteed to treat all of those finding themselves within the categories equally or in a non-discriminatory fashion. Logically, this brand of exclusion has accounted for the majority of juveniles prosecuted in criminal court.

Discretionary Exclusion (another term for transfer to criminal court)

Discretionary exclusion involves the transfer of juveniles to criminal court by a judge or a prosecutor. Transfer is also commonly referred to as waiver or certification (other terms include remand or decline). Unlike mandatory exclusion, in which there is no choice as to where the case will be prosecuted, transfer means the case *could* have been heard in juvenile court but for the judge's or prosecutor's decision to move the proceeding to adult court. In transfer situations the youth is defined legally as a juvenile at the time of the offense, but this legal status was later changed to that of an adult due to the transfer decision. With mandatory exclusion there is no transfer of jurisdiction or change of legal status because the youth already was defined as an adult (and jurisdiction already attached to criminal court) at the time of the offense.

The legislature determines whether mandatory exclusion will exist, whether transfer will be possible, and how it will occur. Legislatures cannot, by themselves, individually select any particular youth, who is younger than the juvenile court's maximum age and not subject to mandatory exclusion, to be tried in adult court. To enable this selection process, legislatures must authorize someone to determine which youth should be adultified. Legislatures in all 50 states, the federal jurisdiction, and the District of Columbia have elected to do precisely that in granting transfer power to judges and/or prosecutors.

The Two Types of Transfer

Transfer has been aimed historically at two populations of juveniles, each of which is associated with a type of transfer. The first population contains youth that do not appear to be amenable to juvenile treatment efforts (the beyond-rehabilitation group); this evaluation is the primary substance of judicial transfer. The second population contains youth that appear to be worthy candidates for the harsh sentencing available in criminal court (the greater-punishment group); prosecutorial transfer mostly entails deciding which juveniles warrant greater punishment. For the most part, judges have been given transfer power over juveniles who are relatively young and whose offenses are not necessarily very serious, yet appear to be beyond the rehabilitative capabilities of juvenile court. It is possible that despite a young age, certain youth have committed many offenses and have experienced numerous dispositions (or efforts at rehabilitation) in the juvenile justice system. Another attempt to rehabilitate these youth could amount to a waste of resources, and could undermine the attempt to rehabilitate other juvenile offenders. Juvenile court judges have been entrusted with this decision-making power. The power prosecutors have enjoyed has been restricted mostly to older youth whose crimes are more serious or chronic in nature, and for whom rehabilitation, per se, is not a critical consideration. If nothing else, the severity of the offenses or their chronic nature may justify the harsh sanctions available in criminal court. The tendency to divide transfer power between judges and prosecutors in this manner is particularly evident in the 42 jurisdictions that have adopted both forms of transfer (see Sanborn, 1996).

Judicial Transfer

Judicial transfer involves a hearing before a juvenile court judge in which the youth's amenability to juvenile court treatment will be evaluated. Judicial transfer exists in 48 jurisdictions; only four states do not provide for judicial transfer and practice only prosecutorial transfer.[4] The transfer hearing is divided into two stages. The first stage typically is called a *probable cause hearing* because the state is obligated to show probable cause to believe the youth committed the alleged offense. The second stage usually is referred to as the *amenability hearing*, which deals with the youth's suitability to rehabilitation. At the amenability stage, the court will examine a number of factors such as the (1) dimensions of the offense (e.g., violence, gun use, extent of injury to victim), (2) previous delinquent acts (3) treatment record (i.e., number of court appearances and how well the youth performed in previous interventions), and (4) age (i.e., how long does juvenile court have to work with the offender). These four factors, although more complex in nature than as just presented, should account for most of the substance that influences judges in their decision to transfer a youth to adult court.

Judicial transfer is either regular or presumptive. With regular judicial transfer, the burden to prove the youth's nonamenability to treatment (or suitability to transfer) is on the state/prosecutor, where it has been placed traditionally since the early days of juvenile court. One recent development within the regular category is to require the holding of a transfer hearing, usually for youth that are older or more chronic offenders and are facing serious charges. This mandatory hearing exists in only Delaware, Florida, Missouri, and Washington so far. The only mandatory aspect of this provision is conducting the hearing itself. Importantly, if the prosecutor elects not to charge the qualifying offense (that triggers the mandatory hearing), the transfer hearing does not have to occur. Other recent changes in the regular category include the legislature's expanding the number of factors that the prosecutor can argue suggest nonamenability, and requiring judges to explain why they denied transfer despite a serious offense/record.

Presumptive judicial transfer involves eliminating or altering the amenability burden. Fifteen jurisdictions have simply shifted the burden from the state to the defendant so as to require the latter to prove amenability to treatment in juvenile court.[5] The transfer is presumptive because it is presumed it will occur unless the youth can sustain the burden. Presumptive transfer has been targeted mostly for older youth that have accumulated a significant delinquent record and/or have been charged with a serious offense. West Virginia allows judges to certify juveniles as adults when prosecutors show probable cause for certain very serious crimes; there is no amenability burden in these select cases. Similarly, Utah requires serious youth offenders to establish that they were not very culpable and did not act in a violent, aggressive, or premeditated manner.

Traditionally, judicial transfer involves a two-stage hearing. If a transfer is granted, the trial is conducted in criminal court. This is what the vast majority of jurisdictions (46 of 48) with judicial transfer continue to do today. Massachusetts and New Mexico are exceptions to this rule. Instead of requiring that the transfer decision be made prior to trial, these states place the judge's decision to transfer at the conviction/sentencing stage, after trial has been completed. Prosecutors in these states (for certain serious offenses in which they lack direct transfer power) can charge the youth as an adult. This charging power makes the process appear to be prosecutorial transfer. Nevertheless, both states have statutes which clearly disclose that the judge delivers the official word on whether the proceeding is criminal or juvenile at the conviction/sentencing stage, which follows the judge's analysis of traditional transfer criteria. These states have simply delayed the judge's transfer decision until after trial instead of after a mere probable cause hearing. Unlike most other states, Massachusetts and New Mexico can delay this decision because both provide juvenile defendants a right to trial by jury.[6] So, Massachusetts and New Mexico can postpone the juvenile-versus-adult conviction question until after the trial since the trial is sufficiently legally sound to support either a juvenile adjudication or a criminal court conviction.

Prosecutorial Transfer

The second type of discretionary exclusion/transfer is prosecutorial transfer, which results from a charging decision made by the prosecutor. It is important to realize just how discretionary the prosecutor's decision to charge is. Although the rehabilitation potential of the youth is not irrelevant, prosecutorial transfer focuses primarily on three factors: offense, delinquent record, and age. Prosecutorial transfer has two versions, one or both of which exists in 46 jurisdictions; only six states completely lack prosecutorial transfer.[7] The first version is forum-oriented because it allows the prosecutor to charge the youth in either juvenile or criminal court, which means the prosecutor is authorized to select the proper forum/court to hear the case. In the 13 states with this version of transfer, legislatures have granted *concurrent jurisdiction* over some crimes committed by juveniles (depending often on age and record) to both courts.[8] Colorado, Florida, and Montana refer to this practice as the prosecutor's authority to "direct file" charges in criminal court. Concurrent jurisdiction is easy to comprehend. The prosecutor simply picks the court in which to prosecute the youth since both courts legally have jurisdiction over the youth/charges.

The second type of prosecutorial transfer is offense-oriented because it provides that the prosecutor's charging of certain offenses automatically initiates criminal court jurisdiction over the juvenile defendant (age and record can be critical too). These crimes have been excluded from juvenile court jurisdiction and cannot be prosecuted there. Forty-two jurisdictions practice offense exclusion,[9] nine of which also have the concurrent version.[10] Although unlike concurrent jurisdiction, offense exclusion means that charging the triggering offense eliminates a prosecution in juvenile court, the two versions are very similar. To be sure, the decision in concurrent jurisdiction appears to be one-dimensional (i.e., simply picking the appropriate court), while offense exclusion seems multidimensional (i.e., selecting both charges and the court). In both contexts, the prosecutor is making the one primary decision: should the youth be adultified? With concurrent jurisdiction, the prosecutor does not need to worry about which particular charge is filed (as long as it qualifies for concurrent jurisdiction), but in offense exclusion, the prosecutor must be sensitive to the charge if the prosecutor wants to keep the youth in juvenile court. That is, to retain the youth in the juvenile system, the prosecutor will have to "undercharge" or prosecute a non-excluded offense. To transfer via offense exclusion, the prosecutor chooses a qualifying offense and selects prosecution in the criminal court.

Although offense exclusion is not inherently complicated, it has been described in the statutes with such different wording that it is difficult to understand. Statutes have phrased offense exclusion in three generic ways (each with multiple variations). The first concentrates on definitions of people and behavior, and declares that certain crimes are excluded from the definition of what is a child[11] or delinquent act[12] or, similarly, that certain crimes convert the child into an adult.[13] An example of this approach is the Pennsylvania statute which declares that delinquent acts do not include murder. A second way focuses on court jurisdiction and holds that juvenile court either does not have jurisdiction or has jurisdiction unless/except or jurisdiction is excluded/divested when certain crimes are charged.[14]

Another way of saying the same thing is to declare that adult court has original jurisdiction over certain crimes[15] or that certain crimes mean the youth will have to be charged as an adult or must be subject to criminal proceedings.[16] Florida and Montana have complicated matters even more by calling their version of offense exclusion, "mandatory direct file." Direct file is associated with the prosecutor's discretion to select one court or another, but adding the word, mandatory, converts this situation into offense exclusion, removing the ability for the prosecutor to file these charges in juvenile court. Important to remember is that, despite the title, this transfer is still discretionary since prosecutors cannot be forced to charge the offense necessary to trigger the mandatory direct file provision.

Finally, the third way offense exclusion is represented in the statutes specifies that the juvenile court judge shall transfer or waive the case to adult court due to the crime charged by the prosecutor.[17] Statutes in Illinois, Ohio, and Texas as well as some critics (Griffin et al., 1998) refer to this version as mandatory transfer, which is inaccurate because the transfer becomes mandatory only if the excluded offense is charged.

In the first two phrasings of offense exclusion, charging the excluded offense strips juvenile court of its jurisdiction. The prosecutor would need to file these charges in adult court. If the prosecutor fails to establish probable cause for the excluded offense, while demonstrating enough proof for a lesser-included, non-excluded crime, the case/jurisdiction reverts back to juvenile court. Similarly, in the third phrasing of offense exclusion, the jurisdiction of juvenile court is limited to finding probable cause to believe the defendant committed the excluded offense. Thus, the preliminary hearing occurs in juvenile court instead of in criminal court. Again, the transfer is not mandatory since the prosecutor's failure to charge or the juvenile court judge's failure to find probable cause for the excluded offense would keep the case in juvenile court.

Not surprisingly, perhaps, the literature is filled with serious misrepresentations of offense exclusion. Instead of recognizing offense exclusion as a second version of prosecutorial transfer, some observers have identified it as a third and distinct type of transfer (Bishop & Frazier, 2000; Clausel & Bonnie, 2000; Feld, 2000; Torbet et al., 1996). The misrepresentation stems from an incorrect assertion that, unlike concurrent jurisdiction, offense exclusion represents an elimination of discretion and an adoption of automatic or mandatory removal from juvenile court because excluded crimes must be prosecuted in criminal court (Allen, 2000; Dawson, 2000; Feld, 1978, 1989). This is clearly erroneous. The exclusion here is purely discretionary and not mandatory; transfer occurs if, and only if, the prosecutor elects to charge the excluded offense rather than a crime that does not require prosecution in criminal court. It is the crime that must be excluded from juvenile court, not the juvenile. Not only is charging necessarily a discretionary act, no one can force a prosecutor to charge an excluded offense in any case.

Another error involves referring to offense exclusion as legislative transfer or legislative/statutory exclusion (Bishop & Frazier, 2000; Dawson, 2000; Feld, 2000; Griffin et al., 1998; Snyder & Sickmund, 1995; Torbet et al., 1996), which is uninformative since all exclusion from juvenile court is legislative in origin and is statutorily based. Offense exclusion involves the legislators' authorizing prosecutors to transfer by virtue of the charge (which is precisely what happens as well in concurrent jurisdiction situations). More important, perhaps, is that legislative transfer can easily be misconstrued to mean that the transfer is non-discretionary and cannot be applied discriminatorily, which is inaccurate.

Designated Proceedings (Combining Judicial, and Prosecutorial Transfer)

Thus far, the process whereby judges and prosecutors transfer cases to adult court for trial has been examined. The only exception to this was the trial-before-transfer (delayed transfer) procedure adopted in Massachusetts and New Mexico. Recently, Michigan added what it calls a designated proceeding. While Michigan has maintained traditional judicial and prosecutorial transfer provisions for delinquents who are at least 14 years old, the designated proceeding has no minimum age. Prosecutors can designate any case that involves a specified juvenile violation (numerous serious offenses that qualify for concurrent jurisdiction) and can request the judge to designate any other criminal charge. In this respect both judges and prosecutors have an opportunity to transfer juveniles to criminal court via this procedure. Designation means the case has been permanently converted into a criminal proceeding even though the trial occurs in juvenile court. Like Massachusetts and New Mexico, Michigan grants juvenile defendants trial by jury so it can secure an adult conviction via the juvenile court process (once it is designated). The designated proceeding differs from the delayed transfer in that any conviction stemming from this proceeding must be criminal. Nevertheless, like delayed transfer, the judge in a designated proceeding uses transfer-like criteria in determining whether the sentence will be imposed via juvenile or adult court.

Aging out of Juvenile Court (Criminal Prosecution by Becoming an Adult)

Throughout the discussion on discretionary exclusion, the focus has been on youth who were juveniles at the time of the offense, but who were later converted to adult legal status due to a decision to transfer the case to adult court. The assumption underlying this analysis has been twofold: one, that the youth's age at the time of the offense is the pivotal age and, two, that the youth has not become an adult by witnessing an eighteenth birthday in the interim between the offense and prosecution. In the vast majority of jurisdictions, age at the time of the crime controls. Even youth that age into adulthood must still be transferred to criminal court in order to be held criminally responsible for behavior committed while a juvenile. Nevertheless, in Delaware, Oregon, and Wisconsin it is the defendant's age at the time of either arrest/charging, and, in Arizona and Washington, it is age at the time of trial that determine actual age. Thus, in these few states, youth that were legally juveniles at the time of the offense can experience adultification literally and only because they became adults by the time they were prosecuted. Similarly, even some jurisdictions that observe the youth's age at the offense provide that if the accused is not prosecuted until clearly of adult age (such as in the twenties), trial must occur in criminal court, without the need for transfer.

Potential Criminal Conviction (Transfer to Juvenile Court's Second Tier)

In addition to a direct transfer to adult court, several states provide for transfer to a second tier of their juvenile courts. This transfer to a higher level of juvenile court is commonly known as an Extended Juvenile Jurisdiction Prosecution/ Proceeding (EJJ) in Arkansas, Illinois, Kansas, Minnesota, and Montana.[18] Connecticut refers to it as a serious juvenile repeat offender prosecution, and Ohio calls it a serious youthful offender disposition. Rhode Island complicates matters by identifying this process as certification, while transfer to adult court is known as waiver.

Except for youth in Ohio and for some in Montana and Rhode Island, a youth has to be transferred to the second tier, and traditional judicial transfer criteria are employed. Most youth eligible for this internal transfer are those that are subject also to transfer to adult court.[19] In addition, trial and sentencing provisions are similar in the eight states that have this process. Of the eight states, only Montana provides all its juvenile defendants a right to jury trial. Unlike first-tier defendants in the other seven states, second-tier youth are granted this critical right.[20] If found guilty, this is regarded as a juvenile adjudication, provided the youth successfully serves the court's sentence. While Rhode Island forces the judge to give either a juvenile or an adult court sentence, the second-tier sentence in the other seven states is a *combined* or *blended* one. This means that the youth is given both a juvenile and an adult court sentence. The latter is stayed or suspended while the court imposes the juvenile disposition. Eventually, the juvenile court will conduct a review hearing to determine how the youth has fared. Successful completion of the juvenile disposition requires dismissal of the adult sentence. Proof of failure to fulfill the terms of the juvenile disposition, however, means the adult sentence (typically together with an adult conviction) can be imposed.

How Juveniles Can End Up Back in Juvenile Court

If a juvenile has experienced mandatory exclusion, there is no choice in the location of the prosecution. The trial, if any, must occur in criminal court. A case that has been transferred to adult court for prosecution, however, does not necessarily have to stay there. Numerous states permit the criminal court judge or prosecutor to send a case back to juvenile court.[21] This procedure amounts to a reversing of the original transfer decision and understandably has been referred to as *reverse transfer*.

Reverse Transfer

Reverse transfer involves the same examination of the youth's amenability to treatment that occurs in judicial transfer, but a criminal court judge (or prosecutor) conducts the examination, and the amenability burden is always on the youth. Typically, this de-adultification is limited to prosecutorial transfer cases. This makes sense since a judge has already evaluated a youth when judicial transfer occurs.

Interestingly, reverse transfer is possible in Connecticut, Montana, Nebraska, and New York that have only prosecutorial transfer. Reverse transfer exists more often in situations in which offense exclusion has occurred, perhaps to compensate for an overly rigid statute or prosecutor. However, de-adultification is also available when concurrent jurisdiction occurs.[22] Also interesting is that six states allow the prosecutor to initiate the reverse transfer, which makes sense only when offense exclusion is involved.[23] This process compensates for the prosecutor's inability to charge the excluded offense and to keep the youth in juvenile court. Delaware, Georgia, New York, and South Carolina permit prosecutors to make this decision on their own. This essentially converts offense exclusion into concurrent jurisdiction. That is, although the offense is excluded from juvenile court jurisdiction, it can be prosecuted there, as long as the prosecutor files the charge initially in adult court and then transfers it back to juvenile court.

If criminal court does not find probable cause for cases sent there via prosecutorial transfer (i.e., the judge has already found probable cause in judicial transfer), the case should have to be sent back to juvenile court. This is equivalent to offense exclusion charges not being sent to criminal court due to a juvenile court judge's failure to find probable cause. Sending the case back to juvenile court in this context occurs because the criminal court loses jurisdiction over the charge (the charge qualifying for adult court has not been demonstrated). This maneuver is not discretionary (and thus is not transfer), but rather is mandatory. Although this is not reverse transfer, it has been interpreted as such (Griffin et al., 1998). Similarly, if an appellate court determines that a judicial transfer to adult court was done unlawfully, the case must also revert back to juvenile court. This also means criminal court loses jurisdiction over the case. It should not be classified as reverse transfer, but it has been called such (Griffin et al., 1998). Both of these are mandated returns to juvenile court due to adult court's losing jurisdiction because the transfer was unlawful rather than a discretionary choice to reverse the transfer.

Delayed Reverse Transfer

De-adultification is also possible after conviction in adult court when the youth can be given a juvenile court disposition at sentencing; this discretionary sentencing is a *delayed reverse transfer*. This post-conviction return to juvenile court is more likely when prosecutors transferred the case to adult court. This sentencing-based return to juvenile court is sometimes mandatory. Several states demand that some youth who are convicted of charges less serious than the charge that qualified for offense exclusion must be returned to juvenile court for disposition.[24] Colorado and Oregon demand the same in comparable situations in judicial transfer cases. Although this is an example of de-adultification or re-juvenilization, it is not delayed reverse transfer (Griffin et al., 1998). This post-conviction provision amounts to adult court's losing jurisdiction over the case because the offense qualifying for adult court jurisdiction was not sustained. The judge does not have the discretion to retain the case in criminal court and thus the youth must be relocated to juvenile court, not transferred there.

Many states have adopted delayed reverse transfer and give adult court judges the discretion to sentence all or nearly all youth convicted there to juvenile court dispositions.[25] Similarly, provided the conviction is a lesser offense than the concurrent/excluded one, a number of states are willing to let the adult court judge impose a juvenile sentence or to return the case to juvenile court for disposition.[26] The statutes of many of these states provide the adult court judge with criteria similar to that used by juvenile court judges in making the transfer decision.[27]

Unlike the pre-trial reversal of jurisdiction, the post-conviction move to juvenile court in Michigan can still be considered a criminal conviction despite the transfer. Moreover, in some states, the adult court judge will impose a juvenile sentence only after an adult sentence is stayed or suspended.[28] This is the mirror image of the sentencing that takes place in Extended Juvenile Jurisdiction (EJJ) prosecutions. Importantly, the adult court usually retains jurisdiction over the youth while the juvenile disposition is served. Eventually, just as with the EJJ juveniles, the youth that have been given a juvenile disposition will be given a review hearing (often in adult court) to determine whether the juvenile disposition has been completed successfully. Failure to satisfy the disposition terms can result in the imposition of the adult conviction and sentence.

Youthful Offender: Neither Juvenile Adjudication nor Criminal Conviction

Even if the youth are not re-juvenilized via either form of reverse transfer, it is possible for them to end up in a position in-between that of juvenile and adult court despite conviction in adult court. At least 17 jurisdictions use the *youthful offender* (YO) status as a special category of disposition (and record) for juveniles prosecuted in adult court, typically for first time offenders. In 14 jurisdictions YOs can be (or must be) juveniles that have been transferred to adult court.[29] Although the standards for eligibility vary considerably, traditional judicial transfer criteria on the youth's amenability to juvenile court treatment typically are employed in determining whether the juvenile will be sentenced as a YO or as an adult.[30]

Most of these jurisdictions have the adult court judge set a criminal sentence, which is then suspended or stayed while the youth serves a juvenile disposition.[31] In addition to the combined sentence, Massachusetts and Oklahoma allow the judge to select a juvenile or adult sentence; this is the only option available to New Mexico judges. Finally, while Florida modifies the YO sentence considerably (compared to an adult sentence), Kentucky imposes an adult sentence, then reviews the youth's status at the age of 18 to decide whether to continue the sentence or to discharge the youth.

Eight jurisdictions extend YO status to young adults who most likely are in adult court for the first time (not as transfers from juvenile court). Three of these jurisdictions are of concern because their maximum juvenile court age is either 15 (CT, NY) or 16 (SC) years of age, and their YO adults can be as young as either 16 or 17 years of age. YO status in these states serves, in part at least, as compensation for having such a young eligibility for criminal court prosecution. In terms of sentencing, while Connecticut and South Carolina provide for the combined sentence format, New York reduces the YO sentence considerably (a four-year prison sentence is the maximum).

Alabama, Connecticut, New York, Oklahoma, and Vermont emphasize that a YO adjudication is not a criminal conviction. So, although a YO designation often is better than having a criminal conviction (although Kentucky and New Mexico consider it as such), it is not quite as good as having a juvenile adjudication. The YO youth has been neither completely re-juvenilized nor fully adultified.

This first section of the chapter has attempted to accomplish two objectives. The first was to remedy the numerous misinterpretations that have surrounded the area of exclusion in the literature. Hopefully, this presentation has effectively, completely, and accurately described the exclusion process. The second goal was to present the myriad ways in which youth are excluded from the juvenile system, as well as the many ways in which they may be returned, one way or another, to the juvenile system from the criminal court. Most jurisdictions in this country have established a complex and paradoxical network of methods by which youth are both sent to and returned from the criminal court.

Perhaps the message in this setup is simply that as eager as states are to enable the prosecution of violent and chronically criminal youth in the adult system, they also are equally concerned that this power is not abused and have adopted liberal provisions in facilitating the return of at least some youth to the juvenile system.

Questioning Whether and When to Criminally Prosecute Juvenile Offenders

Prosecuting juvenile offenders in criminal court must be put into perspective. This is needed because much of the literature has classified the adultification of youth as criminalizing delinquency (Fagan, 1995; Singer, 1996). The suggestion here is that otherwise trivial offending (i.e., delinquency) is being transformed into something more serious (i.e., criminal) than it really is due to a transfer decision. The same can be said of the notion of the adultification of youth (see Sanborn, 2004), in that it suggests that juveniles are being transformed into adults rather than that their criminal behavior is simply being treated as criminal.

Rather than viewing this issue simply and only as which juveniles should be removed from juvenile court, it is important to remember that this also involves which criminal youth should be immune from criminal liability by remaining in juvenile court. Juvenile court was created as a haven from the criminal court system; offenders were given chances to turn behavior patterns around without harming offenders. There was belief in the system's ability to rehabilitate and the youth's malleability to be reformed. This belief, coupled with a desire to invest in delinquent youth and to not destroy their life chances, was sufficient to tell society that exacting revenge (and possibly securing greater protection for society) via the criminal justice system would not be possible in many situations. Despite serious crime, most youth were to be processed in a system that was created to promote their interests. However, this immunity from criminal prosecution was never meant to apply to all juveniles regardless of the number or severity of their crimes. Both mandatory and discretionary exclusion existed from the very first days of juvenile court (Tanenhaus, 2000). Legislatures had never been willing to give the juvenile system *carte blanche*. So, the question is which, if any, young criminals deserve to be diverted from the criminal justice system to the relatively friendly and forgiving confines of juvenile court. In short, the adultification of youth involves which youth should not be granted diversion from criminal court.

Possible Policy Positions on the Criminal Prosecution of Juvenile Offenders

Three potential exclusion policy positions exist. *Zero exclusion* holds that no youth should be criminally prosecuted (total inclusion of youth within the juvenile system), *total exclusion* seeks the removal of all youth from juvenile court (prosecution of all defendants in criminal court), and *selective exclusion* wants only some youth to be prosecuted in criminal court.

Zero Exclusion (Anti-Exclusion)

Zero exclusionists point to three sets of inadequacies in prosecuting juveniles in adult court: (1) inadequate subjects, (2) inadequate housing, and (3) inadequate results. Inadequate subjects refer to the youth in two contexts: as defendants and as culpable actors. Some critics argue that juveniles are not sufficiently competent to serve in the role of defendant in criminal court (Bonnie & Grisso, 2000; Steinberg & Schwartz, 2000). Juveniles are supposedly not able to participate meaningfully in the adjudicative process, ranging from comprehending the nature of the proceedings to consulting effectively with counsel.

The problem with this assertion is twofold. As U.S. Supreme Court cases have demonstrated, the constitutional basis for competency to stand trial involves a level of awareness that virtually any elementary school student could satisfy (assuming no severe mental impairment exists). Even more important, if adjudicative competence is a real concern, then the youth is likely to receive a much more accurate assessment of this element in adult court, where incompetent youth stand out better in comparison to competent adult defendants. Moreover, while incompetence is recognized as an obstacle to prosecution in criminal court, this condition could be interpreted as a need to adjudicate and to rehabilitate in juvenile court.

Supposedly, juveniles are not sufficiently mature to be culpable for their behavior (Steinberg & Schwartz, 2000; Zimring, 1998, 2000). Three interrelated deficiencies contribute to this relative lack of culpability: the cognitive ability to know/use legal rules, the ability to control impulses, and the ability to resist peer pressure (Zimring, 1998). The problem with this assertion is threefold. First, the abilities are immeasurable and thus cannot meaningfully inform policy. Not only are there rapid and reversible changes in maturity levels during adolescence, there is also considerable variability among youth such that it is not possible to generalize about what any particular adolescent's maturity level should be (Steinberg & Schwartz, 2000).

Moreover, there is no way to gauge what the interaction among the three abilities should mean. For example, what if a youth had excellent cognitive ability but had poor impulse control? Even more intriguing would be a youth who has sufficient cognitive ability and impulse control, but just "had" to participate in the gang-related homicide (and thus couldn't resist peer pressure). This inquiry is also impractical. The analysis would have to be done for *every* offender at the time of the offense. To conduct the examination long after the offense would give only a picture of the offender at the later date. Assessments that pre-date the offense would be unusable for the same reasons.

Finally, the reduced culpability proposition lacks foundation since it is simply not true that all juveniles are immature, and commit crime and/or deserve leniency due to this. In addition, penal proportionality or diminished culpability for some youth does not convert into penal immunity for all youth (Zimring, 1998). At best, the inadequate subjects argument militates against wholesale prosecution of youth in adult court. At worst, the argument grants criminal immunity to youth that display cognitive ignorance, poor self-control, and commit crimes with at least one other person.

The second inadequacy involves the failure of some criminal justice systems to deal properly with the juvenile inmate. There is reason for concern when youth are incarcerated with adults (Bishop & Frazier, 2000). This argument ignores the safety of mixing some adults with some violent youth and of institutionalized juveniles retained in the juvenile system if these would-be-adultified youth were placed in juvenile facilities; it also is irrelevant to those who are put on probation by criminal court. Nevertheless, the concern is legitimate and serious. While this perspective calls strongly for the development of adult penal policy that seeks to prevent the inappropriate and harmful mixture of inmate populations (for which age is one but not the only criterion), it does not invalidate the transfer of any particular youth or negate the appropriateness of exclusion policy.

The final inadequacy is results. Some findings from preliminary research suggest that some offenders processed by criminal court will display more recidivistic tendencies than supposedly comparable youth processed by the juvenile system. Two research projects have documented this. The first compared youth who were matched on current offense and record (as well as age, gender, and race, in part) (Bishop & Frazier, 1991, 1996; Bishop et al., 1989). The transferred youth were rearrested sooner, more often, and for more serious offenses than youth retained by juvenile court, although over the long term (seven years) the differences between the two groups were less significant (Winner et al., 1997).

The second study compared 15- and 16-year-old youth charged with robbery and burglary who were processed by juvenile court in New Jersey with youth of the same ages (and charges) who were prosecuted in criminal court in New York (Fagan, 1991, 1995). The data reveal quicker and more numerous arrests by the youth prosecuted in criminal court. It is impossible to know whether there were two sets of equal offenders in both datasets (the accuracy of current charge and delinquent history can be very unreliable in records, and the juvenile court history of the New York sample was unknown). It cannot be ruled out that the population prosecuted in criminal court was more crimogenic than the juvenile court sample.[32] The most serious charges excluded from juvenile court (like murder) were not examined in either project.[33] Finally, there could have been significant differences in other important aspects of these samples (e.g., probation officer's supervision and arresting practices) that could explain some variation in recidivism.

Nevertheless, the studies suggest caution in expecting exclusion from juvenile court to accomplish crime control goals without fail. They also question the type of exclusion that should occur. The second study primarily examined mandatory exclusion because the 16-year-old New York youth (who likely dominated the study) were adults when they committed their crimes, they were not transferred to adult court. Although the nontransfer policy conclusion drawn by the researchers in both studies was compatible with their anti-exclusion viewpoints, this is certainly not the only conclusion to which the data can lead. It is also plausible to infer that juvenile courts may hold onto some youth far too long, that career criminals should be considered to begin their careers as juveniles rather than as adults, and that for their first appearance in adult court, many youth (especially chronic offenders) should not be granted leniency. The point is that research data do not always or only lead to where the researchers point.

Total Exclusion

Total exclusionists advocate the demise of juvenile court (Ainsworth, 1991; Federle, 1990; Feld, 1990, 1993) with the criminal prosecution of all youthful offenders. There appears to be only one, albeit serious, problem that prompts this perspective: the relative lack of due process in juvenile court proceedings. To be sure, there are potential situations in the standard adjudicatory hearing that make it difficult to receive a fair trial in juvenile court (Sanborn, 1994a). These potential fairness problems militate against the imposition of very punitive dispositions in juvenile court, and the granting of substantial weight to juvenile court records when they are used later to enhance criminal court sentences (Sanborn, 1998, 2000). Although these lapses in due process call for remedy, it is far from certain that the abolition of juvenile court is necessary to accomplish this task.

The question awaiting the success of total exclusion is: Now what? One advocate has proposed that juvenile offenders be given a sentence discount by virtue of age (Feld, 1993). The fact that both common sense and the wisdom of developmental psychologists recognize that adolescent offenders are "all over the map" in competence and culpability, there seems to be little prospect for the age-discount-sentencing format to be adopted. This proposal also ignores the caseload burden it would present adult court. The problem that is marginal in zero-exclusion policy (i.e., we can't transfer because this clogs adult court) becomes central if total exclusion prevails. Moreover, assuming a desire to retain ameliorative interventions into most youthful offenders' lives (i.e., frequent probation and humane institutions), as well as the non-permanence of a juvenile court record (when offending is neither serious nor chronic), there is no need for the due process measures available in criminal court to be extended to the vast majority of juvenile defendants. Total exclusion threatens not only the existence of juvenile court, but also the survival of policies geared to avoid permanently harming the life chances of young criminals.

Zero and total exclusion represent extreme viewpoints. The former asks too much of society (and of juvenile court), while the latter asks too much of criminal court (and hurts more than helps youth). Not surprisingly, none of the 52 legislatures in this country has embraced either proposition. One or more examples of selective exclusion occur in all 52 jurisdictions.

Selective Exclusion: Current Policy

Selective exclusion is a compromise between zero and total exclusion; it seems to be the most reasonable policy (Sanborn, 1996). (This might suggest why it is practiced in *every* jurisdiction in this country.) Although exclusion appears to concern only which juvenile offenders should be rehabilitated versus which should be punished, exclusion involves more than merely the "fit" of rehabilitation. This is clear since the juvenile court's "separate existence is warranted not because of proven rehabilitative success but because leniency toward the young is morally justified and because the risk of failure is worth taking" (Bonnie, 1989:206). The task, then, is to identify when this leniency and risk are no longer warranted. For some individuals, the only situation is when the punishment necessary for the offender exceeds that which is possible in the juvenile system (Zimring, 1998, 2000). Although this certainly is a valid rationale for transfer, it is not the only valid one.

Juvenile court is about limited punishment, but not *only* about limited punishment. Juvenile court is also about a system that should further the youth's best interests, primarily if not exclusively. At some point, however, because of violence and/or chronic offending, it seems reasonable that instead of preserving life chances for youth and exploring their room for reform, society's interests should be promoted. It is also reasonable is for society to identify a threshold beyond which tolerance and criminal immunity will not be countenanced despite the relative youth and immaturity of the offender. At some point, violent behavior and chronic criminality become the appropriate targets of society's condemnation. Some juvenile criminals "are morally responsible, criminally blameworthy actors, who happen to be statutorily defined as children" (McCarthy, 1994:661). Promoting society's interests and condemning behavior are missions best served in criminal court. Keeping youth who do not "belong" in juvenile court frustrates these missions, and threatens the fragile parameters and orientation of juvenile court. Prosecuting violent/chronic offenders in juvenile court encourages legislatures to permit judges to impose extended sentences, to provide the victim a (potentially hostile and counterproductive) voice throughout the process (Sanborn, 2001), and to allow juvenile court records to dramatically impact subsequent criminal court sentencing (Sanborn, 1998, 2000). These outcomes violate both the level of rights extended the defendant and the rehabilitation purpose of juvenile court. These measures and other changes in the orientation of the juvenile court (such as pursuing the protection of society) have been cited by individuals (usually total exclusionists) as examples of the *criminalization* of juvenile court (Feld, 1984). This means juvenile court is becoming the clone of criminal court; the implication is that we don't need two courts doing the same thing.

Rationales Supporting Selective Exclusion

Three philosophies that influence juvenile justice suggest when exclusion should exist. Rehabilitation-oriented individuals defend transfer when treating certain youth is a waste of resources, and when these youth undermine the treatment or physical safety of other youth. Some juvenile courts lack the facilities/ programs with which to help some offenders (Bishop, Frazier & Henretta, 1989; Fagan & Deschenes, 1990; Feld, 1978). Critics allege it is wrong for juvenile court to abandon youth to adult court where treatment is not a priority. However, it is unfair to blame juvenile court for the failings of adult court. Moreover, it is unreasonable to force the juvenile system to accommodate all youth, regardless of their problems and the number of years required to resolve them (Sanborn, 1994a). Chronic, less serious offenders are the likely targets for rehabilitation-based judicial transfer, but first- or second-time serious offenders can be candidates as well, especially if the jurisdiction has no (or only limited) prosecutorial transfer. These *beyond-rehabilitation* youth can thus be transferred when they have committed seemingly or relatively non-serious offenses, and the transfer can be granted without an expectation or desire of lengthy sentences if they are convicted in criminal court. Similarly, it should be noted that mandatory exclusion can easily produce the same results. States with reduced ages for criminal court jurisdiction and states that demand criminal prosecution for anyone who has been convicted previously in criminal court will guarantee that many "juvenile" defendants in criminal court will be facing non-serious charges there. These elements are critical to remember since zero exclusionists will often emphasize that juveniles who have committed non-violent crimes are frequently found in criminal court, and that they end up receiving probation or short terms of incarceration (which obviously are quite possible in juvenile court). Of course it is possible that some youth are being inappropriately transferred to criminal court. But what is most likely happening here is that, although multiple potential scenarios legitimately call for the criminal prosecution of juvenile offenders, anti-exclusion types recognize or will allow only one (the need for lengthy sentences for violent juvenile offenders in criminal court) and then cry foul when the sentences are not lengthy and the offenders are not violent.

Crime control advocates support transfer to obtain lengthy sentences and to secure retribution and the condemnation of behavior. Promoting deterrence, incapacitation, and community protection would also be relevant (Bishop & Frazier, 1991; Feld, 1978, 1984; Zimring, 1991). Although crime control individuals neither expect nor want less deterrence to result from transfer, exclusion is not simply a matter of whether recidivism would be prevented better by one court or the other (Arthur & Schwartz, 1993). There might be a decent prospect for acquittal in criminal court vis-à-vis juvenile court, and there is no guarantee that adult court will effectively sentence young criminals convicted there. Regardless, transfer cannot be held hostage to the uncertainties and inadequacies of criminal court. Older and more serious or chronic offenders are usually the ones targeted for transfer by crime control individuals, who tend to prefer prosecutorial transfer.

Due process-oriented persons defend transfer on the grounds that it encourages a more fortified foundation of justice in criminal court. This transfer appears most justifiable either when the charge is very serious or when the jurisdiction's adult court can use a juvenile record to enhance a criminal sentence (Sanborn, 1996). This "greater justice" rationale could explain, in part, why some legislatures have excluded some very serious crimes from juvenile court.

Selecting the Proper Methods of Selective Exclusion

Although various philosophies agree that exclusion should exist, not all forms of exclusion will receive equal support. While mandatory exclusion is attractive for its equal handling of youth, it can be overinclusive. While discretionary exclusion can avoid being overinclusive, youth can end up being handled discriminatorily. Mandatory exclusion includes two very different situations.[34] While it makes sense to let a criminal conviction confer adult status on a youth, it is not clear whether it is wise to reduce the maximum juvenile court age to 15 or 16 years of age. Unless lowering the age reflects when adulthood truly begins, it is unnecessary and counterproductive to have to adultify all 16- and 17-year-olds when transfer can accomplish this task for the most serious or chronic offenders.

The next question is which type of transfer should exist. Those who want to limit transfers tend to prefer judicial waiver because judges are known for not certifying youth as adults for prosecution (McCarthy, 1994; Sanborn, 1994a). A good deal of the recent expansion of prosecutorial transfer (and presumptive judicial transfer) can be explained by judges' failure to exercise their authority. One rationale used to support judges' control of transfer is to declare that it is "more like a sentencing than a charging decision" (Zimring, 2000:218). First and foremost, transfer is a charging decision: Should the youth be charged as a criminal or diverted from criminal court? This decision properly belongs to a prosecutor; granting judges this authority violates separation of powers. There are other problems with relying exclusively upon judicial transfer. At least in cases of serious or chronic offenders, amenability to treatment should not be a primary concern because society's interests should prevail over those of the youth. A murder prosecution should not take place in juvenile court. In judicial transfer, probation officers and/or clinicians conduct treatment analyses, which influence and may determine the outcome of a transfer decision. This arrangement is inappropriate in cases involving serious or chronic offenders because probation officers and clinicians are not accountable to the public, and should not possess such significant charging power. Finally, treatment evaluations entail very subjective estimates of rather vague elements, which should not be controlling in the prosecution of serious or chronic cases; they also lead almost inevitably to considerable disparity in transfer decisions. Transfer becomes a "luck of the draw," depending upon which officials are involved.

Letting the judge make a transfer decision based on the charges is also a problem. In serious or chronic cases, the public deserves to be represented by an advocate; this is a prosecutor's role, not a judge's. Prosecutors see the worst-case scenario and should conduct charging analysis. A judge or jury can correct any overcharging later. Once jeopardy has attached, charges cannot be raised; a judge's tempered view should not initiate charging. Judges are also not in a position to gauge the severity of the charges; they do not interview victims/witnesses and arresting officers. Moreover, judges do not have the sufficient experience with which to evaluate charges. Finally, in large cities (where the majority of transfers occur), unless a single judge transfers, there is little chance to achieve equality in transfer decisions; multiple judges will produce multiple charging views and decisions. Although there is no guarantee of equality if prosecutors control transfers, there is a better chance of achieving it. Larger prosecutors' offices have a charging unit and/or a supervisor who monitors charging decisions. This should enhance the possibility of reaching fairly uniform transfer decisions.

Prosecutors should control the more serious charges and the more chronic felons, while judges should make choices for the younger and less serious chronic offenders. Judges should control cases when it is presumed that the youth's best interests (and diversion to juvenile court) should prevail, while prosecutors should control cases when it is presumed that society's best interests (and adultification/criminal prosecution) should prevail. Perhaps the only unresolved aspect of prosecutorial transfer is whether offense exclusion or concurrent jurisdiction should be practiced. Offense exclusion makes sense for the most serious felonies, particularly for older offenders. One could question the appropriateness of a statute that permitted one 17-year-old to be charged with murder in juvenile court and another (seemingly) comparable youth to face the same charges in adult court. This could be a denial of equal protection. The arrangement that has been adopted by several jurisdictions makes sense. While the most serious charges are subject to offense exclusion (which is a statement that a matter this serious does not deserve to be diverted from criminal court), less serious felonies are eligible for concurrent jurisdiction so prosecutors can elect to send particularly troublesome youth (if not charges) to criminal court. Judges also have the power to send younger, less serious but more intractable juvenile offenders to adult court.

In the end it is important to recognize that exclusion from juvenile court is a rational policy, regardless of whether every youth prosecuted in criminal court should have faced that fate. Much of the motivation in having youth prosecuted in criminal court, especially when it comes to transferring individuals there, will be influenced by the severity and amount of juvenile crime plaguing any one location. Serious crimes, which also receive substantial publicity, are particularly prone to end in criminal prosecution.

The future of this decisionmaking will rely heavily upon just how frequently youth commit those serious crimes. Recently, there has been a decrease in the overall amount of juvenile violence, which not coincidentally has been accompanied by a reduction in legislative initiatives geared to remove youth from the juvenile system. Although this lower crime trend may persist for some time, it is doubtful that the vast machinery of exclusion will be dismantled any time soon. At the same time, the existence of this machinery may be just what the juvenile court must have available to it in order to convince the public that it can serve the interests of both youthful offenders and society, and that it deserves the continued support of the community.

Recent Developments and Future Considerations

Although critics have raised the hue and cry asserting that great injustices have resulted from the transfer of masses of juvenile offenders to criminal court, data suggest something else altogether. The great juvenile crime surge of the mid-80s to mid-90s, which led to the adoption of much of the current legislation on excluding youth from juvenile court, has subsided (although there has been a slight rebound or upswing in the number of juvenile crimes). Not surprisingly, the number of juveniles transferred to criminal court has also dropped. Of course, the severity and volume of juvenile offenses are irrelevant to transfer decisions when mandatory exclusion is involved. Judges and prosecutors cannot be blamed for the presence of juvenile offenders in criminal court when mandatory exclusion has brought about the prosecution of these youth in criminal court.

There has also been a dearth of activity in legislation addressing this issue. There have been no modifications in the area of mandatory exclusion. Alaska, Delaware, Indiana, Montana, and New Jersey have somewhat expanded the scope of their prosecutorial transfer provisions, while South Dakota and Tennessee have slightly expanded their judicial transfer measures. Oklahoma has removed the possibility for 15-, 16-, and 17-year-olds charged with first degree murder to be eligible for reverse transfer. There has been some change in the opposite direction as well. While Illinois has converted some drug-related crimes from the category of offense exclusion to presumptive judicial transfer, Arizona, Arkansas, Connecticut, and Illinois have either adopted or expanded reverse transfer.

Most of the activity in this area is probably the campaign waged by anti-exclusionists. Much of this initiative has been supported by the MacArthur Foundation. For example, the increase in research projects and articles that have supposedly established that juveniles are incompetent to stand trial in criminal court completely lacks credibility. The works in this area tend to be marked more by ideological zeal than scientific analysis. The inquiries into the fate of some youth who end up prosecuted in criminal court, however, reveal serious problems. Although the problems do not call for altogether abandoning the prosecution of juvenile offenders in criminal court (as the ideology suggests), they do disclose the fact that legislatures have not followed through in enacting policy in this area. Essentially, many states have done nothing more than enable the transfer of juveniles into the adult system without ensuring their safety and proper treatment. It is time for legislatures to address this critical omission.

As final thoughts concerning the criminal prosecution of juvenile offenders, one needs to reflect on the "worlds" created by the possible policy positions. In other words, what would the consequences be if any one of the policies were to dominate the decision to prosecute juvenile offenders in criminal court? We already know the answer to this question regarding selective exclusion since it is the policy we have in place. An unresolved question is what adjustments might be necessary to better effectuate the policy? In other words, how can the system ensure the safe and proper treatment of juvenile offenders prosecuted in criminal court? The more intriguing issues concern the consequences for the systems resulting from the adoption of either of the other two policies.

First, there is the world or model of total exclusion or the prosecution of all juvenile offenders in criminal court. This least recommended and least likely scenario could produce some Draconian results. Probably the most dramatic and problematic consequence would be an extreme overload of the criminal court's capacity to prosecute offenders, even if some offenses were decriminalized. A 30 to 40 percent increase in the overall criminal defendant population (via the addition of all juvenile criminal offenders) would very likely result in either massive *nolle prossing* of cases (perhaps primarily the less serious offenses of youth, which was one of the original motivations behind the founding of juvenile court) or even greater pressures to plea bargain and to quickly and informally dispose of the vast majority of cases. It is simply impossible to fathom the additional prosecution of countless numbers of juvenile defendants, especially if great numbers of them exercised their newly found constitutional right to jury trial (merely doubling the current rate in criminal court would be overwhelming). Even the criminal courts' hiring of all the former employees of the juvenile court would not alleviate the problem. In addition to the resource crisis is the prospect that discounted sentencing for youth would not be adopted, juvenile-oriented facilities (or at least those who truly attempt to rehabilitate) would be abandoned, and court records would be very permanent and debilitating.

Embracing the model of zero exclusion (the prosecution of all juvenile offenders in juvenile court) is equally daunting. There would be some concern about the juvenile court's ability to handle the increase in caseload. Dispositional resources would be similarly taxed, if not overwhelmed. More troublesome is the prospect of juvenile court's adjudicating hardcore 17-, 18-, and 19-year-old defendants facing charges of multiple murders or rapes (committed prior to their eighteenth birthday), and perhaps having a lengthy record of equally violent conduct as well. In most states the sentencing power of juvenile courts would have to be enhanced considerably unless the prospect of releasing violent murderers/rapists from custody after serving only a year or two of incarceration would be acceptable (since most states currently lose control/jurisdiction once the offender turns 21 years old). Of course, accepting the latter choice would seem to erase any chance society has of deterring juvenile criminals.

On the other hand, the idea that juvenile courts could incarcerate serious and chronic offenders for a dozen or more years, in punitive-oriented, prison-like facilities without making drastic changes to the court's operation (e.g., requiring jury trials), seems implausible. Nevertheless, it would be interesting to consider the impact that the most violent or chronic juvenile offenders would have on the less serious and more salvageable juvenile offenders. It would also be surprising if the juvenile courts were able to maintain the best-interests-of-the-juvenile-approach they currently employ with the vast majority of offenders processed there. At the same time, it is difficult to imagine that prosecuting all juvenile offenders in juvenile court would accomplish much in the way of protecting society. Indeed, it would seem that adopting a zero exclusion policy would exact very serious costs and consequences for simply avoiding the prosecution of the few violent and chronic juvenile offenders in criminal court.

Endnotes

[1] Although this chapter focuses on youth that are forcibly removed from juvenile court by the state, it is important to note briefly that several states allow juveniles to choose to transfer themselves to criminal court. In addition, some juveniles do not fight the state's effort to forcibly exclude them from juvenile court. Most youth would prefer to be processed by the juvenile court. Nevertheless, some defendants may consider a criminal court prosecution to be preferable for one or more reasons, such as to secure bail, to obtain a jury trial and other trial-related rights, and to be sentenced more leniently. Thus, not all youth that are prosecuted in criminal court have been removed from juvenile court against their will.

[2] The three states that end juvenile court jurisdiction at 15 are: CT, NY, NC. The ten states that end juvenile court jurisdiction at 16 are: GA, IL, LA, MA, MI, MO, NH, SC, TX, and WI.

[3] There are 30 states that consider a juvenile convicted in criminal court to henceforth be an adult in terms of prosecution for criminal behavior. They are: AL, AZ, CA, CT, DE, DC, FL, HI, ID, IN, KS, LA, ME, MI, MS, MO, NV, NH, ND, OH, OK, OR, PA, RI, SD, TN, UT, VA, WA, and WI.

[4] The four states with only prosecutorial transfer are: CT, MT, NE, and NY.

[5] There are 15 jurisdictions that practice presumptive judicial transfer. They are: AK, CA, CO, DC, IL, KS, ME, MN, NV, NH, NJ, ND, PA, RI, and SD.

[6] Actually, both Massachusetts and New Mexico provide defendants in juvenile court a jury of six members, while adult defendants are given 12 jurors. In order to ensure the validity of an adult conviction, should that be the judge's decision, youth in the delayed judicial transfer trial are given jury trials with 12 members.

[7] The six states without prosecutorial transfer are: HI, ME, MO, NH, SD, and TN.

[8] The 13 states practicing concurrent jurisdiction are: AZ, AR, CA, CO, FL, GA, LA, MT, NE, SC, VT, VA, and WY.

[9] Only ten states do not practice prosecutorial transfer. They are: AR, CO, HI, ME, MO, NE, NH, SD, TN, and WY.

[10] The nine states with both offense exclusion and concurrent jurisdiction are: AZ, CA, FL, GA, LA, MT, SC, VT, and VA.

[11] Eight jurisdictions practice offense exclusion by limiting the definition of a child. They are: DC, IL, KS, MN, NM, OH, OK, and SC.

[12] Three states practice offense exclusion by limiting the definition of delinquent act. They are: MS, NV, and PA.

[13] Four states hold that certain crimes convert a child into an adult. They are: MA, NY, OK, and RI.

[14] Eleven states divest juvenile court from having jurisdiction of certain offenses. They are: AL, AK, IL, IN, LA, MD, MA, MS, NV, VA, and WA.

[15] Seven states declare that adult court has jurisdiction over certain offenses. They are: GA, IA, LA, ND, UT, WA, and WI.

[16] Fourteen states declare that certain offenses mean criminal court has jurisdiction. They are: AL, AZ, CA, DE, FL, ID, IL, IA, MT, OK, OR, SC, UT, and VT.

[17] The 16 jurisdictions that employ this language are: CT, GA. FED, IL, IN, KY, MI, MN, NJ, NC, ND, OH, SC, TX, VA, and WV.

[18] Delaware and New Hampshire refer to extended jurisdiction in their statutes. However, this term in both states merely means juvenile court has jurisdiction over youth for a year or two longer than that that applies to typical youth.

[19] Arkansas, Montana, and Rhode Island have significant exceptions to this standard, such as no minimum age for any felony charge (RI), murder (AR) or other serious charges (MT) to be sent to the juvenile court's second tier. Transfer provisions in these states are not that permissive or broad.

[20] Juveniles who demand a jury trial in Connecticut are forced to go to adult court to collect the right. They must waive the right to stay in juvenile court.

[21] There are 17 states that provide for reverse transfer. They are: AR, CT, DE, GA, IA, MD, MS, MT, NE, NV, NY, OK, PA, SC, VT, WI, and WY. Although New Hampshire and Tennessee officially provide for reverse transfer, the provisions are so narrow they are virtually non-existent.

[22] Five states practicing concurrent jurisdiction permit reverse transfer. They are: AR, MT, NE, VT, and WY.

[23] The six states that allow prosecutors to reverse transfer in offense exclusion cases are: CT, DE, GA, NY, OK, and SC.

[24] The six states that demand a return to juvenile court in this context are: AR, KS, NY, VT, VA, and WI.

[25] The nine states that allow the criminal court judge this much discretion are: CA, FL, ID, MI, MO, OK, SC, VA, and WV.

[26] The eight states that allow the criminal court judge to return the case to juvenile court are: AK, CO, GA, IL, MA, NM, OR, and PA.

[27] The eight states that provide criteria to the criminal court judge are: AK, CO, FL, IL, OK, OR, MI, and MO.

[28] The eight states that impose a criminal court sentence prior to a juvenile court one are: ID, IA, MA, MI, MO, OK, VA, and WV.

[29] The 14 jurisdictions that allow or require YOs (youthful offenders) to be transferred from juvenile court are: AL, AR, CO, DC, FL, IA, KY, MA, NM, OK, SC, VT, VA, and WY.

[30] The nine jurisdictions that employ transfer criteria in determining YO status are: AL, AR, DC, FL, MA, NM, OK, SC, and VT.

[31] The 11 jurisdictions that impose an adult sentence first for YOs are: AL, AR, CO, DC, IA, MA, OK, SC, VT, VA, and WY.

[32] Perhaps the most disturbing aspect of the Florida study was the researchers' ability to find 3,000 purportedly matched pairs of youth who apparently were not treated equally in the transfer decision. Some, and perhaps most, of the difference in the charging of these youth – apart from any real differences in the offenders – is the county/court in which the charging occurred. Prosecutors in some court districts believe their juvenile courts work well (Sanborn, 1994a). This could explain their willingness to keep some youth in the juvenile system and explain better performances by some youth.

[33] In addition, anyone from the transferred group who actually served more than a year in prison was purposely excluded from the sample/comparison group, which could have skewed the recidivism rates of this group.

[34] This analysis will not examine the esoteric Florida three-strikes provision.

References

Ainsworth, J. (1991). "Re-imaging Childhood and Reconstructing the Legal Order: The Case for Abolishing the Juvenile Court." *North Carolina Law Review*, 69:1083-1133.

Allen, F.A. (2000). Forward. In J. Fagan & F.E. Zimring (eds.) *The Changing Borders Of Juvenile Justice: Transfer of Adolescents to the Criminal Court*, pp. ix-xvi. Chicago, IL: University of Chicago Press.

Arthur, L.G. & L.J. Schwartz (1993). "Certification: An Overview." *Juvenile & Family Court Journal*, 44(3):61-71.

Bishop, D.M. & C.E. Frazier (2000). "Consequences of Transfer." In J. Fagan & F.E. Zimring (eds.) *The Changing Borders of Juvenile Justice: Transfer of Adolescents to Criminal Court*, pp. 227-276. Chicago, IL: University of Chicago Press.

Bishop, D.M. & C.E. Frazier (1996). "Race Effects in Juvenile Justice Decision-Making: Findings of a Statewide Analysis." *Journal of Criminal Law and Criminology*, 86:392-414.

Bishop, D.M. & C.E. Frazier (1991). "Transfer of Juveniles to Criminal Court: A Case Study and Analysis of Prosecutorial Waiver." *Notre Dame Journal of Law, Ethics & Public Policy*, 5:281-302.

Bishop, D.M., C.E. Frazier & J.C. Henretta (1989). "Prosecutorial Waiver: A Case Study of a Questionable Reform." *Crime & Delinquency*, 35(2):179-201.

Bonnie, R.J. (1989). "Juvenile Homicide: A Study in Legal Ambivalence." In E.P. Benedek & D.G. Cornell (eds.) *Juvenile Homicide*, pp. 185-217. Washington, DC: American Psychiatric Press.

Bonnie, R.J. & T. Grisso (2000). "Adjudicative Competence and Youthful Offenders." In T. Grisso & R.G. Schwartz (eds.) *Youth on Trial: A Developmental Perspective on Juvenile Justice*, pp 73-103. Chicago, IL: University of Chicago Press.

Clausel, L.E. & R.J. Bonnie (2000). "Juvenile Justice on Appeal." In J. Fagan & F.E. Zimring (eds.) *The Changing Borders of Juvenile Justice: Transfer of Adolescents to the Criminal Court*, pp. 181-206. Chicago, IL: University of Chicago Press.

Dawson, R.O. (2000). "Judicial Waiver in Theory and Practice." In J. Fagan & F.E. Zimring (eds.) *The Changing Borders of Juvenile Justice: Transfer of Adolescents to the Criminal Court*, pp. 45-81. Chicago, IL: University of Chicago Press.

Fagan, J. (1995). "Separating the Men from the Boys: The Comparative Advantage of Juvenile versus Criminal Court Sanctions on Recidivism among Adolescent Felony Offenders." In J.C. Howell, B. Krisberg, J.D. Hawkins & J.J.Wilson (eds.) *Serious, Violent, and Chronic Juvenile Offenders: A Sourcebook*, pp. 238-260. Thousand Oaks, CA: Sage Publications.

Fagan, J. (1991). *The Comparative Impacts of Juvenile Court and Criminal Court Sanctions on Adolescent Felony Offenders*. Final Report to the National Institute of Justice. Washington, DC: U.S. Department of Justice.

Fagan, J. & E.P. Deschenes (1990). "Determinants of Juvenile Waiver Decisions for Violent Juvenile Offenders." *Journal of Criminal Law and Criminology*, 81(2):314-347.

Federle, K.H. (1990). "The Abolition of the Juvenile Court: A Proposal for the Preservation of Children's Legal Rights." *Journal of Contemporary Law*, 16:23-51.

Feld, B.C. (2000). "Legislative Exclusion of Offenses from Juvenile Court Jurisdiction: A History and Critique." In J. Fagan & F.E. Zimring (eds.) *The Changing Borders of Juvenile Justice: Transfer of Adolescents to the Criminal Court*, pp. 83-144. Chicago, IL: University of Chicago Press.

Feld, B.C. (1993). *Justice for Children: The Right to Counsel and the Juvenile Court*. Boston MA: Northeastern University Press.

Feld, B.C. (1990). "The Punitive Juvenile Court and the Quality of Procedural Justice: Disjunctions Between Rhetoric and Reality." *Crime & Delinquency*, 36(4):443-466.

Feld, B.C. (1989). "Bad Law Makes Hard Cases: Reflections of Teen-Aged Axe-Murderers, Judicial Activism, and Legislative Default." *Law and Inequality: A Journal of Theory and Practice*, 8:1-101.

Feld, B.C. (1984). "Criminalizing Juvenile Justice: Rules of Procedure for Juvenile Court." *Minnesota Law Review*, 69:141-276

Feld, B.C. (1978). "Reference of Juvenile Offenders for Adult Prosecution: The Legislative Alternative to Asking Unanswerable Questions." *Minnesota Law Review*, 62:515-618.

Griffin, P., P. Torbet & L. Syzmanski (1998). *Trying Juveniles in Adult Court: An Analysis of State Transfer Provisions*. Washington, DC: Office of Juvenile Justice and Delinquency Prevention, Office of Justice Programs.

McCarthy, F.B. (1994). "The Serious Offender and Juvenile Court Reform: The Case for Prosecutorial Waiver of Juvenile Court Jurisdiction." *Saint Louis University Law Journal*, 38:629-671.

Sanborn, J.B. (2004). "The 'Adultification' of Youth." In P.J. Benekos & A.V. Merlo (eds.) *Controversies in Juvenile Justice and Delinquency*, pp. 143-164. Newark, NJ: Lexis-Nexis/Matthew Bender & Co., Inc.

Sanborn, J.B. (2001). "Victims' Rights in Juvenile Court: Has the Pendulum Swung Too Far?" *Judicature*, 85(3):140-146.

Sanborn, J.B. (2000). "Striking out on the First Pitch in Criminal Court." *Barry Law Review*, 1(1):7-61.

Sanborn, J.B. (1998). "Second-Class Justice, First-Class Punishment: The Use of Juvenile Records in Sentencing Adults." *Judicature*, 81(5):206-213.

Sanborn, J.B. (1996). "Policies Regarding the Prosecution of Juvenile Murderers: Which System and Who Should Decide?" *Law & Policy*, 18(1, 2):151-178.

Sanborn, J.B. (1994a). "Certification to Criminal Court: The Important Policy Questions of How, When, and Why." *Crime & Delinquency*, 40(2):262-281.

Sanborn, J.B. (1994b). "Remnants of Parens Patriae in the Adjudicatory Hearing: Is a Fair Trial Possible in Juvenile Court." *Crime & Delinquency*, 40:599-615.

Singer, S.I. (1996). *Recriminalizing Delinquency: Violent Juvenile Crimes and Juvenile Justice Reform*. New York, NY: Cambridge University Press.

Snyder, H. & M. Sickmund (1995). *Juvenile Offenders and Victims: A Focus on Violence*. Washington, DC: Office of Juvenile Justice and Delinquency Prevention, Office of Justice Programs.

Steinberg, L. & R. Schwartz (2000). "Developmental Psychology Goes to Court." In T. Grisso & R.G. Schwartz (eds.) *Youth on Trial: A Developmental Perspective on Juvenile Justice*, pp. 9-31. Chicago, IL: University of Chicago Press.

Tanenhaus, D.S. (2000). "The Evolution of Transfer out of the Juvenile Court." In J. Fagan & F.E. Zimring (eds.) *The Changing Borders of Juvenile Justice: Transfer of Adolescents to the Criminal Court*, pp. 13-43. Chicago, IL: University of Chicago Press.

Torbet, P.M. (1996). *Juvenile Probation: The Workhorse of the Juvenile Justice System. Juvenile Justice Bulletin* March 1996. Washington, DC: U. S. Department of Justice, Office of Juvenile Justice and Delinquency Prevention.

Torbet, P., R. Gable, H. Hurst IV, I. Montgomery, L. Szymanski & D. Thomas (1996). *State Responses to Serious and Violent Juvenile Crime*. Washington, DC: Office of Juvenile Justice and Delinquency Prevention.

Winner, L., L. Lanza-Kaduce, D.M. Bishop & C. Frazier (1997). "The Transfer of Juveniles to Criminal Court: Re-examining Recidivism over the Long Term." *Crime & Delinquency*, 43(4):548-563.

Zimring, F.E. (2000). "Penal Proportionality for the Young Offender: Notes on Immaturity, Capacity, and Diminished Responsibility." In T. Grisso & R.G. Schwartz (eds.) *Youth on Trial: A Developmental Perspective on Juvenile Justice*, pp. 271-290. Chicago, IL: University of Chicago Press.

Zimring, F.E. (1998). *American Youth Violence*. New York, NY: Oxford University Press.

Zimring, F.E. (1991). "The Treatment of Hard Cases in American Juvenile Justice: In Defense of Discretionary Waiver." *Notre Dame Journal of Law, Ethics & Public Policy*, 5:267-280.

CHAPTER 8

Youth Behind Bars:
Doing Justice or Doing Harm?

Eric J. Fritsch
Tory J. Caeti

Introduction

The practice of incarcerating juveniles for delinquent acts has a long history in the United States. Newer strategies and alternative sanctioning systems, such as boot camps, have also become increasingly popular in recent years. However, controversy exists over whether placing youth behind bars does more harm than good. Some argue that incarcerating juveniles protects society from further victimization, while others argue that the criminogenic environment of juvenile institutions and adult prisons only serves to further perpetuate delinquency. Additionally, the increasing availability of alternative sanctions and placements might lead to "net widening" where juveniles who would otherwise receive probation receive terms of incarceration. This chapter will provide a brief history of juvenile institutions as well as a discussion of the changing assumptions that influence juvenile correctional policy. In addition, policy implications will be discussed.

History of the Issue

In the past, there was no distinction between juveniles and adults in the courts or other societal institutions. Prior to the twentieth century, juveniles were essentially chattel (property) in the eyes of society and the courts. Juveniles could be bought, sold, and treated like any other property, with the owner being the person in total control of the child. Not given a separate status in the eyes of the criminal court, a juvenile was treated the same as an adult in the criminal justice system and subject to the same penalties as adults, including death. Juveniles, once convicted of a crime, were sent to the same prisons as adults (Platt, 1969). Therefore, it is important to note that putting juveniles in adult prisons is not, per se, a new correctional strategy but one that has a long history in the United States as well as other countries.

In terms of criminal responsibility, children under the age of seven were assumed to not be accountable for any criminal acts they committed. Therefore, any child over the age of seven could be held criminally responsible for his or her actions. The age of seven was established in early Roman laws, adopted by the English common law, and eventually brought into the American system of justice. In fact, a few states still set seven years of age as the earliest for juvenile court interdiction. Even though juveniles were eligible to receive the same punishments as adults, in practice, the criminal justice system tended to take a more paternalistic approach to handling these cases, and many times the punishments for juveniles were reduced or never imposed (Faust & Brantingham, 1979). When juveniles were sent to adult institutions, however, they were housed with the adult inmates.

In the United States, correctional facilities exclusively designed to house juveniles were developed in the early 1800s. In 1823, the Society for the Prevention of Pauperism advocated the construction of a new facility to deal with the different problems and issues facing children (National Center for Juvenile Justice, 1991). "Houses of refuge" were created in New York, Pennsylvania, and Massachusetts and were designed to take in all children who were in need of greater supervision in the eyes of the state. It was thought that juveniles could be saved through hard work and religious reflection. These ideas were embraced in the houses of refuge, where juveniles would be removed from weak and criminal parents, protected from the evils of street life, and, most importantly, saved from their evil temptations. At the center of the teachings in these houses was the strong Puritan belief that humans are inherently evil and must be taught to be good. It was not the children's fault that they were neglected, abused, or delinquent. Instead, the Puritans, and later the child savers, would rescue juveniles from their environment and instill in them a "moral sense." In these early institutions, the notion that the state was sometimes in a better position than the family to raise a child, and thus had the duty to do so whenever it was in the best interests of the child, began to take root. By the end of the nineteenth century, the belief that juveniles should be housed separately from adults in correctional institutions was widespread. Additionally, the idea that science had progressed enough to correctly diagnose and treat social diseases was firmly established.

The houses of refuge were one of the first attempts to separate juvenile delinquents from adult criminals in a correctional environment. The Houses of Refuge were the predecessors of modern-day juvenile institutions. Institutions today do not reflect many of the practices of the houses of refuge, but these houses were basically the beginning of separate correctional institutions for juveniles – a practice that continues today.

Assumptions Influencing Correctional Policy in the Juvenile Justice System

Correctional policies in the United States designed to deal with juveniles are based on assumptions regarding a juvenile's level of culpability, the presumed causes of delinquency, the role of the state in controlling juvenile delinquency, and the goals of the juvenile justice system. These assumptions influence policy decisions and as they change over time, so do the correctional policies designed to deal with juvenile offenders. In fact, it can be argued that policy shifts in the juvenile justice system are more about changing perceptions than they are about actual practice, empirical study, or philosophic reasoning (Fritsch, Hemmens & Caeti, 1996).

The history of the juvenile justice system in the United States is typically divided into three distinct time periods: The traditional model (1899-1960s), due process model (1960s-1980s), and the punitive model (1980s-Present) (Fritsch et al., 1996). The traditional model of juvenile justice was based on the need to treat and handle juvenile offenders separately and with greater attention to the individual than the criminal justice system could provide. The early juvenile justice system was founded on the belief that the state could and should act *in loco parentis* (in place of the parents) under the doctrine of *parens patriae* (state acting as parents). Instead of an adversarial contest whose fundamental purpose was to determine facts, assess blame, and punish the guilty, the juvenile system was to be more of an inquisitorial system whose purpose was to determine cause, diagnose illness, and prescribe treatment. The emerging juvenile justice system reflected the belief that science had progressed to such a degree that it was possible to accurately and effectively diagnose and treat juveniles with the goal of curing delinquency. Although juveniles were incarcerated in juvenile institutions at the time, the presumed focus inside institutions was on providing treatment to the juvenile.

An examination of the early juvenile justice system reveals that, for the most part, there was a wide gap between what was intended by progressive reformers and actual system operation (Schlossman, 1977). Several studies about the juvenile justice system prior to the due process revolution of the 1960s argued that the system was far from its paternalistic and benevolent ideal (Albanese, 1993). Indeed, some legal scholars contended that the juvenile court was nothing more than a junior criminal court where juveniles were denied basic due process rights (Tappan, 1946). These arguments, combined with several high-profile cases, led the U.S. Supreme Court to more closely examine the operation and administration of the juvenile justice system. Eventually, however, the criticisms of the juvenile court began to outnumber the accolades, and the juvenile justice system became a substantial target of the due process movement during the turbulent decade of the 1960s.

National trends indicate that the juvenile justice system is growing more formal, restrictive, and punitive. The perceived inability of the juvenile justice system to deal with chronic and violent offenders resulted in a wave of get tough legislation that began in the 1970s and continues today. The agenda of deinstitutionalization, diversion, and reform has been openly questioned and criticized from several sources (Bazemore, 1992; Hirschi & Gottfredson, 1993; Krisberg et al., 1986) and many states have de-emphasized rehabilitation in favor of punishment, justice, accountability, and public protection (Anderson, 1992; Feld, 1980, 1981; Gardner, 1987; Sanborn, 1994; Torbet et al., 1996). New policies and codes are based on assumptions that are markedly different from those of the founders of the juvenile justice system.

Under the punitive model of juvenile justice, the function of the system has shifted to assessing the level of harm to society from the actions of a juvenile and imposing the appropriate level of punishment to deter the juvenile from future delinquency. This change led to increased incarceration of juvenile offenders in institutions and adult prisons in the 1990s. The number of delinquents held in public facilities rose 36 percent from 1991 to 1999 but then dropped 13 percent by 2003 (Snyder & Sickmund, 2006). Similarly, between 1997 and 2004, while prison populations grew, the number of prisoners under age 18 fell 54 percent (Snyder & Sickmund, 2006).

The assumptions regarding juveniles and the juvenile justice system varied during each of these three eras, which influenced the correctional policies of the time (See Table 8.1). First, during the traditional model of juvenile justice, it was assumed that juveniles as a group did not possess the same mens rea as adults. Proponents argued that juveniles had diminished intent and were not capable of forming the same level of intent as adults. The assumption, which led to correctional policies that focused on the treatment of juveniles in the system, has changed radically in recent years due to the shift in thinking that juvenile crime is no less serious than adult crime. Under the current punitive model of juvenile justice, it is assumed that certain juveniles, especially violent or chronic offenders, are just as culpable as adults, and therefore just as deserving of increased punishment in the system. This belief has influenced the increased use of adult sanctions on juveniles in recent years. For example, between 2000 and 2004, the number of judicially waived delinquency cases increased 21 percent in the United States (Stahl et al., 2007).

Another assumption of the traditional model of juvenile justice is based on the positivistic assumption that the causes of delinquency come from the broader social environment – the neighborhood, the family, and the specific child rearing practices in the family. The idea that the causes of delinquency were external to the individual led to the belief that delinquency was an illness brought on by the social diseases of poverty, parental neglect, ignorance, and urban decay. Because the causes were beyond the control of the juvenile, rehabilitation rather than punishment was appropriate. Under a punitive model of juvenile justice, however, it is assumed that juveniles commit delinquent acts because they have made a rational choice to do so. With a shift from an offender-based to offense-based system, the reason a juvenile engages in delinquency is secondary to the offense the juvenile committed. This premise leads to increased punishment, especially the use of incarceration as a correctional strategy.

Table 8.1 **Assumptions Influencing Correctional Policy**

Variable	Traditional Model (1899-1960s)	Due Process Model (1980s-Present)	Punitive Model (1960s-1980s)
Juvenile's Culpability	Diminished, juveniles are not capable of forming the same *mens rea* as adults	Recognized that the system viewed juveniles as less culpable, but net result of process was criminal culpability	Certain juveniles, especially violent or multiple offenders, are just as culpable as adults
Causes of Delinquency	The broader social environment – the neighborhood, poverty, urban decay, the family, and child rearing practices	Belief in positivism withstood judicial modifications, the causes of delinquency are essentially unimportant as long as juveniles are treated fairly in the system	In general, delinquency is a matter of a juvenile choosing to commit a crime for which he/she must be held accountable
Role of the State	The state could and should act in *loco parentis*, and in the best interests of the child	To act in *loco parentis* and in the best interests of the child while providing fundamental fairness and due process	To act in *loco parentis* for the best interests of society. The more serious the crime committed, the more society needs protection
Goals of the System	Prevention of future delinquency through treatment and rehabilitation	Prevention of future delinquency, rehabilitation, and protection of a juvenile's rights	Prevention of future delinquency through punishment, incapacitation, deterrence, and holding juveniles accountable

Source: Robert W. Taylor, Eric J. Fritsch & Tory J. Caeti (2007). *Juvenile Justice: Policies, Programs, and Practices*, Second Edition, p. 40. Boston, MA: McGraw-Hill Publishers.

Another assumption of the traditional model of juvenile justice was that the legal concept of *parens patriae* meant that the role of the state was to act *in loco parentis*. The early juvenile justice system advocates believed that intervention was "in the best interests of the child." Indeed, the philosophy of the juvenile court was that the wayward child was to be taken in hand by the state, and the state was to act as a protector. Today the interventions are still occurring, but for a different reason – the protection of society. The punitive model of juvenile justice assumes that the role of the state is to act in the best interests of society, not the child. Justifying intervention on the basis of community protection gives further support to the idea that the causes, diagnosis, prescribed treatment, and rehabilitation of juveniles are not as important under a punitive model of juvenile justice as is incapacitating the child so that no further harm results to society. Once again, this assumption leads to the increased use of incarceration as a means to deal with delinquency.

Finally, the goals of the system are based on the conceptualization detailed above. Perceptions about juveniles, their delinquency, and what to do about them led to the assumption that the goal of the system was treatment and rehabilitation. Hence, the mission, objectives, and effectiveness of the juvenile justice system were based on rehabilitation. The due process model left these explanations intact, changing only the process by which these goals would be reached. Legislation based on the punitive model's assumptions changes the fundamental goals of the system, and subsequently affects the system's operation. The new goals incorporate community protection, retribution, restitution, and punishment. While many state statutes still espouse the goal of rehabilitation, it is either secondary or must be done in concert with the new goals of the system.

Secure Detention Facility: Intake

Different Perspectives on the Issue

The following section will discuss and analyze the controversies surrounding the use of three correctional strategies for juveniles: confinement in juvenile institutions, placement in boot camps, and incarceration in adult prisons.

Juvenile Institutions

Secure placements for juveniles represent the most severe and intrusive sanctions in the juvenile justice system. These placements can include short-term facilities such as detention centers or boot camps, and long-term facilities such as youth ranches or state institutions. According to the Census of Juveniles in Residential Placement, there are more than 1,100 public and 1,600 private juvenile facilities throughout the country (Snyder & Sickmund, 2006).

The trends in residential placement in recent years mirror the changing assumptions previously discussed. Over a 20-year period between 1985 and 2004, the number of adjudicated delinquency cases that resulted in out-of-home placement rose from 105,200 to 140,700. However, the number of cases involving out-of-home placements peaked in 1997 at 175,900 cases and then decreased 20 percent by 2004. The largest decreases occurred among property offense cases (34%) and drug offense cases (25%) (Stahl et al., 2007). Of the juveniles committed to a secure correctional facility in 2004,

25 percent had committed a violent offense while the remaining 75 percent committed property offenses (34%), drug offenses (10%), and public order offenses (31%) (Stahl et al., 2007).

It is important to note, however, that commitment to an out-of home placement is the most serious sanction available to a juvenile judge and typically only a small portion of the juveniles arrested is eventually committed to a residential placement. For example, in the United States in 2004, police took 2.2 million juveniles into custody and 1.6 million cases were processed by the juvenile court system. However, only slightly more than 140,000 juveniles were placed in out-of-home placements (Stahl et al., 2007).

Most states have a central juvenile correctional authority that governs the administration and operations of juvenile correctional facilities in the state. If a judge decides to send a juvenile to a secure placement, the judge issues an order of commitment whereby the juvenile is removed from the custody of his or her parent or guardian and placed in the custody of the state juvenile correctional authority. The correctional authority determines placement, correctional treatment plan, time spent in the institution, and release from secure confinement. In some instances, the judge retains the authority to release the juvenile. Most state correctional authorities have a variety of placement options that address the offense committed, the risk associated with the juvenile, and the treatment needs of the juvenile. The most prominent secure placement for youth usually involves confinement in a state institution. However, does institutional confinement do more harm than good?

State institutions and schools are typically very self-contained and provide a variety of services for juveniles including rehabilitation, health, education, counseling, recreation, and employment training. Historically, these facilities have been very large, housing up to 300 youth drawn from wide geographic regions of the state. The trend of placing juveniles in remote state institutions is not universal, however. Many states rely on a combination of privately operated community placements and programs and state-operated community facilities and group homes.

Some in the juvenile justice community argue that institutionalizing juveniles does more harm than good. In the 1970s, practices in juvenile institutions began to be questioned, and civil action was initiated in some states. Lawsuits alleged that juvenile institutions were brutal environments that violated the cruel and unusual punishment clause of the Eighth Amendment. For example, in *Morales v. Turman* (1974), a federal court ruled that actions and practices within the then-Texas Youth Council constituted cruel and unusual punishment. Among the areas addressed by the court were physical brutality and other forms of abuse, inadequate disciplinary procedures, substandard medical and psychiatric care, and poor academic and vocational education (*Morales v. Turman*, 1974). As a result of similar lawsuits throughout the country, many states have moved away from large, rural juvenile institutions in favor of more community-based facilities for offenders not needing placement in a juvenile institution. This policy response will be discussed in greater detail in a later section.

It is important to note that conditions of confinement and violations of civil rights are still controversial issues in juvenile institutions. For example, the Justice Department recently sued the State of Louisiana over the conditions of its juvenile institutions, citing instances of repeated juvenile abuse and failure to heed repeated warnings to improve. The suit claimed that the state held juveniles in solitary confinement, and provided them poor medical and mental health care, and little education. According to the suit, juveniles were unreasonably vulnerable to abuse from fellow inmates and correctional officers (Taylor, Fritsch & Caeti, 2007).

Another controversy is whether juveniles have a right to treatment and, if so, what services have to be provided to them in an institution. Does a juvenile have to be provided with treatment services in a juvenile institution? While the right to treatment is grounded in the historical development of the juvenile court, it only developed recently into a legal right for challenging the conditions in juvenile facilities (Pattison, 1998). Several cases focused on complaints about conditions of confinement in juvenile facilities. These attempted to enforce the juvenile court's promise to provide rehabilitative care by asserting a "right to treatment" (Pattison, 1998). Many courts have determined that juveniles do have a right to treatment under the Constitution and some state statutes. However, the form of treatment and how treatment should be prescribed is generally still left to correctional authorities.

Juvenile Boot Camps

A correctional sanction that has generated a significant amount of controversy in recent years is juvenile boot camps. A boot camp is a secure correctional facility that emphasizes military-style discipline, physical training, and an extremely regimented schedule. The boot camp correctional philosophy is essentially guided by the idea that a juvenile delinquent needs structure and discipline in his or her life. Therefore, just like military boot camps, the juvenile must be broken down and then built back up into a more productive model citizen. The regimens at the juvenile correctional boot camps vary, but the guiding principles are remarkably consistent; strict discipline, structure, and "tough love." The first correctional boot camps began in Georgia and Oklahoma in 1983 and by the end of the 1980s, 16 states had operational correctional boot camps (MacKenzie & Souryal, 1994). Boot camps began with adult prisoners but were soon implemented for juvenile offenders. They were established at state-level juvenile correctional systems, at the county-level operated by either law enforcement or probation officials, and in private juvenile correctional corporations. Like other correctional panaceas, boot camps were extraordinarily popular during an era when the public and politicians perceived the need to get tough on juvenile crime. Several controversies exist regarding the use of boot camps as a correctional alternative for juveniles.

One of the largest controversies is whether boot camps are effective in reducing recidivism. Some studies have shown that boot camps have little impact on recidivism. For example, the Office of Juvenile Justice and Delinquency Prevention sponsored three demonstration boot camps for juvenile offenders in Cleveland, Ohio; Denver, Colorado; and Mobile, Alabama. The boot camps targeted nonviolent offenders and operated a 90-day program that embraced military-like discipline and structure in a comprehensive residential setting followed by supervised aftercare in the community for up to nine months (Felker & Bourque, 1996). In all three, physical fitness, basic education, and life skills training were part of each day's regimen (Felker & Bourque, 1996).

The juveniles selected for the boot camps at the three sites varied somewhat in terms of their criminal history and socioeconomic status, however, most of the juveniles who went through the program were similar. Researchers compared the recidivism rates for juveniles who participated in the pilot programs with those of control groups. Most juvenile boot camp participants completed the residential program and graduated to aftercare. Program completion rates were 96 percent in Cleveland, 87 percent in Mobile, and 76 percent in Denver. In Cleveland and Mobile, substantial improvements in academic skills were noted (Felker & Bourque, 1996). None of the three programs researched demonstrated a reduction in recidivism. In Denver and Mobile, no difference was found between the recidivism rates of juvenile boot camp participants and those of youth confined in state or county institutions or released on probation. In Cleveland, boot camp graduates had higher recidivism rates than juveniles confined in traditional juvenile correctional facilities (Felker & Bourque, 1996).

Another controversy surrounding boot camps involves the issue of cost. Communities often implement juvenile boot camps, in part to reduce costs. Research indicates that when boot camps are used as an alternative to traditional confinement, costs can be reduced considerably because of the significantly shorter residential stay. However, if boot camps are used as an alternative to probation, savings will not be realized. Several studies of boot camps have noted that the overall cost savings are minimal, primarily due to the fact that many youth sent to boot camps would have otherwise been placed on probation (Peters, Thomas & Zamberlan, 1997).

Additional criticism has been directed at the concept of boot camps. One commentator concluded that the nature of the boot camps do not fit well with the basic principles of adolescent development. Boot camps do not allow juveniles to have a voice in their treatment, and they tend to be very negative, especially at the outset (Beyer, 1996). In a broader sense, boot camps violate a primary principle of the juvenile justice system: individualized treatment. In response to the criticism that boot camps were too harsh and provided little if any rehabilitative treatment, many began to offer educational and psychological services as part of their mission.

In addition to these controversies surrounding the appropriateness and effectiveness of juvenile boot camps, incidents of physical abuse and concerns about excessive discipline prompted some states to close their juvenile boot camps (Blair, 2000). A Maryland Task Force concluded that confirmed cases of physical abuse of youth and the failure of the juvenile boot camp program in general warranted termination of that state's juvenile boot camps. Citing abuses, other states – Colorado, Arizona, and North Dakota – also dropped their boot camp programs, and some states (such as Georgia) have acknowledged the harmful effects of the paramilitary model and restructured their programs to minimize the military regime (Blair, 2000).

Perhaps the most salient criticism of the juvenile boot camp system is the idea of putting a juvenile through a short program and then expecting the juvenile to be reformed without follow-up or aftercare. Recently established boot camps have embraced a more holistic philosophy that includes a range of programming and aftercare services. In addition, offenders that are selected for boot camp are screened more carefully than they were when the facilities first came into operation. Finally, future evaluations will determine if boot camps are a viable alternative sanction that reduces recidivism and costs less than traditional secure facilities. Until that research is compiled, boot camps remain controversial.

Juveniles in Adult Prisons

On occasion, juveniles are sentenced to adult prison. In order to be eligible for this sentence, juveniles must typically first be waived to adult court for processing. Waiver to adult court is the procedure by which a juvenile is processed in the criminal justice system instead of the juvenile justice system (see Chapter 7). With the get tough on juvenile crime attitude that is prevalent in many states, the use of waiver to adult court for serious and violent juvenile offenders has become popular. Although the use of waiver to adult court increased 21 percent between 2000 and 2004 (Stahl et al., 2007), it is still a relatively rare event. Only about 1.7 percent of all violent offense cases formally processed in juvenile court were waived to adult court for prosecution in 2004 (Stahl et al., 2007). The percentages are even smaller for drug offenses (1.3%), property offenses (1.0%), and public order offenses (0.3%).

State statutes stipulate who is eligible to be waived to adult court. The offender's age and current offense have usually been used to determine transfer to adult court. Some states permit only older juvenile offenders (15-, 16-, and 17-year-olds) to be waived to adult court, while some allow any juvenile to be waived regardless of age. Some states identify only offenders who have committed violent offenses while other states allow juveniles who have committed property and drug offenses to be eligible for such waiver. Once waived to adult court, juveniles are usually subject to the same penalties as adults. This includes life sentences, and in most states, the possibility of life without parole. With the U.S. Supreme Court decision in *Roper v. Simmons* (2005), juveniles are no longer eligible for the death penalty.

The increased use of waiver has led to an increased use of prison as a correctional sanction for juveniles in the 1990s. The number of juveniles admitted to state prison more than doubled from 3,400 in 1985 to 7,400 in 1997 (Austin, Johnson & Gregoriou, 2000). Although prison populations continued to grow between 1997 and 2004, the number of prisoners under the age of 18 fell 54 percent (Snyder and Sickmund, 2006). It is estimated that approximately 2,400 juveniles are incarcerated in adult prisons on any given day (Sabol, Minton & Harrison, 2007). Most of these offenders have been convicted of a violent offense. In 2002, 61 percent of the juveniles admitted to prison committed a violent offense while the remaining committed property offenses (23%), drug offenses (9%), and public order offenses (5%) (Snyder & Sickmund, 2006). In addition to these attributes, juveniles sentenced to prison are becoming younger. Although the vast majority of juveniles admitted to prison are age 17, admissions in the 13-16 age group increased from 20 percent in 1985 to 26 percent in 1997. Beginning in 1995, offenders age 14 and younger were being sentenced to prison (Austin et al., 2000).

One of the largest controversies surrounding the practice of incarcerating juveniles in prison involves where the juvenile should be placed. Should the juvenile be placed in a separate juvenile facility, which is run by the state prison system, or should he or she be placed in a facility that houses adults as well? In practice, almost all states allow juveniles who have been sentenced as adults to be sent to an adult prison facility. Of the 50 states and the District of Columbia, 44 house juveniles in adult prisons (Austin et al., 2000). In some states, the juvenile is housed in the general adult population (straight adult incarceration) while other states house the juvenile in a separate facility for younger adult offenders, usually between the ages of 14 and 25 (segregated incarceration).

Of the 44 state prison systems that house juveniles as adults, 18 states maintain designated youthful offender housing units (Austin et al., 2000). These housing units do not typically house juveniles exclusively. They usually house youthful offenders ranging in age from 14 to 25. It is rare that a youth would be kept in a separate facility run by the state prison system which only houses juveniles. Therefore, the most common placement for juveniles in adult prison is straight adult incarceration. In other words, most juveniles sentenced to prison are incarcerated in a prison unit that houses older offenders. This is perhaps not surprising when the rationale for sending juveniles to prison is taken into consideration: the severity of their crimes, the failure of rehabilitation, and the difficulty in managing their behavior in the facility. Inside these units, juveniles are also not typically segregated from other offenders. One study estimated that 51 percent of the juvenile offender population was housed in a dormitory setting, 30 percent in single cells, and 19 percent in double cells (Austin et al., 2000).

Usually juveniles incarcerated in adult prisons are subject to the same policies and procedures as other inmates regarding housing, health care services, education, vocation and work programs, and recreational activities (United States General Accounting Office, 1995). In other words, they are treated the same as the rest of the inmates, and special services to meet the special needs of juvenile offenders are typically lacking. The lack of specialized treatment for juveniles in prison is a controversial issue, but juveniles in adult prison represent a small percentage of all inmates. As previously mentioned, fewer than 2,500 individuals under the age of 18 are held in state prisons (Sabol, Minton & Harrison, 2007). It is important to note that some of these 17-year-olds are technically adults as classified by state law. For example, in states such as Georgia, Illinois, Louisiana, Massachusetts, Michigan, Missouri, New Hampshire, South Carolina, Texas, and Wisconsin the maximum age of juvenile court jurisdiction is 16. Similarly, in Connecticut, New York, and North Carolina the maximum age is 15. In these states, 17-year-olds are technically adults. In 2007, however, Connecticut raised the age of juvenile court jurisdiction from 16 to 18 for nonviolent juvenile offenders. This leaves New York and North Carolina "as the only states that automatically try 16- and 17-year-olds as adults" (Center for Policy Alternatives, 2007:2).

Another major concern regarding the incarceration of juveniles in adult prison involves their increased risk of victimization. Research has shown that juveniles in adult facilities are at much greater risk of victimization, especially violent victimization, than youth housed in juvenile institutions (Austin et al., 2000). It has been reported that youth in adult prison are just as likely as youth in juvenile institutions to be victims of property crimes while incarcerated. However, a juvenile in adult prison is much more likely to be a victim of a violent crime than a juvenile incarcerated in juvenile institutions. In 1988, 47 percent of the juveniles in prison suffered violent victimization, including violence at the hands of correctional staff. In comparison, 37 percent of youth in juvenile institutions experienced similar victimizations. Sexual assault was five times more likely in prison, beatings by staff nearly twice as likely, and attacks with weapons almost 50 percent more common in adult facilities (Austin et al., 2000). In addition, the suicide rate for juveniles in prison is five times the rate of the general youth population and eight times the rate for juveniles in juvenile facilities (Austin et al., 2000).

Another controversy is that the general public does not favor sending juveniles to prison once they are convicted in adult court. According to a recent Gallup Poll, when respondents were asked how juveniles between the ages of 14 and 17 who commit violent crimes should be treated, 59 percent of the respondents stated that juveniles should be treated the same as adults, while 32 percent advocated more lenient treatment (Sourcebook of Criminal Justice Statistics, 2003). Although the survey does not include respondents' opinions about the treatment of juvenile property and drug offenders, it is assumed that fewer people would advocate the same treatment for property and drug offenders in comparison to violent offenders.

Other studies have found that the public does not always prefer long sentences of incarceration for youthful offenders and is generally supportive of rehabilitation (Applegate & Davis, 2006; Nagin, Piquero, Scott & Steinberg, 2006; Moon, Cullen & Wright, 2000). In their survey of Florida citizens, Applegate and Davis concluded that respondents distinguished the differences in seriousness of juvenile violent offending, and in most cases were supportive of short sentences of incarceration (2006:55). In her commentary on "public opinion and juvenile justice policy," Bishop observed that "the American public (has) remained steadfast in its support for juvenile rehabilitation" (2006:657). While the public expects accountability and punishment for violent juvenile offenders, it also recognizes the benefits of therapeutic interventions (Bishop, 2006). Based on this public opinion and the evidence of harmful effects of incarceration of youth in adult prisons, should juveniles continue to be confined with adult offenders?

Policy Responses and Implications

There are several policy responses and implications to the practices previously discussed. Some policies will lead to the increased incarceration of juveniles, while others will lead to less. These policy responses and implications are discussed below.

Move to Community-Based Facilities

Starting in the 1970s, some states opted to eliminate or reduce their dependence on large institutions. Instead, they developed smaller, community-based facilities serving 10 to 50 youth. These smaller facilities typically allow youth to be placed closer to their homes and to the communities to which they will return upon release (Office of Juvenile Justice and Delinquency Prevention, 2000). This process is frequently termed "deinstitutionalization." Within the past 25 years, states such as Massachusetts, Maryland, Pennsylvania, and Utah have decreased their reliance on large juvenile institutions and have even closed some of their institutions. For example, only a small percentage of the youth committed to the State Department of Youth Services in Massachusetts are placed in an institution. Most are placed in community-based programs, including group homes, day treatment programs, and forestry camps (Krisberg & Austin, 1993). In addition, most of the community-based programs have been privatized, and the residential programs are small in size, with usually fewer than 30 youth per facility (Krisberg & Austin, 1993). These practices have led to fewer youth being placed in institutions in some states.

Use of Legal Interventions

One method that is increasingly being used as an attempt to ensure the civil rights of incarcerated juveniles is civil action by the Department of Justice against a juvenile facility under the Civil Rights of Institutionalized Persons Act (CRIPA). CRIPA allows the United States Attorney General to file a federal complaint against a juvenile facility when there are systemic violations of the rights of youth. Since Congress enacted CRIPA, several juvenile correctional institutions have been investigated. Some of the investigations were closed before any litigation ensued, because the Justice Department concluded that a pattern or practice of unlawful conditions did not exist or because the facility closed its doors (Puritz & Scali, 1998). The use of legal interventions does not necessarily decrease the number of juveniles confined in institutions, but it certainly is a mechanism that can be used to improve their conditions of confinement.

Increased Use of Waiver to Adult Court

As previously mentioned, waiver to adult court is being used more frequently than in the past because it is viewed as a means to get tough on juvenile offenders. From 1998 through 2002, 18 states passed laws making it easier to try juveniles as adults (Snyder & Sickmund, 2006). Many of the changes can be classified into three types. First, laws have been passed that have lowered the age at which a juvenile can be waived to adult court. Second, laws have been enacted that have expanded the number of offenses eligible for waiver to adult court. Some states that have targeted primarily violent offenders for waiver to adult court have now allowed more property offenders to be eligible for waiver. Third, states have enacted or modified legislative or prosecutorial waiver statutes. Because legislative waiver automatically waives certain offenders to adult court, this mechanism fits well with the current get tough attitude toward juvenile offenders. In addition, prosecutorial waiver bypasses the waiver hearing used in judicial waiver and therefore expedites the process. These trends point to the more frequent use of waiver in the future and also point to potential increases in the number of youth incarcerated in prisons. In other words, because more juveniles are eligible for waiver than was the case 10 years ago, more juveniles may be incarcerated in prison in the future.

Blended Sentencing

Traditionally, the juvenile justice system has been completely separate from the criminal justice system. There has not been any crossover between the two systems. If a person was processed in juvenile court, the maximum punishment available would be a term of confinement in a juvenile institution until the individual reached the age of majority, usually 18 to 21 years of age depending on the state. At that point, the juvenile had to be released from the institution and was no longer under the jurisdiction of the juvenile court. The only way to impose a longer sentence on the individual was to waive the juvenile to adult court and sentence the juvenile to prison upon conviction. If convicted in adult court, the juvenile could potentially receive life imprisonment.

In recent years, however, a new form of disposition and sentencing has become popular. It is known as blended sentencing and it refers to the imposition of juvenile and/or adult correctional sanctions for serious and violent juveniles who have either been processed in the juvenile or adult court (Torbet et al., 1996). It blurs the traditional dividing line between the juvenile and criminal justice systems and allows certain juveniles processed in juvenile court to receive adult sanctions, and juveniles waived to adult court to receive juvenile sanctions. Blended sentences are unprecedented in the history of the juvenile justice system. Few court cases have tested the constitutionality of blended sentencing statutes, and few studies have been conducted to assess their effectiveness. Under blended sentencing, a juvenile can potentially receive a mix of both juvenile and adult sanctions.

There are five types of blended sentencing. In three of the types, the juvenile is processed in juvenile court but is eligible to receive an adult punishment (e.g., incarceration in prison). In the other two types, the juvenile is processed in adult court but is eligible to receive a juvenile punishment (e.g., incarceration in a juvenile institution). The models vary based on two factors: first, where the case is processed (juvenile or adult court); and second, which sentencing options are available. The following are the five types of blended sentencing:

(1) *Juvenile-Exclusive Blend*. The case against the juvenile offender is processed in juvenile court. If the individual is adjudicated, the juvenile is eligible to receive either a sentence in the juvenile correctional system or the adult correctional system (Griffin, 2003). That is why it is known as exclusive blend, because the judge must decide between either a juvenile or adult sanction. The judge cannot impose both a juvenile sanction and an adult sanction under this type of sentencing. New Mexico has this type of blended sentence (Griffin, 2003).

(2) *Juvenile-Inclusive Blend*. The case against the juvenile offender is processed in juvenile court. The difference between this type of sentencing and the first one is the type of sanction that is available after adjudication. A judge can simultaneously impose both a juvenile and adult correctional sanction. The adult correctional sanction is suspended pending a revocation or further criminal activity, at which point the juvenile will be required to complete the adult sanction (Griffin, 2003). For example, a juvenile is convicted of aggravated robbery and the judge sentences the individual to a term of incarceration in a juvenile institution and 10 years in adult prison. The juvenile will be sent to the juvenile institution and will only be required to complete the juvenile sanction unless the person does not satisfactorily adjust in the juvenile institution. In this case, the judge can revoke that sentence and force the juvenile to

serve the 10-year prison sentence in an adult correctional facility. This type of blended sentence is used in Alaska, Arkansas, Connecticut, Illinois, Kansas, Massachusetts, Michigan, Minnesota, Montana, Ohio, and Vermont (Griffin, 2003).

(3) *Juvenile Contiguous*. Once again, the case against the juvenile offender is processed in juvenile court. After adjudication, the judge can impose a sentence on the juvenile offender that can exceed the jurisdictional age limit of the juvenile corrections agency (Griffin, 2003). Before the juvenile reaches the jurisdictional age limit, the sentence is continued in the adult correctional system. As previously discussed, each state has a jurisdictional age limit of its juvenile corrections agency, most frequently 21 years of age. All juveniles incarcerated in a juvenile institution must be released by this age. The juvenile contiguous type of blended sentencing allows correctional sanctions to be continued from the juvenile to the adult system. Colorado, Rhode Island, and Texas all have this type of blended sentence (Griffin, 2003). For example, in Texas, juveniles who commit certain offenses can receive up to a 40-year sentence from the juvenile court judge. Juveniles remain in juvenile institutions until they reach 17, at which time they are eligible for transfer to an adult prison unit for the remainder of their sentence.

(4) *Criminal-Exclusive Blend*. The last two types of blended sentencing are different than the previous three because the case against the juvenile offender is processed in the adult criminal court. Under the criminal exclusive blend, the judge must decide whether to impose a juvenile or adult correctional sanction, but not both, after the juvenile is convicted in adult court (Griffin, 2003). If the judge believes that the juvenile should be sent to adult prison, then the judge can sentence the individual to prison. However, if the judge decides to sentence the person using a juvenile correctional sanction such as confinement in a juvenile institution, then the judge will impose this disposition despite the fact that the case was processed in adult court. This is similar to the juvenile exclusive type of blended sentencing previously discussed except the case is processed in adult court. This type of blended sentence can be found in California, Colorado, Illinois, Kentucky, Massachusetts, Nebraska, New Mexico, Oklahoma, West Virginia, and Wisconsin (Griffin, 2003).

(5) *Criminal-Inclusive Blend*. A case processed under a criminal inclusive type of sentencing is processed in adult criminal court. After conviction, the judge will impose both a juvenile and an adult correctional sanction but suspend the adult sanction pending a violation or revocation. Therefore, the juvenile will begin to serve his or her sentence in a juvenile institution. If a violation or revocation occurs, the judge can impose the adult sanction (Griffin, 2003). This is similar to the juvenile inclusive type of blended sentencing previously discussed except the case is processed in adult court. States that have this type of blended sentencing as an option include Arkansas, Florida, Idaho, Iowa, Michigan, Missouri, and Virginia (Griffin, 2003).

What impact will these sentencing options have in the future? Their use may lead to the increased use of adult prison, but can also be seen as a mechanism for minimizing the controversy of putting young offenders in prison. For example, with the contiguous type of blended sentence, juveniles can stay in juvenile institutions until they are older and perhaps more prepared to handle prison. Likewise, under the inclusive blend of sentencing, the adult sanction is suspended in an effort to give the juvenile one last chance by incarcerating the juvenile in a juvenile institution. However, if the juvenile fails to make appropriate adjustment, the adult sanction is imposed. Under the exclusive blend, the judge decides between confinement in adult prison or a juvenile institution.

This gives a judge much more flexibility in sentencing. Under a typical waiver to adult court statute, a judge may only impose adult sanctions. If a judge believes that a juvenile needs to be incarcerated but not necessarily in adult prison, the judge has no other incarceration option. Under blended sentencing, the judge may impose a sentence of confinement in a juvenile institution. When a judge believes that prison may be inappropriate for the juvenile, blended sentencing offers an alternative that previously did not exist.

Future Directions

A study of the system clearly demonstrates that the fundamental assumptions about juveniles, juvenile delinquency, and how best to respond have changed dramatically. The new assumptions of juvenile justice rest on the fundamental beliefs that juvenile crime is out of control, that juvenile criminals are just as dangerous if not more so than adults, and that the system is not doing an adequate job of protecting the public from violent juvenile offenders. Less emphasis is placed on how intellectually, socially, or morally developed a juvenile is when facing certain criminal charges. This is a reflection of the shift from an *offender*-based to an *offense*-based juvenile system. Rehabilitation is taking a back seat to public protection. Perhaps the greatest philosophical shift concerns the disposition of juveniles. The current practices now assume that punishment and accountability *are* rehabilitative. Regardless of the merits of this idea, it is a marked shift from the original assumptions of the juvenile court. The changing goals of the juvenile justice system are more a function of our changing assumptions about the nature of juvenile crime itself rather than problems regarding the original goals themselves.

A cyclical pattern between rehabilitation and punishment in juvenile justice policies is generated by several aspects of the system that have remained consistent since its founding (Bernard, 1992). Juveniles will continue to be in a high-crime group and will continue to receive less punishment than adults who commit similar crimes, and most people will claim that there is a juvenile crime wave that began in the recent past (Bernard, 1992). These beliefs foster the punitive assumptions that have been outlined in this chapter and will continue to result in pressure to increase punishment for juvenile offenders. It is unknown whether incarcerating youth in adult and juvenile facilities, including boot camps, does more harm than good. Some states are restricting the use of the most severe sanction, confinement in adult prison, by requiring juveniles to be a certain age before being sent to prison and by providing judges with more sentencing options. These practices are based on the assumption that incarcerating a youth in prison may do more harm than good in some instances.

Conversely, most states have enacted statutes that make more juveniles eligible for waiver to adult court. This expanded eligibility may also increase the number of youth confined in prison. It appears that for the near future the increased incarceration of juveniles in both institutions and adult prisons will likely continue.

Endnotes

[1] Some courts found the right to treatment in the Eighth or Fourteenth Amendments of the U.S. Constitution. Other courts based the right to treatment on state juvenile court statutes. In these latter cases, the court examined the promise of rehabilitation in the statutes authorizing juvenile court jurisdiction over youthful offenders. Because the stated purpose of the statutes was to rehabilitate young offenders, the courts held states accountable for providing services to youth in confinement. In *Jackson v. Indiana* (1972), the Supreme Court stated that "at the least, due process requires that the nature and duration of commitment bear some reasonable relation to the purpose for which the individual is committed." Because the stated purpose of confinement was rehabilitation or treatment, due process required that treatment be provided to confined juveniles. However, the Court in another case limited the right to treatment and declared that judges should defer to the professionals in charge of the facilities.

The Eighth Amendment basis for the right to treatment has also been limited in lower court decisions. In *Morales v. Truman* (1974), a Texas district court explained that while the Eighth Amendment protects juveniles from abusive conditions, it does not necessarily include a right to a certain kind of treatment because treatment options are open to discretionary interpretation. While the *Morales* court recognized that the Eighth Amendment requires adequate food, shelter, clothing and medical care, it decided that the failure to provide these services only reached a constitutional violation when it was sufficiently dangerous and a result of an institution official's disregard of the juvenile's health and safety. In *Alexander S. v. Boyd* (1995), a federal appellate court ruled that under the Fourteenth Amendment, "a minimally adequate level of programming is required in order to provide juveniles with a reasonable opportunity to accomplish the purpose of their confinement, to protect the safety of the juveniles and the staff, and ensure the safety of the community once the juveniles are released." Furthermore, the court defined "minimally adequate training" to be services "designed to teach juveniles the basic principles that are essential to correcting their conduct." These generally recognized principles include: (1) taking responsibility for the consequences of their actions; (2) learning appropriate ways to respond to others (coping skills); (3) learning to manage their anger; and (4) developing a positive sense of accomplishment. (See Pattison, 1998.)

References

Albanese, J. (1993). *Dealing With Delinquency: The Future of Juvenile Justice*. Chicago, IL: Nelson-Hall Publishers.

Alexander S. v. Boyd, 876 F. Supp. 773, 802 (D.S.C. 1995).

Anderson, G.M. (1992). "Punishing the Young: Juvenile Justice in the 1990s." *America*, 166(7) February 29:158-163.

Applegate, B.K. & R.K. Davis (2006). "Public Views on Sentencing Juvenile Murders: The Impact of Offender, Offense, and Perceived Maturity." *Youth Violence and Juvenile Justice*, 4(1):55-74.

Austin, J., K.D. Johnson & M. Gregoriou (2000). *Juveniles in Adult Prisons and Jails: A National Assessment*. Washington, DC: Bureau of Justice Assistance.

Bazemore, G. (1992). "On Mission Statements and Reform in Juvenile Justice: The Case of the 'Balanced Approach'." *Federal Probation*, 56(3):64-70.

Bernard, T.J. (1992). *The Cycle of Juvenile Justice*. New York, NY: Oxford University Press.

Beyer, M. (1996). *Juvenile Boot Camps Don't Make Sense*. American Bar Association.

Bishop, D.M. (2006). "Public Opinion and Juvenile Justice Policy: Myths and Misconceptions." *Criminology & Crime Policy*, 5(4):653-664.

Blair, J. (2000). "Boot Camps: An Idea Whose Time Came and Went." *New York Times*, (January 2):A3.

Center for Policy Alternatives (2007). "Connecticut Raises the Age of Juvenile Court Jurisdiction." (July 5). www.stateaction.org/blog/?cat=15 [Retrieved February 3, 2008].

Faust, F.L. & P.J. Brantingham (1979). *Juvenile Justice Philosophy: Readings, Cases and Comments*. St. Paul, MN: West Publishing.

Feld, B.C. (1980). "Juvenile Court Legislative Reform and the Serious Young Offender: Dismantling the 'Rehabilitative Ideal'." *Minnesota Law Review*, 65:167-242.

Feld, B.C. (1981). "Legislative Policies toward the Serious Juvenile Offender: On the Virtues of Automatic Adulthood." *Crime & Delinquency*, 27:497-521.

Felker, D.B. & B.B. Bourque (1996). "The Development of Boot Camps in the Juvenile System: Implementation of Three Demonstration Programs." In D.L. MacKenzie & E.E. Hebert (eds.) *Correctional Boot Camps: A Tough Intermediate Sanction*. Washington, DC: National Institute of Justice.

Fritsch, E.J., C. Hemmens & T.J. Caeti (1996). "Violent Youth in Juvenile and Adult Court: An Assessment of Sentencing Strategies in Texas." *Law and Policy*, 18(1-2):115-136.

Gardner, M.R. (1987). "Punitive Juvenile Justice: Some Observations on a Recent Trend." *International Journal of Law and Psychiatry*, 10:129-151.

Griffin, P. (2003). *Trying and Sentencing Juveniles as Adults: An Analysis of State Transfer and Blended Sentencing Laws*. Pittsburgh, PA: National Center for Juvenile Justice.

Hirschi, T. & M. Gottfredson (1993). "Rethinking the Juvenile Justice System." *Crime & Delinquency*, 39:262-271.

Jackson v. Indiana, 406 U.S. 715 (1972).

Krisberg, B., I.M. Schwartz, P. Litsky & J. Austin (1986). "The Watershed of Juvenile Justice Reform." *Crime & Delinquency*, 32:5-38.

Krisberg, B. & J. Austin (1993). *Reinventing Juvenile Justice*. Newbury Park, CA: Sage Publishing Company.

MacKenzie, D.L. & C. Souryal (1994). *Multisite Evaluation of Shock Incarceration*. Washington, DC: National Institute of Justice.

Moon, M.M., F.T. Cullen & J.P. Wright (2000). "Is Child Saving Dead? Public Support for Juvenile Rehabilitation." *Crime & Delinquency*, 46(1):38-60.

Morales v. Turman, 383 F.Supp. 53 (1974).

Nagin, D.S., A.R. Piquero, E.S. Scott & L. Steinberg (2006). "Public Preferences for Rehabilitation Versus Incarceration of Juvenile Offenders: Evidence from a Contingent Valuation Survey." *Criminology & Crime Policy*, 5(4):627-652.

National Center for Juvenile Justice (1991). *Desktop Guide to Good Juvenile Probation Practice*. Pittsburgh, PA: National Center for Juvenile Justice.

Office of Juvenile Justice and Delinquency Prevention (2000). *Employment and Training for Court-Involved Youth*. Washington, DC: Office of Juvenile Justice and Delinquency Prevention.

Pattison, B. (1998). "Minority Youth in Juvenile Correctional Facilities: Cultural Differences and the Right to Treatment." *Law and Inequality*, 16:573-598.

Peters, M., D. Thomas & C. Zamberlan (1997). *Boot Camps for Juvenile Offenders*. Washington, DC: Office of Juvenile Justice and Delinquency Prevention.

Platt, A. (1969). "The Rise of the Child-Saving Movement: A Study in Social Policy and Correctional Reform." *American Academy of Political and Social Science*, 381:21-38.

Puritz, P. & M.A. Scali (1998). *Beyond the Walls: Improving Conditions of Confinement for Youth in Custody*. Washington, DC: Office of Juvenile Justice and Delinquency Prevention.

Roper v. Simmons, 543 U.S. (2005).

Sabol, W.J., T.D. Minton & P.M. Harrison (2007). *Prison and Jail Inmates at Midyear 2006*. Washington, DC: Bureau of Justice Statistics.

Sanborn, J.B. (1994). "Remnants of *Parens Patriae* in the Adjudicatory Hearing: Is a Fair Trial Possible in Juvenile Court." *Crime & Delinquency*, 40(4):599-615.

Schlossman, S.L. (1977). *Love and the American Delinquent: The Theory and Practice of "Progressive" Juvenile Justice, 1825-1920*. Chicago, IL: University of Chicago Press.

Snyder, H.N. & M. Sickmund (2006). *Juvenile Offenders and Victims: 2006 National Report*. Pittsburgh, PA: National Center for Juvenile Justice.

Sourcebook of Criminal Justice Statistics (2003). Washington, DC: Bureau of Justice Statistics. www.albany.edu/sourcebook [Retrieved November 29, 2007].

Stahl, A.L., C. Puzzanchera, S. Livsey, A. Sladky, T.A. Finnegan, N. Tierney & H.N. Snyder (2007). *Juvenile Court Statistics 2003-2004*. Pittsburgh, PA: National Center for Juvenile Justice.

Tappan, P.W. (1946). "Treatment without Trial." *Social Forces*, 24:306-327.

Taylor, R.W, E.J. Fritsch & T.J. Caeti (2007). *Juvenile Justice: Policies, Programs, and Practices*, Second Edition. New York, NY: McGraw-Hill Publishers.

Torbet, P., R. Gable, H. Hurst IV, I. Montgomery, L. Szymanski & D. Thomas (1996). *State Responses to Serious and Violent Juvenile Crime*. Washington, DC: Office of Juvenile Justice and Delinquency Prevention.

United States General Accounting Office (1995). *Juvenile Justice: Juveniles Processed in Criminal Court and Case Dispositions*. Washington, DC: United States General Accounting Office.

CHAPTER 9

Race, Delinquency, and Discrimination: Minorities in the Juvenile Justice System

Donna M. Bishop

Introduction

One of the most well-documented and controversial features of the juvenile justice system is the overrepresentation of minority youth. African American, Hispanic, and Native American juveniles are arrested in numbers greatly disproportionate to their numbers in the general population. They are overrepresented among those held in secure detention and petitioned to juvenile court. Among those adjudicated delinquent, they are more often sentenced to incarceration. When confined, they are more often housed in large public institutions rather than privately run group homes or specialized treatment facilities. And, finally at the "end of the line," they are more apt to be transferred to criminal court for prosecution and punishment as adults. In a nation committed to principles of justice, fairness, and equality under the law, such disparities are, and should be, a matter of grave concern.[1]

Although considerable research has been conducted on minority overrepresentation, no clear consensus has emerged regarding its causes. Some have concluded that it fairly accurately reflects race differences in offending (see for example, Hindelang, 1978; Blumstein, 1982; Langan, 1985). According to this view, minority youth are more likely to be arrested and more often penetrate to the deep end of the juvenile justice system because they are the most serious and chronic offenders. Others claim that minority overrepresentation is the result of racial bias. They contend that official responses to youth crime reflect either racial prejudice or more subtle forms of discrimination. These two views ("differential offending" and "system bias") are often pitted as opposing, even mutually exclusive claims. To the contrary, it will be suggested here that they are complementary and mutually reinforcing and that they share common origins in the structure and culture of American society.

The purpose of this chapter is to conduct an analysis of minority overrepresentation in the juvenile justice system. The inquiry begins with a discussion of the magnitude of the problem. This section is followed by a review highlighting research and theory on differential offending and system bias. The chapter concludes with a discussion of policy implications, including an assessment of the merits of alternative remedial strategies.

The Extent of Minority Overrepresentation in the Juvenile Justice System

Data on minorities in the juvenile justice system are not without shortcomings. For the most part, race categories are limited to white, black, and "other," with Asians, Native Americans, and Pacific Islanders included in the latter group. Information on ethnicity is generally unavailable. For example, youth of Hispanic ancestry represent a substantial (15%) and growing segment of the minority population, but are coded "white" more than 90 percent of the time (Snyder & Sickmund, 2006:2). As a result, the overrepresentation of minorities appears smaller than it really is.

In studying minority overrepresentation, it is important to examine the juvenile justice system as a series of decision points, because overrepresentation is more pronounced at some stages than others and because it tends to compound as we move from the beginning phases of processing to later ones. The overrepresentation of minorities in institutions is best understood as a product of actions that took place early on, at arrest and at juvenile court intake.

Table 9.1 presents national data on the processing of young people by police (from the FBI's *Uniform Crime Reports*) and the juvenile courts (from *Juvenile Court Statistics*) for 2003, the most recent year for which data from arrest to court disposition are available.[2] The first two rows of the table show the racial composition of the population at risk (i.e., 10- to 17-year-olds) and of juvenile arrestees. It can be seen that white youth who make up 78 percent of the youth population, are underrepresented among arrestees (71%) (Puzzanchera et al., 2007). Blacks, on the other hand, make up 16 percent of the youth population but account for 27 percent of all juvenile arrests. Those in the "other" category make up a small fraction of both the youth and arrestee populations.

Arrest rates (per 100,000 youth in the 10- to 17-year age category) are presented next. Rates adjust for differences in group population size and permit direct comparisons across groups. The arrest rate for blacks (10,865 per 100,000 youth) is much greater than that for whites (6,040 per 100,000 youth). As shown in the row labelled Relative Risk, the probability of a black juvenile being arrested in 2003 was nearly twice as great as the risk for whites.

Table 9.1 **The Processing of Juveniles by Race, 2003**

	White	Black	Other
Population age 10-17[a]	26,097,451	5,517, 053	1,913,984
	(77.8%)	(16.5%)	(5.7%)
Arrested[b]	1,576,413	599,481	66,609
	(71%)	(27%)	(03%)
Arrest Rate[c]	6,040	10,865	3,480
Relative Risk, Black : White = 1.8 : 1			
Referred to Court[d]	1,099,011	494,444	49,608
	(67%)	(30%)	(03%)
% Arrestees Referred	70	82	74
Referral Rate	4,211	8,962	2,592
Relative Risk, Black : White = 2.1 : 1			
Detained[d]	211,269	127,467	11,084
	(60%)	(36%)	(03%)
% Referrals Detained	19	26	22
Detention Rate	809	2,310	579
Relative Risk, Black : White = 2.9: 1			
Formally Charged[d]	597,325	316,787	28,558
	(63%)	(34%)	(03%)
% of Referrals Charged	54	64	58
Rate of Formal Charging	2,288	5,741	1,492
Relative Risk, Black : White = 2.5 : 1			
Adjudicated Delinquent[d]	417,527	197,428	21.209
	(66%)	(31%)	(03%)
% of Charged Adjudicated	70	62	74
Adjudication Rate	1,599	3,578	1,108
Relative Risk: Black : White = 2.2 : 1			
Placed Out of Homed	90,869	52,709	5,756
	(61%)	(35%)	(04%)
% of Adjudicated Placed	22	27	27
Placement Rate	348	955	301
Relative Risk, Black : White =2.7 : 1			
Waived to Adult Court[d]	5,205	3,809	300
	(56%)	(41%)	(03%)
% of Charged Waived	0.9	1.2	1.0
Waiver Rate	20	69	16
Relative Risk, Black : White = 3.5 : 1			

[a] Source: Puzzanchera, C., T. Finnegan & W. Kang (2007). *Easy Access to Juvenile Populations*. Available Online: http://www.ojjdp.ncjrs.org/ojstatbb/ezapop/.

[b] Source: Snyder, H., R. & M. Sickmund (2006:125). *Juvenile Offenders and Victims: 2006 National Report*. Washington, DC: Office of Juvenile Justice and Delinquency Prevention.

[c] All rates are calculated per 100,000 juveniles age 10-17 in the general population.

[d] Source: National Center for Juvenile Justice (2007). *National Juvenile Court Data Archive: Juvenile Court Case Records 1985-2004* [machine-readable files]. Available online: http://www.ojjdp.ncjrs.gov. ojstatbb/ezajcs.

There are also differences in the kinds of offenses for which blacks and whites are apprehended (data not shown). Although blacks account for 27 percent of all juvenile arrests, they make up a much greater portion of those arrested for serious crimes of violence (45%). However, serious violent crimes contribute only a small fraction (4%) of all arrests. Serious property crimes are more common (21% of arrests) and, in this category, black juveniles are over-represented to a lesser degree (28% of arrestees). The vast majority (75%) of juvenile arrests are for 21 lesser crimes, the most common are simple assault, drug offenses, disorderly conduct, and liquor law violations. For these offenses, blacks make up 27 percent of arrestees. In all, blacks are overrepresented in 26 of the 29 UCR offense categories. They are underrepresented only for liquor law violations, drunkenness, and driving under the influence.

Referral to Juvenile Court

Of the 2.24 million juvenile arrests made in 2003, 1.64 million (about 73%) were referred to juvenile court intake.[3] As shown in Table 9.1, racial disparities are quite pronounced at this stage. Seventy-three percent of arrests involving blacks, compared to 60 percent of those involving whites, were referred to the court. Expressed in terms of youth at risk, blacks were referred at a rate of 8,962. The comparable rate for whites was 4,211 and for other minorities, 2,592. Of the youth population at risk, blacks were more than two times as likely as whites to be referred to court.

Detention

Twenty-one percent of all juvenile referrals were held in secure detention awaiting the outcome of their cases. Among black referrals, 26 percent were detained, compared to 19 percent of whites and 22 percent of other races. Expressed in terms of the total population at risk, black youth were nearly three times as likely to be detained as white youth. The use of detention varied considerably by offense type (see Table 9.2). Although blacks were more likely than whites to be detained in all offense categories, racial disparities were especially pronounced for drug crimes: 30.7 percent of blacks referred for drug offenses were detained, compared to 16.5 percent of whites. Black youth arrested for drug offenses were even more likely to be detained than youth arrested for crimes against persons.

Formal Charging

Forty-three percent of all referrals were dropped or diverted at intake, while the remaining 57 percent were formally charged or "petitioned." Whites and blacks were not petitioned at equal rates. As shown in Table 9.1,

64 percent of black referrals were petitioned, versus 54 percent of whites. Table 9.2 shows that, for all offense types, black youth were more likely to be petitioned than whites. However, as was the case for detention, racial disparities were especially pronounced for drug crimes. Petitions were filed in 77 percent of the drug cases involving blacks, compared to 53 percent of the drug cases involving whites and youth of other races. This represents a very substantial race differential.

Table 9.2 **Juvenile Court Processing by Race and Offense Type, 2003**

Offense Type	Detained[a]			Petitioned[b]			Placed[c]		
	White	Black	Other	White	Black	Other	White	Black	Other
Person	23.4	28.0	28.7	56.3	65.6	61.1	24.8	26.7	32.5
Property	15.2	21.8	16.8	52.6	61.3	52.2	20.8	24.5	28.8
Drug	16.5	30.7	17.1	53.3	76.6	52.9	15.5	32.0	18.8
Public Order	23.0	26.9	28.6	55.8	62.1	65.8	23.7	27.5	23.0
Total	19.2	25.8	22.3	54.4	64.1	57.6	21.8	26.7	27.1

[a] Numbers shown refer to the percent detained among those referred within each race and offense category.

[b] Numbers shown refer to the percent petitioned among those referred within each race and offense category.

[c] Numbers shown refer to the percent placed among those adjudicated delinquent within each race and offense category.

Source: Author's calculations are based on data provided in: Stahl, A., T. Finnegan, and W. Kang (2007). *Easy Access to Juvenile Court Statistics, 1985-1994.* Available Online: http://www.ojjdp.ncjrs.org/ojstatbb/ezajcs.

Adjudication

After formal charging, juvenile defendants either plead guilty (the vast majority of cases) or proceed to a hearing where evidence is presented and a verdict is returned. If a determination of guilt is made, either by plea or by verdict, a juvenile is said to be "adjudicated delinquent." Unlike earlier stages in processing, the probability of being adjudicated is *lower* for blacks than for whites (62% of petitioned cases involving blacks resulted in adjudication, compared to 70% of cases involving whites and 74% of cases involving youth of other races). Even though blacks were less likely to be adjudicated delinquent than whites, blacks are nevertheless overrepresented at this stage in processing. Table 9.1 shows that the risk of being adjudicated delinquent among blacks is 2.2 times greater than the risk for whites. This greater risk reflects the cumulative effects of disparities that disadvantaged blacks at earlier stages in processing.

Disposition

An increase in minority overrepresentation occurs again at disposition, although to a lesser degree than at the initial stages of processing. Most youth who are adjudicated delinquent receive probation or some other community-based disposition. Less frequently used is the more severe disposition of commitment/residential placement. Black youth received less of the former and more of the latter. Of the cases that proceeded to disposition, 27 percent of cases involving blacks, versus 22 percent of cases involving whites, were sentenced to out-of-home placement (see Table 9.1). Table 9.2 shows that this pattern held true for all offense categories but was especially pronounced for drug crimes. Thirty-two percent of black drug offenders but only 15.5 percent of white drug offenders were removed from their homes by the courts.

The effect of racial disparities that have accumulated over multiple decision points is noteworthy. As shown in the row labeled Relative Risk, by the time a juvenile reaches the disposition stage, disparities at each stage in processing have compounded to the point that blacks are 2.7 times as likely as whites to wind up in residential placement.

Youth in Juvenile Correctional Facilities

Youth of color are greatly overrepresented among delinquents confined in juvenile correctional institutions. Biannually, the federal Office of Juvenile Justice and Delinquency Prevention conducts a biannual *Census of Juveniles in Residential Placement* (CJRP), which produces a count of youth incarcerated on a single day during the year. Unlike the data sources discussed thus far, CJRP includes information on both race and ethnicity. The results for 2003 showed 96,655 juvenile offenders confined in residential facilities; 68 percent were housed in public facilities and 32 percent in private facilities. Of the 96,655, 39 percent were non-Hispanic whites, while racial and ethnic minorities made up 61 percent of the incarcerated youth population. This is significantly out of proportion to their numbers in the general population. A comparison of incarceration rates across groups brings the problem of disproportionate minority confinement into sharp relief. The custody rate for non-Hispanic whites was 190 per 100,000 juveniles in the general population. For blacks, it was 754, for Native American youth, the rate was 496, and for Hispanic youth, 348. In other words, the incarceration rate for blacks was four times the rate for non-Hispanic whites, while the rates for Native American and Hispanic youth were 2.6 and 1.8 times the white rate, respectively. Among minorities, only Asians were incarcerated at a rate comparable to whites (113). Moreover, whites were far more likely than minorities to be held in private facilities, which are generally smaller and better equipped than public institutions (Snyder & Sickmund, 2006:214).

Transfers to Criminal Court

Transfer to criminal court is the harshest method of processing a juvenile defendant. Youth who are transferred are considered adults and are generally eligible for the same punishments as apply to adult offenders. Although they are no longer eligible for the death penalty,[4] they can be sentenced to prison and, in many states, to terms including life without possibility of parole. Counts of transferred youth are difficult to obtain. At one time, a judicial waiver hearing in juvenile court was the primary method of removing youth to the adult system. Reliable records of cases waived by the juvenile court have been published for many years in *Juvenile Court Statistics*. However, beginning in the 1970s, the vast majority of states opted to create more expedient transfer mechanisms that bypass the juvenile court by allowing prosecutors to file cases directly in criminal courts. Unfortunately, data collection efforts have not kept pace with reforms. Most cases today are transferred by prosecutors, who generally do not maintain separate records for juvenile defendants.

Data on judicially waived cases are presented in Table 9.1. Although waiver is a rare event, it is applied disproportionately to minority defendants. Forty-four percent of cases waived in 2003 involved black defendants (41%) or youth of other races (3%), while whites were greatly underrepresented (56%) relative to their proportions in the general population.

How Pervasive Is Minority Overrepresentation?

Thus far, the analysis has been confined to national data, which do not tell us how common minority overrepresentation is among the states. (The problem might be concentrated in a few large states.) A 1992 amendment to the federal Juvenile Justice and Delinquency Prevention Act required all states to assess and take steps to reduce disproportionate minority confinement (DMC). Reporting on the early phases of the DMC initiative, Donna Hamparian and her colleagues gathered data on disproportionality at multiple points in processing for those states that had completed assessments (Community Research Associates, 1997). For each stage, they calculated an Index of Disproportionality, which reflects the percentage of minority youth at that point divided by the percentage of minority youth age 10-17 in the state. An index of 2.0, for example, means that minorities are represented at a rate twice what would be expected based on their proportion in the at-risk population.

In 34 of 36 states reporting data for arrest, minority youth were overrepresented, with an average index of disproportionality of 1.7. Forty-four states reported detention data and, in all but one, minority youth were overrepresented, with an average index of 2.8. In 42 states reporting juvenile institutional corrections data, all but two showed minority overrepresentation, with an average index of 2.6. As was true for the nation as a whole, overrepresentation was greatest for blacks and somewhat less for Hispanics, while Asian youth were most often underrepresented. (Data for Native Americans were too scant for computation.) Parallel to the cumulative effects mentioned earlier for the nation, in nearly every state the overrepresentation of black and Hispanic youth increased from arrest to residential commitment.

Evidence of Race Differences in Offending

As discussed above, blacks are more likely to be arrested than whites in nearly every offense category. Some, however, have questioned whether arrest data reflect bias against blacks. Fortunately, we have other sources of data on youth crime with which to address the issue of race differences in offending. If these other sources reveal race differences in crime that are in basic agreement with arrest data, we can have more confidence that race differences in arrest reflect real differences in offending. If they do not, then the system bias thesis becomes more plausible.

Self-reports and victimization surveys are alternative methods of measuring crime. Unfortunately, they too are not without shortcomings. Self-reports ask high school and other samples of youth to anonymously report any offenses they have committed, whether or not they were apprehended. However, self-reports may not be equally valid for blacks and whites. Some researchers have suggested that blacks tend to underreport serious misconduct (Hindelang, 1981; Huizinga & Elliott, 1986), while others have found no differences in the accuracy of reporting across racial groups (Farrington et al., 1996). Victimization surveys ask household residents to report personal victimizations, regardless of whether they reported these crimes to the police. Victims, though, can tell researchers about characteristics of offenders only when there has been face-to-face contact. For so-called "victimless" crimes (e.g., drug offenses, curfew violations), property crimes (e.g., burglary, auto theft), and homicides, victim descriptions of offenders are unavailable. Furthermore, even for crimes involving face-to-face contact, victims may not always be able to accurately identify the offender's age and race. With these caveats in mind, we look briefly at what these data tell us about race differences in offending.

The National Youth Survey is a self-report administered to a nationally representative sample of teens. Based on the data for 17-year-olds, Elliott and his colleagues (Elliott, 1994; Elliot & Ageton, 1990) found that black youth admitted greater involvement in violent behavior than Hispanic youth, who in turn reported greater involvement than whites. These findings are consistent with those from the Denver, Pittsburgh, and Rochester Youth Studies, where white youth reported involvement in violent crimes at lower rates than Hispanic youth, and black youth reported the highest levels of involvement (Huizinga, Loeber & Thornberry, 1994). Although the self-reported race differences in violent offending across all these studies are substantial, they are not nearly as great as those found in police arrest data.

Another national self-report study examined patterns for lesser offenses (Snyder & Sickmund, 2006). Thirty-nine percent of white youth and 33 percent of blacks reported that they had vandalized property; 44 percent of whites and 38 percent of blacks reported that they had committed thefts worth less then $50. There were no differences by race in the proportion of youth who admitted carrying guns. With drug offenses, *Monitoring the Future* – an annual national survey of high school students begun in 1975 – has consistently shown that the highest proportions of drug use of all kinds are found among whites, followed by Hispanics, with blacks reporting the lowest levels of illicit drug use. These race differences in self-reported crime are not at all consistent with police arrest data, which show substantial overrepresentation of minorities for vandalism, theft, and drug offenses.

Victim reports, obtained from the annual National Crime Victimization Survey (NCVS), indicate that minorities are overrepresented among offenders who commit serious violent crimes (sexual assault, robbery, and aggravated assault) (Greenfield, 1999). For robbery, the proportion of juvenile offenders whom victims identified as black is only slightly lower than the proportion shown in police data. For sexual and aggravated assaults, blacks are also overrepresented, although the proportion of blacks is considerably lower than indicated in arrest data.

Taken together, self-report and victimization data suggest that black youth are considerably more likely to commit violent crimes than whites, although the disparities are not as great as those reported in official arrest data. For property and drug crimes (for which victimization data are not available), self-reports indicate minimal race differences in offending. The differences that do appear more often suggest greater delinquent involvement among whites. In sum, these comparisons of arrest data with self-report and victimization data seem to support the following general conclusion: racial disparities in arrest are attributable both to differential offending and to differences in the way justice officials respond to white and minority juveniles who engage in the same sorts of behaviors. In the next section, explanations for race differences in offending are explored.

Explaining Race Differences in Offending

In their recent analysis of race differences in offending, the National Research Council and Institute of Medicine concluded that minority youth are more often exposed than whites to "contexts of risk," that is, social structural conditions that contribute to delinquency and crime (National Research Council and Institute of Medicine, 2001). This explanation focuses on the economic status of racial and ethnic minorities, the effects of poverty and disorder on the family, and the impact of neighborhood conditions on the development of traditions of crime and delinquency in urban areas (See Walker et al., 2000; Wilson; 1987, 1993; Hawkins et al., 1998; Sampson & Groves, 1989; Sampson & Lauritsen, 1997; Sampson & Wilson, 1995).

The roots of this perspective are found in social disorganization theory, developed in the 1940s by Clifford Shaw and Henry McKay (1969). Shaw and McKay spent years mapping residences of youth referred to the Chicago juvenile court during the 1920s and 1930s. Their research showed that rates of delinquency were highest near the center of the city and declined as the distance from the city center increased. High-crime neighborhoods were inhabited primarily by recent immigrants who lacked the funds to live in more desirable areas. Although politicians and even some scholars tended to attribute crime to the moral inferiority of the immigrants themselves, Shaw and McKay demonstrated the fallaciousness of this kind of thinking. As different immigrant groups became upwardly mobile and moved to areas more removed from the inner-city, they did not take their high crime rates with them. Instead, the same inner-city neighborhoods continued to have high rates of delinquency for decades, despite undergoing major change in racial and ethnic composition. Shaw and McKay concluded that it must be something about these neighborhoods, rather than the people within them, that contributed to offending.

High-crime areas were characterized by high population density, poverty, and unemployment; racial and ethnic heterogeneity; and highly transient populations. Shaw and McKay argued that these structural features produced "social disorganization," referring to a condition in which social networks – both informal intergenerational ties and friendships and formal neighborhood organizations – were attenuated and unable to provide the supervision and control necessary for the effective socialization of children. This explanation is similar to the notion, popularized today, that "it takes a village to raise a child." When the neighborhood is constantly in flux, when most residents are poor and unemployed, when families are broken and isolated from one another, neighborhood residents mistrust each other and do not forge networks of association that might help them to deal more effectively with local community problems. They fail to support each other, to look out for each other's children, and to work together to control crime in their neighborhoods. Because crime flourishes in these areas, children are routinely exposed to deviant role models. They see persons involved in drugs, gambling, prostitution, theft, and violence, which become behavioral options they might not otherwise have thought of or chosen. In this way, structural conditions give rise to traditions of crime and delinquency that are passed on from one generation of young residents to the next.

The social disorganization perspective has recently been applied to an understanding of race differences in offending in contemporary America, especially by Sampson and his colleagues (see e.g., Sampson & Groves, 1989; Sampson & Wilson, 1995; Sampson et al., 1997; Sampson et al., 1999). They note that the inner city has undergone a social transformation in the past few decades, resulting in the ghettoization of an impoverished black population – consisting especially of single-mother families – who live in relative social isolation in pockets of concentrated poverty. While, in the past, poor inner-city residents were able to secure fairly well paying jobs in manufacturing and other industries (e.g., steel and textile mills) that allowed them eventually to move out of the urban core, this is no longer possible for vast numbers of urban residents. In the 1970s and 1980s, the urban industrial sector of the nation's economy largely shut down. While economic growth continued, it relocated primarily to suburban areas, which are generally beyond the reach of public transportation from the inner city. Jobs that remain in the city tend to be either professional-level (requiring higher education) or, far more often, jobs in the retail sales and service sectors (e.g., salesclerk, cashier, nurse's aide, waiter, and housekeeper) (Sklar, 1995:32). Most of these latter jobs pay only a minimum wage. At that rate, a single breadwinner supporting three dependents will live far below the official poverty level (Walker et al., 2000:69). Even if two parents work, they will barely rise above the poverty line. The result is that the poor are essentially trapped in the inner city, where unemployment rates are high and available jobs are marginal.

The inner-city poor today are disproportionately black. Following World War II, there was a mass migration of blacks from the South to northern cities. At about the same time, the establishment of interstate highways and new housing and mortgage policies facilitated the development of suburbs. Many whites and middle-income and upper-income blacks left the inner city for these more desirable areas.

Further contributing to the development of a largely minority urban under-class are practices of residential segregation that relegate poor minorities to urban ghettoes, where they live in relative isolation from the more affluent majority (Wilson, 1987). To be sure, many poor white families live in cities as well, but they are less apt to live in areas where everyone else is poor.

For blacks, poverty and residential segregation have had devastating effects on the family. The strains of poverty, high rates of male unemployment, and child welfare policies that disallow payments to mothers who reside with a spouse, have combined to produce high rates of family disruption:

> Although the national rate of family disruption and poverty among blacks is two to four times higher than among whites, the number of distinct ecological contexts in which blacks achieve equality to whites is striking. In not one city over 100,000 in the United States do blacks live in ecological equality to whites when it comes to these basic features of economic and family organization. Accordingly, race differences in poverty and family disruption are so strong that the "worst" urban contexts in which whites reside are considerably better off than the average context of black communities (Sampson & Lauritsen, 1997:337).

Family disruption means that youth have little sustained exposure to conventional role models, such as married males working in blue- and white-collar occupations who return home to parent their children.

Poverty in the inner-city has many additional ramifications. While pregnant women cannot afford health insurance, they often fail to receive prenatal care, increasing the risk that their children will be born with neurological deficits that impair learning and social development both of which have been linked to antisocial behaviour (see, e.g., Fishbein, 2001:63-70). Inner-city neighborhoods tend also to be characterized by "critically low performing" schools which do little to improve youth's life chances, and by a dearth of recreation programs and other organized activities for adolescents. It is difficult if not impossible for a single parent, especially one who must work to support the family, to provide the instruction needed to compensate for inferior schools, to organize and supervise her children's after-school activities, and to provide guidance sufficient to counterbalance the negative influence of deviant role models on the streets (e.g., knife- and gun-wielding gangs, drug dealers, addicts, pimps, and prostitutes). These factors in combination are believed to contribute heavily to minority youth crime.

Evidence of Bias in the Juvenile Justice System

We turn now to evidence of racial bias/discrimination in the juvenile justice system. At the outset, it is important to be clear about terminology, especially with regard to disparity and discrimination. "Disparity" refers simply to differences in outcomes between groups, irrespective of their origins. Suppose, for example, that among youth found delinquent in a juvenile court, 30 percent of blacks and 15 percent of whites are committed to residential placements. Clearly, there is a difference in outcomes between groups (disparity). Nevertheless, it would be incorrect to conclude from this fact alone that the court acted in a racially discriminatory fashion. Perhaps black youth commit more serious offenses or have lengthier prior records. Most people would agree that these offense-related differences would justify differential treatment.

"Discrimination" refers to disparities that are the product of illegal or illegitimate considerations (National Research Council and Institute of Medicine, 2001:230-231. See also Walker et al., 2000:15-18). Identifying discrimination is complicated by the fact that people do not agree on what factors are legitimate. To understand why this is the case, we need to consider the nature of the juvenile court.

Adult courts operate differently than juvenile courts. Their goal is to punish those who have committed crime. Justice demands that like cases be treated alike, that the court's response should fit the crime (the "principle of offense") (Matza, 1964; Feld, 1988, 1993a, 1993b). The defendant's background (e.g., whether he or she comes from a broken home, failed in school, or has criminal friends) is irrelevant. There is general agreement that criminal court decisions should be based only on legal factors (e.g., the nature of the crime, the strength of the evidence, and the offender's prior record).[5]

The juvenile court, on the other hand, was founded on a different principle, the doctrine of *parens patriae*. It was designed as a therapeutic system whose primary task is to treat or rehabilitate youth who have gone astray so they will grow up to become law-abiding adults. What this means for decisionmaking is perhaps best expressed in the words of Judge Julian Mack, who served on the juvenile bench in the early twentieth century:

> The problem for determination . . . is not, Has this boy or girl committed a specific wrong, but What he is, how he has become what he is, and what had best be done in his interest and in the interest of the state to save him from a downward career (Mack, 1909:119).

According to this view, except at adjudication (when proof of the offense is at issue), juvenile justice officials should try to serve each youth's best interests, guided by a consideration of his or her background, family relationships, school performance, peer influences, and other factors bearing on the youth's needs and rehabilitative potential.

Complicating the matter, critics (including the U.S. Supreme Court) have argued that, while the juvenile justice system may be rehabilitative in theory, it has failed to achieve that goal in practice and is in fact a punitive system (see e.g., *In re Gault*, 1967; Feld, 1999). Most states still aspire to the rehabilitative ideal. However, in the wake of highly publicized media accounts of increased violent juvenile crime in the 1980s, many also began endorsing "get tough" policies that are decidedly punishment oriented.[6] The juvenile justice system today tries to both treat and punish (often punishing in the name of treatment).

To the extent that the juvenile justice system has become a punitive system, it can be argued that, like the criminal justice system, it should follow the "principle of offense." From this perspective, officials have no business basing decisions on family relationships, school performance, and other criteria that are not offense-related. To the extent that application of these criteria works to the disadvantage of minority youth, they are racially discriminatory. They are examples of institutionalized racism, referring to practices that, while not racist in intent, are discriminatory in effect. On the other hand, if one grants that the juvenile justice system is and should aspire to remain a treatment-oriented system, then factors like family background and school performance are legitimate considerations. Basing decisions on them may produce racial disparities, but they are not racially discriminatory.

Consider, for example, family status. There is considerable evidence that juvenile court officials are more likely to charge and incarcerate offenders from single-parent families because of concern about the inadequacy of parental supervision. Because black youth are more likely than white youth to reside in single-parent homes, they are more likely to be charged and incarcerated than white youth who have committed identical crimes. Is this racial discrimination? Or is this a legitimate practice that should be condoned even though it contributes to minority overrepresentation in processing? The answer depends on your view of what the juvenile justice system is, or should be, about.

The analysis now turns to a review of the evidence of disparity and discrimination in juvenile justice processing. Space considerations do not allow complete coverage of all of the research. Instead, this section highlights robust findings that hold up across multiple studies.

Evidence of Discrimination in the Juvenile Justice System

An appraisal of bias in the juvenile justice system would not be complete if we did not look briefly beyond the operation of police, court, and correctional agencies to consider the politics of race and crime. Enforcement of the law is obviously constrained by the law itself. The conservative political climate of the last few decades has spawned legislation and strategic initiatives that, while perhaps not racist in intent, have definitely had a differential impact on minorities.

The "war on drugs" is one of the best examples. Although self-report studies showed little change in drug use during the 1970s compared to earlier periods, legislatures – responding to a media-created moral panic – targeted drug offenders for stepped up enforcement and harsher penalties (see e.g., Tonry, 1995). Whites and blacks reported similar levels of drug use, yet the media portrayed the drug problem as an urban black male phenomenon (Walker et al., 2000:45). In other words, the problem was "racialized." While drug arrest rates were higher among white than black youth throughout the 1970s, following the initiation of the war on drugs, drug arrests among whites dropped while arrests of blacks skyrocketed. By the early 1990s, the drug arrest rate for black youth was 4-5 times the white rate. The National Criminal Justice Commission concluded: "Police found more drugs in minority communities because that is where they looked for them" (Donziger, 1996:115).

There are numerous other examples of laws with built-in race bias. In many states, legislatures have enacted enhanced penalties for crimes committed within close proximity to public housing. One study found that all of the juveniles to whom such a provision was applied were black (Clarke, 1996:9). Enhanced penalties for gang members and curfew laws that apply only in urban communities also differentially weigh upon minority youth. Clearly, the current politico-legal climate has fostered policies and practices that exacerbate minority overrepresentation in the juvenile justice system.

Race and Policing

The nature of police work provides a great deal of potential for bias. Although officers are constrained by statutes, regulations, and the informal norms of their departments, rules cannot possibly cover all situations, and many situations are legally ambiguous (Lipsky, 1980). The vast majority of contacts with juveniles are for minor offenses, for which officer discretion is great (Engel et al., 2000; Terrill, 2001; Worden & Myers, 1999).

That police decisions often must be made quickly adds to the potential for bias. Officers draw on their personal backgrounds and experiences in making on-the-spot decisions (see, e.g. Smith & Visher, 1981). Differentiation between suspicious and nonsuspicious persons is essential to good police work, but in the context of a society suffused in race prejudice and inequality, race and class may become shorthand cues upon which decisions are based (Lipsky, 1980).

Unfortunately, we know very little about police handling of juveniles prior to arrest. The lack of information is especially distressing because police are the primary gatekeepers of the juvenile court. Bias introduced by them is likely to influence outcomes at later stages, even if there is no bias at later stages. Moreover, police bias is easily hidden. For example, if police more often arrest youth of color in situations where white youth are released or handled informally, this will translate into race differences in prior record. Court officials generally accept prior record as a legitimate basis on which to premise more severe dispositions. Similarly, if minority youth are subject to overcharging by the police, they will penetrate deeper into the juvenile court system. Seriousness of the arrest offense is a key predictor of outcomes at nearly every stage in court processing, and its validity as a proxy for actual behavior is seldom questioned.

Racial disparities in police handling of juveniles have been attributed in part to deployment decisions. Patrol officers are disproportionately dispatched to geographic areas that have the highest crime rates, which tend to be areas with higher concentrations of poor and minority youth. Such deployment practices may be rational and defensible for some purposes, but by increasing surveillance of minority populations, they selectively increase the risk of detection and arrest (Werthman & Piliavin, 1967).

Observational studies of police suggest that neighborhood characteristics affect the exercise of officer discretion in ways that render youth of color more vulnerable to being stopped and arrested (Sampson, 1986; Smith, 1986; Smith et al., 1984; Conley, 1994). Officers develop shorthand "typifications" of neighborhoods based on race and class as a way of identifying dangerous places and suspicious persons. Officers tend to impute to people who reside in "bad neighborhoods" the negative characteristics of the areas themselves, resulting in a more aggressive stance toward minorities. A recent survey of Cincinnati residents found that 47 percent of blacks, compared to 10 percent of whites, reported that they had been stopped or watched by the police when they had done nothing wrong. Among young people, the race difference was even more dramatic (Browning et al., 1994:9; Kennedy, 1997).

Although there have been few studies of police-juvenile encounters, most suggest that for minor offenses, race has an indirect effect on arrest that operates through youth's demeanor. A study conducted in two states showed that minority suspects were twice as likely as whites to be perceived as disrespectful by the officer, which significantly elevated the probability of arrest (Worden & Myers, 1999). There is fairly consistent evidence across a number of studies that youth of color are (or are perceived to be) more belligerent and uncooperative (see e.g., Bell & Lang, 1985; Kurtz et al., 1993, Wordes & Bynum, 1995; Worden & Shepard, 1996). Officers tend to interpret hostile demeanor as an indicator of criminal propensity, or as a signal that the situation may get out of control (Bittner, 1990:336). Demeanor can be misleading, however, because juveniles frequently hang out in groups, and police-juvenile encounters routinely occur in situations in which youth are "on stage" before an audience of their peers. In such settings, an attitude of toughness or hostility may be a face-saving tactic rather than a harbinger of danger. Hostile attitudes may also be a response to real or perceived police prejudice, especially if police concentrate surveillance in underclass areas and make frequent stops of minority youth. Research indicates that such practices generate anger and perpetuate a vicious cycle (Anderson, 1990; Griffiths & Winfree, 1982).

Other research has examined police charging decisions. The most common finding is that blacks and whites who have engaged in similar behavior are not treated the same. Kurtz et al. (1993) assessed whether the charges police recorded at arrest were the most serious that could have been made. They found that black and lower-class youth were charged with more serious offenses because they were perceived to be more hostile (Kurtz et al., 1993). Another study presented vignettes based on actual police-juvenile encounters to officers in several police departments (Sutphen et al., 1993). Officers were asked whether they would make an arrest and what charges they would record. Even though the vignettes were identical in all other respects save race, officers indicated they would arrest black suspects more often and charge them with more counts and more serious crimes (Sutphen et al., 1993).

Intake Decisionmaking

The consensus of prior research is that legal (offense-related) variables are the strongest predictors of intake decisions to refer cases for formal handling (see, e.g., Bishop & Frazier, 1988, 1996; DeJong & Jackson, 1998; Kempf et al., 1990; Leiber, 1994, 1995). However, there is also considerable evidence of racial and ethnic disparity that cannot be explained by legal factors. Researchers have identified several non-legal factors that help to explain why minority youth are less likely to be filtered out of the system. One involves criteria for diversion. As a matter of policy in many jurisdictions, juveniles are ineligible for diversion if their parents do not appear for an interview. In a Florida study, Bishop & Frazier (1996) reported that minority families were less likely to have phones, access to transportation, access to childcare, and the ability to take time from work without loss of pay – all of which made it more difficult for them to comply with official policy.

Family assessments also play an important role in decisions to refer youth for formal processing. A study of juvenile court case records in Missouri showed that parents of minority youth were described as less willing to supervise their children and less capable of exercising proper control even when they expressed a willingness to do so (Kempf et al., 1990). Although it is unclear on what basis these judgments were made, the danger of racial stereotyping is unmistakable. Several studies report that blacks are disadvantaged at intake because their parents are perceived as uncooperative and incapable of providing adequate supervision.

Financial considerations also contribute to racial disparities. Intake officials have indicated that middle-class families are able to purchase private services for their children (e.g., counseling, substance abuse treatment) and avoid formal processing, while comparable services for lower class can only be obtained by court order following an adjudication of delinquency (Bishop & Frazier, 1996; see also Bortner et al., 1993). Officials most often defend this practice of differential handling on the grounds that it enables them to provide services for the poor that more affluent families can purchase on their own. In their view, the goal of obtaining treatment supersedes concerns about selective prosecution of poor (disproportionately minority) youth.

School problems (low grades, suspensions) also influence intake decisions to refer youth for formal processing. While low academic performance is common among delinquent youth, it is more common among blacks, Native Americans, and Hispanics (for whom English is frequently a second language). Suspensions are also more common for minorities, both because inner-city schools tend to use suspension much more liberally as a response to student misconduct and because suspension is used more often when the misbehaving student is black (Williams, 1989; McFadden et al., 1992).

Detention

Detention is the decision point at which substantial race effects that cannot be explained by offense-related variables are most often found (see, e.g., Bishop & Frazier, 1988, 1996; Bortner & Reed, 1985; Bridges et al., 1993; Wordes & Bynum, 1995). Some studies show that race is more strongly correlated with being detained than either offense or prior record. Several factors contribute to race differences in treatment. These include perceptions that minorities are involved in drugs or gangs, that students perform poorly in school, and that parental supervision is inadequate. Unfortunately, discrimination at this point in the system has serious repercussion for later outcomes. Youth who are detained are more likely to be adjudicated delinquent, and more likely to receive harsher sanctions at disposition, than youth who are equivalent in all other respects.

Prosecutorial Charging

Very few studies have explored the influence of race/ethnicity on prosecutorial decisions to file formal charges, and they have produced mixed results. Some have found that minorities are more likely to be charged even after controlling for other variables (see, e.g., MacDonald & Chesney-Lind, 2001; Leonard & Sontheimer, 1995). Others have found that blacks are more likely to be formally charged only because they are more likely to be detained (Bishop & Frazier, 1988, 1996). Still others report that minority youth are less likely to be formally charged because they are more often arrested on the basis of weak evidence (Bridges et al., 1993).

Adjudication

Contrary to the results at virtually every other decision point, most studies report that, even after controlling for referral offense and prior record, minority youth are less likely to be adjudicated delinquent than whites (see, e.g., Johnson & Secret, 1990; Secret & Johnson, 1997; Wu et al., 1997). A plausible explanation is that minority youth more often progress to the adjudicatory stage despite having been arrested and charged on the basis of weaker evidence. Judges may compensate at adjudication for the differential treatment that occurred earlier, especially since adjudicatory decisions focus on evidence of guilt, rather than on characteristics of youth and their social backgrounds (Dannefer & Schutt, 1982). At all stages at which a youth's background and life circumstances are considered, black, Hispanic, and Native American defendants are disadvantaged relative to whites.

Judicial Disposition

The juvenile codes of most states specify that dispositions are to be guided by consideration of both the risk offenders pose for public safety and their treatment needs. There is a fair degree of consensus that prior record is the strongest predictor of disposition outcomes. (From the standpoint of risk assessment, this makes good sense. Past behavior is generally a pretty good indicator of how people will behave in the future.) Previous dispositions are also highly influential, more so than the current offense. (From the standpoint of treatment needs, this also makes fairly good sense. Courts generally look to what treatments or sanctions they have tried in the past. When these have failed, dispositions that are more lengthy and intensive are selected the next time around.) (see e.g., Henretta et al., 1986; Thornberry & Christensen, 1984) These considerations put minorities at a disadvantage compared to whites. Youth of color are more vulnerable to arrest and formal processing than whites. Consequently, compared to white youth who have engaged in identical behaviors, youth of color more readily accumulate offense histories and dispositions from which unfair inferences about risk and needs are drawn.

It is also the case that youth who are detained generally receive more severe sanctions. For a variety of reasons, most of which have little to do with the offenses with which they are charged, minority youth are more likely to be detained than whites. Other fairly strong predictors of more severe dispositions include conviction for a drug offense and being from a family that is perceived as dysfunctional. Youth of color are disadvantaged on all counts.

In making disposition decisions, judges frequently rely heavily on predisposition reports prepared by probation departments. In a fascinating study, Bridges & Steen (1998) examined these reports to determine whether there were differences in the ways that black and white offenders were described. Controlling for offense and prior record, they found pronounced racial differences in the attributions made by probation officers regarding the causes of offending. Offending among whites was more often attributed to external factors, while blacks' offenses were most often attributed to moral character flaws and personality defects. Since defects of character or personality are enduring traits, minority youth were viewed as more fully responsible for their bad acts, as less treatable, and as more likely to re-offend. Whites were viewed as more sympathetic figures: they were judged to be less responsible for their behavior because it was due to factors outside of their control. Consequently, they were regarded as less threatening and as more promising candidates for treatment and rehabilitation. Consistent with these perceptions, whites received more lenient sentencing recommendations than blacks.

Correctional Placement

The juvenile corrections systems in most states include a wide variety of facilities and programs, ranging from large and generally very secure training schools to small, community-based group homes and halfway houses. In one of the few studies to report on race and ethnic differences in correctional placement while controlling for offense-related variables, Leonard and Sontheimer found that blacks and Hispanics were more often sent to large institutions, and whites to small, privately run group homes, foster homes, and drug and alcohol treatment programs (Leonard & Sontheimer, 1995:120). Another study examined placements made by the Texas Youth Commission. White youth were more likely than Hispanic or black youth to be diagnosed with emotional disturbances. Among those diagnosed as disturbed and "in high need for treatment," 39 percent of whites actually received specialized treatment, compared to only 14 percent of blacks and Hispanics (Jeffords et al., 1993).

Other Sources of Bias

Thus far, we have examined studies of the processing of individual cases *within* juvenile courts. Research has also uncovered important differences in processing *across* courts that redound to the disadvantage of minorities. For example, urban courts tend to be more formal and bureaucratic than suburban and rural ones. That is, cases involving both black and white offenders referred to urban courts are more likely to progress to formal adjudication and disposition than those referred to courts in other areas. Research has also found that counties with greater underclass poverty and racial inequality more often place youth in detention and make greater use of out-of-home placements (Sampson & Laub, 1993:293). Each of these differences works to the disadvantage of blacks and Hispanics because they are more likely than whites to reside in underclass urban areas marked by racial inequality.

Explaining Bias in the Juvenile Justice System

There are two primary explanations for race bias in the juvenile justice system. The first, drawn from conflict theory (see e.g. Chambliss & Seidman, 1971; Blalock, 1967), draws attention to racial stereotypes that portray poor minority youth as especially threatening (see, e.g., Tittle & Curran, 1988). We have seen that police officers apply stereotypes to places and people. Lower-class neighborhoods inhabited by racial and ethnic minorities tend to be perceived as disreputable, and so too the people within them. Police officers patrol these neighborhoods especially heavily, make more investigative stops, and attend to demeanor in making judgments about who is dangerous and who is not. Disproportionately, they find signs of danger in the demeanor of minority youth.

At juvenile court intake, detention, formal charging, and disposition, officials also make judgments about youth's character and his or her propensity for future offending. The risk that youth of color will be perceived differently than whites based on factors other than offense and prior record is particularly great. "Character" is an amorphous concept and stereotypes of minority offenders as particularly dangerous and menacing are deeply embedded in popular culture. Nowhere is the evidence of racial stereotyping more apparent than in Bridges' and Steen's research on probation officers' attributions, risk predictions, and sentencing recommendations. Research in other contexts (e.g., simulated juror decisionmaking) has also linked race with attributions of culpability (see e.g., Bodenhausen & Wyler, 1995; Pfeifer & Ogloff, 1991). These studies corroborate the idea that race differentials in processing are supported by popular stereotypes of minority offenders as more dangerous than their white counterparts.

An alternative explanation for race and ethnic disparities in processing is that the juvenile justice system is more paternalistic toward minorities because they are perceived as more needy than whites.[7] We have seen that studies that control for personal and social factors (e.g., family structure, ability of parents to provide control and supervision, school performance) report that these variables influence court referral, detention, and disposition decisions. From the perspective of juvenile justice officials with a social-welfare orientation, these indicators of need are legitimate considerations.

There are several troubling aspects to the court's responsiveness to the needs of youth. First, it seems unreasonable that the economically disadvantaged should have to accrue a record of conviction as the *quid pro quo* for services they cannot purchase on their own, while middle- and upper-class children can avoid a delinquency record because their parents can arrange for these services privately. The result is what Bortner has called a "two-track" juvenile justice system – one for youth from largely middle-class white families and a second for the children of low-income families who are largely black, Hispanic, and Native American (Bortner et al., 1993:73; see also Eisenstein, 1994:43).

Second, there is a real danger that racial stereotypes will enter unwittingly into needs assessments. Qualitative research indicates, for example, that single-parent minority families are perceived as more dysfunctional than single-parent white families and that, irrespective of family structure, parental supervision in minority families is perceived as less adequate (Frazier & Bishop, 1995). By legitimating the assessment of treatment needs, the juvenile court may be an especially receptive host to subtle forms of racial discrimination:

> When decisions to process juveniles formally as opposed to infor-
> mally, or harshly as opposed to leniently, hinge on evaluations of
> the social circumstances in which juveniles live, officials are in a
> precarious position. They must somehow evaluate comparatively
> perceived differences in family structure, neighborhood reputation,
> demeanor of juveniles and their families – indeed, the culture of vari-
> ous groups from which defendants come. Almost invariably, there is
> a reliance on common stereotypes of the nonwhite community, fam-
> ily, and interpersonal styles (Frazier & Bishop, 1995:35-36).

Third, because each of the needs to which justice officials attend (e.g., broken homes, dysfunctional and/or uncooperative families, even living in a high crime neighborhood (Frazier & Bishop, 1995) is (or is perceived to be) more characteristic of youth of color, it is inevitable that minority youth will more often penetrate the system and receive more severe dispositions than whites. In other words, race and ethnic differentials are virtually built into a system that purports to respond to the needs of delinquent youth. This is nothing new. From its very beginnings at the turn of the twentieth century, the juvenile justice system was preoccupied with immigrant children living in conditions of poverty in inner-city America. Minority youth from impov-erished backgrounds have always been the key "beneficiaries" of services of the juvenile court.

A key issue is whether youth actually receive services that benefit them. If treatment is the justification for greater intrusion into the lives of minority youth, is effective treatment actually provided? Probation, the most com-mon "treatment," has become little more than a monitoring system involving periodic phone checks to insure that youth are attending school and living at home. Probation caseloads are so high that officers rarely have time to meet with youth one-on-one.[8] When youth fail on probation, they eventually wind up in institutions. To a youth who has been cut off from his or her home, fam-ily, and friends, this feels like punishment. To be sure, some of what happens to youth in the best institutions is positive (e.g., social skills training, anger management classes, academic education, vocational training), but many insti-tutions are little more than warehouses. Overcrowding is a pervasive problem (Parent et al., 1994) and it contributes to violence (see e.g., Feld, 1977; Miller, 1998). Many institutions are operating under consent decrees in settlement of class-action lawsuits detailing the abuse of incarcerated youth and unconsti-tutional ("cruel and unusual") conditions of confinement.

With regard to treatment effectiveness, recidivism rates are high, especially among youth who are committed to residential placement. Although no national recidivism data are available, individual programs and some states track re-offense rates. One of the most systematic data collection efforts occurs in Florida. There, a report on more than 10,000 youth who successfully completed commitment programs showed that 63 percent were rearrested within one year of release (Florida Department of Juvenile Justice, 1999). This poor rate of success cannot justify differential selection of minorities for institutionalization.

High rates of recidivism are not surprising when one considers that the vast majority of young offenders return to the same criminogenic environments from which they came. This point leads to an even more important one. If, as has been suggested above, the roots of crime lie in social and economic conditions, race differentials in juvenile court responses cannot be justified in the name of "treatment" when the juvenile justice system is powerless to alter these conditions that cause crime.

In conclusion, it appears that the same structural factors responsible in large part for race differences in offending (poverty, racial inequality, social disorganization, family disruption) are also responsible for racial disparities in juvenile justice processing. "Differential offending" and "system bias" are mutually reinforcing, and both are rooted in underlying social and economic conditions that are beyond the reach of the juvenile court (National Research Council and Institute of Medicine, 2001; Bortner et al., 2000).

Policy Implications

The problem of minority overrepresentation in the juvenile justice system is complex and does not lend itself to easy solutions. Efforts to reduce racial disparity would seem to require a multi-pronged approach aimed at altering structural factors that limit the opportunities of poor and minority youth. Effective, long-term solutions cannot come from within the juvenile justice system itself, for the source of the problem lies in social and economic conditions. Change will require a national focus on the problems faced by impoverished inner-city families.

Efforts to reduce minority overrepresentation would include such things as improving inner-city schools by incorporating skilled trades curricula; updating equipment and educational materials; providing incentives to attract more qualified teachers; replacing out-of-school suspension with in-school behavioral management; and providing after-school tutoring for at-risk youth. Improving schools might help youth be better prepared for higher education and for positions other than dead end, minimum-wage jobs in the service sector. It will be necessary also to make efforts to create employment opportunities (e.g., by providing industry incentives to relocate to the urban core, including tax breaks and employee subsidies). Efforts to organize and empower residents in minority communities are also essential. There are numerous strategies that might be employed (beginning with community policing and enlisting the support of local churches) to assist inner-city residents to come together in civic organizations. It will take neighborhood organization to bring community problems to the attention of local and state officials and to exert sufficient pressure to institute change (e.g., removing drug dealers from the streets; rehabilitating abandoned houses that become havens for illicit activity; establishing day-care centers, free clinics, and recreational programs).

Youth living in isolated inner-city ghettoes might benefit greatly from sustained contact with conventional adult role models. Big Brother/Big Sister programs, and similar efforts to establish meaningful long-term relationships between impoverished minority youth and middle- and upper-class minority adults, would help to expose at-risk youth to conventional values and to persons who can show them pathways to success in conventional terms.

There are some things that can be done within the justice system, but these are ancillary to the social and economic changes required to promote lasting change. Because stereotyping of minority neighborhoods, families, and youth by justice officials increases the probability of arrest, referral, formal charging, and intrusive dispositions, efforts need to be undertaken to combat myths and misconceptions, especially those that portray minority offenders as threatening and morally defective, or their families as disinterested or incapable of providing effective guidance and supervision.[9] Requiring training for justice officials in cultural sensitivity and awareness would help them become aware of their own attitudes and beliefs and facilitate more objective assessments of youth and their families.

Juvenile justice officials also need to identify and take steps to change formal and informal agency policies that, even if well intended, work to the disadvantage of minority youth. The common intake requirement of a face-to-face interview with a parent as a precondition for diversion and release is a case in point. Arrangements could be made instead to talk to parents by phone or visit them in their homes. Premising processing decisions on youth's demeanor during the period immediately before and after arrest is another informal policy that should be reconsidered. Demeanor is transitory and situational. A youth's reactions are highly dependent on the personal characteristics (including race) and demeanor of the official(s) with whom he or she interacts.

Finally, whether a youth is diverted or adjudicated delinquent should not depend on his or her parents' ability to pay for counseling or substance abuse treatment. This practice violates fundamental principles of equality under the law. As a solution, juvenile court resources could be allocated to the front end of the system in the form of vouchers for mental health and other services available in the community. These services could then be accessed by financially disadvantaged youth and their families without legal penalty.

Conclusion

In summary, several observations are worth noting. Minority overrepresentation in the juvenile justice system appears to be attributable both to race differences in offending and to inequities in the response of the juvenile justice system to white and minority offenders who are legally equivalent. Higher rates of offending among minority youth are attributable in part to the impoverished conditions in which minority families disproportionately reside – in socially disorganized areas where drugs, theft, and violence are pervasive features of everyday life.

Race differences in offending, however, cannot fully account for racial disparities in official responses. It has been suggested here that disparities in processing stem from the juvenile court's dual focus on protecting the public from dangerous offenders and on rehabilitating offenders with the greatest needs. On both counts, minorities are disadvantaged.

Politicians and the media have linked race, drugs, and violence in public perceptions, creating stereotypical images of minority youth as especially dangerous. These images have contributed to the enactment of laws that differentially target minority youth, to selective police surveillance of minority neighborhoods, and to harsher court responses to youth of color.

Disparities in processing are also produced by the juvenile court's *parens patriae* orientation, which legitimates greater solicitude toward "needy" offenders. Compared to whites, minority youth more often have school problems and are more likely to reside in single-parent homes. In addition, stereotypes of minority families as dysfunctional – as unable or unwilling to provide proper guidance and support for their children – contribute to processing disparities. So too do inner-city schools, which are of inferior quality and use suspension liberally (and in a racially discriminatory manner) in response to student misbehavior.

Harsher court responses to minority youth also reflect the police tendency to arrest youth of color for minor crimes that would be informally adjusted if committed by whites, and to overcharge when recording arrests. As a result, minorities more readily accrue arrest records, for more serious crimes, to which the courts respond by imposing more intrusive sanctions.

It has been suggested here that race differentials in both offending and system response have common origins in social and economic features of contemporary American life and the neighborhood traditions of delinquency and crime to which they give rise. Consequently, minority overrepresentation in the juvenile justice system cannot be addressed adequately through reforms in the justice system itself. It is essential that we attend to structural conditions (poverty, unemployment, racial segregation, family disruption). Reducing minority overrepresentation will require nothing less than making the problems faced by impoverished inner-city families a national priority. Until "other people's children" are recognized as "our children," there can be little hope of substantial change.

Endnotes

[1] It is only in the past 15 years that the federal government has identified minority overrepresentation as a high priority issue. In 1988, Congress passed an amendment to the Juvenile Justice and Delinquency Prevention (JJDP) Act of 1974 requiring that states which receive federal funds under the Formula Grants Program to take steps to reduce the disproportionate minority confinement in detention centers, jails, lockups, and secure commitment facilities (Public Law 93-415, 42 U.S.C. 5061 et seq.). In the 1992 Amendments to the JJDP Act, reducing disproportionate minority confinement and contact (DMC) was elevated to a "core requirement" and future funding was made contingent on state compliance.

[2] Data are reported for 2003 because this is the last year for which complete data on the racial distribution of arrests and youth incarcerated in prisons are currently available. Although there are more recent juvenile court and corrections data, the racial distributions are similar to those reported here. The advantage of using data from a single year is that we can see the movement of a cohort of cases through the entire system.

[3] In the remaining 27 percent of cases, police let the suspect go with a warning, turned the youth over to his or her parents, or otherwise handled the matter informally. Consistent with the "get-tough" era of juvenile justice, the proportion of cases that the police choose to handle informally has been steadily declining.

[4] In 2005, in the landmark case of *Roper v. Simmons*, the U. S. Supreme Court declared that because of their youth and immaturity, the death penalty is an unconstitutional punishment for persons under the age of 18.

[5] Indeed, to ensure fidelity to the principle of offense, many states have adopted determinate sentencing and sentencing guidelines (which tell the judge what sentence should be imposed based on characteristics of the offense and the defendant's prior record).

[6] These include the adoption of graduated sanction policies, determinate and mandatory sentencing, and broadened criteria for transfer to criminal court.

[7] It is noteworthy that studies of the adult criminal justice system, which does not focus on defendants' needs, report much less evidence of race effects than studies of the juvenile court.

[8] The most recent national report indicates a median active caseload size of 41.

[9] For example, justice officials would benefit by learning about extended kin networks as resources for minority youth, rather than focusing on disruption and dysfunction within the nuclear family.

References

Anderson, E. (1990). *Street Wise: Race, Class, and Change in an Urban Community*. Chicago, IL: University of Chicago Press.

Bell, D., Jr. & K. Lang (1985). "The Intake Dispositions of Juvenile Offenders." *Journal of Research in Crime and Delinquency*, 22:309-328.

Bishop, D.M. & C.E. Frazier (1996). "Race Effects in Juvenile Justice Decisionmaking: Findings of a Statewide Analysis." *Journal of Criminal Law and Criminology*, 86:392-414.

Bishop, D.M. & C.E. Frazier (1988). "The Influence of Race in Juvenile Justice Processing." *Journal of Research in Crime and Delinquency*, 25:242-263.

Bishop, D.M., C.E. Frazier, L. Lanza-Kaduce & L. Winner (1996). "The Transfer of Juveniles to Criminal Court: Does it Make a Difference." *Crime & Delinquency*, 42(2):171-191.

Bittner, E. (1990). "Policing Juveniles: The Social Context of Common Practices." In E. Bittner (ed.) *Aspects of Police Work*, pp. 322-247. Boston, MA: Northeastern University Press.

Blalock, H. (1967). *Toward a Theory of Minority-Group Relations.* New York, NY: John Wiley.

Blumstein, A. (1982). "On the Racial Disproportionality of the U.S. States' Prison Population." *Journal of Criminal Law and Criminology*, 73:1259-1281.

Bodenhausen, G.V. & R.S. Wyler (1995). "Effects of Stereotypes on Decision Making and Information Processing Strategies." *Journal of Personality and Social Psychology*, 48:267-304

Bortner, M.A., C. Burgess, A. Schneider & A. Hall (1993). *Equitable Treatment of Minority Youth: A Report on the Overrepresentation of Minority Youth in Arizona's Juvenile Justice System.* Phoenix, AZ: Arizona Juvenile Justice Advisory Council, Minority Youth Issues Committee.

Bortner, M.A., M.S. Zatz & D.F. Hawkins (2000). "Race and Transfer: Empirical Research and Social Context." In J. Fagan & F.E. Zimring (eds.) *The Changing Borders of Juvenile Justice*, pp. 277-320. Chicago, IL: University of Chicago Press.

Bortner, M.A. & W.L. Reed (1985). "The Preeminence of Process: An Example of Refocused Justice Research." *Social Science Quarterly*, 66:413-425.

Bridges, G.S., D. Conley, G. Beretta & R.L. Engen (1993). *Racial Disproportionality in the Juvenile Justice System: Final Report.* Olympia, WA: State of Washington, Department of Social and Health Sciences.

Bridges, G.S. & S. Steen (1998). "Racial Disparities in Official Assessments of Juvenile Offenders: Attributional Stereotypes as Mediating Mechanisms." *American Sociological Review* 63:554-570.

Browning, S.L., F.T. Cullen, L. Cao, R. Kopache & T.J. Stevenson (1994). "Race and Getting Hassled by the Police: A Research Note." *Police Studies*, 17:1-11.

Chambliss, W.J. & R.B. Seidman (1971). *Law, Order, and Power.* Reading, MA: Addison-Wesley.

Clarke, E. (1996). "A Case for Reinventing Juvenile Transfer." *Juvenile and Family Court Journal*, 47(4):3-21.

Community Research Associates (1997). *Disproportionate Confinement of Minority Juveniles in Secure Facilities: 1996 National Report.* Washington, DC: U. S. Department of Justice, Office of Juvenile Justice and Delinquency Prevention.

Conley, D.J. (1994). "Adding Color to a Black and White Picture: Using Qualitative Data to Explain Racial Disproportionality in the Juvenile Justice System." *Journal of Research in Crime and Delinquency*, 31:135-148.

Dannefer, D. & R.K. Schutt (1982). "Race and Juvenile Justice Processing in Court and Police Agencies." *American Journal of Sociology*, 87:1113-1132.

DeJong, C. & K.C. Jackson (1998). "Putting Race into Context: Race, Juvenile Justice Processing, and Urbanization." *Justice Quarterly*, 15:487-504.

Donziger, S.R. (ed.) (1996). *The Real War on Crime: The Report of the National Criminal Justice Commission.* New York, NY: Harper Collins.

Eisenstein, Z. (1994). *The Color of Gender: Reimaging Democracy.* Berkeley, CA: University of California Press.

Elliott, D.S. (1994). "Serious Violent Offenders: Onset, Developmental Course, and Termination—The American Society of Criminology 1993 Presidential Address." *Criminology*, 32(1):1-21.

Elliott, D.S. & S. Ageton. (1990). "Reconciling Race and Class Differences in Self-Reported and Official Estimates of Delinquency." *American Sociological Review*, 45:95-110.

Engel, R.S., J.J. Sobol & R.E. Worden (2000). "Further Explanation of the Demeanor Hypothesis: The Interaction Effects of Suspects' Characteristics and Demeanor on Police Behavior." *Justice Quarterly*, 17:235-258.

Farrington, D.P., R. Loeber, M. Stouthamer-Loeber, M. VanKammen & L. Schmidt (1996). "Self-reported Delinquency and a Combined Delinquency Seriousness Scale Based on Boys, Mothers, and Teachers: Concurrent and Predictive Validity for African-Americans and Caucasians." *Criminology*, 34:493-514.

Feld, B.C. (1999). *Bad Kids: Race and the Transformation of the Juvenile Court*. New York, NY: Oxford University Press.

Feld, B.C. (1993a). "Criminalizing the American Juvenile Court." In M. Tonry (ed.) *Crime and Justice: A Review of Research*, Volume 17, pp. 107-280. Chicago, IL: University of Chicago Press.

Feld, B.C. (1993b). "Juvenile (In)Justice and the Criminal Court Alternative." *Crime & Delinquency*, 39(4):403-424.

Feld, B.C. (1988). "The Juvenile Court Meets the Principle of Offense: Punishment, Treatment, and the Difference It Makes." *Boston University Law Review*, 68:821-915.

Feld, B.C. (1977). *Neutralizing Inmate Violence: Juvenile Offenders in Institutions*. Cambridge, MA: Ballinger Publishing.

Fishbein, D. (2001). *Biobehavioral Perspectives in Criminology*. Belmont, CA: Wadsworth.

Florida Department of Juvenile Justice (1999). *DJJ Recidivism Report for Commitment Programs FY 1997-98*. (Management Report 99-5). Tallahassee, FL: Florida Department of Juvenile Justice, Bureau of Data and Research.

Frazier, C.E. & D.M. Bishop (1995). "Reflections on Race Effects in Juvenile Justice." In K.K. Leonard, C.E. Pope & W.H. Feyerherm (eds.) *Minorities in Juvenile Justice*, pp. 16-46. Thousand Oaks, CA: Sage Publishing Company.

Greenfield, L.A. (1999). "Juvenile Offending as Reported by Victims of Violence." Unpublished paper presented to the National Research Council Workshop on Racial Disparity in the Juvenile Justice System. Reported in National Research Council and Institute of Medicine.

Griffiths, C.T. & L.T. Winfree, Jr. (1982). "Attitudes toward the Police – A Comparison of Canadian and American Adolescents." *International Journal of Comparative and Applied Criminal Justice*, 6:128-141.

Hawkins, D.F., J.H. Laub & J.L. Lauritsen (1998). "Race, Ethnicity, and Serious Juvenile Offending." In R. Loeber & D. P. Farrington (eds.) *Serious and Violent Juvenile Offenders: Risk Factors and Successful Interventions*, pp.30-46. Thousand Oaks, CA: Sage Publishing Company.

Hawkins, J.D., J.M. Jenson, R.F. Catalano & D. Lishner (1988). "Delinquency and Drug Abuse: Implications for Social Service." *Social Service Review*, 62:258-284.

Henrettta, J.C., C.E. Frazier & D.M. Bishop (1986). "The Effect of Prior Case Outcomes on Juvenile Justice Decisionmaking." *Social Forces*, 65:554-562.

Hindelang, M.J. (1978). "Race and Involvement in Common-Law Personal Crimes." *American Sociological Review*, 43:93-109.

Hindelang, J.M. (1981). "Variations in Sex-Race-Age-Specific Incidence Rates of Offending." *American Sociological Review*, 46:461-474.

Huizinga, D. & D. Elliott (1986). "Re-assessing the Reliability and Validity of Self-Report Delinquency Measures." *Journal of Quantitative Criminology*, 2:293-327.

Huizinga, D., R. Loeber & T. Thornberry (1994). *Urban Delinquency and Substance Abuse. Initial Findings*. Washington, DC: Office of Justice Programs, Office of Juvenile Justice and Delinquency Prevention.

In re Gault, 387 U.S. 1, 87 S. Ct. 1428, 18 L. Ed.2d 527 (1967).

Jeffords, C., J. Lindsey & S. McNitt (1993). *Overrepresentation of Minorities in the Juvenile Justice System*. Huntsville, TX: Department of Research and Planning, Texas Youth Commission.

Johnson, J.B. & P.E. Secret (1990). "Race and Juvenile Justice Decision Making Revisited." *Criminal Justice Policy Research*, 4:159-187.

Kempf, K.L., S.H. Decker & R.L. Bing (1990). *An Analysis of Apparent Disparities in the Handling of Black Youth Within Missouri's Juvenile Justice Systems*. to St. Louis, MO: Department of Administration of Justice, University of Missouri-St. Louis.

Kennedy, R. (1997). *Race, Crime, and the Law*. New York, NY: Pantheon Books.

Kurtz, P.D., M.M. Giddings & R. Sutphen (1993). "A Prospective Investigation of Racial Disparity in the Juvenile Justice System." *Juvenile and Family Court Journal*, 44:43-59.

Langan, P. (1985). "Racism on Trial: New Evidence to Explain the Racial Composition of Prisons in the United States." *Journal of Criminal Law and Criminology*, 76:666-683.

Leiber, M.J. (1995). "Toward Clarification of the Concept of 'Minority' Status and Decision-Making in Juvenile Court Proceedings." *Journal of Crime and Justice*, 18:79-108.

Leiber, M.J. (1994). "A Comparison of Juvenile Court Outcomes for Native Americans, African Americans, and Whites." *Justice Quarterly*, 11:257-279.

Leonard, K.K. & H. Sontheimer (1995). "The Role of Race in Juvenile Justice in Pennsylvania." In K.K. Leonard, C.E. Pope & W.H. Feyerherm (eds.) *Minorities in Juvenile Justice*, pp. 98-127. Thousand Oaks, CA: Sage Publishing Company.

Lipsky, M. (1980). *Street-Level Bureaucracy*. New York, NY: Russell Sage.

MacDonald, J.M. & M. Chesney-Lind (2001). "Gender Bias and Juvenile Justice Revisited: A Multiyear Analysis." *Crime & Delinquency*, 47:173-195.

Mack, J. (1909). "The Juvenile Court." *Harvard Law Review*, 22:104-122.

Matza, D. (1964). *Delinquency and Drift*. New York, NY: Wiley.

McFadden, A., G. March, B. Price & Y. Hwang (1992). "A Study of Race and Gender Bias in the Punishment of School Children." *Education and Treatment of Children*, 15:140-146.

Miller, J.G. (1998). *Last One Over the Wall*, Second Edition. Columbus, OH: Ohio State University Press.

National Center for Juvenile Justice (2007). *National Juvenile Court Data Archive: Juvenile Court Case Records 1985-2004* [machine-readable files]. Available online: http://www.ojjdp.ncjrs.gov.ojstatbb/ezajcs.

National Research Council and Institute of Medicine. J. McCord, C.S. Widom & N.A. Crowell (eds.) (2001). *Juvenile Crime, Juvenile Justice.* Panel on Juvenile Crime: Prevention, Treatment, and Control. Committee on Law and Justice and Board on Children, Youth, and Families. Washington, DC: National Academy Press.

Office of Juvenile Justice and Delinquency Prevention. *Census of Juveniles in Residential Placement for 2003.* Washington, DC: Bureau of the Census.

Parent, D.G., V. Leiter, S. Kennedy, L. Livens, D. Wentworth & S. Wilcox (1994). *Conditions of Confinement: Juvenile Detention and Corrections Facilities.* Washington, DC: U. S. Department of Justice, Office of Juvenile Justice and Delinquency Prevention.

Pfeifer, J.E. & J.R. Ogloff (1991). "Ambiguity and Guilt Determinations: A Modern Racism Perspective." *Journal of Applied and Social Psychology,* 21:1713-1725.

Puzzanchera, C., T. Finnegan & W. Kang (2007). *Easy Access to Juvenile Populations.* Available Online: http://www.ojjdp.ncjrs.org/ojstatbb/ezapop/[Retrieved April 4, 2008].

Roper v. Simmons, 543 U. S. 551 (2005).

Sampson, R.J. (1986). "Effects of Socioeconomic Context on Official Reaction to Juvenile Delinquency." *American Sociological Review,* 51:876-885.

Sampson, R.J. & J.H. Laub (1993). "Structural Variations in Juvenile Court Processing: Inequality, the Underclass, and Social Control." *Law and Society Review,* 27:285-311.

Sampson, R.J. & J.L. Lauritsen (1997). "Racial and Ethnic Disparities in Crime and Criminal Justice in the United States." In M. Tonry (ed.) *Crime and Justice: A Review of Research,* Volume 21, pp. 311-374. Chicago, IL: University of Chicago Press.

Sampson, R.J., J.D. Morenoff & F. Earls (1999). "Beyond Social Capital: Spatial Dynamics of Collective Efficacy for Children." *American Sociological Review,* 64:633-660.

Sampson, R.J., S.W. Raudenbush & F. Earls (1997). "Neighborhoods and Violent Crime: A Multilevel Study of Collective Efficacy." *Science,* 277(August 15):918-924.

Sampson, R.J. & W.B. Groves (1999). "Community Social Disorganization and Crime." In F.T. Cullen & R. Agnew (eds.) *Criminological Theory: Past to Present,* Chapter 7, pp. 71-76. Los Angeles, CA: Roxbury Publishing.

Sampson, R.J. & W.B. Groves (1989). "Community Structure and Crime: Testing Social-Disorganization Theory." *American Journal of Sociology,* 94:774-802.

Sampson, R.J. & W.J. Wilson (1995). "Toward a Theory of Race, Crime, and Urban Inequality." In J. Hagan & R. Peterson (eds.) *Crime and Inequality,* pp. 37-54. Stanford, CA: Stanford University Press.

Secret, P.E. & J.B. Johnson (1997). "The Effect of Race on Juvenile Justice Decision Making in Nebraska: Detention, Adjudication, and Disposition, 1988-1993." *Justice Quarterly,* 14:445-478.

Shaw, C. & H. McKay (1969). *Juvenile Delinquency and Urban Areas,* Revised Edition. Chicago, IL: University of Chicago Press. [originally published in 1942]

Sklar, H. (1995). *Chaos or Community?* Boston, MA: South End Press.

Smith, D.A. (1986). "The Neighborhood Context of Police Behavior." In A.J. Reiss & M. Tonry (eds.) *Communities and Crime,* pp. 313-342. Chicago, IL: University of Chicago Press.

Smith, D.A. & C.A. Visher (1981). "Street-Level Justice: Situational Determinants of Police Arrest Decisions." *Social Problems,* 29:167-177.

Smith, D.A., C.A. Visher & L.A. Davidson (1984). "Equity and Discretionary Justice: The Influence of Race on Police Arrest Decisions." *Journal of Criminal Law and Criminology*, 75:234-249.

Snyder, H.R. & M. Sickmund (2006). *Juvenile Offenders and Victims: 2006 National Report*. Washington, DC: U.S. Department of Justice, Office of Justice Programs, Office of Juvenile Justice and Delinquency Prevention.

Stahl, A., Finnegan, T. & W. Kang (2007). *Easy Access to Juvenile Court Statistics, 1985-1994*. Available Online: http://ojjdp.ncjrs.org/ojstatbb/ezajcs [Retrieved April 4, 2008].

Strom, K. (2000). *Profile of State Prisoners under Age 18, 1985-97*. Washington, DC: U.S. Department of Justice, Bureau of Justice Statistics.

Sutphen, R.P., D. Kurtz & M. Giddings (1993). "The Influence of Juveniles' Race on Police Decision-Making: An Exploratory Study." *Juvenile and Family Court Journal*, 44:69-78.

Terrill, R. (2001). *Police Coercion: Application of the Force Continuum*. New York, NY: LFB.

Thornberry, T. & S. Christensen (1984). "Criminal Justice Decisionmaking as a Longitudinal Process." *Social Forces*, 632:433-444.

Tittle, C.R. & D.A. Curran (1988). "Contingencies for Dispositional Disparities in Juvenile Justice." *Social Forces*, 67:23-58.

Tonry, M. (1995). *Malign Neglect: Race, Crime, and Punishment in America*. New York, NY: Oxford University Press.

Torbet, P.M. (1996). *Juvenile Probation: The Workhorse of the Juvenile Justice System. Juvenile Justice Bulletin* March 1996. Washington, DC: U. S. Department of Justice, Office of Juvenile Justice and Delinquency Prevention.

Torbet, P., R. Gable, H. Hurst IV, I. Montgomery, L. Szymanski & D. Thomas (1996). *State Responses to Serious and Violent Juvenile Crime*. Washington, DC: Office of Juvenile Justice and Delinquency Prevention.

Walker, S., C. Spohn & M. DeLone (2000). *The Color of Justice: Race, Ethnicity and Crime in America*. Belmont, CA: Wadsworth Publishing.

Werthman, C. & I. Piliavin (1967). "Gang Members and the Police." In D. Bordua (ed.) *The Police: Six Sociological Essays*, pp. 56-98. New York, NY: Wiley.

Williams, J. (1989). "Reducing the Disproportionately High Frequency of Disciplinary Actions Against Minority Students: An Assessment-Based Approach." *Equity and Excellence*, 24:31-37.

Wilson, W.J. (1987). *The Truly Disadvantaged*. Chicago, IL: University of Chicago Press.

Wilson, W.J. (ed.) (1993). *The Ghetto Underclass*. Newbury Park, CA: Sage Publishing Company.

Worden, R.E. & S.M. Myers (1999). "Police Encounters with Juvenile Subjects." Unpublished paper commissioned by the Panel of Juvenile Crime: Prevention, Treatment, and Control. Washington, DC: National Academy of Sciences.

Worden, R.E. & R.L. Shepard (1996). "Demeanor, Crime, and Police Behavior: A Re-examination of the Police Services Study Data." *Criminology*, 34:61-82.

Wordes, M. & T.S. Bynum (1995). "Policing Juveniles: Is there Bias against Youths of Color?" In K.K. Leonard, C.E. Pope & W.H. Feyerherm (eds.) *Minorities in Juvenile Justice*, pp.47-65. Thousand Oaks, CA: Sage Publishing Company.

Wu, B., S. Cernkovich & C.S. Dunn (1997). "Assessing the Effects of Race and Class on Juvenile Justice Processing in Ohio." *Journal of Criminal Justice*, 25(4):265-277.

CHAPTER 10

In Trouble and Ignored: Female Delinquents in America

Ruth Triplett
Dianne Cyr Carmody
Peggy S. Plass

Introduction

A curious mixture of attention and neglect characterizes the history of the treatment of girls by the juvenile justice system (Chesney-Lind & Shelden, 1998; Leonard, 1982). Since its inception, the juvenile justice system has been interested in the behavior of females, particularly when that behavior is seen as inappropriate in terms of traditional gender roles and expectations. Though arrested and institutionalized much less often than boys, as researchers have demonstrated time and time again (Chesney-Lind & Shelden, 1998), the police and juvenile justice system have demonstrated a remarkable attention to the pre-delinquent behaviors of girls, arresting and incarcerating them for behaviors often ignored in boys. In fact, the idea that girls receive differential treatment has led many researchers in this area to argue that the juvenile justice system's treatment of females is often characterized by both paternalism and sexism.

The attention paid by the juvenile justice system to the behavior of girls has been strangely countered by neglect in the areas of theory, research, resources, policy, and programs. Criminological and criminal justice research, both past and present, ignores females relative to males (for example, see Smart, 1976; Naffine, 1996; Belknap, 2001). Many traditional criminological theories were actually developed to explain the delinquency of boys, while others that supposedly focused on the delinquency of both males and females are in fact not well suited to explicate the delinquent activities of females (see

Leonard, 1982, for a review of the stance of traditional criminological theory on females and crime). Empirical research follows this trend with analyses often based on data that do not include females.

The lack of concern shown in theory and research is reflected in the level of resources, programming, and policies for males and females in the juvenile justice system. Although it is difficult to find out just how resources are distributed across males and females, an oft-cited study by Lipsey (1990) gives some indication. In reviewing program evaluations of delinquency prevention programs since 1950, Lipsey found that of the 443 programs examined, approximately 34 percent only admitted males, 42 percent served "mostly males," and six percent "some males;" only two percent served females only. In addition, of the programs that are available for females, evidence suggests that many of them were actually designed around the needs of males. The result of this lower level of theory, research, and resources is a juvenile justice system that deals with girls but whose policies and programs are designed for boys.

This combination of attention and neglect is a dangerous one both for the girls affected by it and for society. First there are the girls who need prevention, treatment, and re-entry programs. They need protection from the sexual, physical, and emotional abuse so common among pre-delinquent and delinquent girls. They need safe places to turn to when home is not safe. Left on their own, these girls may turn to pre-delinquent or delinquent behavior for survival. Then, there are the girls who have committed serious offenses. The treatment needs of these girls should not be ignored, and yet they so often are. Finally there is society, concerned about crime and implementing policies designed to get tough on offenders in general and violent female offenders in particular.

In today's climate of continuing concern about violent crime and "get-tough" style policies, it is particularly important to look at the juvenile justice system's treatment of girls. What exactly is the state of juvenile justice policies and programs for females? Where should progress for the future be made? These are the questions addressed in this chapter. Addressing these questions requires an understanding of two areas – the extent and nature of female offending, and the historical treatment of girls by the juvenile justice system.

The Extent and Nature of Delinquent Offending for Girls

Girls and boys are involved in criminal offending in quite different ways. Not only in the present, but historically as well, both the extent and nature of female delinquency appear to be quite different from that of boys. In this section, we will examine ways in which female delinquency is unique – both in terms of its "quantity" and its "quality" – and discuss some of the implications of this uniqueness.

The Extent of Female Delinquency

Perhaps the most notable feature of female delinquency is its rarity – that is, girls commit considerably fewer crimes than do boys. In 2003, for example, although girls accounted for about 50 percent of the juvenile population, they accounted for only about 29 percent of all juvenile arrests. In addition, girls comprised only 18 percent of juveniles arrested in 2003 for violent index offenses, while they accounted for 32 percent of all property index offenses (Federal Bureau of Investigation, 2004). This pattern of considerably greater involvement in delinquent offenses on the part of boys is consistent across time; that is, females have always been underrepresented as "clients" of the juvenile justice system.

One should note, however, that in recent years the involvement of girls in delinquency appears to be increasing. Much of the increase in the number of arrests for girls overall between 1994 and 2003 was in minor crime categories – for example, arrests of girls for disorderly conduct increased by 46 percent

Figure 10.1 **Juvenile Arrest Rates for Violent Crime Index Offenses by Sex, 1980-2006.**

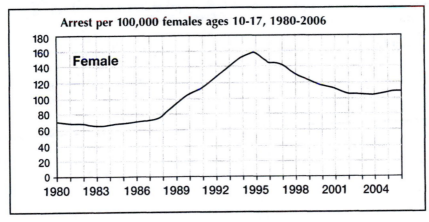

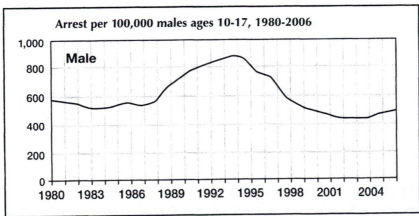

Source: OJJDP Statistical Briefing Book. Online. Available: http://ojjdp.ncjrs.org/ojstatbb/crime/JAR_Display.asp?ID=qa05231. December 13, 2007.

(while those for boys increased only 2%), those for liquor law violations increased by 26 percent for girls (compared with a 5% decline for boys), and for drug abuse violations, arrests of girls increased almost 60 percent (compared with a 13% increase for boys) (Snyder, 2005).

Of more concern are the arrest figures for violent offenses. According to FBI statistics, in 2003, females accounted for 24 percent of juvenile arrests for aggravated assault and 32 percent of juvenile arrests for simple assaults and intimidations. Between 1997 and 2002, the number of arrests (for all crimes) of girls in the United States remained stable, while those for boys fell 15 percent. In the same period, there was a 7 percent increase in the number of arrests of girls for violent index offenses (compared with a 5% decline in arrests of boys for this category of offense) (Snyder & Sickmund, 2006). In comparison, the data in Figure 10.1 indicate that the male arrest rate for violent index offenses still remains four times the arrest rate for females (Snyder & Sickmund, 2006).

At first glance, these arrest statistics might indicate the rise of a new "breed" of female offender. A closer examination of the trends, however,

Figure 10.2 **Juvenile Arrest Rates for Aggravated Assault by Sex, 1980-2006.**

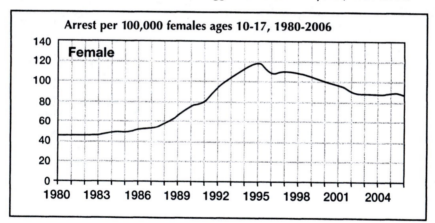

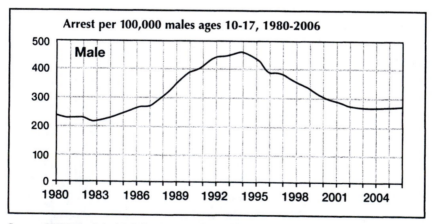

Source: OJJDP Statistical Briefing Book. Online. Available: http://ojjdp.ncjrs.org/ojstatbb/crime/JAR_Display.asp?ID=qa05235. December 13, 2007.

Figure 10.3 **Juvenile Arrest Rates for Simple Assault by Sex, 1980-2006.**

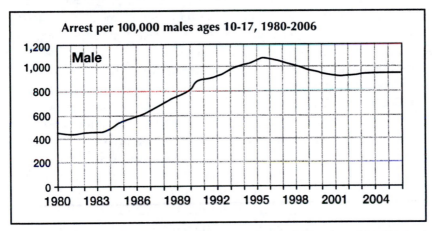

Source: OJJDP Statistical Briefing Book. Online. Available: http://ojjdp.ncjrs.org/ojstatbb/crime/
JAR_Display.asp?ID=qa05241. December 13, 2007.

suggests a different picture. First, much of the increase in the number of arrests for girls between 1994 and 2003 was in minor crime categories. Second, in the context of violent index offenses, almost all of the arrests of girls were for assault (they represented 85 percent of the violent index arrests). Assault was also the only category of violent index crime in which the number of female arrests increased in the 1990s – arrests actually declined for murder, rape, and robbery. (See Figures 10.2 and 10.3).

Some criminologists assessing these trends (i.e., the increase in arrests for assaults) suggest that society has become more attentive to female offending. In other words, this view suggests that the arrest data reflect a change in societal response to female offending rather than a substantive change in female delinquency. This does not, however, overlook the evidence that females do commit serious offenses. Researchers have linked violent offending among girls to two interesting developments which will be discussed below.

Thus, while the number of arrests of girls undeniably increased, much of this increase came in the area of minor offenses. Even the most alarmist interpretation of these recent trends, however, would still ultimately be that females are a decided minority among juvenile arrests, and this relative rarity of their criminal offending remains a defining feature of female delinquency.

The Nature of Female Delinquency

Females are not only different in the extent of their delinquent behavior but also in the nature of the acts they commit and for which they are likely to be processed through the juvenile justice system. Many of these differences parallel those between adult men and women – for example as noted above, girls (like women) are much less likely to be involved in violent crimes. Arguably the most significant feature of female involvement in juvenile crime comes in an area in which girls are distinct from their adult counterparts as well: the arrest rates for status offenses.

Status offenses are behaviors which are illegal for children but not for adults (e.g., running away from home, skipping school, violating curfews, the use of alcohol or tobacco, or even just being "incorrigible"). Since the development of the juvenile court, status offenses have been an important part of girls' offending. Further, if we compare the nature of the offenses of female delinquents with those of males (both historically and in the present), it is clear that girls are considerably more likely to be arrested for status offenses. In 2001, for example, 19 percent of the arrests of females were for status offenses (running away or curfew violations), while only 8 percent of the arrests of boys were in those categories (Snyder & Sickmund, 2006). Girls comprised more than one-half of the arrests for running away from home (59 percent) – one of only two offenses recorded by the FBI for which females are more than one-half of the arrests (the other being prostitution) (Snyder 2005).

Running away from home was, in fact, the second most likely offense for which girls were taken into custody in 2003 ("prostitution and commercialized vice" was the most likely offense) (Snyder & Sickmund, 2006:125). This difference in arrest rates for status offenses is striking because self report data suggest that boys and girls commit these offenses at similar rates. This strongly suggests that girls are more likely to be arrested for behavior such as running away from home and incorrigibility than boys (Chesney-Lind & Pasko, 2004). The difference in response to status offending, however, does not stop with arrests and the police. It also involves parents and the courts. Chesney-Lind (1989) has found that conflict with parents, and their insistence that the child be arrested, is a significant factor in police arrests of girls. In addition, she reports on research that shows that girls are more likely to be referred to the juvenile court than boys by sources other than the police, a significant group of which is parents.

There is also evidence that when they are accused of status offenses, girls are likely to be dealt with more harshly by the justice system. In spite of the fact that the 1974 Juvenile Justice and Delinquency Prevention Act specifically recommended the deinstitutionalization of status offenders, a significant number of girls continues to be sentenced to public or private juvenile institutions for these acts (Snyder & Sickmund, 2006). In 2003, for example, 13 percent of all girls in residential placement had a status offense as their most serious violation. Only four percent of boys in residential placement were there for status offenses (Snyder & Sickmund, 2006). In other words, in 2003, of all the females held in residential placement, 14 percent were delinquent and 40 percent were status offenders (Snyder & Sickmund, 2006:210). Overall, girls are a small minority of the juveniles in the United States who are in residential placement (only about 15% in 2003). They are, however, quite close to a majority of youth who are incarcerated for status offenses (40% in 2003). Clearly, the nature of the offenses that bring girls to a residential placement is different from that for boys. Girls are more likely to be institutionalized for a minor offense.

Understanding Girls' Delinquency: Victimization and Running Away

A final finding important in understanding girls' delinquency is the relationship that their offending has to victimization and running away from home. There is ample evidence that status or "pre-delinquent" offenses (like running away) are likely to stem from victimizations such as physical or sexual abuse or neglect in the family. Much research has shown that many girls who run away from home are fleeing physical or sexual abuse (Widom, 2000; Flowers, 2001). Once they have run away, girls may become involved in a variety of delinquent (as opposed to status) offenses as well – theft, prostitution, drug use and the like (Flowers, 2001; Chesney-Lind & Pasko, 2004; Gilfus, 1992). Pre-delinquent "survival strategies" thus become status offenses, which may in turn lead to more serious delinquency. Chesney-Lind (1989) refers to the connection between abuse at home, running away, offending and the response of the police and court as the "criminalization of girls' survival". Criminologists have frequently used this "pathways" approach to explain how childhood abuse and neglect may set young people on the road to homelessness and crime (Goodkind, Ng & Sarri, 2006; Siegel & Williams, 2003; Holsinger, Belknap & Sutherland, 1999).

Studies suggest that child sexual abuse and/or physical abuse or neglect may play an important role in the development of delinquent behavior among girls. Widom noted that "When compared with girls who have not been abused and neglected during childhood, abused and neglected girls are nearly twice as likely to be arrested as juveniles" (2000: 29). We know that about 70 percent of child sexual abuse victims are female (Tyler, Hoyt & Whitbeck, 2000).

Generally, research on female criminality has found that a much larger proportion of incarcerated females than males report having been physically or sexually abused in their childhoods, with many reporting this abuse before the age of 18 (Siegel, 2000). For example, in one study, 37 percent of female inmates in state prisons reported physical or sexual abuse before they were 18 years old (compared with only 14% of males in state prisons) (Harlow, 1999). Another study of juveniles found that 62 percent of girls who were in juvenile institutions had experienced physical abuse, and 54 percent had experienced sexual abuse (American Correctional Association, 1990). While it is reasonably clear that victimization and offending are interrelated for all delinquents, it appears that the role of victimization in leading to offending for juvenile females is more substantial than it is for males. Theorists recognize that girls who are victims of violence and abuse are more likely to become offenders and have identified girls' victimization as an explanation for their offending.

The above examination of both the extent and nature of female offending demonstrates three distinct features of the delinquent behavior of girls. First, female delinquency is relatively rare. In spite of the fact that there have been increases in the arrests of girls in recent years, females show no signs of "catching up" with their male counterparts in their levels of involvement in delinquency. Second, female delinquency is qualitatively different from that of males. In spite of an increase in arrests for assault, girls are still relatively less likely to be involved in violent offenses. It is status offenses that have historically played the largest role in female offending. If self-report studies are correct, however, girls are no more likely to be involved in status offenses than boys and yet they are more likely to be arrested for them. Third, many of these status or pre-delinquent offenses appear to grow out of victimization (e.g., sexual and physical abuse in the home) and to lead to more offending as well as more victimization for these girls. Indeed, studies of both girls and women who are incarcerated indicate that their levels of physical and sexual victimization are substantial (Siegel & Williams, 2003). It is likely that victimization plays a relatively greater role in the delinquent activities of girls than boys.

Girls, Paternalism, and the Juvenile Court

Examination of the extent and nature of female offending shows a pattern distinct from that of males. Differences are also found in the way in which males and females are treated by the juvenile justice system. An examination of the history of the juvenile court system reveals its paternalistic roots and exposes the use of the juvenile court to control the sexuality of girls and "keep them in their place." It also provides an understanding of the current situation of girls in the juvenile justice system in terms of the allocation of resources, programming, and policies. This section of the chapter traces the history of the juvenile court in the United States, with special attention to these practices, from Colonial times to today.

Laying the Groundwork:
Parens Patriae *and the Stubborn Child Law*

Within the United States, paternalistic governmental control of juveniles can be traced back to the legal doctrine of *parens patriae*. This doctrine supplies the legal basis for court intervention into the relationship between children and their parents (Teitelbaum & Harris, 1977; Krisberg & Austin, 1993). When it first originated, *parens patriae* gave the king, in his presumed role as the "father" of his country, the legal authority to take care of "his" people, especially those who were unable, for various reasons (including age) to take care of themselves (Chesney-Lind & Shelden, 1998). Originally used to deal with the administration of the property of orphans, the doctrine was soon expanded to allow the state control over children whose parents were unable to care for them. The idea of the state as parent was reflected in the laws of Colonial America, providing the basis for the states' treatment of juveniles.

Shelden (1998), an important scholar in the area of juvenile justice, argues that it is important to think about exactly what the doctrine of *parens patriae* means for the state's authority over juveniles and, in particular, girls. Two of the important points regarding *parens patriae* concern who is the object of parental authority. First, it is clearly men, the state as "father" or the father himself, who have the parental authority recognized by *parens patriae* and, second, just as clearly, women and children who are the objects of that authority. *Parens patriae* thus strongly supported the patriarchal system of male authority over females.

This paternalistic notion of the state as parent (or "father") plays out as shown in the Stubborn Child Law. Passed in 1646 in Massachusetts, the Stubborn Child Law made it a capital offense for a child to disobey his or her parents.[1] This law, which grew out of the notion of *parens patriae*, was the first statute in the United States to define the legal regulation of children and also to require parents to bring disobedient children before the court. It was copied into the codes of several states, and while substantially amended, it remained in force in Massachusetts until 1973.[2] In many ways, the government continued for centuries to use *parens patriae* and the Stubborn Child Law to support intervention in the lives of young people. Often, this governmental involvement was described as "for their own good," "for their own protection," or "in the best interests of the child" (Chesney-Lind & Shelden, 1998:126).

Continuing State Control:
Houses of Refuge *and* Ex Parte Crouse

During the eighteenth and nineteenth centuries, the United States experienced increased rates of immigration, and the population in urban areas grew especially quickly. At this time, the state control over the lives of young people continued to expand. With immigration came large numbers of poor, homeless youth, the majority of which were also uneducated. A variety of reformist associations emerged in response to the growing number of "unsupervised" youth. In 1823, for example, the Society for the Reformation of Juvenile Delinquents was founded in New York City (Sutton, 1988:69). This group pressured the New York legislature to establish the New York House of Refuge, the first correctional institution for children in the United States. Children committed to the House of Refuge had not committed any crime; they were simply seen as "incorrigible" or "beyond control."

Similar reformist associations emerged in other cities (Platt, 1969) and played an instrumental role in the establishment of more houses of refuge in Boston (1826), Philadelphia (1828), and Baltimore (1830) (Bremmer, 1970:679-682). These houses were to "provide education, religious instruction, training for future employment, and parental discipline" (Chesney-Lind & Shelden, 1998:127). In reality, these institutions were harsh environments where many children experienced abuse. Further, the young people sent to such institutions had few rights and were sent away after only informal hearings. Clearly, there were separate standards of justice in place for adults and children.

One of the most important early legal challenges to the state's control of juveniles involved a little girl named Mary Ann Crouse. The importance of this case stems from the fact that it was the first court decision to invoke the doctrine of *parens patriae*. In 1838, Mary Ann Crouse was committed by her mother to the Philadelphia House of Refuge. Mary Ann Crouse's father, asking for the release of his daughter, filed a petition of *habeas corpus*. He argued that because she had not received a jury trial, her incarceration was illegal. The Supreme Court of Pennsylvania disagreed, basing its decision on the *parens patriae* doctrine (Pisciotta, 1982; Shelden, 1998). This ruling was based on the assumption that the Philadelphia House of Refuge had a beneficial effect on its residents; an assumption that since has been called into question by researchers who argue that abuse was commonplace in these institutions (Pisciotta, 1982; Hawes, 1971; Bremner, 1970).

Saving Children: The Progressive Era and the First Juvenile Court

The Progressive Era (1890-1920) led to increased governmental involvement in the lives of adolescents (Teitelbaum & Harris, 1977). A separate juvenile court was established in Chicago in 1899, supported by a vocal group of reformers known as the "child savers." It provided the blueprint for juvenile courts in other states, and by the end of the 1920s, nearly every state had a juvenile court (Chesney-Lind & Shelden, 1998; Bremner, 1970). It was assumed at the time that the juvenile court, acting in place of the child's parents, would act in the best interests of the child. From its inception, then, the juvenile court has dealt with "offenses" that do not qualify as crimes. Specifically, the first juvenile courts had three areas of concern: (1) children who violated laws applicable to adults, (2) children who committed status offenses, and (3) children who were abused, neglected or abandoned, or had "unfit" parents.[3]

It is important to note the role of women in the child-saving movement and the establishment of the juvenile courts in this country. In terms of the child-saving movement, many of the leaders were women from the "privileged" classes. Of great concern to these reformers was the issue of "wayward" girls. Many considered it the responsibility of the juvenile courts to protect the virtue of innocent young women. When juvenile courts came into being in the early 1900s, women were appointed as "referees" in the courts, responsible for the girls' cases and acting with nearly as much power as judges (Chesney-Lind & Shelden, 1998). Women were also employed at the girls' detention facilities, and much attention was given to controlling the "sexual behavior among working class girls" (Odem & Schlossman, 1991:190).

The "child saving" movement is of particular importance to understanding the treatment of girls by the juvenile justice system. The movement focused on a variety of social problems, many of which were centered on the "problems" of females, such as prostitution. From its initiation, then, the juvenile court was interested in the sexual behavior of the girls that came to its attention. "Immorality" was the most common charge against girls at this time. Other charges included "coming home late at night," "masturbating," "using obscene language," "riding at night in automobiles without a chaperone," and "strutting about in a lascivious manner" (Schlossman & Wallach, 1978:72). These inappropriate behaviors often resulted in incarceration. The first reform school for girls opened in Lancaster, Massachusetts, in 1856. The majority of the girls sent to this institution had been accused of moral rather than criminal offenses.[4]

Even a brief examination of the history of the American juvenile court system shows the long-standing concern of the system with the behavior of girls. Coupled with the juvenile court's great powers to detain, punish, and "treat" children and its paternalistic stance toward girls, this concern led to a "double standard" of juvenile justice. Under the "double standard," girls' behavior (offenses such as running away from home and incorrigibility) was often sexualized, judged "inappropriate," and dealt with harshly.

More Recent Legislative Changes and the Juvenile Justice System

Historically, the juvenile court has been quick to incarcerate girls, many of whom have committed only status or pre-delinquent offenses. Girls are still more likely than boys to be placed in custody for status offenses, although there is evidence that this may be changing (Law Enforcement Assistance Administration, 1998). In 2003, girls were twice as likely to be held for status offenses as were boys. The proportion of girls held for these offenses, however, has declined markedly in recent years, while that of boys has remained relatively unchanged. In 1991, for instance, 33 percent of incarcerated girls were held for status offenses, compared with 13 percent of girls held for this type of offense in 2003 (Snyder & Sickmund, 2006). While the apparent move toward a decreased likelihood of institutionalizing girls for status offenses is promising, it is still apparent that these behaviors continue to be more likely to result in serious intervention for girls than for boys. This punitive treatment of girls is likely linked to an overly paternalistic concern about girls' sexuality. In 1975, a report published by the Law Enforcement Assistance Administration Task Force on Women drew increased attention to this problem and emphasized the importance of deinstitutionalizing status offenders.[5]

The Juvenile Justice and Delinquency Prevention (JJDP) Act of 1974 addressed some of these issues. Central to this law was the "separation of adult and juvenile offenders and the removal of status offenders from secure incarceration" (Law Enforcement Assistance Administration, 1998:25). The deinstitutionalization of status offenders most strongly affected females because a larger proportion of the girls involved with the juvenile justice system were, and continue to be, status offenders. Unfortunately, the move to deinstitutionalize status offenders has been resisted by some officials in the juvenile justice system. Court officials have found two ways in particular to continue the institutionalization of status offenders – "bootstrapping" and transinstitutionalization (Chesney-Lind & Shelden, 1998). Bootstrapping occurs when youth, originally in court for a status offense, violate a court order and are then re-labeled "delinquent" (Federle & Chesney-Lind, 1992; Girls, Inc., 1996). Data from 2003 may well reflect this – 20 percent of girls who were in custody in that year were being held for technical violations, compared with 14 percent of boys (Snyder & Sickmund, 2006). Transinstitutionalization occurs when youth are placed in private facilities (such as mental health facilities) as alternatives to institutionalization by the justice system (Federle & Chesney-Lind, 1992). A larger proportion of girls (36%) than boys (31%) were, in fact, housed in private institutions in 2003 (Snyder & Sickmund, 2006).

Though it had a tremendous impact on the treatment of females by the juvenile justice system, the JJDP Act of 1974 did not specifically target the needs of girls. It was in the 1992 reauthorization of the JJDP Act that the specific needs of girls were addressed for the first time. Through the Challenge E section of the 1992 act, Congress identified two areas in need of particular attention (Office of Juvenile Justice and Delinquency Prevention, 1998). The first area asks that states develop and adopt policies that would prohibit gender bias in the juvenile justice system. The second asks for the development of programs for females that would give them access to a complete range of programming. The 2002 reauthorization of the Juvenile Justice and Delinquency Prevention Act also reflected this, offering block grants for programs that focused on the needs of young girls at risk for delinquency or status offenses (JJDPA, 42 U.S.C. 5651 § 241). It also included provisions for preventing gender bias. Further, it emphasized deinstitutionalization of status offenders (DSO), separation of juveniles from adults in institutions (separation), removal of juveniles from adult jails and lockups (jail removal), and reduction of disproportionate minority contact (DMC), where it exists.

The Current Status of Juvenile Court

Despite the move to deinstitutionalize in 1974, the emphasis in the Challenge E section of the 1992 reauthorization of the JJDP Act, and the 2002 reauthorization, evidence suggests that the traditional double standard within the juvenile justice system still exists. These legislative attempts to deal with the inequality of the system in its focus on status offenses for girls have met considerable resistance both within the juvenile justice system and among the general public (MacDonald & Chesney-Lind, 2001). Chesney-Lind and Okamoto (2001) report that several sessions of congress in the late twentieth and early twenty-first centuries sought overhauls of the Juvenile Justice and Delinquency Prevention Act that "were ominous for girls" (2001:14). These sessions included discussions that attempted to refocus attention on violent and repeat offending and to reconsider the deinstitutionalization of status offenders.

Girls still face a higher risk of incarceration for status offenses than do boys. It has also been noted that girls enter the juvenile justice system at younger ages than do boys (Law Enforcement Assistance Administration, 1998:21; Snyder & Sickmund, 2006). During the same time, the arrest rates for females grew at a faster rate (or decreased at a lower rate) than have arrests of males (Poe-Yamagata & Butts, 1996; Snyder & Sickmund, 2006). Some have suggested that the increase in female arrest rates is more a function of a change in our response to girls' behavior than a change in the behavior itself (American Bar Association and National Bar Association, 2001). These patterns are especially troubling, given the historically punitive treatment of girls by the juvenile courts.

The juvenile justice system, then, still remains focused on status offenses for girls but also demonstrates paradoxical behavior of neglect and attention. Neglect is particularly apparent in term of resources and understanding of the causes of female offending while attention remains focused on status offenses. If the system is really so concerned with the pre-delinquent behavior of

Young girl appears before Juvenile Court Judge.

girls, this should be seen in efforts at prevention and treatment. Historically, prevention and treatment have often boiled down in practice to incarceration with little in the way of programming. When programming was available, it came in the form of programs designed for boys and their needs. Has this changed since 1974? If girls are still being incarcerated for pre-delinquent offenses, is it because of the development of programs that effectively deal with this behavior? These are questions to keep in mind as the discussion moves to programming and policies for girls.

Policies and Programs for Girls: What Is Available Today; Recommendations for Tomorrow

The smaller numbers of girls in the juvenile justice system and the historically paternalistic attitude of the system toward girls are important parts of the explanation for the odd combination of attention and neglect girls have traditionally received. Though equity has not yet been achieved, since the 1970s there have been changes in the level of attention and resources given to girls in the system. We need to examine this change and discuss what still remains to be done. We start this section of the chapter then with an examination of some of the ideas about programming for girls that developed since the 1970s and the 2002 reauthorization of the JJDP Act.

Changing Ideas

Over the nearly 40 years since the passage of the 1974 JJDP Act, there has been a slowly increasing (and hard won) attention paid to the programming needs of girls. Today, three ideas are at the forefront of discussions on policy and programming for pre-delinquent and delinquent girls. These three ideas are that (1) the needs of boys and girls are different, (2) what is needed for the prevention and treatment of juvenile delinquency is gender-specific programming, and (3) gender specific programming must include a focus on the pathways to offending, including child abuse and running away from home.

The idea that girls and boys have different needs is central to recent discussions of the program and policy needs for girls in the juvenile justice system (American Bar Association and National Bar Association, 2001; OJJDP, 1998; Chesney-Lind, 2001). The discussion calls attention to the construction of gender in our society and, in particular, the expectations we have for girls and the special problems they face. Attention has begun to focus programming on the importance of such factors as self-esteem and self-image, body image, and dealing with physical changes that occur as one matures. Attention also focuses on factors that place girls at risk for delinquency – trouble at school, early involvement in sex, pregnancy, drug use, and unstable families. Also central to discussions of programming for girls is how to deal effectively with the problems girls may have to face. First and foremost is the physical, sexual, and emotional abuse these girls often receive both outside of and inside the juvenile justice system (American Bar Association and National Bar Association, 2001). Many also have to deal with the difficulties caused when they become teen mothers.

Connected to the idea that girls and boys have different needs is the call for gender-specific programming. A report by Greene, Peters, and Associates (1998) on programming for girls discusses the need for gender-specific programming and what exactly that means. They write (Chapter 2):

> Gender-specific programming refers to program models and services that comprehensively address the special needs of a targeted gender group, such as adolescent girls. Such programs foster positive gender identity and development. Gender-specific programs recognize the risk factors most likely to impact the targeted gender group and the protective factors that can build resiliency and prevent delinquency.

Those interested in gender-specific programming are interested as well in equity in programming and resources for boys and girls. Equity in programming does not mean that boys and girls receive the same types of programs. Because boys and girls have different needs, they will need different programs. It does mean, however, that there should be equity in the availability of programs. It also means that the programs girls receive should be rooted in their experiences and not those of boys.

More recently Bloom, Owen, and Covington (2003) have outlined key aspects of a "new vision" for gender-responsive programming based on research which was sponsored by the National Institute of Corrections. The guiding principles of this vision include an acknowledgement that gender makes a difference in the need to provide a safe environment, the need to help develop and maintain healthy connections to family, friends, and community, and to provide programming that deals with drug abuse and the trauma of child abuse. In addition, this programming must include a focus on the factors that research has identified as the important pathways to delinquent behavior of girls. This includes preventing child abuse, establishing safe havens for runaways, and dealing effectively with the consequences of each (Bloom et al., 2003).

There are signs then of increased attention to the needs of girls, but just how far have we progressed in the development and implementation of programs for girls? Are we carrying out the ideas that boys and girls have different needs and that gender-specific programming is necessary for the prevention and treatment of delinquency? It is difficult to determine what exactly is happening across the 50 states in programming for girls. However, as we will see in the next section of the chapter, there is evidence that the 1980s and 1990s saw an increase in the development and implementation of some innovative programs for pre-delinquent and delinquent girls.

The Changing Availability of Programs for Girls

An important source of support for both national and local programs for at-risk girls at least since the 1980s is Girls Inc., a national organization for girls once known as Girls Clubs of America (Girls Inc., 1996). At the national level, this organization sponsors a wide variety of programs designed to assist girls living in environments that place them at risk for delinquent behavior. Programs aimed at teaching resistance to drug use and preventing teen pregnancy are key to their national efforts. In addition, they have sponsored such local programs as P.A.C.E. (Practical and Cultural Education Center for Girls, Inc.) in Florida, which is now one of the few programs for girls that has been evaluated (Acoca, 1998). Established in 1985, P.A.C.E is a non-residential, community-based comprehensive education program serving at-risk girls age 14-18 (Burke, 1991; Girls, Inc., 1996). The centerpiece of the P.A.C.E. program is education; it requires that each girl attends school. In addition, there are independent living classes in the areas of health and physical education, life skills, career development, and home economics. Aimed at increasing self-esteem through the development of pride and accomplishment, girls also participate in two or three community service projects a month.[6]

There is evidence of change across the states outside of such national organizations as Girls Inc. In several states, an interest in programming for girls began prior to the 1992 reauthorization of the Juvenile Justice and Delinquency Prevention Act. For example, Oregon and Minnesota are two leaders in the recognition of the needs of girls and the development and implementation of programs. According to a 1998 report, Minnesota formed its first task force for the examination of the needs of women offenders in 1978, soon expanding it to consider the needs of girls (Greene, Peters & Associates, 1998). Three years later, the state passed a statute on parity for women and girl offenders, and developed the Advisory Task Force on Adult and Juvenile Female Offenders in Corrections. By 1989, Minnesota had already reported on the gap in programming for girls and established an annual conference on adolescent females, the goal of which was to seek innovative solutions. In 1993, the state began awarding model program grants to community-based programs with gender-specific programming. One notable program in Minnesota is Milwaukee's Community-Based Out-of-Home Care,[7] which began operation in 1987. It serves girls 12 to 17 years of age who are usually court ordered into the program. The goal of the program is to provide short-term, community-based care and services that allow diversion of girls from institutional placements.

Oregon is also an early leader among the states in programming for girls. In 1987, the state began to examine the services it provided for girls (Greene, Peters & Associates, 1998). Legislation was enacted to reduce the number of status offenders in institutions and to develop programs for at-risk youth. Oregon also established a task force to help identify where gaps in programming for girls might exist and ways to diminish them. Oregon, like Minnesota, introduced legislation requiring equity in programming (Greene, Peters & Associates, 1998). This act requires ". . . equal access for both males and females less than 18 years of age to appropriate facilities, services and treatment" (Girls, Inc., 1996:26). Oregon has also been noted in the literature for one of its programs for girls – Emancipation Program for Girls in Portland.[8] Established in the late 1980s, the Emancipation Program for Girls was set up by the Portland YWCA. Its aim is to provide a short-term program that would help pre-delinquent and delinquent girls prepare for independent living. The six-month program, which accepts girls from any source, helps them progress from dormitory living to independent life in an apartment.

As part of a recent and broader movement at both the national and state level, there has been increased attention on the "re-entry" of girls as they move from institutional and residential control back to the community. The focus on re-entry stems from the realization that re-entry is not, as Travis (2005) writes, an option, but reflects what he calls the "Iron Law of Imprisonment" which is that "they all come back."

Progress and Uncertainty

With the reauthorization of the Juvenile Justice and Delinquency Prevention Act in 1992, attention among the states in programs specifically aimed at girls increased. Whether that progress will continue after the 2002 reauthorization remains uncertain. A 1998 report from the Office of Juvenile Justice and Delinquency Prevention reported on the progress that has been made at the state level in addressing the Challenge E section of the 1992 Act (Office of Juvenile Justice and Delinquency Prevention, 1998). At the time of the report, 23 states had applied for and received grants in Challenge E section of the Act. The report also noted a number of states that had indeed completed studies of gender bias in their state juvenile justice systems and developed programs for girls. More recently, Chesney-Lind has summarized state activities under the Challenge E section. She found that out of the 21 states for which information was available, 95 percent had completed a needs assessment, 38 percent had initiated new programs, 28 percent had special conferences and specialized training, 23 percent had convened special committees, and 10 percent had introduced new legislation or policies (Chesney-Lind, 2000).

Progress has certainly been made in the past 35 years, but it has not been steady. Further, there is no guarantee that it will continue. Three points can be used to illustrate the need for continued diligence in efforts to ensure effective programming for girls. First, rapid changes can occur at the federal level in terms of attention and resources. Shelden (1998), in a paper on the 1996 reauthorization of the Juvenile Justice and Delinquency Prevention Act, reports that the focus now is turning back to research and programs for violent offenders and, simultaneously, a "gutting" of deinstitutionalization – both of which will dramatically affect girls. The focus on violent offenders turns attention largely to boys because of their greater involvement in violent delinquent acts. The lack of attention to deinstitutionalization would impact on girls because, as we saw, status offenses make up a large proportion of their offenses. Stepping back from the goals of deinstitutionalization means a continuation (and perhaps an increase) in the number of girls incarcerated for pre-delinquent offenses such as running away. Though the 1996, 1998, and 2000 reauthorizations continued to include the Challenge E section of the Act, recent events have turned a great deal of public and legislative attention to violent delinquents, gangs, and school violence, all indicative of attention on males.

The uncertainty of progress is also reflected in reports that we have not made the progress we need in the development and implementation of programming for pre-delinquent and delinquent girls. One such report was issued jointly by the American Bar Association (ABA) and the National Bar Association (NBA) in 2001 (American Bar Association and National Bar Association, 2001). The report begins by noting the continued growth of the numbers of girls entering the system. It suggests the possibility that it is not simply a change in the behavior of the girls but a change in the system's response that accounts for this increase. In particular, the report lists changes in the system response that include re-labeling girls' family conflicts as violent offenses, changes in police practices regarding domestic violence, and gender bias in the processing of misdemeanor cases. Perhaps most importantly, the report argues that the increase may be the result of a continued failure of the juvenile justice system (and, in fact, of society) to understand the needs of young girls and the problems many of them face.

In terms of programs, the ABA/NBA report notes a number of problems that remain. These include the fact that alternatives to incarceration are still lacking, especially for status offenders. There are simply not enough of these alternative programs for the number of boys and girls each year whose pre-delinquent offenses might be illustrating their need for assistance. It notes further that of those alternatives that do exist, many are still based on programs for males and are not the types of gender-specific programming that has been called for in the literature. The result is that what is available in terms of programming at both the institutional and community levels may not be "developmentally sound, culturally competent or responsive to the special needs of girls" (American Bar Association and National Bar Association, 2001:13). The report also notes that many programs, even for runaways, focus on control rather than support. Finally, the report notes that few of these programs receive funding for careful evaluation. Without this, the ability to evaluate what works is limited.

Finally, not everyone recognizes or acknowledges the bias in the system or the need for gender-specific programming. One of the disappointments of recent years was the GAO report on gender bias in the system (GAO, 1995). The report's main conclusion was that there is minimal gender bias in the juvenile justice system. Albrecht, however, points out correctly that the report defined bias in terms of outcomes, ignoring bias in processes (Albrecht,

1996). Focusing on outcomes, the report then missed two important forms of gender bias in the system – it is designed for males and it fails to take into account differences by gender. Another development reported by Chesney-Lind and Okamoto (2001) is an initiative in some states to make it easier to institutionalize girls.

Where Do We Go from Here?

There is no doubt that progress has been made. Researchers and officials connected with the juvenile justice system are beginning to pay attention to the needs of girls, but they still face many challenges. If we are to continue to develop and implement programs and policies that will assist pre-delinquent and delinquent girls, what should these gender-specific programs and policies look like? What challenges do we need to be aware of as we proceed?

One of the first recommendations made by a number of recent reports on the state of programming is the need for a continuum of care.[9] These reports note that many youth in the juvenile justice system were also involved in child care, mental health, or other systems earlier on. Collaboration among these systems may help provide programs not easily available in the justice system. This would allow more successful prevention services at one end of the continuum, early intervention and diversion in the middle, and juvenile justice intervention and aftercare at the other end. As OJJDP (1998) argues, however, a basic principle underlying the effective use of this continuum-of-care model has to be that girls be treated in the least restrictive setting possible.

In terms of programs and policies, one critical area that is so often neglected in the rush to "do something about crime" is prevention. As few programs as there are for pre-delinquent and delinquent girls, there are even fewer for those at risk. The need to develop programs for high-risk girls ages eight to 12 has been noted (Acoca, 1998). Most girls between these ages do not quality for entry into the already established programs. In addition, many researchers are convinced that important strides would be made in the prevention of delinquency if we dealt more effectively with child abuse (Acoca, 1998). Programming that might well reduce child abuse in all its forms would include maternal and child care programs (Acoca, 1998) as well as programs designed to assist victims of child abuse in dealing with the trauma.

For pre-delinquent girls, scholars have made a number of recommendations. First, there is agreement that we need more alternative, community-based programs and services. At the same time, we need to continue the emphasis on deinstitutionalization. This is not as easy as it may seem at first for two reasons. First, there are groups who oppose deinstitutionalization. In particular, some have noted a long history of resistance by court officials (Shelden, 1998) while others recognize that this opposition continues to persist (Chesney-Lind & Okamato, 2001). Second, as noted above, researchers have warned that even when deinstitutionalization does seem to be working because of reduced numbers of status offenders in the juvenile justice system, this may be the result of bootstrapping or transinstitutionalization.

At the other end of this continuum is the need for re-entry programs that assist girls who have been incarcerated. The increasingly large body of work on re-entry for adult offenders could be instructive in developing programs that would facilitate successful re-entry. These include addressing the problems of housing, education, and employment, and returning to the family as well as continuing treatment for drug abuse and relapse prevention.

Beyond the need for more programming, three important recommendations for existing programs come from Shelden (1998). First, he suggests the need for more stable funding of innovative programs. Many of these innovative programs are begun with federal grant monies. When that money runs out, how many are actually able to survive? Second, he recommends programs be culturally specific as well a gender-specific. We must be aware of the fact that girls from different ethnic groups have different experiences and needs that should be taken into consideration in programming. Finally, and incredibly important, is his recommendation that programs receive careful scrutiny to ensure that they remain alternatives to institutionalization. As he notes, history has taught us that there is a danger that these new programs will become concerned with social control and security and will lose their interest in innovation.

Conclusion

In a time where public perceptions of a "new breed" of female offender proliferate despite evidence to the contrary, it is important to take a step back and examine the juvenile justice system's treatment of female offenders. It has been argued in this chapter that the juvenile justice system has a long history of attention to the behavior of girls and yet a neglect of girls in terms of theory, research, resources, policies, and programs. Fortunately, some progress has been made in the recognition of the needs of girls. The JJDP Act of 1974 and its reauthorizations in 1992 and 2002 were important steps in the right direction. Though resisted by some, the fight continues for the deinsitutionalization of status offenders and the provision of alternative programming. The fight continues as well for the development of innovative programs that recognize and are designed around the needs of girls.

At the same time, we have also emphasized the need to continue the progress that has been made. There is always a danger that the attention of the public, the legislature, and even reformers will shift to more "exciting" and "pressing" concerns. There is always a danger that with this change in attention will go the funding that supports innovative ideas and programs as well as their evaluation. We need also to be wary of the dangers history has shown us. Innovative ideas can turn to nothing if those who are to implement them have no stake in their implementation or if they see the ideas as nothing more than a new and "soon to be passing," fad in correctional treatment. In this context, innovative programs designed as alternatives to incarceration can easily turn into another form of detention.

There is much that remains to be done, and history suggests continuing progress will not be easy. In the long run, though, the potential benefit to girls and to society requires that we continue. It is imperative to pay attention to policies, resources, theory, and research concerning delinquent and pre-delinquent girls and to eliminate the unnecessary pain that many of these girls have to go through. As numerous authors have noted, the girls that end up in our juvenile justice system are often victimized by family and then victimized again by the system. No child should have to suffer sexual and physical abuse, especially when the result of that abuse is then treated as a crime rather than an attempt at survival.

In addition, we should continue to keep in mind the connection between child abuse, delinquency, and parenting. So often, many of us end up parenting our children the same way our parents taught us. As Widom reminds us: "Women play a unique role in society. They produce children. . . . The behavior and health risks . . . these young adult women face are of particular concern – especially because the environments they create will affect the physical and psychological development of their children" (Widom, 2000:34). Although we can continue to ignore the implications of this cycle in our policies and programs, ignoring the implications does not mean the results will not follow. Alternatively, we can implement reforms, save the children, and feel the effects for generations to come.

Endnotes

[1] The Stubborn Child Law states:

> If a man have a stubborn or rebellious son, of sufficient years and understanding (viz) sixteen years of age, which will not obey the voice of his Father, or the voice of his Mother, and that when they have chastened him will not harken unto them: then shall his Father and Mother being his natural parents, lay hold on him, and bring him to the Magistrates assembled in Court and testify unto them, that their son is stubborn and rebellious and will not obey their voice and chastisement, but lives in sundry notorious crimes, such a son shall be put to death (Sutton, 1988:11).

[2] The Stubborn Child Law was also adopted by Connecticut, Rhode Island, and New Hampshire (Sutton, 1988).

[3] Laws applicable to adults included robbery, burglary, and larceny. Status offenses included "vicious or immoral conduct," "incorrigibility," "profane or indecent behavior," and "growing up in idleness" (Chesney-Lind & Shelden, 1998:129-130).

[4] These offenses included vagrancy, wanton and lewd conduct, and running way (Brenzel, 1983:81).

[5] The report stated that girls were more likely than boys to be committed to an institution if there was any evidence of sexual activity, regardless of the original offense that brought them before the court (Law Enforcement Assistance Administration, 1998).

[6]   There is evidence that there is a continuing concern for programming for girls by national organizations. A recent article by Hirsch et al. (2000) describes the gender equity initiative of a Boys and Girls Clubs of America regional affiliate.

[7]   See the program description in Friedman and Sampson, 1991

[8]   See the program description in Chesney-Lind and Shelden, 1998.

[9]   See the recommendation by American Bar Association and National Bar Association, 2001; OJJDP, 1998; Girls, Inc., 1996.

References

Acoca, L. (1998). "Outside/Inside: The Violation of American Girls at Home, on the Streets, and in the Juvenile Justice System." *Crime & Delinquency*, 44(4):561-589.

Adler, F. (1975). *Sisters in Crime*. New York, NY: McGraw Hill Book Company.

Albrecht, L. (1996). "Gender Specific Programming in Juvenile Detention and Corrections." *Journal of Juvenile Justice and Detention Services*, 11(2):55-63.

American Bar Association and National Bar Association (2001). *Justice by Gender: The Lack of Appropriate Prevention, Diversion and Treatment Alternatives for Girls in the Justice System*. Washington, DC: American Bar Association and National Bar Association.

American Correctional Association (1990). *The Female Offender: What Does the Future Hold?* Washington, DC: St. Mary's Press.

Belknap, J. (2001). *The Invisible Women: Gender, Crime and Justice*, Second Edition. Belmont, CA: Wadsworth Publishing.

Bloom, B., B. Owen & S. Covington (2003). *Research, Practice, and Guiding Principles for Women Offenders: Gender Responsive Strategies*. Washington, DC: U.S. Department of Justice. National Institute of Corrections.

Bremner, R.H. (ed.) (1970). *Children and Youth in America*. Cambridge, MA: Harvard University Press.

Brenzel, B. (1983). *Daughters of the State*. Cambridge, MA: MIT Press.

Burke, V. (1991). "P.A.C.E. Center for Girls, Inc." In I. Schwartz & F. Orlando (eds.) *Programming for Young Women in the Juvenile Justice System*, pp. 4-8. Ann Arbor, MI: Center for the Study of Youth Policy.

Chesney-Lind, M. (2001). "What about Girls? Delinquency Programming as if Gender Mattered." *Corrections Today*, (February) 63(1):38-40, 42, 44-45.

Chesney-Lind, M. (2000). "What to Do About Girls? Thinking about Programming for Young Women." In M. McMahon (ed.) *Assessment to Assistance: Programs for Women in Community Corrections*, pp. 139-170. Lanham, MD: American Correctional Association.

Chesney-Lind, M. (1995). "Girls, Delinquency, and Juvenile Justice: Toward a Feminist Theory of Young Women's Crime." In B.R. Price & N.J. Sokoloff (eds.) *The Criminal Justice System and Women: Offenders, Victims and Workers*, Second Edition, pp. 71-88. New York, NY: McGraw Hill.

Chesney-Lind, M. (1989). "Girls' Crime and Woman's Place: Toward a Feminist Model of Female Delinquency." *Crime & Delinquency*, 35:5-29.

Chesney-Lind, M. & S. Okamoto (2001). "Gender Matters: Patterns in Girls' Delinquency and Gender Responsive Programming." *Journal of Forensic Psychology Practice*, 1:1-28.

Chesney-Lind, M. & L. Pasko (2004). *The Female Offender: Girls, Women and Crime*, Second Edition. Thousand Oaks, CA. Sage Publications.

Chesney-Lind, M. & R. Shelden (1998). *Girls, Delinquency and Juvenile Justice*, Second Edition. Belmont, CA; Wadsworth Publishing.

Federal Bureau of Investigation (2004). *Crime in the United States: 2003*. Washington, DC: U.S. Department of Justice.

Federal Bureau of Investigation (2001). *Crime in the United States: 2000*. Washington, DC: U.S. Department of Justice.

Federle, K. & M. Chesney-Lind (1992). "Special Issues in Juvenile Justice: Gender, Race and Ethnicity." In I. Schwartz (ed.) *Juvenile Justice and Public Policy: Toward a National Agenda*, pp. 165-295. New York, NY: Lexington Books.

Friedman, J. & J. Sampson (1991). "Community-Based Out-of-Home Care: A Milwaukee Model." In I. Schwartz & F. Orlando (eds.) *Programming for Young Women in the Juvenile Justice System*, pp. 21-25. Ann Arbor, MI: Center for the Study of Youth Policy.

Flowers, R.B. (2001). *Runaway Kids and Teenage Prostitution: America's Lost, Abandoned, and Sexually Exploited Children*. Westport, CT: Greenwood Press.

Gilfus, M. (1992). "From Victims to Survivors to Offenders: Women's Routes of Entry and Immersion into Street Crime." *Women and Criminal Justice*, 4(1):63-89.

Girls, Inc. (1996). *Prevention and Parity: Girls in Juvenile Justice*. Indianapolis, IN: Girls Incorporated National Resource Center.

Goodkind, S., I. Ng & R. Sarri (2006). "The Impact of Sexual Abuse in the Lives of Young Women Involved or at Risk of Involvement with the Juvenile Justice System." *Violence Against Women*, 12(5):456-477.

Government Accounting Office (1995). *Report of Juvenile Gender Bias, 1994-1995*. Washington, DC: General Accounting Office, General Government Division.

Greene, Peters & Associates (1998). *Guiding Principles for Promising Female Programming: An Inventory of Best Practices*. Washington, DC: U.S. Office of Juvenile Justice and Delinquency Prevention.

Harlow, C.W. (1999). *Prior Abuse Reported by Inmates and Probationers*. Washington, DC: U.S. Department of Justice.

Hawes, J. (1971). *Children in Urban Society*. New York, NY: Oxford University Press.

Hirsch, B., J. Roffman, N. Deutsch, C. Flynn, T. Loda & M. Pagano (2000). "Inner-City Youth Development Organizations: Strengthening Programs for Adolescent Girls." *Journal of Early Adolescence*, 20(2):210-230.

Holsinger, K., J. Belknap & J. Sutherland (1999). *Assessing the Gender Specific Program and Service Needs for Adolescent Females in the Juvenile Justice System*. Columbus, OH: Office of Criminal Justice Services.

Juvenile Justice and Delinquency Prevention Act of 2002. 42 U.S.C. 5651 § 241.

Krisberg, B. & J. Austin (1993). *Reinventing Juvenile Justice*. Newbury Park, CA: Sage Publishing Company.

Law Enforcement Assistance Administration (1998). *Women in Criminal Justice: A Twenty-Year Update*. Rockville, MD: National Criminal Justice Reference Service (NCJ 173416).

Leonard, E. (1982). *A Critique of Criminological Theory: Women, Crime and Society*. New York, NY: Longman Publishing Press.

Lipsey, M. (1990). *Juvenile Delinquency Treatment: A Meta-Analytic Inquiry into the Variability of Effects*. New York, NY: Russell Sage.

MacDonald, J.M. & M. Chesney-Lind (2001). "Gender Bias and Juvenile Justice Revisited: A Multiyear Analysis." *Crime & Delinquency*, 47:173-195.

Miller, J. (2001). *One of the Guys: Girls, Gangs and Gender*. Oxford: Oxford University Press.

Naffine, N. (1996). *Feminism and Criminology*. Philadelphia, PA: Temple University Press.

Odem, M.E. & S. Schlossman (1991). "Guardians of Virtue: The Juvenile Court and Female Delinquency in Early 20th Century Los Angeles." *Crime & Delinquency*, 37:186-203.

Office of Juvenile Justice and Delinquency Prevention Statistical Briefing Book. Online. Available: http://ojjdp.ncjrs.org/ojstatbb/crime/JAR_Display.asp?ID=qa05235

Office of Juvenile Justice and Delinquency Prevention Statistical Briefing Room. Online. Available: http://ojjdp.ncjrs.org/ojstatbb/crime/

Office of Juvenile Justice and Delinquency Prevention (1998). *Juvenile Female Offenders: A Status of the States Report*. Washington, DC: Office of Juvenile Justice and Delinquency Prevention.

Pisciotta, A.W. (1982). "Saving the Children: The Promise and Practice of *Parens Patriae*, 1838-98." *Crime & Delinquency*, 28:410-425.

Platt, A. (1969). "The Rise of the Child-Saving Movement." *American Academy of Political and Social Science*, 381:21-38.

Poe-Yamagata, E. & J.A. Butts (1996). *Female Offenders in the Juvenile Justice System*. Pittsburgh, PA: National Center for Juvenile Justice.

Schlossman, S. & S. Wallach (1978). "The Crime of Precocious Sexuality: Female Delinquency in the Progressive Era." *Harvard Educational Review*, 48:65-94.

Shelden, R. (1998). "Confronting the Ghost of Mary Ann Crouse: Gender Bias in the Juvenile Justice System." *Juvenile and Family Court Journal*, (Winter) 49(1):11-26.

Siegel, J.A. (2000). "Aggressive Behavior Among Women Sexually Abused as Children." *Violence and Victims*, 15:235-255.

Siegel, J. & L. Williams (2003). "The Relationship Between Child Sexual Abuse and Female Delinquency and Crime: A Prospective Study." *Journal of Research in Crime and Delinquency*, 40(1):71-94.

Smart, C. (1976). *Women, Crime and Criminology: A Feminist Critique*. London: Routledge and Kegan Paul.

Snyder, H. (2005). *Juvenile Arrests 2003*. Washington, DC: U.S. Department of Justice, Office of Juvenile Justice and Delinquency Prevention.

Snyder, H. & M. Sickmund (2006). *Juvenile Offenders and Victims: 2006 National Report*. Washington, DC: U.S. Department of Justice, Office of Justice Programs, Office of Juvenile Justice and Delinquency Prevention.

Snyder, H. & M. Sickmund (1999). *Juvenile Offenders and Victims: 1999 National Report*. Washington, DC: Office of Juvenile Justice and Delinquency Prevention.

Snyder, H. & M. Sickmund (1995). *Juvenile Offenders and Victims: A Focus on Violence*. Washington, DC: U.S. Justice Department, Office of Juvenile Justice and Delinquency Prevention.

Sutton, J.R. (1988). *Stubborn Children: Controlling Delinquency in the United States, 1640-1981*. Berkeley, CA: University of California Press.

Teitelbaum, L.E. & L.J. Harris (1977). "Some Historical Perspectives on Governmental Regulation of Children and Parents." In L.E. Teitelbaum & A.R. Gough (eds.) *Beyond Control: Status Offenders in the Juvenile Court*. Cambridge, MA: Ballinger Publishing.

Travis, J. (2005). *But They all Come Back: Facing the Challenges of Prisoner Reentry*. Washington, DC: The Urban Institute.

Tyler, K.A., D.R. Hoyt. & L.B. Whitbeck (2000). "The Effects of Early Sexual Abuse on Later Sexual Victimization Among Female Homeless and Runaway Adolescents." *Journal of Interpersonal Violence*, 15:235-250.

Widom, C.S. (2000). "Childhood Victimization and the Derailment of Girls and Women to the Criminal Justice System." In National Institute of Justice, *Research on Women and Girls in the Justice System: Plenary Papers of the 1999 Conference on Criminal Justice Research and Evaluation-Enhancing Policy and Practice Through Research, Volume 3*, pp. 27-36. Washington, DC: National Institute of Justice.

CHAPTER 11

Sentenced to Die: Controversy and Change in the Ultimate Sanction for Juvenile Offenders

Alexis J. Miller
Richard Tewksbury

Introduction

The punishment of death is one of the most frequently and intensely debated issues in America, particularly when the offender facing capital punishment was a juvenile. This chapter will address the controversies of imposing the death penalty on juveniles. We start by summarizing the history of capital punishment for juveniles and discuss juveniles who faced execution prior to the landmark 1972 capital punishment case of *Furman v. Georgia*. Then we examine the late twentieth century developments including the 2005 Supreme Court case of *Roper v. Simmons* when the death penalty for juveniles was ruled unconstitutional by the U.S. Supreme Court. Finally, we will also discuss the case law relevant to the juvenile death penalty and summarize the research that addressed public opinion and attitudes regarding the execution of juvenile offenders.

The Juvenile Death Penalty: 1642-1959

Juveniles facing execution prior to 1960 very often were under the age of 18 at the time of their death, whereas the appeal process today delays the execution date well past the age of majority. In 1642, Thomas Graunger was executed in Plymouth Colony, Massachusetts. That day marked the beginning of America's history with juvenile executions; however, it was another 120 years before another juvenile faced execution (Hale, 1997). The time span between Graunger's death and Gourd's death (the second juvenile executed) was at least partly due to the ambivalence that colonists had regarding how to deal with juveniles. Similar to today, some argued for harsh discipline, while others looked toward compassion as a better way to address juvenile offenders. Furthermore, executions during this time, regardless of the offender's age, meant the executed was a potentially productive worker being removed from the already small labor force. As a result of the times and the ambivalence, death and imprisonment were rarely used during early colonial days for either adults or juveniles.

Early penalties in America mirrored many of the same laws and legal customs found in England. In an effort to minimize the power of government, one distinct difference with juveniles was that colonists chose not to adopt the chancery courts which England used "to govern over the welfare of children" (Hale, 1997:35). Regardless, many of the laws retained by the colonists did have a religious emphasis that followed the customs and norms found in England. This allowed for the punishment of death in some extreme and biblical cases. Both Graunger and Gourd were charged and convicted of bestiality which, according to a passage in most versions of the Bible, calls for death (Landau, 1992).

Other early laws dealing with juveniles recognized their lack of maturity and corresponding inability to form criminal intent, or *mens rea* (Horowitz, 2000; Hale, 1997). According to English Common Law, seven has been the age designated for when children are considered capable of forming criminal intent. In other words, children six years of age and younger are considered incapable of understanding the consequences of their actions and thus, are not held responsible for those actions, while children seven and older are legally considered capable of understanding the consequences of their behavior and therefore can be held responsible in a court of law. Also according to English Common Law, for children under the age of 14 but over the age of six, the court had to prove criminal intent (Hale, 1997). Children over the age of 14 were always considered able to form *mens rea*. Graunger and Gourd were both 17 years old at the time of their execution. They were tried and convicted in what today constitutes an adult criminal court, because the first juvenile court was not established until 1899. From 1642 until 1925 (when all states had established a juvenile court system), 210 juveniles under the age of 18 were executed (Hale, 1997).

In 1899, the first Juvenile Court was established in Chicago, Illinois. The Juvenile Court was intended to "protect the state's right to use *parens patriae* for official intervention in the juvenile's life, especially if the youth was neglected" (Elsea, 1995:137). The goal of the juvenile court would be to protect neglected children and rehabilitate delinquent children. *Parens patriae* was the rationale used that gave the state these powers. This doctrine was interpreted to mean that "because children were not of full legal capacity, the State had the inherent power and responsibility to provide protection for children whose natural parents were not providing appropriate care or supervision" (Snyder & Sickmund, 2006:94). Essentially, juvenile courts were developed in an effort to protect children from parents who were not reasonably taking care of their children. The court's focus was on the welfare of the child, which included dependent, neglected, abused, and delinquent children (see Chapter 6).

The goal of the juvenile justice system early on was identified as rehabilitation (Hale, 1997). Juveniles were not considered small adults, rather juveniles were deemed as incapable of making sound decisions because of their young age. Thus, a juvenile's age at the time of his or her crime was one of the most important factors in developing another system. It was believed that this system would protect young people from the harsh punishments of the adult system, while also offering an alternative: rehabilitation. Nonetheless, the juvenile death penalty remained a part of the legal system. From 1922 until 1959, 140 juveniles were executed. Even with the protections of *parens patriae* and the juvenile court system, children still found themselves facing the death penalty. As with adult executions, 80 percent of the juveniles executed between 1922 and 1959 were non-white (Hale, 1997). On April 10, 1959, Leonard Shockley became the last juvenile under the age of 18 to be executed.

Changes in the Death Penalty: 1960-1988

By the 1960s, support for the death penalty (for all types of offenders, both adult and juveniles) had declined by almost 20 percent from 1937 (Vidmar & Ellsworth, 1982). The U. S. Supreme Court case of *Weems v. United States* (1910) marked the beginning of both legal and practical changes regarding the death penalty. In *Weems*, and then later in *Trop v. Dulles* (1958), the Court ruled that the Eighth Amendment was not a static clause. In other words, according to the "evolving standard of decency" punishments that were found constitutional in the eighteenth century would not necessarily always be considered constitutional (Hale, 1997). Partly due to the lack of public support for the death penalty during the 1960s and partly due to the legal changes in what has been called the "evolving standard of decency," no juveniles were put to death between 1966 and 1972. Furthermore, during that same time period only two adults were executed (Bedau, 1982). During this moratorium period for executions, the Supreme Court decided a number of landmark cases regarding the death penalty. Although some of these decisions are not directly related to juveniles, they do apply for juveniles as well as adults.

In 1972, the Court decided the case of *Furman v. Georgia*. Contrary to popular misconception, the Supreme Court did not rule that the death penalty in its entirety was unconstitutional. Rather, the Court found that sentencing procedures that allowed juries to have too much discretion violated the

Eighth Amendment. The Justices did not establish any guidelines in their ruling regarding capital punishment; however, they did send a message to the states that their death penalty procedures must be revised. The decision further stipulated that when capital punishment is applied, it must meet the goals of retribution and deterrence.

After *Furman*, states were forced to rewrite their statutes concerning the death penalty and address the issues that the Court identified in *Furman*. Then, in 1976, the Supreme Court again reviewed a number of newly revised statutes on capital punishment. In a series of cases argued before the Court, under the lead case of *Gregg v. Georgia* (1976), a number of decisions were made. In *Gregg*, the Court established a standard three-pronged test for judging when a criminal punishment (including the death penalty) is appropriate. Specifically, in *Woodson v. North Carolina* (which accompanied *Gregg*) the Court stated (1976):

1. The punishment must not have been forbidden at the time the Bill of Rights was adopted.

2. The punishment must not violate the evolving standards of decency that marked the progress of a maturing society

3. The punishment must not be so excessive or disproportionate as to be inconsistent with the basic concepts of human dignity.

Additionally, the Court struck down mandatory sentences of death as unconstitutional, while upholding what is called "guided discretion" (*Woodson v. North Carolina*, 1976). Further, the Court decided that both aggravating and mitigating circumstances surrounding the crime and the criminal must be included within the decision-making process. While *Furman* and *Gregg* did not address juveniles specifically, the rulings of these cases do affect juveniles facing the death penalty.

Three cases dealt directly with juveniles during this time frame: *Eddings v. Oklahoma*, (*Eddings v. Oklahoma*, 1982), *Thompson v. Oklahoma* (*Thompson v. Oklahoma*, 1988), and *Stanford v. Kentucky* (*Stanford v. Kentucky*, 1989). In 1982, the Supreme Court Justices reviewed *Eddings v. Oklahoma* and ruled that an offender's age, as well as his or her mental and emotional development, must be included as a mitigating factor in the sentencing process. The Court recognized that adolescents are not as mature, responsible, and self-disciplined as adults. The Court did not, however, decide that age alone would prohibit the death penalty, rather that the jury must include age as a mitigating factor in determining whether to sentence an offender to death.

In *Thompson v. Oklahoma* (*Thompson v. Oklahoma*, 1988), the Court went a step further and did mandate a threshold age. Specifically, the Court prohibited offenders who were 15 years of age or younger at the time of their crime to be sentenced to death. Furthermore, in *Thompson*, the court found that because 15-year-olds lack the responsibility and maturity of adults, the traditional goals that justified the death penalty – retribution and deterrence

– did not apply. Thus, offenders who were 15 years of age at the time of their offense would not be eligible for capital punishment. This threshold was tested and confirmed one year later in *Stanford v. Kentucky* (1989). In *Stanford*, the Court reaffirmed its view that persons 16 and 17 years of age at the time of the offenses were sufficiently mature and responsible to face the possibility of a death sentence.

During this time period (1960-1988) only three juveniles were executed in the United States. All three of these youth were 17 years old when convicted; and they were in their mid-twenties when executed. In 1979, Charles Rumbaugh was sentenced to die by lethal injection in Texas. He was executed on September 11, 1985, at the age of 28. In 1986, J. Terry Roach and Jay Pinkerton followed in South Carolina and Texas, respectively. As already mentioned, in 1959, Leonard Shockley was the last offender to be executed while still under the age of 18. At the end of this period, juveniles sentenced to death would almost certainly remain on death row for a much longer time during their appeal process. This extended time, perhaps 10 years or longer, was just one of the issues around which the public debate focused.

The Rebirth and End of the Juvenile Death Penalty: 1989-2004

Since the moratorium on the death penalty from 1972 to 1976, and through 2005, when the juvenile death penalty was ruled unconstitutional by the U.S. Supreme Court, a total of 22 juveniles were executed in the United States (see Table 11.1). Juveniles facing capital punishment during that period had a more elaborate judicial process to work through before actually facing execution. The time required to process the waiver into adult court, the capital trial, the sentencing, and the appeal procedures could be exceptionally lengthy. For instance, Joseph Cannon was sentenced to death in 1977 in Texas. He was not executed until 1998, 21 years after the crime took place. While a juvenile at the time of his crime, conviction, and sentencing, Cannon was approaching middle age when his sentence was finally carried out. He was 17 years old at the time of his crime and 38 at the time of his execution (Death Penalty Information Center, n.d.).

Another landmark juvenile execution after the moratorium was the execution of Sean Sellers in 1999. Sean was 16 years old when he was sentenced to death in 1986 in Oklahoma. There was an outcry from advocacy groups and people who opposed the execution because of Sean's age when the crime took place. Furthermore, other groups spoke out because Sean had been diagnosed with multiple personality disorder, which was not explained to the jury at his trial. However, despite the controversy, Sean Sellers became the first juvenile to be executed since Leonard Shockley in 1959 for a crime committed by a 16-year-old.

Table 11.1 **Juveniles Executions 1985-2003**

Name of Executed	Date of Execution	Place of Execution	Race of Executed	Age at Crime	Age at Execution
Charles Rumbaugh	9/11/85	Texas	White	17	28
J. Terry Roach	1/10/86	South Carolina	White	17	25
Jay Pinkerton	5/15/86	Texas	White	17	24
Dalton Prejean	5/18/90	Louisiana	Black	17	30
Johnny Garrett	2/11/92	Texas	White	17	28
Curtis Harris	7/1/93	Texas	Black	17	31
Frederick Lashley	7/28/93	Missouri	Black	17	29
Ruben Cantu	8/24/93	Texas	Latino	17	26
Chris Burger	12/7/93	Georgia	White	17	33
Joseph Cannon	4/22/98	Texas	White	17	38
Robert Carter	5/18/98	Texas	Black	17	34
Dwayne Allen Wright	10/14/98	Virginia	Black	17	24
Sean Sellers	2/4/99	Oklahoma	White	16	29
Douglas C. Thomas	1/10/00	Virginia	White	17	26
Steven Roach	1/13/00	Virginia	White	17	23
Glen McGinnis	1/25/00	Texas	Black	17	27
Shaka Sankofa (Gary Graham)	6/22/00	Texas	Black	17	36
Gerald Mitchell	10/22/01	Texas	Black	17	33
Napoleon Beazley	5/28/02	Texas	Black	17	25
T.J. Jones	8/8/02	Texas	Black	17	25
Toronto Patterson	8/28/02	Texas	Black	17	24
Scott A. Hain	14/03/03	Oklahoma	White	17	32

Source: Streib, 2005.

Juveniles, like Sellers, facing the death penalty prior to 2005 had to be transferred, or "waived," into adult court from the state's juvenile justice system. Even with the constitutional ban on the juvenile death penalty, there are still juveniles transferred to adult criminal court to face other adult sentences. There are several ways that a juvenile can be waived into adult court. Every state has guidelines – established in statutory law – that allow juveniles who commit certain felony offenses to be waived into the adult criminal court (see Chapter 7). The first way a juvenile can be transferred into the adult court system is by a judge's decision. Typically, this depends on the state's laws determining what age a juvenile must be before he or she can be transferred; however, there are several states that specify no age limit on transfers. Sometimes states have further criteria focusing on prior convictions and/or adjudications or the seriousness of the offense in question. This is called a judicial waiver (see Table 11.2). States have a variety of ages that allow for transfer into adult court; however, prior to the *Roper* (2005) decision, a juvenile had to be 16 years of age at the time of the crime before he or she could face the death penalty. Then and now, the juvenile can still be transferred into adult court in some states if he or she is under the age of 16. In these instances, the state can seek any adult punishment other than capital punishment.

Table 11.2 **Minimum Age for Judicial Waiver for Capital Crimes (or Murder) in 2004**

Minimum Age for Judicial Waiver	States
No age Specified (17 States)	Alaska, Arizona, Delaware, Hawaii, Idaho, Maine, Maryland, Montana, Nebraska, Oklahoma, Oregon, Rhode Island, South Carolina, South Dakota, Tennessee, Washington, West Virginia
Age 10 (3 States)	Indiana, Kansas, Vermont
Age 12 (2 States)	Colorado, Missouri
Age 13 (7 States)	Georgia, Illinois, Mississippi, New Hampshire, New York, North Carolina, Wyoming
Age 14 (19 States)	Alabama, Arkansas, California, Connecticut, Florida, Iowa, Kentucky, Louisiana, Massachusetts, Michigan, Minnesota, Nevada, New Jersey, North Dakota, Ohio, Pennsylvania, Texas, Virginia, Wisconsin
Age 15 (1 State)	New Mexico plus District of Columbia
Age 16 (1 State)	Utah

Source: Snyder, H. & M. Sickmund (2006).

Another way juveniles can be placed into adult court is a relatively new method. Some state legislatures have replaced the judicial waiver with an automatic or mandatory waiver into adult criminal court jurisdiction for certain serious offenses (see Table 11.3). For instance, in North Carolina, juveniles are automatically transferred into adult criminal court at the age of 16. North Carolina has a statute that specifies juvenile court jurisdiction only for children under the age of 16. However, even before *Roper*, in North Carolina, a 16-year-old could not face capital punishment; in North Carolina prior to *Roper*, an offender had to be at least 17 at the time of the offense for the death penalty to be considered. Judicial transfer is based on the discretion of the juvenile court judge; an automatic transfer is usually based only on age.

Even before the Court addressed the juvenile death penalty in *Roper v. Simmons*, three states (Missouri, South Dakota, and Wyoming) raised their age limit for death penalty eligibility. In effect, this eliminated the juvenile

Table 11.3 **State Juvenile Justice Profiles**

	Judicial Waiver			Direct File	Statutory Exclusion	Reverse Waiver	Once/ Always	Juvenile Blended	Criminal Blended
	Discretionary	Presumptive	Mandatory						
Total States	45	15	15	15	29	25	34	15	17
Alabama	x				x		x		
Alaska	x	x			x			x	
Arizona	x			x	x	x	x		
Arkansas	x			x		x		x	x
California	x	x		x	x	x	x		x
Colorado	x	x		x		x		x	x
Connecticut			x			x		x	
Delaware	x		x		x	x	x		
District of Columbia	x	x		x			x		
Florida	x			x	x		x		x
Georgia	x		x	x	x	x			
Hawaii	x						x		
Idaho	x				x		x		x
Illinois	x	x	x		x	x	x	x	x
Indiana	x		x		x		x		
Iowa	x				x	x	x		x
Kansas	x	x					x	x	
Kentucky	x		x			x			x
Louisiana	x		x	x	x				
Maine	x	x					x		
Maryland	x				x	x	x		
Massachusetts					x			x	x
Michigan	x			x			x	x	x
Minnesota	x	x			x		x	x	
Mississippi	x				x	x	x		
Missouri	x						x		x
Montana				x	x	x		x	
Nebraska				x		x			x
Nevada	x	x			x	x	x		
New Hampshire	x	x					x		
New Jersey	x	x	x						
New Mexico					x			x	x
New York					x	x			
North Carolina	x		x				x		
North Dakota	x	x	x				x		
Ohio	x		x				x	x	
Oklahoma	x			x	x	x	x		x

Table 11.3 *(continued)*

	Judicial Waiver			Direct File	Statutory Exclusion	Reverse Waiver	Once/ Always	Juvenile Blended	Criminal Blended
	Discretionary	Presumptive	Mandatory						
Total States	**45**	**15**	**15**	**15**	**29**	**25**	**34**	**15**	**17**
Oregon	x				x	x	x		
Pennsylvania	x	x			x	x	x		
Rhode Island	x	x	x				x	x	
South Carolina	x		x		x				
South Dakota	x				x	x	x		
Tennessee	x					x	x		
Texas	x						x	x	
Utah	x	x			x		x		
Vermont	x			x	x	x		x	
Virginia	x		x	x		x	x		x
Washington	x				x		x		
West Virginia	x		x						x
Wisconsin	x				x	x	x		x
Wyoming	x			x		x			

© 2000 (original copyright); © 2007 (most recent copyright) National Center for Juvenile Justice.

Source: Griffin, Patrick (2007). "National Overviews." *State Juvenile Justice Profiles.* Pittsburgh, PA: National Center for Juvenile Justice. Online. Available: http://www.ncjj.org/stateprofiles/

death penalty in their states. On March 3, 2004, the governors of both South Dakota and Wyoming signed legislation raising the minimum age for capital punishment to 18 (Human Rights Watch, 2004). Previously, South Dakota and Wyoming had the juvenile death penalty set at the minimum age limit specified by the Court, 16, although neither state executed any children between 1985 and 2003, the last year of a juvenile execution in the United States (see Table 11.4).

Children Facing Execution in the Late Twentieth Century

When considering the lives experienced by many of the children facing the death penalty in the late twentieth century, the debate against executing children becomes even more rational. Children are incapable of deciding that their parents are neglecting them, abusing them, or teaching them poor habits. A 16-year-old child of a drug addict is not allowed to move out, get a full-time job, and escape the criminal lifestyle in which he or she is being raised. In fact, many children in such environments do not totally comprehend that their lives are different or problematic (Horowitz, 2000). Unless the state steps in with charges of abuse or neglect, neglected children are

Table 11.4 **Minimum Age for Death Penalty Eligibility as of February 28, 2005**

Minimum Age for Death Penalty Eligibility	States
Age 16 (14 States)	Alabama, Arizona, Arkansas, Delaware, Idaho, Kentucky, Louisiana, Mississippi, Nevada, Oklahoma, Pennsylvania, South Carolina, Utah, Virginia
Age 17 (5 States)	Florida, Georgia, New Hampshire, North Carolina, Texas
Age 18 (18 States and the Federal Government)	California, Colorado, Connecticut, Illinois, Indiana, Kansas, Maryland, Missouri, Montana, Nebraska, New Jersey, New Mexico, Ohio, Oregon, South Dakota, Tennessee, Washington, Wyoming, Federal Government
States with No Death Penalty (12 States and D.C.)	Alaska, District of Columbia, Hawaii, Iowa, Maine, Massachusetts, Michigan, New York, North Dakota, Rhode Island, Vermont, West Virginia, Wisconsin

Source: Streib, 2005.

very often left to grow up in such environments. Even if the state steps in and removes children from biological parents due to abuse or neglect, and places them in foster homes, states still often refuse to consider the consequences of the lifestyle children have been living prior to the new arrangements. A critique of the environment offered by foster care is beyond the scope of this chapter; however, suffice it to say that states that allow for the sentencing of juveniles to death often do not address the full make-up of children's lives when facing such decisions.

Robert Carter, a 17-year-old offender from Texas, was executed on May 18, 1998. Carter,

> . . . one of six children living in an impoverished Houston neighborhood, had been whipped and beaten with wooden switches, belts, and electrical cords by both his mother and step-father. When he was five, he was hit on the head with a brick; when he was ten, a baseball bat smashed his head so hard that the bat broke; and when he was seventeen, his brother shot him in the head, lodging a bullet near his temple. When he was arrested for the murder of an eighteen-year-old female, the police held this seventeen-year-old brain damaged boy incommunicado and convinced him to confess to the murder as well as to waive his right to a lawyer (Amnesty International, 1998: Section 6).

When Carter faced sentencing in Texas, the "jury was not invited to consider as mitigating evidence Carter's age at the time of his crime" (Amnesty International, 1998: Section 6). The jury was also not informed of Carter's possible mental retardation, his brain injury, the brutal abuse he suffered as a child, or that this was his first offense. The jury arrived at a sentence of death in less than 10 minutes.

Carter was never allowed to pursue a life outside of his childhood or the prison system. Mitigating circumstances, such as domestic violence and sexual abuse, are often included for the jury's consideration during the sentencing process in adult capital cases. When these circumstances are not included during the sentencing for children, the court is assuming that children are rational and capable of making informed choices regardless of their background.

Carter did not have a chance to move out and start a new life, free of violence. He had no opportunity to remove himself from his violent childhood or family. There may be years between an adult's abusive childhood and his or her crime, but the jury may still be allowed to hear the mitigating evidence that he or she was abused as a child. Children have no time span between their violent childhoods and their crimes, nor do they have the experiences adults have, which allow for maturity, after moving out of the house. It is believed that this time span between childhood and adulthood is what assists in discerning between right and wrong and what consequences will be faced for criminal behavior (Horowitz, 2000).

Even more so, a child's world will typically revolve solely around himself or herself. In the Supreme Court case of *Stanford v. Kentucky* (1989), Justice Brennan's dissenting opinion focused on the idea that the age of 18 is a conservative line for people moving into their adulthood. Brennan believed that most psychological and emotional changes that bring maturity do not occur until later in life. Thus, he considered the sentence of death inappropriate for a juvenile because of his or her inability to mature truly and properly prior to the age of 18. Essentially, Justice Brennan believed that the existing laws for children that cited the age of majority at 18 were at the lowest age possible when considering the maturity and life experiences gathered beyond those years.

Prior to the *Roper* decision, the age of the child facing the death penalty was the most prominent mitigating circumstance included during the sentencing phase; however, sometimes the age of the offender was used as an aggravating factor when presented by the prosecution (Amnesty International, 2001). As previously mentioned, the Justices determined that when imposing the death penalty the goals of retribution and deterrence must be met for both juveniles and adults (*Furman v. Georgia*, 1972; *Stanford v. Kentucky*, 1989). The Court found that juveniles 15 years of age and younger had limited intellectual capabilities and thus could not be held fully responsible for their actions. The Justices also found, though, that starting at the age of 16, juveniles were capable of understanding the consequences of their actions (*Stanford v. Kentucky*, 1989; *Thompson v. Oklahoma*, 1988). These rulings did not reflect universal beliefs, however. Dissenting in the *Stanford* decision, Justice Brennan found that attempting to place a culpability line between offenders who are 15 and those that are 16 or 17 made no sense (Horowitz, 2000). He believed that juveniles (under the age of 18) lacked the ability to understand a punishment so extreme. Therefore, executing any offender for a crime committed while under the age of 18 did not follow the goals of retribution.

The Evolving Standards of Decency: *Atkins* and *Roper*

Among the arguments debated by death penalty opponents and proponents that apply to both children and adults are the rationale for keeping the death penalty as a punishment. According to *Furman v. Georgia* (1972), the punishment of death must meet the goals of both retribution and deterrence. Furthermore, the Court determined that the constitutionality of the death penalty must adhere to the "evolving standards of decency." Essentially this means that the courts must be able to demonstrate that the use of the death penalty furthers the goals (retribution and deterrence) *and* is still acceptable through the eyes of the public or society.

In 2002, the Court applied the "evolving standard of decency" to the execution of the mentally retarded. The Court ruled in *Atkins v. Virginia* that because 60 percent of the states did not allow for execution of the mentally retarded (which includes the 12 states that did not allow for the death penalty at all), this provided "powerful evidence that today our society views mentally retarded offenders as categorically less culpable than the average criminal" (*Atkins v. Virginia*, 2002:123). The Supreme Court decided in this case that the "evolving standard of decency" called for an end to the execution of the mentally retarded because the majority of the public was in disagreement with the sanction.

Some abolitionists contended that these same standards should also apply to the use of capital punishment for juveniles. If the mentally retarded are excluded from eligibility for the death penalty because they have less culpability, this could also be said of children. The belief that children, or people under the age of 18, are incapable of making sound decisions is applied in many other areas of American law. Juveniles are prohibited from many activities that are permitted for adults (drinking, voting, and viewing certain movies) because of their presumed less developed intellectual abilities, immature decision-making skills, and abilities to avoid harm. After the *Atkins* decision, it was expected that the Court would address the juvenile death penalty under the same "evolving standards of decency." This would constitute a strong argument for extending the prohibition on the death penalty to juveniles. The Court's decision, however, did not come soon enough for some juveniles.

After *Atkins*, there were three juvenile executions pending in the summer and fall of 2002 and another in the spring of 2003. Toronto Patterson was the first of the juveniles to address the Court. On August 26, 2002, just over two months after the *Atkins* decision, a petition on behalf of Patterson was filed with the U.S. Supreme Court citing *Atkins v. Virginia* and the "evolving standard of decency." Prior to the petition, and after the *Atkins* decision, some of the Justices stated they would like to review the juvenile death penalty based on the "evolving standards of decency." Nonetheless, the Court refused to hear Patterson's appeal and he was executed on August 28, 2002 (American

Bar Association, n.d.). The second post-*Atkins* petition to the Court was from Kevin Stanford (*In re Stanford*, 2002). This was the same Stanford in the *Stanford v. Kentucky* (1989) decision that established a precedent for the minimum age that juvenile offenders could face the death penalty. Like Patterson, Stanford filed a *habeas corpus* appeal with the U.S. Supreme Court and, on October 22, 2002, in a 5-4 decision, the Court declined to hear the appeal. Unlike Patterson, however, Stanford was not executed. Paul Patton, then-governor of Kentucky, commuted his death sentence to life (Aronson, 2007).

Patterson and Stanford were not the last juveniles to face execution in the United States. In 2003, almost a year after the *Atkins* decision, the Court refused to hear the case of Scott Hain of Oklahoma (James & Cecil, 2004). Oklahoma, like Kentucky, also had a history of using the juvenile death penalty. As previously noted, in 1999, Sean Sellers was the first, and only, juvenile since 1959 to be executed for a crime committed before his seventeenth birthday. At the time of his offense, Hain was 17 years old; he was executed on April 3, 2003 (James & Cecil, 2004). It was not until *Roper v. Simmons* that the Court would again address the issue of the juvenile death penalty.

In September, 1993, Christopher Simmons planned and carried out a brutal murder. He was 17 at the time of his crime. Simmons was found guilty and sentenced to death by a Missouri trial court. Facing execution, Simmons filed a petition for post-conviction relief with the state arguing for the prohibition of juvenile executions based on the finding in *Atkins v. Virginia*. As Benekos and Merlo (2005) stated, Simmons asked the Missouri Supreme Court to make a "prediction" on what the U.S. Supreme Court might decide in the future regarding the juvenile death penalty. Based on *Atkins*, the Missouri Supreme Court vacated the death sentence and resentenced Simmons to life in prison without the possibility of parole.

> Using the reasoning from the *Atkins* case, the Missouri court decided, 6-to-3, that the U.S. Supreme Court's 1989 decision in *Stanford v. Kentucky*, which held that executing minors was not unconstitutional, was no longer valid. The opinion in *Stanford v. Kentucky* had relied on a finding that a majority of Americans did not consider the execution of minors to be cruel and unusual. The Missouri court, citing numerous laws passed since 1989 that limited the scope of the death penalty, held that national opinion had changed. Finding that a majority of Americans were now opposed to the execution of minors, the court held that such executions were now unconstitutional (The Oyez Project, n.d.).

Using the "evolving standards of decency," the Missouri Supreme Court ruled that the juvenile death penalty did not meet the goals of either retribution or deterrence and therefore disregarded case precedent established in *Stanford* (1989).

Unlike most death penalty appeals, *Roper* was appealed by the Attorney General of Missouri instead of the sentenced offender because at this point, Simmons was no longer on death row. The Attorney General appealed the Missouri State Supreme Court ruling primarily because the state court relied on a future ruling by the U.S. Supreme Court and demonstrated complete disregard for case precedent. At the time of the Missouri Supreme Court ruling, the case precedent clearly stated that the execution of juveniles (ages 16 or 17 at the time of their crime) was constitutional.

The U.S. Supreme Court heard arguments on October 13, 2004, and released its decision on March 1, 2005. Prior to the ruling, there was some conjecture that the Court would ignore the lower court's blatant overruling of case precedent (Richey, 2003). Others argued that the juvenile death penalty issue was secondary to the obvious disregard of case precedent. Nonetheless, the Court agreed with the Missouri Supreme Court concluding that children are "categorically less culpable than the average criminal" (*Roper v. Simmons*, 2005:2). The Court noted that a majority of states had rejected the juvenile death penalty and, in fact, executions of juveniles were infrequently carried out. As an additional consideration for finding that juvenile executions were unconstitutional, the Court also cited international opinion that strongly opposed the juvenile death penalty. According to Greenhouse (2004), the last five executions of juveniles in the world all occurred in the United States. Finally, the Court also stated that juveniles are "vulnerable to influence and susceptible to immature and irresponsible behaviors" thus juveniles have a diminished culpability and "neither retribution nor deterrence provides adequate justification for imposing the death penalty" (*Roper v. Simmons*, 2005:6).

Roper and Beyond: 2005-Present

Executing juveniles is largely an ethical/moral debate for most people. Is it right to sentence a child to death? For some who believe the execution of an adult offender is acceptable, when the offender is a "child," their acceptance of this criminal penalty wanes or disappears. In American culture, children often are viewed as different from adults. Consequently, children are held to different standards of conduct and provided with different forms and degrees of assistance and punishment.

Not all of the controversy focuses on ethical/moral issues. Capital punishment is one of the most common topics of research in criminal justice; however, most of the research available about the death penalty focuses on adults facing execution. The issues surrounding children facing the death penalty in the United States are under-researched (Hale, 1997). Nevertheless, most of the issues cited above that are debated for adults can also be applied to children who were facing execution. Equally controversial are many other issues involving children that do not apply to adults.

Deterrent Effects

In addition to retribution, the second goal for capital punishment is deterrence. A deterrent effect can be found when an offender is a rational, informed decisionmaker who can insightfully discern between his or her action and the consequence (*Stanford v. Kentucky*, 1989). Otherwise, the person will be incapable of understanding why the action resulted in such a harsh punishment. Deterrence occurs when an individual who knows the possible punishment for a crime makes a decision not to commit that crime so as to avoid suffering the punishment. This is clearly a process of rational thinking. Whether a juvenile's behavior can be influenced by the possibility that he or she may receive a sentence of death is an issue of debate. Many believe juveniles are less likely than adults to consider consequences of actions, especially long-term consequences. In *Roper v. Simmons*, the Court ruled that because juveniles were "vulnerable to influence, and susceptible to immature and irresponsible behavior" neither "retribution nor deterrence provides adequate justification for imposing the death penalty" (2005:2).

Furthermore, because the majority of juveniles who were facing execution in America came from communities where they faced the possibility of death everyday, the possibility that they *may* get caught and then *may* face capital punishment rarely affected their behaviors. Juveniles typically believe they are invincible (*Stanford v. Kentucky*, 1989); therefore, imposing such a sanction has no significant deterrent value, even for juveniles from a middle-class background.

Finally, prior to *Roper v. Simmons*, the American Bar Association (ABA) cited strong opposition for the juvenile death penalty (Streib, 1998). In August, 1983, the ABA House of Delegates ascertained its opposition for executing persons who were under the age of 18 at the time of their offense. Later, in 1997, the ABA supported a complete moratorium on the death penalty until it could be administered fairly and impartially (Horowitz, 2000; Streib, 1998). Essentially, the ABA decided that juveniles, along with those who are mentally retarded, should not be treated the same as adults who are not suffering from mental retardation. The ABA argued that other laws generally do not treat them the same (as previously mentioned, the right to vote, drink, and marry), and that capital punishment should follow the same guidelines. Interestingly enough, in 1998, Streib contended that "the national movement to ban the death penalty for juvenile offenders is much further along than that for retarded offenders" (1998:57). In 2002, however, contrary to Streib's view, the Supreme Court struck down the death penalty for mentally retarded offenders but refused to review the use of capital punishment for juveniles until 2004. Arguably, the long-standing opposition voiced by the American Bar Association had little effect on juvenile death penalty laws in the U.S. While public opinion alone did not have much effect on the juvenile death penalty, public opinion did affect state legislators who changed state laws which effectively were a significant factor in Court's deliberations in *Roper*.

Public Opinion

Over the years, public support has varied between 64 and 80 percent in favor of capital punishment (Gallup Poll, 2007). However, when questions about the death penalty include factors such as mental illness, mental retardation, and age of the offender, support for the death penalty declines. For instance, a 2006 Gallup Poll reports that 69 percent of those surveyed support the death penalty for persons convicted of murder (Gallup Poll, 2007). However, when participants are given a sentencing alternative, such as life without the possibility of parole, support for the death penalty declined. In fact, the Gallup Poll showed greater support for life without the possibility of parole (48%) than for the death penalty (47%). As indicated by the Gallup Poll, support for life without the possibility for parole over the death penalty continues to increase.

Academic research has mirrored what public opinion surveys have found regarding executing juveniles. Skovron, Scott, and Cullen (1989) found that even with a growing rate of violent juvenile crimes, most people disagree with the execution of juvenile offenders. A similar result was demonstrated by Finkel, Hughes, Smith, and Hurabiell (1994), who determined that only 35 percent of those surveyed supported the execution of juveniles between the ages of 16 and 18. Finally, researchers have also found that respondents favor less punitive punishments over the death penalty for juveniles (Moon, Wright, Cullen & Pealer, 2000; Vito & Keil, 1989). These studies illustrate that public sentiment is against executing juvenile offenders. Even more indicative of the lack of support for the juvenile death penalty, a 1995 Hart Research Poll of police chiefs in the United States found that the majority of police chiefs do not believe that the death penalty is an effective tool in decreasing violent crime (Dieter, 1995).

The effect of public opinion is minimal when it comes to laws regulating or ending the death penalty. "Legislatures do not rely solely on public opinion, nor should they" (Seis & Elbe, 1991:476), but the Supreme Court's "evolving standards of decency" does, in some sense, rely on public support. The decisions in *Atkins v. Virginia* and *Roper v. Simmons*, focused on the fact that the evolving standards of decency disapproved the execution of the mentally retarded and children. As previously mentioned, the decisions in these cases were based on changes in public opinion for executing the mentally retarded and youth under the age of 18 at the time of their offense.

Prior to *Roper*, there was considerable debate on the direction of the juvenile death penalty. Some jurisdictions supported lowering the age for execution to even younger juvenile offenders. For instance, Florida and Arkansas legislators supported lowering the age requirement to 14 (Strater, 1995). Furthermore, one Los Angeles District Attorney stated he would support the death penalty for children no matter what their age (Amnesty International, 1998). These proposals were primarily based on reactions to recent high-profile juvenile crimes, such as children killing other children and mass murders in schools.

Even with evidence of support for lowering the age limit of the juvenile death penalty in some jurisdictions, other states began to initiate legislative changes in the opposite direction. On March 26, 2002, the Governor of Indiana signed into law a bill requiring offenders to be at least 18 at the time of their crime to face capital punishment. Similarly, Montana enacted legislation in 1999 that increased the minimum age for death penalty eligibility to 18. When New York reinstated death penalty laws in 1995, legislators excluded children from the law (Streib, 2005). Furthermore, in 2004, prior to the *Roper* decision, both South Dakota and Wyoming raised the minimum age for capital punishment to 18 (Human Rights Watch, 2004).

Before the 2005 *Roper* decision, 14 states specified death penalty eligibility for juveniles who were 16, five states specified it for juveniles who were 17, and the remaining 18 states and the federal government allowed the death penalty only if the offender had reached the common age of majority, 18 (Streib, 2005). Therefore, prior to *Roper*, the death penalty for juveniles was available in only 19 states. While 37 states (and the federal government) had the death penalty available for adults, only 51 percent (19) of those jurisdictions with the death penalty extended that option to juvenile offenders.

Conclusion

Prior to *Roper*, the likelihood that a juvenile would be sentenced to the death penalty, even after committing a violent crime, was minimal. Between 1973, when executions were resumed, and 2005, when executions for juveniles were deemed unconstitutional, approximately 7,528 death sentences were handed down by the courts for both juveniles and adults (Streib, 2005). Of this total, only 226 or three percent were for juvenile offenders (Streib, 2005). Of those death sentences, only 22 (10%) of the total 226 sentences were actually carried out. The other cases were either reversed and/or the sentences were commuted to life imprisonment before or after the *Roper* decision. Essentially, even when the death penalty was available for children, the likelihood of a juvenile actually being executed was remote.

Because the actual application of the death penalty for juveniles was so low, the retributive and deterrent effects of the punishment were questionable. For a punishment to be a deterrent, juveniles must understand that their specific punishment fits the degree of their crimes. Because juveniles are typically considered incapable of understanding such an extreme punishment, the retributive aspect of the death penalty was not present. Furthermore, for retribution to apply, juveniles who commit violent felony murders should all face the death penalty. The reality, however, is that capital punishment, in the past for juveniles and currently for adults, is applied inconsistently. According to Pierce and Radelet (2005), in California, the likelihood of a defendant being sentenced to death increased if the victim was white rather than Black or Latino.

Following the *Furman* and *Gregg* decisions, the Supreme Court reviewed several cases that dealt solely with juveniles facing execution. Prior to *Roper*, the most important decisions were *Eddings*, *Thompson*, and *Stanford*, because these cases respectively allowed for mitigating circumstances (i.e., age) to be brought into the sentencing process, halted executions of 15-year-old offenders, and reinstated the standard that only juveniles 16 and 17 years of age could face the death penalty. In the decision of *Patterson v. Texas*, the Court denied a stay of execution for Patterson. Justice Stevens (joined by Justices Ginsburg and Breyer) dissented and referred to the 1989 decision in which he joined Justice Brennan in the majority opinion issued for *Stanford v. Kentucky* (*Patterson v. Texas*, 2002:1-2):

> Since that opinion was written, the issue has been the subject of further debate and discussion…Given the apparent consensus that exists among the States and in the international community against the execution of a…juvenile offender, I think it would be appropriate for the Court to revisit the issue at the earliest opportunity.

The dissent in *Patterson* by Stevens, Ginsburg, and Breyer, the views expressed in the *Atkins* decision, and the fact that most state statutes prohibited juvenile executions presented the Court with an opportunity to review the juvenile death penalty and to interpret this sanction in the context of the evolving standards of decency. In October, 2002, however (*Patterson v. Texas* 2002:5341), the Court refused to consider the constitutionality of executing juvenile offenders. As a result, two more offenders who had been sentenced for crimes committed as juveniles, Patterson and Hain, were executed.

The juvenile death penalty existed in the colonies before American independence from England. In 1642, Thomas Graunger faced execution, just as 22 other juveniles faced execution through April 3, 2003, when the last juvenile was executed in the United States. Since then, significant changes have been made in death penalty statutes but arguably, none has been more important than the decision in *Roper v. Simmons* in 2005, to end the death penalty for children. The emergent question now is what to do with violent juvenile offenders (Benekos & Merlo, 2005). Does life without parole warrant the same attention and scrutiny as the juvenile death penalty? Both sentences (death and life without parole) have the same result. Are children who are sentenced to life without parole facing punishment too harsh for crimes committed at such young ages?

According to Human Rights Watch (2005), in 2005, there were more than 2,225 children serving life without parole in the United States. Furthermore, 16 percent of the 2,225 youth were under the age of 15 at the time of their offense. This is younger than was the acceptable age (prior to *Roper*) for imposing the death penalty on juveniles. In *Roper*, the Justices considered the development and maturity of an adolescent in determining whether juveniles should be held to the same standard as adults. Their decision that adolescents operated with diminished competency justified excluding juveniles from capital punishment. Does the "evolving standard of decency" also apply to juveniles sentenced to life without parole? In other words, "is the decency of life imprisonment the next policy issue to be confronted by the Court?" (Benekos & Merlo, 2005:330).

References

American Bar Association (n.d.). "Juvenile Death Penalty Toronto Patterson." This report is electronically available at http://www.abanet.org/crimjust/juvjus/patterson.html [Retrieved November 1, 2007].

Amnesty International (2001). *United States of America: Too Young to Vote, Old Enough to Be Executed.* New York, NY. This report is available electronically at: http://www.amnesty.org/en/library/info/AMR51/105/2001 [Retrieved February 22, 2008].

Amnesty International (1998). *United States of American: Robert Anthony Carter – Juvenile Offender Scheduled to be Executed in Texas.* New York, NY. This report is available at: http://www.asiapacific..amnesty.org/library/Index/ENGAMR510241998?open&of=ENG-2M4 [Retrieved November 1, 2007].

Aronson, J. (2007). "Brain Imaging, Culpability and the Juvenile Death Penalty." *Psychology, Public Policy, and Law,* 13(2):115-142.

Bedau, H.A. (ed.) (1982). *The Death Penalty in America,* Third Edition. New York, NY: Oxford University Press.

Benekos, P.J. & A.V. Merlo (2005). "Juvenile Offenders and the Death Penalty." *Youth Violence and Juvenile Justice,* 3(4):316-333.

Death Penalty Information Center (n.d.). Available http://www.deathpenaltyinfo.org. [Retrieved on December 1, 2008].

Dieter, R.C. (1995). *On the Front Line: Law Enforcement Views on the Death Penalty.* Washington, DC: Death Penalty Information Center. This report is available at: http://www.death penaltyinfo.org/article.php?did=545&scid=45 [Retrieved November 1, 2007].

Elsea, K.K. (1995). "The Juvenile Crime Debate: Rehabilitation, Punishment or Prevention." *The Kansas Journal of Law and Public Policy,* 5(1):135-146.

Finkel, N.J., K.C. Hughes, S.F. Smith & M.L. Hurabiell (1994). "Killing Kids: The Juvenile Death Penalty and Community Sentiment." *Behavioral Sciences and the Law,* 12(1):5-20.

Gallup Poll (2007). This report is electronically available at: http://www.gallup.com/poll/1606/Death-Penalty.aspx [Retrieved November 1, 2007].

Greenhouse, L. (2004). "Court to Review Using Execution in Juvenile Cases." *New York Times,* (27 January):A1.

Griffin, P. (2007). "National Overviews." State Juvenile Justice Profiles. Pittsburgh, PA: National Center for Juvenile Justice. Online. Available: http://www.ncjj.org/stateprofiles [Retrieved on April 5, 2008].

Hale , R.L. (1997). *A Review of Juvenile Executions in America.* Lewiston, NY: The Edwin Mellen Press.

Horowitz, M.A. (2000). "Kids Who Kill: A Critique of How the American Legal System Deals with Juveniles Who Commit Homicide." *Law and Contemporary Problems,* 63(3):133-177.

Human Rights Watch (2004). *U.S.: Two More States Abolish Juvenile Death Penalty*, March 4, 2004. This report is available at http://www.hrw.org/campaigns/deathpenalty/docs/update030404.htm [Retrieved February 22, 2008].

Human Rights Watch (2005). *United States: Thousands of Children Sentenced to Life without Parole*, October 12, 2005. This report is available at http://www.hrw.org/english/docs/2005/10/12/ usdom11835.htm [Retrieved November 1, 2007].

James, A & J. Cecil (2004). "Out of Step: Juvenile Death Penalty in the United States." *The International Journal of Children's Rights*, 11(3):291-303.

Landau, E. (1992). *Teens and the Death Penalty*. Hillside, NJ: Enslow.

Moon, M.M., J.P. Wright, F.T. Cullen & J.A. Pealer (2000). "Putting Kids to Death: Specifying Public Support for Juvenile Capital Punishment." *Justice Quarterly*, 17(4):663-683.

National Center for Juvenile Justice (2006). *State Juvenile Justice Profiles*, Office of Juvenile Justice and Delinquency Prevention. This report is available at http://www.ncjj.org/stateprofiles/ [Retrieved November 1, 2007].

Pierce, G.L. & M.L. Radelet (2005). "Empirical Analysis: The Impact of Legally Inappropriate Factors on Death Sentencing for California Homicides, 1990-1999." *Santa Clara Law Review*, 46:1-47.

Richey, W. (2003). "Sniper Case Revisits Juvenile Death Penalty." *Christian Science Monitor*, (21 November). This report is available at http://www.csmonitor.com/2003 /1121/p02s 01-usju.html [Retrieved November 1, 2007].

Seis, M.C. & K.L. Elbe (1991). "The Death Penalty for Juveniles: Bridging the Gap between an Evolving Standard of Decency and Legislative Policy." *Justice Quarterly*, 8(4):466-487.

Skovron, S.E., J.E. Scott & F.T. Cullen (1989). "The Death Penalty for Juveniles: An Assessment of Public Support." *Crime & Delinquency*, 35(4):546-561.

Snyder, H. & M. Sickmund (2006). *Juvenile Offenders and Victims: 2006 National Report*. Washington, DC: Office of Juvenile Justice and Delinquency Prevention.

Strater, S.D. (1995). "The Juvenile Death Penalty: In the Best Interest of the Child?" *Human Rights*, 22(2):10-15.

Streib, V.L. (2005). *The Juvenile Death Penalty Today: Death Sentences and Executions for Juvenile Crime, January 1, 1973 – February 28, 2005*. This report is electronically available at: http://www.law.onu.edu/faculty_staff/faculty_profiles/coursematerials/streib/juvdeath.pdf [Retrieved November 1, 2007].

Streib, V.L. (1998). "Moratorium on the Death Penalty for Juveniles." *Law and Contemporary Problems*, 61(4):55-74.

The Oyez Project, *Roper v. Simmons*, 543 U.S. 551 (2005). http://www.oyez.org/cases/2000-2009/2004/2004_03_633/ [Retrieved February 23, 2008].

Vidmar, N. & P. Ellsworth (1982). "Public Opinion and the Death Penalty." In H.A. Bedau (ed.) *The Death Penalty in America*, pp 68-84. New York, NY: Oxford University Press.

Vito, G.F. & T.J. Keil (1989). "Selecting Juveniles for Death: The Kentucky Experience." *Journal of Contemporary Criminal Justice*, 5:181-198.

Cases Cited

Atkins v. Virginia, 122 S. Ct. 2242 (2002).

Eddings v. Oklahoma, 455 U.S. 104 (1982).

Furman v. Georgia, 408 U.S. 238 (1972).

Gregg v. Georgia, 428 U.S. 157 (1976).

In re Stanford, 537 U.S. 968 (2002).

Patterson v. Texas, 536 U.S. ___ (2002).

Roper v. Simmons, 543 U.S. 551 (2005).

Stanford v. Kentucky, 109 S. Ct. 2969 (1989).

Thompson v. Oklahoma, 487 U.S. 815 (1988).

Trop v. Dulles, 356 U.S. 86 (1958).

Weems v. United States, 217 U.S. 349 (1910).

Woodson v. North Carolina, 482 U.S. 280 (1976).

CHAPTER 12

Comparative Juvenile Justice Policy: Lessons from Other Countries

Audry Passetti
Alida V. Merlo
Peter J. Benekos

Introduction

As reviewed in Chapter 1, juvenile justice policy in the United States is somewhat paradoxical. Although there is evidence of excessively harsh sanctions, there are also indications of a softer approach to dealing with youth. It is useful to examine other countries' juvenile justice systems to contrast similarities or differences in their policies. This chapter presents a brief summary and comparison of juvenile justice in five countries: Canada, Sweden, Russia, Japan, and China. There are limitations to comparing countries: the definitions of offenses, the categories of offenses, the age or mental status when youth are considered juveniles, and the record keeping vary from country to country (Reichel, 2002; Finckenauer, 2001:196; Zalkind & Simon, 2004). In addition, the differences in history, governments, culture, economics, and politics affect how youth are perceived and the philosophy of juvenile justice. These constraints preclude comparing every aspect of juvenile justice policy. Nonetheless, there is an opportunity to discuss observations about juvenile justice in other countries.

Canada

Youth Policies

In describing the "birth" of juvenile justice in Canada, Winterdyk portrays the response to young offenders in the late 1800s as a shift away from years of neglect or punishment toward a "more benevolent attitude" that was in part the result of the "child-saving movement" (2002 :63). In 1894, the Youthful Offenders Act gave the government authority to intervene when "families failed to raise their children properly" (2002:63). The legislation emphasized that youthful miscreants were "misdirected and misguided" children who should not be punished as adults but rather be diverted from the judicial process. By 1908, a more formalized Juvenile Delinquents Act was passed that emphasized treatment, *parens patriae*, and a "welfare model" that included informality, indeterminate sanctions, preference for individualized treatment, and reliance on social workers and childcare experts to treat youth (Winterdyk, 2002:64).

By the mid 1960s, dissatisfaction with youth courts, and increased public concern about youthful offending, facilitated reform efforts that culminated in the Young Offenders Act (YOA) that was eventually implemented in 1984. The "new" philosophy was characterized as a "neo-classical" approach that rejected the "welfare model" of the previous legislation and promoted a "modified justice model" that emphasized adherence to due process, greater accountability, and punishment (Winterdyk, 2002:67). The YOA eliminated status offenses and established separate court jurisdiction for youth ages 12 through 17 (Bertrand, Paetsch & Bala, 2002:31).

Additional principles of the 1984 Act included: accountability, protection of society, recognition of special needs of youth, protection of legal rights for youth, and use of least possible interference (Bertrand et al., 2002:32). Under the YOA, youth had the right to counsel and were to be kept confined separately from adults. However, offenders ages 16 and 17 years old who were charged with "the most serious offenses" were to be dealt with in adult court and youth who were transferred and convicted could be sent to adult correctional facilities (Bertrand et al., 2002:34).

This Act was an attempt to balance public safety with rehabilitation and reintegration, and to consider a range of sentences that recognized the importance of community-based alternatives. However, controversies over the perceived ineffectiveness of the 1984 YOA came from liberals, who believed that the welfare-treatment model was being ignored, as well as conservatives who lamented the lack of accountability and concern for public safety. From both sides, the Act was seen as vague, ineffective, and unclear on how to prioritize the guiding principles. As a result, the Act was amended three times: 1986, 1992, and 1995 (Canadian Department of Justice, 2002b:6).

In 1992, the sentence for murder was increased from three to five years less one day and in 1995, it was again extended to ten years. In addition, the 1995 amendment established that for violent crimes (murder, attempted murder, manslaughter, and aggravated sexual assault), the presumptive age for youth to be handled in the adult system was 16 (Canadian Department of Justice, 2002b:6). The 1992 and 1995 amendments "responded to public concerns that the Act (1984 YOA) was too lenient" (2002b:6).

Continuing dissatisfaction with the YOA prompted the Minister of Justice to initiate a fundamental review of the Act. Even though recommendations from that study were proposed to modify and enhance the existing policies, criticisms and concerns were so prevalent that an entirely new Act was introduced to ensure "significant reforms" to the youth justice system. The 2001 legislation, the Youth Criminal Justice Act (YCJA), which was implemented in April, 2003, was designed to replace the Young Offenders Act with a system that is "fairer and more effective" and one which articulates that "the system's response to an offense should reflect the needs and individual circumstances of a young person" (Canadian Department of Justice, 2002a: Preamble and Declaration of Principle:1).

In addition, "the objectives of the youth justice system are to prevent crime; rehabilitate and reintegrate young persons into society; and ensure meaningful consequences for offenses" (2002a:1-2). Essentially, the YCJA is designed to prevent crime by treating youth and holding them accountable while recognizing their reduced level of maturity. The new Act prescribes sanctions that are the "least restrictive alternative" and "encourage the repair of harm done" (Canadian Department of Justice, 2002a: Preamble and Declaration of Principle:2).

> "The YCJA contains new policy directions in several areas, including the philosophical underpinnings of the youth justice system; the use of the court versus less formal responses to youth crime; conferencing; restrictions on pre-trial detention; sentencing principles; sentencing options; elimination of transfer of cases to the adult courts; and custody and reintegration of youth into society" (Barnhorst, 2004:232).

This new act has been found to be more specific in conveying key decision points in the juvenile justice process, which was lacking under the YOA (Barnhorst, 2004). Unlike the United States, Canada mandates that no juvenile will ever be detained with adult offenders. Rather, Canada creates an educational and safe experience for youthful offenders (Zalkind & Simon, 2004). In the years since YCJA was implemented, the rate of incarceration and detention has declined at all stages of the juvenile justice process (Barnhorst, 2004). Thus far, Canada has observed positive developments in juvenile justice since changing from the YOA to YCJA (Barnhorst, 2004).

Youth Crime and Dispositions

In 1999, youth represented 18 percent of all individuals charged for offenses. This includes 27 percent of all property and 16 percent of all violent offenses (Bertrand et al., 2002:29). A 12-year trend (1988-1999) of youth crime arrests reveals an increase in late 1980s and early 1990s with subsequent decreases through the 1990s. Data reviewed by Bertrand, Paetsch, and Bala on youth arrest rates indicate that other than for robbery and nonsexual assault, violent and property crime arrests decreased throughout the 1990s (2002:30). Homicide rates were consistent at two arrests per 100,000 youth and thefts decreased from 1,618 per 100,000 youth in 1988 to 906 per 100,000 youth in 1999. Based on their assessment, they concluded that "while public concern in Canada over youth offending remains high, it would appear that in the late 1990s youth crime rates slightly declined" (2002:31).

Additional data suggest similar conclusions. In 1997, 4,927 youth out of 100,000 were charged for all offenses compared to 4,656 in 2001 and 3,327 in 2006 (Statistics Canada, 2008a). For crimes of violence (homicide, attempted murder, assaults, robbery) rates declined from 919 per 100,000 in 2002 to 794 in 2006. The property crime rates decreased from 1,714 arrests for every 100,000 in 2002 to 998 for every 100,000 in 2006 (Statistics Canada, 2008a).

The most notable arrest rate for property crimes was for theft of $5,000 or less (355 for every 100,000 in 2006) (Statistics Canada, 2006a). For crimes of violence in 2006, assaults represented the highest rate at 548 per 100,000 (compared to 670 per 100,000 in 2002). In 2006, however, the homicide rate for youth was 3.2 per 100,000 (up from 1.7 in 2002) compared to 1.7 for adults per 100,000 population (Statistics Canada, 2008a).

In 2003/2004, Canadian youth courts handled 70,465 cases which is a 17 percent decrease from 2002/2003 (Thomas, 2005). In addition, the number of cases resulting in "guilty findings" in youth court decreased from fiscal year 2000/2001 (60,041) to fiscal year 2005/2006 (34,628) (Statistics Canada, 2008b). About 18 percent (6,355) of the 2005/2006 cases, resulted in sentences of secure custody compared to a similar pattern in 2000/2001 when 17 percent of the cases were sentenced to secure custody (10,458). In 2000/2001, about 34 percent of all cases disposed of in youth court resulted in either secure or open custody (Statistics Canada, 2008b; Statistics Canada, 2002b). Approximately, 5,000 youth are in custody in Canada on a daily count (Winterdyk, 2002:89).

For youth transferred to adult court, Winterdyk reports that in fiscal year 1991/92, 71 cases were transferred. In 1994/1995, the number increased to 123 but then dropped to 79 in 1997/1998 (2002:82). Bertrand, Paetsch, and Bala report that in fiscal year 1999/2000 the number of cases dropped again to 52, which represents less than one percent of the case dispositions in youth court (2002:36).

Sweden

Overview

As one of the Scandinavian countries, Sweden maintains a social welfare approach to handling young offenders and is committed to policies which emphasize children's rights. Sweden endorses the recommendations of the United Nations Committee on the Rights of the Child (CRC) and has a "child policy" that is directed toward improving social and economic conditions and the quality of life for children and youth (Ministry of Health and Social Affairs, 2001). This doctrine recognizes that the best interests of the child are a necessary and basic principle for government legislation and polices. While individuals are considered children up to the age of 18, the age of criminal responsibility is 15, and "social authorities rather than the police handle youth under the age of 15" (Winterdyk, 2002:xvii). Because the Swedish language does not have an equivalent concept for "juvenile delinquent," youthful offending is referred to as "juvenile criminality" (Winterdyk, 2002:xvii).

For all youth under the age of 18, "the main responsibility for young offenders devolves on social services, and these offenders shall as far as possible be excluded from the prison and probation system generally and from prisons in particular" (Ministry of Health and Social Affairs, 2001:13). In most cases for youth under the age of 15, social welfare services provide for care and protection, not punishment. Youth 15 to 18 years of age are also seen as in need of care and are rarely imprisoned. Guidance and social services are provided in shelters and schools. For youth under the age of 18 who commit criminal offenses and require more than fines and probation, a sanction of "closed juvenile care" was established in 1999 and is maintained by the National Board of Institutional Care (Ministry of Health and Social Affairs, 2001).

While youth between the ages of 18 and 21 may be sentenced to imprisonment, this is relatively rare and depends on special circumstances. When youth are incarcerated, they are housed separately from adult prisoners (Ministry of Justice, 2000:1). As a general rule, Sweden subordinates sanctions to treatment and relies on social services rather than prosecution to handle young offenders (Becker & Hjellemo, 1976:109).

Sweden does not have a special court for juveniles and "does not formally recognize status offenses" (Winterdyk, 2002:xvii). When youth are referred to general court, Swedish prosecutors have authority to consult with social welfare agencies to determine if a waiver of prosecution is appropriate. Collaboration among child welfare boards, schools, and the police is seen as a viable approach to developing acceptable remedial responses (Becker & Hjellemo, 1976:96).

As observed by Sarnecki, "the social services play a considerably greater role in the society's response to criminal acts committed by young people, in comparison with most other countries" (2006:192). Police exercise limited influence on offenders less than 15 years of age. For example, police cannot interrogate youth unless the crime involved an adult. More recently, police are expected to investigate crimes committed by those over 12 years of age while still collaborating with the social service agencies (Sarnecki, 2006).

Youth Crime

The total number of reported crimes in Sweden increased from 1975 to early 1990 and then remained fairly stable throughout the 1990s. This was also the case for most other European countries. In 2000, 58 percent of the reported offenses in Sweden were thefts and 12 percent were crimes against person (National Council for Crime Prevention, 2001a:21; 2001b).

Trends in youth crime followed a similar pattern up to 1995, when there was a "steep drop" that continued through the end of the 1990s. As in other countries, however, female criminality increased during the 1990s (Winterdyk, 2002). While youth aged 15 to 20 represent about 8 percent of the Swedish population, this group comprised about 25 percent of all suspected offenders in 2001. This proportion of youth population to young offenders (i.e., 8:25) was also similar to the proportion in 1990 (National Council for Crime Prevention, 2001a:21).

The most common offenses committed by youth are property offenses: break in, criminal damage, and shoplifting (National Council for Crime Prevention, 2001b:9). A study by the National Council for Crime Prevention of 4,500 youth aged 15 to 17 found that the number of reported robberies committed by youth increased in the late 1990s (2000a:81). Similarly, use of drugs among youth also reportedly increased in the 1990s (National Council for Crime Prevention, 1999a:45). The National Council for Crime Prevention noted, however, that changes in public attitude and in the tendency to report crimes may account for these increases (2000a). In general, the pattern of youth criminality has been relatively stable, with a slight increase in the early 1990s followed by a drop to levels approaching those in the 1970s (National Council for Crime Prevention, 2001b:10).

In 2001, 20 percent of all convicted persons were between the ages of 15 and 20. (Conviction refers to a court sentence, a fine issued by the prosecutor, or a prosecutorial cautioning – i.e., the youth is found guilty of the offense without any further legal action being taken) (National Council for Prevention, 2000b:44). Between 1980 and 1998, more than one-half of the convictions of young persons were theft- related offenses: shoplifting, car theft, burglary (National Council for Crime Prevention, 2000b:44). While convictions for theft are the most common, the percent of convictions for assaults increased from 4 percent of youth convictions in 1980 to 15 percent of youth convictions in 1998 (National Council for Crime Prevention, 2000b:44).

In her analysis of trends in youth offending, however, Durrant found that the proportion of convictions for assault and aggravated assault for individuals age 15 to 17 years did not increase between 1975 and 1996 (2000). In addition, she found that convictions for theft-related offenses declined during this period and that there was no increase in the proportion of youth convicted of homicide (2000:449). She observed that "the prosecution rate has not increased, and out-of-home placements of children have shown a steady and substantial decline" since 1979 (2000:439).

Assaults committed by youth ages 15 to 17 increased in the 1980s and 1990s and peaked in the mid-1990s. From 1998 to 2002, there was a drastic decrease in youth who were guilty of theft (Sarnecki & Estrada, 2004). In 2005, the National Council for Crime Prevention reported that 25,400 individuals ages 15 and 20 were registered as suspects representing the largest age group of suspects compared to older individuals (Wittrock, 2006). Thefts constitute the most common offense for youth, whereas theft and traffic offenses are the most common offenses registered for those over 20 years of age (Wittrock, 2006).

The National Council for Crime Prevention reported that in 2006, youth ages 15 to 20 accounted for ten percent of the population and 24 percent of persons suspected of crime (2007a). As also noted by Wittrock (2006), the National Council for Crime Prevention reported that theft was the most common offense for this age cohort.

In his discussion of the trends in the level of violence by juveniles, von Hofer cites Estrada's observation that too much emphasis is placed on official crime statistics in a country that has other data like self-report studies and victim surveys, which in some cases indicate different data (2003). Since 1995, self-report surveys have been administered regularly to ninth-grade students who are approximately 15 years of age. In his analysis, von Hofer found that there has been a decrease in crimes like shoplifting and destruction of property while crimes of violence have been stable over time (2003). He concludes that there has been an increase in adolescents who "refrain" from crime.

Sanctions

A study of youth sanctions by the National Council for Crime Prevention found that most convictions between 1980 and 1998 resulted in "prosecutorial fines (40-50 percent) or cautions (30-40 percent) (National Council for Crime Prevention, 2000b:44). The trend, however, suggests a reduction in the use of cautions from 50 percent of all convictions (in 1985) to 30 percent (in 1998) for youth without prior convictions and 20 percent for youth with prior convictions. The National Council for Crime Prevention concluded that this decrease in cautions probably reflected the increased number of youth charged with assaults and a "reflection of a shift in attitudes toward young offending in general" (National Council for Crime Prevention, 2000b:45). Nonetheless, the most common sanctions are still fines and social services.

Overall, incarceration is used infrequently in Sweden. In 2005, 130 youth were sentenced to custody, which has increasingly been used for youth as an alternative to prison (closed juvenile care) (Wittrock, 2006). By comparison, in 2006, approximately 100 youth received this sentence (National Council for Crime Prevention, 2007b).

> "For youths aged fifteen to twenty, it has been possible since 1999 for the courts to combine a sentence involving remand into the care of the social services with a requirement that the youth carry out unpaid work or similar, a sanction referred to as youth service" (Wittrock, 2006:18). In 2005, approximately 2,900 youth were sentenced to social services care and 20 percent (590) were also required to complete youth service (Wittrock, 2006).

Observations

The prevailing approach for handling young offenders in Sweden is to seek nonpunitive responses that rely on social welfare services to divert youth away from court. Legislation in the 1980s and 1990s, however, signaled a trend toward more accountability and formal sanctioning. In a report assessing sanctions for young offenders, the National Council for Crime Prevention concluded that "reforms have been intended to make the sanction system applied to young offenders more like that applied to adults" (2000b:43).

While trends in youth crime did not vary dramatically in the 1990s, the increase in the number of arrests of youth for committing violent crimes and an increase in the number of 15-year-old offenders going to court reflect shifts in both public attitudes and crime policy toward youth. In 1985, 270 youthful offenders who were age 15 received court sentences compared to 1,100 in 1998 (National Council for Crime Prevention, 2000b:45). Fines and referral to social services remain the most common sanctions but cautions (i.e., warnings) have decreased and more cases are presented to the courts.

Nonetheless, Winterdyk reports that 80 percent of juvenile crimes are dealt with informally (e.g., cautioning). About 50 percent of these cases result in day fines "without a trial procedure being used" (2002:xvii). Overall, less than 10 percent of young offenders are placed on probation. In addition, the introduction of mediation for young offenders suggests elements of restorative justice and continued commitment to informal, treatment-oriented responses for handling juvenile criminality. Most youth participating in mediation report that they do not perceive the experience to be a punishment and "gained greater insight into the consequences" of their behavior (National Council for Crime Prevention, 1999b:14). In addition, in 1994, the country assumed responsibility for youth in specialized youth homes where institutionalized youth can serve from 14 days to 4 years depending on the severity of the crime (Sarnecki & Estrada, 2004). These institutions are intended to reduce prison time for individuals under the age of 18.

This review suggests that Sweden, like other countries, is re-evaluating and reforming policy on how best to respond to young offenders. While social welfare still appears prevalent, shifts in sanctioning practices indicate more formal responses and less tolerance for youthful offending. Although conflicting conclusions on trends in youth crime have been reported (e.g., Durrant 2000; Winterdyk 2002; von Hofer, 2003; Wittrock, 2006), official crime data do not seem to indicate that youth are becoming more violent or criminal. However, policy changes suggest that attitudes toward youth have changed. Sarnecki and Estrada noted that

> "in 1993, the Commission on Juvenile Crime presented its proposals for society's response to juvenile crime, which were essentially that there should be fixed, clear responses and that they should guarantee the citizen's protection under the law" (2004:4).

Juvenile Justice in Five Countries

NASA. Reprinted with permission.

Russia

Transition in Russia

There are four challenges to understanding juvenile justice in Russia (Finckenauer, 2001:193). First, it is a country in transition. Prior to 1991, it had been a part of the Soviet Union. Now, Russia is the largest of the 15 separate countries that comprise the former Soviet Union. Second, the dissolution of the Soviet Union has resulted in some dramatic transformations. Economically and politically, the country is no longer the same. Third, there has been a lot of crime during this period of change (Finckenauer, 2001:193). Fourth, the data are not systematically collected and are sometimes contradictory (Finckenauer, 2001). Finally, the populations of the United States and Russia are not comparable. In the early 1990s, there were more than 64 million youth under the age of 18 in the United States and 39.9 million in Russia (Finckenauer, 2001:194, citing Snyder & Sickmund, 1995). Cognizant of these limitations, comparisons are presented and discussed.

The Russian Federation has experienced an economic crisis that will probably continue for the next few years. The educational system is funded by local governments, and most of them do not have the resources for construction, teachers' salaries, or adequate educational materials (Pridemore, 2002:191). Unemployment is high, and it is likely to persist. The rate of unemployment appears to exacerbate alcohol consumption among young men. Some researchers suggest that these factors affect the incidence of violent crime, which they predict will continue unabated (Kangaspunta, Joutsen, & Ollus, 1998:pxiii; Gilinsky, 1998:203). According to Blum, nation-building requires the development of new institutions and systems to facilitate order, including efforts to improve the socialization of youth (2006:95). He argues that in order to succeed the "loyalty and active participation of young people" are necessary (2006:95).

Alcoholism is a long-standing problem in Russia, and alcohol use by minors is reported to be increasing. Juveniles who are publicly drunk in Russia are not included in the criminal statistics. Instead, Finckenauer reports that they are usually subjected to "administrative handling" which refers to the fact that they are handled outside the criminal justice system (Finckenauer, 2001:196). In Russia in 1992, 113,557 youth were apprehended for being publicly drunk (Finckenauer, 2001:196). In 1999, "on average, more than 3 out of every 100 adolescents aged 14 to 17 years were taken into custody for the consumption of alcohol or public intoxication" (Pridemore, 2002:205). According to Osborn (2005:1), "Russian boys are particularly prone to tobacco, substance, and alcohol misuse, a fact that means average male life expectancy stands at just 58, 15 years lower than for women." Russia experienced an increase in youth crime in the early 1990s. Beginning in 1989, juveniles comprised 16 to 17 percent of all the convictions. Terrill notes that "according to the Ministry of Internal Affairs, the number of juvenile offenders in 1994 increased 50 percent over the course of the previous five years" (Terrill, 2003:542). In 1995, there were 626,227 youth between the ages of 14 and 17 who were involved in criminal activity (Shestakov & Shestakova, 2001:424). In 1999, Russian youth comprised approximately 11 percent of all convictions (Shestakov & Shestakova, 2001:423). Pridemore reports that in the late 1990s, Russian youth involvement in all violent crime (except rape) and drug offenses increased (2002:200-201).

The Ministry of Internal Affairs reported that there are 360,000 teenagers who are officially "registered" as juvenile offenders (Terrill, 2003:542), that is, juvenile offenders who have been apprehended by the police. According to Finckenauer, being "registered" is equivalent to being arrested in the United States (2001:195-196). The Ministry of Internal Affairs contends that 80 percent of the crimes committed by youth are felonies (Terrill, 2003:542).

In 2002, 88,300 youth in the Russian Federation were sentenced for criminal activity, a decrease from 142,000 in 2001 and 150,000 in 2000 (UNICEF, 2004). The total registered crime rate in 2002 was 1,760 for every 100,000 citizens, while juveniles aged 14 to 17 had a registered crime rate of 1,423 for every 100,000 youth (UNICEF, 2004).

Young Russian offenders appear to be involved primarily in three types of criminal activity, most of which is property crime, specifically theft (Finckenauer, 2001:198). For example, Shestakov & Shestakova found that property crimes comprised more than 60 percent of delinquent activity, hooliganism and vandalism accounted for 25 percent, and violent crimes accounted for 15 percent of juvenile crime (2001:421). According to Terrill, . . . "hooliganism refers to violations of public disorder that are associated with threats to people and the destruction or damage of property" (Terrill, 2003:543).

Russian Youth and the Adult System

In Russia, a youth who is 16 years of age at the time of the offense is considered capable of forming the necessary *mens rea* and cognitively capable of determining the seriousness of the act. Article 10 of the Criminal Code in Russia stipulates that youth who are between the ages of 14 and 16 may be held responsible for their actions (Shestakov & Shestakova, 2001:418). However, there is "diminished responsibility" for youth in this specific age group, as well as "reduced culpability" (Shestakov & Shestakova, 2001:418). However, Russia does not subject youth under the age of 14 to the full impact of the adult criminal justice system. The kinds of offenses for which Russian youth can be held criminally responsible range from homicide, taking a hostage, extortion, and other violent crimes, as well as theft, burglary, vandalism, and hooliganism (Terrill, 2003:543; Shestakov & Shestakova, 2001:418). Recent evidence suggests that the public may be supportive of treatment versus punishment of youth. In a study of attitudes toward youth crime, McAuley and MacDonald were surprised to find that Russian citizens expressed a welfare orientation toward youth (2007:2). While they noted some softening in punishments, they believe "welfare-oriented juvenile justice still awaits legislative approval" (2007:2).

Adjudication of Youth

Juveniles in Russia who are involved in delinquent activity appear before the district court or commissions on juvenile affairs. In order for a case to be handled by the district court, the youth must be 14 years of age or older and be involved in a very serious crime. A judge, along with two peoples' assessors, presides in the district court (Terrill, 2003:544). Assessors are laypersons who are elected to serve by the local constituency for a set term, usually five years. The assessor system provides a way for the public to be represented in the justice system. The assessor's responsibilities usually entail participating in hearings for about two weeks a year. Typically, assessors rely on the presiding judge's counsel (Terrill, 2003:494). However, in those communities where no judge is available, assessors can conduct hearings (Terrill, 2003:494).

Youth under the age of 14, or older youth apprehended for less serious crime, are referred to the Commission on Juvenile Affairs CJA). The commission has played an important role in juvenile justice since 1918 (Terrill, 2003:544). Commissions are comprised of community members appointed by local officials and they typically serve for two years. The commission includes residents from a variety of professions and occupations, including teachers, factory workers, and police. The commission also has an oversight role and supervises some of the institutions that deal with youthful offenders, protects the rights of children and youth, and helps develop programs to prevent child neglect (Terrill, 2003:544). These efforts in delinquency prevention and community treatment appear to have dissipated in recent years. According to Finckenauer, the vast majority of the CJA no longer operates (Finckenauer, 2001:198-199).

In the early 1990s, President Boris Yeltsin (who died in 2007) attempted to create an effective youth policy to address the problems that the newly liberated country was experiencing. After little success by Yeltsin, in 1999 the new President, Vladimir Putin, launched a National Youth Policy which was to be established through the Ministry of Education and Sciences (Blum, 2006). The government also created the State Commission for Youth Affairs whose responsibility included addressing proposals from the Department of Youth Policy. Proposals for youth policy reforms were reviewed for their effectiveness and relevancy by Putin's State Council (Blum, 2006). In 2006, the *Strategy of State Youth Policy in the Russian Federation* (2006–2016) was approved as a plan for bringing youth into social practice, "fostering youth creativity, and incorporating youth in difficult situations into society" (Blum, 2006:101). Kuzio (2006) compared youth attitudes in Russia and the Ukraine and found support for Putin's "managed democracy." He concluded that "Russia's youth back Putin, not democratic revolution, and do not feel empowered to make sweeping political changes" (2006:72).

According to Zalkind and Simon, although Russia's juvenile justice system is in need of improvements, it is not for lack of caring. The country's economic abilities fall short in providing effective rehabilitative care. The issue is not mistreatment or abuse but rather the lack of funds to provide youth with the care that is needed. "Sadly, very few of the children forced into impoverished conditions have been found guilty of violent crimes (Ward cited in Zalkind & Simon, 2004:72). Support for noncustodial care, where youth remain at home but still receive rehabilitation occurs because more expensive residential interventions are too costly (Zalkind & Simon, 2004).

Dispositions

When imposing a sanction, the judge is expected to adhere to Article 38 of the Criminal Code. In particular, the judge evaluates the youth's character and the risk or extent of public danger that occurred as a result of the criminal behavior. The Criminal Code mandates that the judge consider the personality and character of the youth when deciding the sentence (Shestakov & Shestakova, 2001:434). The objective is to prevent crime through the application of the appropriate dispositions (Shestakov & Shestakova, 2001:436).

The types of punishment are stipulated in Articles 21 through 23 of the Criminal Code. According to Shestakov and Shestakova, they include

> ". . . custody, correctional work without imprisonment (e.g., communi-
> ty service work), fine, absolute discharge, entrusting a duty to redress
> committed harm (e.g., victim reconciliation), confiscation of personal
> property thought to interfere with the rehabilitation process, depriva-
> tion of the ranks, and--as an exclusive punishment--capital punish-
> ment" (Shestakov & Shestakova, 2001:434). The Criminal Code does
> not delineate differences in punishments intended for both youthful

and adult offenders, except that Article 23, Part 2, of the Code precludes execution for any offender under the age of 18, and Article 24
limits the length of incarceration to not more than 10 years for anyone
under 18 (Shestakov & Shestakova, 2001:434). With respect to the last
two provisions on capital punishment and length of sentence, there are
no exceptions to the statute (Shestakov & Shestakova, 2001:234).

In Russia, individualized justice is a part of the process. Judges try to
determine the best possible sentence for the youth and can use alternative
sanctions where appropriate. For example, when a first-time offender has
been sentenced to less than three years, the judge is required by statute to
review alternative sanctions in lieu of prison incarceration. In particular, they
attempt to use dispositions which are aimed at re-education and are geared
toward preventing future criminal offending (Shestakov & Shestakova,
2001:435-436). Judges can suspend the sentence and place the youth on
probation, order re-education in lieu of incarceration, require community service, or impose fines (Shestakov & Shestakova, 2001:435-436). It should be
noted, however, that in the Russian Federation, community service is really
"educative labor." The judge allows the offender to keep working at his or
her place of employment, but a portion of the wages or salary is deducted as
the sanction (Kangaspunta, Joutsen & Ollus, 1998:xix). This is also referred
to as "correctional tasks." Judges may also decide to impose fines when the
youth has the means to pay them (Terrill, 2003:546).

The use of alternative sanctions appears to be a significant departure from
the previous policies in the Soviet Union. In fact, there is some literature that
suggests that incarceration is still pervasive in Russia. According to Gilinsky,
from 1986 to 1993, 1,742,855 offenders were sentenced to imprisonment, of
which 181,479 were minors who were 14-17 years of age (1998:200). Similarly, Nikiforov (2002) reports that there were 19,100 juveniles in reforming
labor institutions in the beginning of 1994. Sturova's data indicate that there
are more than 40,000 juveniles in correctional facilities in Russia (2001:36).

Incarceration appears to be a common disposition in Russian juvenile justice. Terrill reports that more than one-half of the youth found guilty in court
are deprived of their liberty, and the usual setting is an educational colony.
Nikiforov (2002) reported that there were 60 educational-labor institutions for
juveniles in 1994. Manual labor is the main feature of these colonies. The length
of incarceration varies, but the average length is reported to be about three years
(Terrill, 2003:545). According to Terrill, only a few youth actually serve three
years; most are usually released after less than one year (2003:545).

An important component of the juvenile institution is education. Offenders are required to complete the secondary education program while they
are incarcerated (Nikiforov, 2002). The compulsory education program is
interesting because the 1992 law "On Education" in Russia no longer requires
completion of secondary education by Russian youth (Sturova, 2001:36). In
fact, Sturova contends that this legislation has contributed to the increase
in delinquency in Russia and notes that 60 percent of the juveniles recently

sentenced to education colonies were neither working nor attending school at the time of their criminal involvement (2001:37).

The use of correctional strategies that are designated as educational measures is controversial. For example, Gilinsky contends that educational facilities can be just as harsh as adult institutions. "In such youth institutions, the minors are subject to beatings, are locked in punishment cells, are under-nourished, and are often sexually assaulted and raped by their 'correctors'" (Gilinsky, 1998:203).

Juvenile incarceration is a serious problem in Russia, especially since there is no classification system for juvenile delinquents. Violent and more serious offenders are routinely in custodial institutions with youth involved in less serious delinquent behavior, and younger and older offenders are indiscriminately placed in the same institutions (Finckenauer, 2001:200). The custody and care of mentally retarded or mentally ill youth are espe-cially troublesome. Typically, these youth are integrated into these same institutions, and there is little or no treatment staff available. According to Finckenauer, "There are staff psychologists in only 7 of 46 special educational institutions" (2001:200). These problems are exacerbated by problems with the sewage systems, heat, running water, and bed space (Finckenauer, 2001:200).

Given the economic crisis in Russia, it is not surprising that there is very little money to fund community programs aimed at prevention and treatment. According to Finckenauer, more than 5000 state-run summer youth camps (that operated prior to the collapse of the Soviet Union) are now closed. In addition, those youth who have mental health problems do not have a single facility available for treatment. There is a serious lack of community criminal justice agencies to divert youth or work with them and their families.

Nonetheless, there are indications that conditions are beginning to improve. Gilinsky reports that there are a number of nongovernmental agencies and organizations offering assistance. These agencies establish self-help groups such as Alcoholics Anonymous, legal services, and social services for distinct populations like drug addicts and the homeless (Gil-insky, 1998:203).

In the summer of 2007, a team of representatives from the Department of Internal Affairs and employees of the Adolescent Affairs Commission travelled to Seattle to acquire knowledge about the juvenile justice system in the United States. Their goals were to become acquainted with models of juvenile court systems, to understand the procedures in court decisions, to learn about methods of correction and social rehabilitation for juvenile offenders, and to study the role of the public in solving juvenile justice prob-lems (USAID, 2007). This endeavor suggests possible interest in reforming Russia's juvenile justice policies and adopting a model that incorporates ideals and practices from the United States. Nonetheless, McAuley and Mac-Donald suggest that legislative reforms are still forthcoming (2007).

Japan

In Japan, there is a long history of treating youthful offenders differently from adults. According to Yokoyama, as early as the eighth century, the criminal laws either exempted youth from sanctions or stipulated reduced sentences (Yokayama, 2002:323). However, it was not until 1922 that the first major Juvenile Law was created. In 1948, a new Juvenile Law was enacted which retained some of the 1922 principles, most notably, *parens patriae*. In the late 1990s, there was widespread demand for new laws which would hold youth accountable for their offenses. Ironically, the demand for new legislation did not coincide with the highest peak in officially record-ed delinquency; this occurred in 1983, 17 years prior to the new statute (Yokoyama, 2002:325-326).

From the mid-1980s until the mid-1990s, juvenile delinquency in Japan decreased. However, beginning in the late 1990s, official delinquency rates began to increase. Media portrayal of youth involved in violent behavior in the late 1990s suggested that the problem was widespread. In a few well-publi-cized cases, youth between the ages of 14 and 17 who engaged in particularly egregious acts were portrayed as part of a new generation of violent offenders. These "new" offenders were depicted as engaging in random murders without feeling remorse. Simultaneously, crime victims became more vocal. The vic-tims questioned the rights afforded juvenile offenders while they were being neglected by the system. The result was a demand for harsher sanctions and a revision of the juvenile justice process (Shimbum, cited in Johnson, 2002:269; Yokoyama, 2002:327). The revised Juvenile Law became effective in 2000 (Yokoyama, 2002:327, 347). In 2004, 219 youth under age 14 were taken into custody for crimes including murder, robbery, and arson (Kakuchi, 2005). As a result, the traditional concern with the welfare of youthful offenders was supplanted by a new emphasis on punishment (Fenwick, 2006:146).

Japanese juvenile justice is emblematic of its culture. Japan is a very homogeneous country; more than 99 percent of the population is Japanese (Reichel, 2002). The Japanese emphasize family and maintaining solidarity, as well as a respect for authority and hierarchy. The country is characterized by low unemployment, informal social control, very tight controls on fire-arms and drugs, a cooperative attitude toward law enforcement efforts, and effective criminal justice agencies (Terrill, 2003:432; Reichel, 2002:307; Shikita & Tsuchiya, 1990).

Recent increases in juvenile crime, however, have generated a renewed focus on juvenile policy. "In 2003, police recorded 212 serious cases involving juve-niles who had committed serious crimes, such as homicide and robbery figures that were up 47 percent in 2002" (Fenwick, 2006:156). Heinous crimes like the stabbing of an 11-year-old girl by a fellow female classmate in 2004 and the mur-der of a 4-year -old by a 12-year-old boy in 2003 have the Japanese government considering new reforms in juvenile law (Fenwick, 2006; *China Daily*, 2004).

Age of Responsibility

The Juvenile Law of 1948 clearly incorporated the philosophy of *parens patriae* (Yokoyama, 1997:5). It embodied the welfare rehabilitation models and sought to help youth develop their abilities through educative measures (Yokoyama, 2002:325). In Japan, youth under the age of 20 are referred to as juveniles. The legislation created categories of juveniles who engage in delinquent and status offender behaviors. For example, "pre-offense juveniles" are those who are under 20 years of age and are perceived as likely to commit delinquent acts. This would include running away, being incorrigible, or loitering. By contrast, a "law-breaking child" is defined as a youth under the age of 14 who has been involved in a very serious act. The "juvenile offender" is between the ages of 14 and 19 and has engaged in a criminal act found in the Penal Code or in some other law in Japan (Terrill, 2003:435; Yokoyama, 2002:325).

By law, the police are mandated to refer all "pre-offense juveniles" to the family court or to the child guidance center (Yokoyama, 1997:16). Japan established child guidance centers in 1952. These centers rely heavily on volunteers to help patrol the streets, provide counseling for parents and youth, and improve the social environment for socializing youth soundly (Yokoyama, 1997:14-15).

All cases for alleged juveniles aged 14 to 19 are sent to family court. Juvenile hearings are not held in public and are intended to have a light atmosphere with contemplation. However, "… juveniles have the right to counsel, but the counselor need not be a lawyer – a parent, teacher, volunteer, or other competent person can serve as counsel" (Dammer & Fairchild, 2006:348). Youth rarely spend time in prisons and by law cannot be sentenced to prison if they are under the age of 16 (Dammer & Fairchild, 2006). Clearly, Japan has a rehabilitative philosophy "… reflected by the presence of nearly 50,000 probation officers who assist professional officers" (Dammer & Fairchild, 2006:349).

Adjudication in Japan

Youth who are involved in delinquent activity can be brought to the family courts or district courts. Family courts are established in each district and deal with both delinquency and domestic affairs. In nonserious cases, after the probation officer screens the cases, the judge can make a decision to dismiss the case without the youth appearing. In other cases, the judge will meet with the youth. After reviewing the recommendations from the probation officer and the specialist from the detention and classification home, the judge will decide if educative measures are warranted (Yokoyama, 2002:343). Family court proceedings are informal and confidential. Rather than focusing on guilt or involvement, these courts are more concerned with choosing the best intervention strategies. Interestingly, no information about the youth can be publicized by the media (Terrill, 2003:435). By contrast, district courts are reserved for more serious delinquent behavior and tend to be more formal.

Juvenile detention and classification homes were established in 1949. The number of youth sent to juvenile classification homes has varied over the years. For example, in 1951, there were 49,000 placements; and in 1998, 19,421 youth were admitted (Yokoyama, 2002:342; Shikita & Tsuchiya, 1990:344-345). These institutions were created "to conduct scientific treatment of juvenile delinquents" (Shikita & Tsuchiya, 1990:285). In particular, the classification home staff assists the family court judges prior to the hearing and disposition of the case (Shikita & Tsuchiya, 1990:257). The staff engages in observation, diagnostic services, medical treatment, and research. Under this law, youth can be held in detention at a classification home for a maximum of eight weeks, but typically the process only takes four weeks (Yokoyama, 2002:328).

Police refer juveniles who are involved in minor delinquent behavior to the family courts; they refer more serious cases to the public prosecutors. After an investigation has been completed and it has been determined that there is sufficient evidence to proceed, the public prosecutor must submit the case to the family court judge. The provisions of the old law precluded judges from referring youth younger than age 16 to the prosecutor, and they were prohibited from directing prosecution of youth who were involved in offenses punishable by fines or lesser penalties (Shikita & Tsuchiya, 1990:261). As noted above, the age for referral back to the prosecutor has been lowered from 16 to 14.

In homicide cases, the family court judge is mandated to refer the case back to the prosecutor (Yokoyama, 2002:328). In addition, all juveniles who are 16 years of age or older and are accused of murder are to be referred to the public prosecutor and afforded a criminal trial just like adults. It is only in exceptional cases that the judge will be able to retain those cases in the family court (*Japan Times*, 2000). Despite the provisions of the legislation, it was reported in the *Japan Times* that between April of 2001 and February of 2002, not one youth age 14 or 15 was returned to the prosecutor for criminal trial (*Japan Times*, 2002).

In January, 2005, several proposals were announced which would reduce the youthful protection principle by initiating "counter-veiling values." According to Fenwick (2006), the objective is to blur the distinction between adult and youth justice and to emphasize punishment for youthful offenders. "Under the new recommendations, a family court will be able to send young offenders who are found to have committed serious offenses to reformatory institutions" (Fenwick, 2006:156). As Ito reported, by lowering the "minimum age at which a child can be sent to a reformatory" to 12, the new juvenile crime laws move in the direction of "harsher punishment" (2007:para 1, 5).

Dispositions

Family court judges have three dispositional alternatives. The judge can place a youth on probation, commit the youth to a training school, or commit the youth to facilities available under the Child Welfare Law for children younger than 18 years of age (Yokoyama, 2002:344). Historically Japan utilizes volunteer probation officers along with professional probation officers. According to Yokoyama, there are more than 48,000 volunteer officers in Japan and 900 professional probation-parole officers (2002:346; 1997:22-23). Youth can remain on probation until they reach 20 years of age. However, with the introduction of short-term probation in 1994, some youth can now remain on probation for six or seven months (Yokoyama, 2002:345-346).

In addition to formal probation, youth in Japan can also be placed on tentative probation. Family court judges place a youth on tentative probation prior to the adjudication, and the youth is frequently under the guidance of a volunteer probation officer (Yokoyama, 2002:342). When the youth completes the tentative probation, he or she appears in family court for the hearing. Typically, the judge will not sentence the youth to any additional penalties after successful completion of tentative probation (Yokoyama, 2002:342).

For more serious offenders, Japan has 54 training schools. Judges can refer youth to either a short-term or long-term training school. As evidenced by the increase in the number of admissions, judges appear to be utilizing training schools more extensively in recent years. In 1998, there were 2,216 youth admitted to short-term training schools (up from 1,678 in 1991), and 3,172 youth admitted to long-term training schools (up from 2,651 in 1991). In 2001, 3.8 percent of the 137,161 youth adjudicated were placed in a training school (Fujino, 2002). Youth in the short-term training schools are usually released after a stay of six months or less, and youth in long-term training schools are usually released after one year (Yokoyama, 2002:345; Moriyama, 2002).

Training schools offer academic education, vocational skills training, life skills programs, and medical care (Shakita & Tsuchiya, 1990:295). Juvenile training schools in Japan include some type of classification where youth are separated by age, seriousness of offense, mental and physical condition, and whether they are chronic offenders (Shakita & Tsuchiya, 1990:296). There is also an assumption that individualized treatment will occur, and a specific plan is established for each youth. The Japanese government has successfully reintegrated youth released into their home communities by working with various agencies (Shakita & Tsuchiya, 1990:299).

The Child Welfare Law is the basis for Homes for Dependent Children and Child Education and Training Homes in Japan. The family court judge may determine that it is in the child's best interests to place him or her "in a home for dependent children or a home to support children's independence" (Yokoyama, 2002:344). There are 57 of these Homes for Dependent Children throughout Japan, and although they are primarily for younger and dependent (orphaned, abandoned, neglected, or abused) children, delinquent youth are also sometimes placed in these facilities (Fujino, 2002; Yokoyama, 2002:344).

Offenders who are younger than 14 and those between the ages of 14 and 18 can also be placed in Child Education and Training Homes in Japan. When a youth is placed in a Child Education and Training Home, the term is indefinite.

Rather than the court, it is the facility's staff that decides the optimum release date for each youth. Both the Home for Dependent Children and the Child Education and Training Home are based on social welfare (Fujino, 2002).

If the youth is to be handled by the adult court, he or she is subject to the same sanctions as adults. There are eight juvenile prisons in Japan (Moriyama, 2002). In order to be admitted to a juvenile prison, the youth must be at least 16 years of age, and have been adjudicated in a District Court. When a 14- to 16-year-old youth is treated as an adult, the maximum sentence of life imprisonment usually results in parole after seven to 10 years. On some occasions, parole may be denied, but the offender can re-apply after a specified period (Fujino, 2002).

Recently, media attention has focused on a few youth who have been sentenced in the District Court to prison. For example, a 19-year-old was sentenced to life in prison for murder and robbery in March of 2002 (*Japan Times*, 2002). In reality, the number of youth sentenced to penal institutions is very low, and young offenders up to the age of 26 are typically housed in juvenile prisons (Yokoyama, 2002:340). Youth are provided with academic education, vocational education and training, and "living guidance," which occurs through counseling, lectures, and physical, cultural, and leisure activities (Shikita & Tsuchiya, 1990:309, 347).

While juvenile arrests decreased in 2005 (Ito, 2007), incidents of youth violence, especially murder, have changed public opinion about the way to handle juvenile offenders (*Japan Times*, 2004; *Japan Times*, 2006). Young killers have provoked new debates about capital punishment and citizens are calling for harsher punishments for juvenile criminals (Negishi & Shimizu, 2006). According to Negishi and Shimizu, "death sentences can be handed down to people aged 18 and older, but the Juvenile Law states that life imprisonment should be meted out when sentencing someone who was under 20 when the crime was committed" (2006:para 23). They note that since World War II, eight offenders under age 20 were sentenced to death (2006: para 24). Based on Ito's review, the traditional role of Juvenile Law has been to help youth; however, this appears to be shifting toward more punitive sanctions (2006:para 3).

People's Republic of China

Youth Policy

Laws in ancient China provided for the protection of youthful offenders. In the Zhou Dynasty (1066 B.C.-221 B.C.), children under seven years of age were exempt from punishment. In the later Han Dynasty (206 B.C.-220 A.D.), the age of exemption was increased to eight, but not if the crime was murder (Zhao, 2001). Later dynasties used height requirements for determining adult status. In their review of Chinese policy toward youth, Dammer and Fairchild observed that "the underlying foundation for the correctional system in China is based on two ancient traditions: Confucianism and legalism" (2006:270). Confucians believe that children must be taught how to be human and allowed to develop their innate goodness. Confining children in prison was considered an impediment to prevent them from developing their potential humanity. In spite of these values, recent concerns about juvenile crime and the need to establish a formal juvenile justice system are reflected in juvenile policy.

While distinct laws were established for juveniles, a separate juvenile justice system was not established in China (Zhao, 2001). After the Chinese Civil War in 1949, China became the People's Republic with a single-party system. Even under the early Republic, a juvenile justice system was not developed but rather youth policy was a function of the family, schools, or other non-justice institutions (Ren, 1996). The history of China's post-civil war juvenile justice is designated into three periods: "the rise of juvenile reform schools and the child welfare system (1948-1965); the void of juvenile justice during the Cultural revolution (1966-1978); and the emergency of juvenile crime and the formalization of the juvenile justice system (1979-1994)"(Ren, 1996:57).

According to Yue, "the first main source of law concerning juvenile justice was the *Law of Protection of Minors* (LPM)" which was adopted in 1991 (2002:107). The "goal" of LPM was the protection of youth under age 18 who committed crimes. Elements of the law were both legalistic and participatory, and demonstrated efforts to protect minors (e.g., separate detention from adults and confidentiality of suspect information) (Yue, 2002:106). Wang characterizes the Chinese juvenile justice system as having both a child welfare model and an adult justice model: "education is the main measure; punishment is a supplemental measure" (2006:11). In China, a system of tribunals handles youthful offenders.

In 1999, in response to perceived increases in delinquency, the *Law on Prevention of Juvenile Crimes* was adopted to provide education, training, and crime prevention efforts, and to promote legal responsibility of youth (Yue, 2002). Youth between 14 and 18 years of age were targeted for initiatives which also included family directives for preventing juvenile crime.

While criminal responsibility in China begins at age 14, youth are not held fully responsible until age 16 unless they commit serious or violent crimes (e.g., homicide, rape, robbery, drug trafficking). Yue reports, however, that youth under age 18 receive mitigated punishment and "may not be convicted and sentenced as adults" (2002:108). His review of Chinese legislation suggests that policy toward youth is somewhat inconsistent and procedures for handling youth can be contradictory. In spite of legislation, Yue finds only limited provisions in criminal law which are specifically related to juvenile delinquency; but he contends that legalism has become more prevalent in juvenile justice (2002:p.105). While relying on 2,400 tribunals to handle youth, China has only recently begun to explore the use of specialized juvenile courts (Mosher, 2004).

Juvenile Crime

In response to the increase in juvenile crime from 2000 to 2004, judges and legal scholars have recognized the need for a separate juvenile justice system (Li, 2005). Mosher (2004) reports that in 2003, more than 69,000 juveniles were arrested; this represents a 13 percent increase from 2002. The majority of arrests (75%) were for property offenses, and most offenders (95%) were between 15 and 16 years of age. In 2003, juveniles accounted for nine percent of all criminal arrests (Mosher, 2004). In comparison, in the United States in 2006, juveniles represented 16 percent of all arrests (*OJJDP Statistical Briefing Book*, 2007).

The deputy secretary general of the Chinese Society of Juvenile Delinquency, Li Guiming, reported that juvenile criminals are becoming younger, committing new types of crimes, and joining more gangs (*USA TODAY*, 2007). Chinese officials report that juvenile arrests have doubled from 33,000 arrests in 1998 to 80,000 in 2007. This trend is attributed to an increase in "broken families" and social disorganization, including emotional neglect and increased violence in homes and schools (*USA TODAY*, 2007).

Drugs present a growing concern in China and youth represent a significant segment of drug users. While heroin was traditionally the drug of choice, drugs such as amphetamines and ecstasy are also prevalent (Chuan, 2005). Based on admission to treatment between 1990 and 1995, youth represented 61 percent of drug addicts (Yue, 2002). Mosher reports that in 2003, juveniles comprised "85 percent of China's drug addicts" (2004:para 5). In his review, Yue characterized these youth as school dropouts, unemployed, younger, and increasingly female (2002:116). The phenomenon is also a peer-group-related process that reflects social and cultural changes and the availability of drugs. The resulting increase in addiction and drug-related crimes has focused greater efforts on enforcement and interdiction as well as prevention (Chuan, 2005).

Juvenile Offenders and Sanctions

In China, a "juvenile delinquent" is between the ages of 14 and 25 while a "juvenile criminal" is between the ages of 18 and 25 (Terrill, 2003:639). The United Nations Convention on the Rights of Children of 1989 established that the age of responsibility should be 18 (Ren, 1996). As noted above, if youth 14 to 16 years of age commit serious crimes (e.g., homicide, rape, robbery, drug trafficking, arson) they could be held fully responsible (Terrill, 2003). The Criminal Law, however, requires "lighter" sentences for those between 14 and 17 years of age. Juvenile delinquents under the age of 14 cannot be held criminally responsible, but they can be disciplined by parents or guardians, or placed by the government in rehabilitation centers. According to Yue, the purpose of placement is not punishment but to receive "educative instruction" (2002:119).

While China is recognized as "the world's leader in executions" (Death Penalty Information Center, 2006:6), offenders under the age of 18 cannot receive the death penalty (Zhao, 2001). In 1997, China revised the law to forbid execution of youth under the age of 18. Amnesty International reports that since 2004, China, Iran, Pakistan, and Sudan have put child offenders to death (n.d.). The report identifies that one man who was either 16 or 17 at the time of the offense was executed in 2004. According to the Death Penalty Information Center, "juveniles continue to be executed due to insufficient care in determining the age of defendants" (2008:3).

When confining youth, the primary objective is education; and punishment is secondary (Zhao, 2001). Young people who have engaged in "minor criminal activity" such as stealing, fighting, and incorrigibility are placed in special work-study schools managed by educational departments (Reichel, 2002:298). Youth spend about two years in the school studying and working in a factory and are only permitted to go home on Sundays and holidays (Reichel, 2002). This informal method is called banf-jiao and is used to "prevent or curb" delinquent behavior in the immediate community (Terrill, 2003: 640). "Help-education teams" comprised of people who know the youth and can have a positive influence work with the youth until he/she is considered rehabilitated (Reichel, 2002).

A procuratorate is assigned to a juvenile who must been seen in the courts. He will appear in the court with the juvenile and serve to protect the youth's legal rights (Zhao, 2001:185). Currently there are 6,000 procuratorates used for juveniles and more than 3,000 juvenile courts (Zhao, 2001:185). Occasionally, juvenile offenders are sentenced to prison (Terrill, 2003:642).

For criminal cases involving juveniles, there are two kinds of violations: those that are committed against a criminal law or those that violate the Public Security Regulation (Ren, 1996). In 1991, a total of 580,272 youth were adjudicated; 271,529 were for crimes violating a criminal law while 308,743 were Public Security violations (Ren, 1996). These data reflect a decrease in adjudications from the prior year. A majority of prison sentences are for 5 years or fewer; and a rare 0.5 percent to 1.4 percent of juveniles received the death penalty between the years of 1983-1989 (Ren, 1996). The period of 1984 up to and including the present demonstrates the increase in the crime rate (Wong, 2001). In fact, Wong (2001:493) contends that "Despite the fight-against-crime campaign launched in 1983, delinquency rose rather than fell."

Comparing the United States to Other Countries

Juvenile Offenders and Punitive Sanctions

From indications noted in this review, Japan, China, and the United States have become more punitive in their treatment of youth in recent years. Ironically, this stance has not always coincided with an increase in violent juvenile offending. In Japan, an increase in violence occurred in the 1990s, and the rate continues to rise (Nakanishi, 2003). In China, even though some policies may look progressive, the country has had numerous human rights violations (Zalkind & Simon, 2004). In all six countries, juvenile offending overwhelmingly reflects property crimes. Although the United States has abolished capital punishment for minors, it still has one of the lowest ages of criminal responsibility. While some developments suggest that the United States may be moving toward less punitive measures, it continues to treat youth more harshly than many other countries. The available evidence suggests that offense trends will not change dramatically in the future. Canada's implementation of *YCJA* has considerably lessened its once harsh disciplinary policies.

There is, however, some variation in offending. Although robbery increased in Sweden, Russia, and Japan in recent years, it decreased in Canada and the United States (National Council for Crime Prevention, 2000a:81; Pridemore, 2002:200; Yokoyama, 2001:4). Specific increases in countries are not easily compared to other countries. For example, drug offending reportedly increased in Sweden and Russia in the late 1990s, but it did not reach the same proportions as it did in the 1990s in the United States (Finckenauer, 2001:196; Shestakov & Shestakova, 2002:436; Terrill, 2003).

In all six countries, violent offenses attract extensive media attention. Rather than being treated as isolated events, youth violence is portrayed as commonplace with random victims. After a few highly publicized murders committed by a small number of youth in Japan, the media portrayal was remarkably similar to the "superpredator" image widely publicized in the early 1990s in the United States (Shimbun, cited in Johnson 2002:269; Yokoyama, 2002:327). These images are powerful and may have helped fuel the legislative changes that have occurred.

Government leaders, influenced by these media characterizations, often react by drafting strict sanctions for juvenile offenders. One manifestation of these policy initiatives is the trend toward the "adultification" of youth. In the 1990s, in the United States, legislatures enacted statutes and established procedures that made it easier to transfer youth into adult court. In reviewing legislation, Sanborn (see Chapter 7) found significant variation in the age at which youth can be transferred into adult court. In a number of states there is no minimum age established by statute for transferring cases to adult court, whereas some statutes authorize transfer at the age of 10, 14, or 16.

Although there is evidence of a harsher attitude toward youth, none of the countries has emulated the approach adopted by the United States where youth who are 12 and 13 years of age can be convicted in adult court and sentenced to prison. This could be changing, however, as Russian Internal Affair representatives recently travelled to the United States to observe and learn more about the juvenile justice system. In Japan, the new Juvenile Law authorizes youth who are 14 years of age at the time of the offense to be handled in the district court. In Russia, a youth who is 14 years of age can be referred to the district court and, in Sweden, the age of criminal responsibility is 15 years of age. Canada authorizes youth to be handled by the adult system at the age of 16. As in Japan and Russia, China's age of responsibility is 14 years old but only for serious crimes; the usual age is 16. It should be noted that transferring youth into adult court is a relatively rare occurrence. In Canada, less than one percent of juvenile cases were transferred into adult court in 1999/2000 (Bertrand et al., 2002:36). In sum, the United States is the only country that allows youth who are younger than 14 years of age to be treated exactly as adults.

The sanctions that can be imposed in other countries also differ dramatically from those in the United States. Legislators have determined that youth who are handled as adults are to be sentenced like adults. In some states, youthful offenders with long sentences are incarcerated first in juvenile (up to age 16 or 18) and then adult institutions or they may be sentenced directly to adult prisons. There is no evidence that the other countries sentence juveniles to a lengthy term of incarceration or place them in an adult prison prior to their sixteenth birthday. In Canada, a youth sentenced as an adult cannot be incarcerated for more than 10 years (Canadian Department of Justice, 2002b:6). In Sweden, no one under the age of 18 can ever be sentenced to life imprisonment, and only in extraordinary circumstances can someone under the age of 18 be sentenced to prison (Terrill, 2003:364). In Japan, a youth tried as an adult and sentenced to life imprisonment is eligible for parole after seven years. Juveniles in Japan cannot be placed in a juvenile prison until their sixteenth birthday. In Russia, no one under the age of 18 can be sentenced to life imprisonment, and the maximum sentence for those under the age of 18 is 10 years (Gilinsky, 1998:198). In China, youth age 14 to 18 have limited liability for their crimes, and are not fully responsible until 18 years of age (Zalkind & Simon, 2004).

In comparing juvenile incarceration rates, the United States and Russia commit more juveniles to institutions than Canada, Japan, Sweden, or China. In addition to having such high incarceration rates, the United States and Russia are also distinguished by the inmate/staff ratio. Norway, Sweden, Italy, and the Netherlands typically have one or more prison employees for every inmate in their adult system. By contrast, the United States and Russia have a high inmate/staff ratio with large numbers of inmates held with fewer staff members (Marshall, 1998:66). Although juvenile institutions have more staff than adult institutions, the ratio is not usually the same as that found in other countries.

Death Penalty

Capital punishment for juveniles as well as adults is widely criticized internationally, especially in Western countries. According to Kuhn, "a de facto moratorium on capital punishment has been in force in all Council of Europe member states since 1 January 1997" (Kuhn, 1998:116). With the abolition of the juvenile death penalty in the United States in March, 2005, all six of the nations reviewed now agree that the death penalty for children is unlawful. In fact, in Russia, youth under the age of 18 cannot be executed or sentenced to life imprisonment (Shestakov & Shestakova, 2001:417).

When a country decides to "adultify" youthful offenders, it involves a major transformation in perceptions about delinquency, crime, and youth. The assumptions about childhood and adolescent development erode. In their stead, pronouncements are made that youth ought to be held accountable and subject to the same punishment as adults. Suddenly, youth are perceived as rational, mature, and responsible individuals who make decisions the same way as adults.

In her historical analysis of the evolution of juvenile offenders in early nineteenth century Britain, Shore discussed how working-class boys were categorized as "embryonic adults" (Shore, 1999:80). They were viewed as different from other children, more masculine, and not deserving of the same consideration (Shore, 1999:80-81). This shift appears to be occurring in Canada and Japan, and there is some evidence that Sweden is also reassessing its approach to juvenile offending. However, their recent policies are not as punitive as those in the United States. They appear to have a greater tolerance for youthful indiscretions and a greater appreciation of childhood development.

Although accountability and stricter sanctions are the major features of the transformation of juvenile justice policy in the United States, Canada, Japan, and possibly Sweden, there is evidence of some positive developments. This is evident in Canada with the YCJA, and in the United States with the abolition of the juvenile death penalty. Other initiatives will be reviewed in the next section.

Trends in Juvenile Justice

In the United States, Canada, Japan, and China there has been an increasing emphasis on victims. One manifestation is the use of the term "accountability" in juvenile statutes. Rather than focusing soley on the offender's rehabilitation and treatment, statutes now include references to holding the juvenile accountable to the community and the victim. There are programs established to allow victims to have some input into the disposition of the case or, at least, to be informed about the judge's decision.

Restorative Justice

Criticisms of juvenile justice and the search for alternative strategies have helped propel the restorative justice movement internationally. The juvenile justice system is an excellent milieu for restorative justice programs. These programs provide an alternative to the continuation of the "get tough" ideology and excessively punitive responses while simultaneously recognizing the importance of the victim and the community. In reviewing the evolution of restorative justice, Walgrave suggests that societies are usually less rigid in their reactions to youth versus adult crime and more likely to implement experimental and nontraditional interventions. In this context, restorative justice emerges as an appropriate response (Walgrave, 1998:15).

Restorative justice frequently involves some type of meeting between offender and victim. Victim offender mediation is rooted in restorative justice theory, and "is primarily 'dialogue driven' with the emphasis upon victim healing, offender accountability, and restoration of losses" (Umbreit & Bradshaw, 1997:34). The first victim-offender mediation program in North America began in Kitchener, Ontario, in 1974 (Umbreit & Bradshaw, 1997:34). In Sweden, a police officer is credited with establishing one of the first victim-offender mediation programs in 1987 in Hudiksvall (Lindstrom & Svanberg, 1998:253). Umbreit and Bradshaw reported that by 1996, there were approximately 700 programs in Europe and more than 300 juvenile programs in the United States and Canada (Umbreit & Greenwood, cited in Umbreit & Bradshaw, 1997:34,39). China, Bulgaria, Albania, and Russia also have created victim-offender programs (Friday, 1999).

In comparing juvenile versus adult victim mediation conferences, Umbreit and Bradshaw examined an adult program in Winnipeg, Canada, and a juvenile program in Minneapolis, Minnesota (1997:37-38). They found that when victims met with juvenile offenders they were more satisfied with their participation in the justice process and less likely to fear further victimization by the juveniles than were victims who participated in adult mediation conferences. Victims also indicated that they had significantly improved attitudes toward the offender than victims of adult offenders (Umbreit & Bradshaw, 1997:37-38). Their data provide empirical support for the development of restorative justice programs that incorporate victim-offender mediation in the process (Umbreit & Bradshaw, 1997:38).

Other countries have utilized "family conferencing" as a way to deal with juvenile offending. The Children, Young Persons, and Families Act in New Zealand established "family group conferences" for young offenders in 1989 (Sarre, 1999:261). Its success contributed to the enactment of a new Young Offenders Act, which took effect in 1994 in Australia. The new legislation stipulates that the needs of the victims and the community must be considered in the dispositions, and it provides for the implementation of a "family conference" based on the New Zealand model. Although the family conference model is used primarily for less serious offenders, its aim is to allow youth reconciliation and reparation (Sarre, 1999:261). In China, the family and community take an active role in the juvenile justice system making it more informal than the United States and other countries (Dammer & Fairchild, 2006).

Victim-offender mediation has become very popular in juvenile justice. Mediation between a crime victim and the offender ". . . is now becoming a supplementary or alternative response within the judicial system" (Lindstrom & Svanberg, 1998:257). Sweden and some other countries have been evaluating their effectiveness. The results of their research will help to modify and improve existing programs.

Community Involvement

In addition to victim-offender mediation programs and family conferencing, the community plays a major role in juvenile justice. In Japan, the community is heavily invested in delinquency prevention through juvenile guidance centers. There are more than 700 juvenile guidance centers and more than 74,000 volunteers who patrol streets in the amusement areas to guide youth, counsel youth and their parents, and improve the social environment to make it possible for youth to be properly socialized (Yokoyama, 2002:335, 337). Volunteer probation officers in Japan also make a significant effort to prevent delinquency and help youth.

The commitment and involvement of the volunteers in Japan is unparalleled. There is some indication that volunteer social service groups are emerging in Russia, but they usually deal with specific types of offenders (e.g., drug offenders) (Gilinksy, 1998). In the United States, volunteers only minimally work with juveniles. Typically, social service agencies recruit volunteers to mentor youth or act as a "Big Brother/Big Sister." Volunteers do not play a dominant role formally, and they are not perceived as integral to juvenile justice as are the volunteer workers in Japan. Clearly, there are lessons to be learned.

China incorporates a "participatory model" in responding to youth. This is articulated in the different chapters of the Protection of Minors Act. For example, the Act includes Chapter II, Protection by the Family, Chapter III, Protection by the School, Chapter IV, Protection by Society, and Chapter V, Judicial Protection (Reichel, 2002:296). Education is also a key feature in the rehabilitation of minors who commit minor offenses.

Other countries rely on the police to work with youth. In order to improve relations between law enforcement and youth in Sweden, the police participate in diversion through a special unit which is called the "social police." The social police offer classes on drug abuse, law, and justice in the schools; establish and participate in recreation programs in the schools; patrol streets with social workers; seek to help adults and juveniles who may need assistance; and share information with the local social board about youth and families who need intervention (Terrill, 2003:370). The coupling of social workers and police to work within the community is an interesting strategy which might be emulated in the United States and some other countries. By involving the police in diversion and soliciting their help in identifying families in need of services, the Swedish model provides an alternative proactive role for law enforcement.

The Role of Parents

In the Crime and Disorder Act of 1998, Britain established a procedure through which a magistrate can direct a parent or parents to participate in some kind of guidance or counseling program (Henricson, Coleman &

Roker, 2000:325). Although there is some controversy regarding mandatory participation of parents in workshops and training sessions, several programs recognizing family diversity have been implemented. There has also been some emphasis to determine which kinds of parenting strategies work best for adolescents versus younger children and to assess which programs are most appropriate for youth and families (Henricson, Coleman & Roker, 2000:334-336). Although the long-term evaluations of these kinds of programs are not yet completed, parenting skills programs appear to be a part of a larger initiative which focuses on early intervention.

Under the provisions of the new Japanese law, judges remind juvenile offenders about their offense and make them reflect on the harm caused during their adjudication. In addition, the judges involve parents and inform them that they have responsibility for the offense. The juvenile and the parents are officially admonished by the judge, and the judge can instruct both parent and child about treatment programs and the ramifications of future delinquent behavior (Yokoyama, 2001:9).

As noted by Dutton, individuals who teach and live with delinquent minors are most likely to be aware of their behaviors, their needs, and ways to approach their problems (2005:228). This is why the official rationale in China emphasizes a family and community approach, and relies more on education than on punishment (Dutton, 2005).

In the United States, there have been incidents when a judge has punished parents for their children's misconduct. Unfortunately, these sanctions tend to be reactive in nature and do little to improve the quality of the family life or the parenting capabilities of the parents. By intervening earlier in a child's life and providing parents with some of the requisite skills to deal effectively with their children, the United States could emphasize a different approach. Once research on the effectiveness of the British program is determined, it may provide a model for the United States.

Conclusion

Controversies in the United States on how to deal with juvenile offenders appear to be influencing other countries. Although the United States abandoned capital punishment for youth, it retains a much harsher stance in its treatment of youthful offenders. This review suggests that other countries also may have become more punitive in recent years. In the United States and Japan, new sanctions are in effect, and in other countries, such as Canada, they were initiated in 2003. Sweden has not yet moved to stricter sanctions, but the Swedish Committee on Juvenile Delinquency recommended fixed, fair, and swift sanctions which are proportional to the acts committed. Although Sweden is disinclined to support harsh sanctions and imprisonment for youth, there is evidence that some reconsideration of its approach to juvenile offenders is occurring (Terrill, 2003:369). In China, which purports to support family and education, there is evidence that juveniles have been sentenced to severe punishments (Zalkind & Simon, 2004).

One of the most intriguing findings of this chapter is the uniqueness of the juvenile justice policies of the United States. Canada, a country most like the United States in terms of culture, geographic proximity, and customs does not treat youth as harshly as the United States. Japan, a country that is homogeneous, geographically distant, and economically prosperous, does not treat youth as harshly. Sweden, too, another prosperous country, does not treat juveniles as harshly. In fact, Sweden embodies the welfare model more than any of the other countries. Even Russia, the most economically depressed country of the selection, with the highest unemployment rate, undergoing the greatest transition of all the countries compared, does not incarcerate for life a youth under the age of 18, or allow any youth under the age of 14 to be treated as an adult. And China, notwithstanding its record of human rights violations and use of life imprisonment (although the prevalence is low), does designate a rehabilitative stance on juvenile justice, and may be considered less punitive than the United States. In short, none of these countries surpasses the United States in terms of punitive sanctions. How is it that the United States achieved this singular distinction, and what are the long-term consequences?

This chapter suggests that some of the punitive policies did not coincide with increases in juvenile violence but rather were the result of media characterizations of violent youth and the perception that random killings were occurring. Politicians reacted to these images by proposing stricter and more adult-like sanctions for youth. There is no evidence that these stricter penalties will have an effect on juvenile offending in any of the countries.

In reassessing juvenile justice policy, legislators and policymakers in the United States can incorporate strategies that other countries are successfully utilizing. In particular, expanded roles for volunteer participation, greater emphasis on early intervention strategies, and more police-youth interaction programs offer promise and deserve attention. These are but a few of the lessons to be learned from studying juvenile justice policies in other countries.

References

Amnesty International (n.d.). *Death Penalty: Executions of Child Offenders since 1990.* http://www.amnesty.org/en/death-penalty/executions-of-child-offenders-since-1990 [Retrieved March 21, 2008].

Barnhorst, R. (2004). "The Youth Criminal Justice Act: New Directions and Implementation Issues." *Canadian Journal of Criminology and Criminal Justice,* (April):231-250.

Becker, H.K. & E.O. Hjellemo (1976). *Justice in Modern Sweden.* Springfield, IL: Charles C Thomas.

Bertrand, L.D., J.J. Paetsch & N. Bala (2002). "Juvenile Crime and Justice in Canada." In N. Bala, J.P. Hornick, H.N. Snyder & J.J. Paetsch (eds.) *Juvenile Justice Systems: An International Comparison of Problems and Solutions*, pp.19-42. Toronto, ON: Thompson Educational Publishing, Inc.

Blum, D. (2006). "Russian Youth Policy: Shaping the Nation-State's Future." *SAIS Review* 26(2):95-108. Johns Hopkins University Press.

Canadian Department of Justice (2002a). *YCJA Explained.* (July 3) www.canada.justice.gc.ca/en/ps/yj/repository/2overvw/2010001a.html [Retrieved July 16, 2002].

Canadian Department of Justice (2002b). *Concerns about the Current Youth Justice System.* www.canada.justice.gc.ca/en/ps/yj/yoas6.html [Retrieved July 16, 2002].

China Daily (2004). "Japanese Girl Stabbed to Death in School." http://www.chinadaily.com.cn/english/doc/2004-06/02/content_335813.htm [Retrieved November 13, 2007].

Chuan, Q. (2005). "Drug Crime Rise Sparks Calls for Crackdown." *China Daily*, (April 5).http://www.chinadaily.com.cn/english/doc/2005-04/05/content_431066.htm [Retrieved March 20, 2008].

Classical Chinese Philosophy (n.d.). http://www.geocities.com/tokyo/springs/6339/philosophy.html [Retrieved November 3, 2007].

Dammer, H.R. & E. Fairchild with J. Albanese (2006). *Comparative Criminal Justice Systems*, Third Edition. Belmont, CA: Thompson/Wadsworth Publishing.

Death Penalty Information Center (2008). "Reported Executions of Juvenile Offenders in Other Countries since 1990." http://www.deathpenaltyinfo.org/article.php?scid=27&did=203#execsworld [Retrieved March 20, 2008].

Death Penalty Information Center (2006). *The Death Penalty in 2006: Year End Report.* http://www.deathpenaltyinfo.org/2006YearEnd.pdf [Retrieved March 20, 2008].

Durrant, J.E. (2000). "Trends in Youth Crime and Well-Being since the Abolition of Corporal Punishment in Sweden." *Youth & Society*, (June), 31(4):437-455.

Dutton, M. (2005). "Toward a Government of the Contract: Policing in the Era of Reform." In B. Bakken (ed.) *Crime, Punishment, and Policing in China*, pp. 189-234. Lanham, MD: Rowman & Littlefield Publishers, Inc.

Fenwick, M. (2006). "Japan: from Child Protection to Penal Populism." In J. Muncie & B. Goldson (eds.) *Comparative Youth Justice: Critical Issues*, pp. 146-158. London: Sage Publications.

Finckenauer, J.O. (2001). "Two Worlds of Deviance: Russia and the United States." In S.O. White (ed.) *Handbook of Youth and Justice*, pp. 193-206. New York, NY: Kluwer Academic/Plenum Publishers.

Friday, P.C. (1999). World Society of Victimology. International Scientific and Professional Advisory Council (ISPAC) of the United Nations Crime Prevention and Criminal Justice Programme. http://www.restorativejustice.org.uk/International_RJ/pdf/res.pdf [Retrieved December 6, 2008].

Friday, P.C. & X. Ren (eds.) (2006). *Delinquency and Juvenile Justice Systems in the Non-Western World.* Monsey, NY: Criminal Justice Press.

Fujino, K. (2002). Personal correspondence, December 10, 2002.

Gilinsky, Y. (1998). "The Penal System and Other Forms of Social Control in Russia: Problems and Perspectives." In K. Aromaa (ed.) *The Baltic Region: Insights in Crime and Crime Control*, pp. 197-204. Oslo, Norway: Pax Forlag.

Guo, J., G. Xiang, W. Zongxian, X. Zhangrun, P. Xiaohui & L. Shuangshuang (n.d.). *World Factbook of Criminal Justice Systems: China*. http://www.ojp.usdoj.gov/bjs/pub/ascii/wfbcjchi.txt [Retrieved January 16, 2008].

Henricson, C., J. Coleman & D. Roker (2000). "Parenting in the Youth Justice Context." *The Howard Journal*, 39(4):325-338.

International Centre for Prison Studies (2002). Prison Brief for Sweden. (October 15). www.kcl.ac.uk/depsta/rel/icps/worldbrief/europe_records.php?code=47 [Retrieved November 21, 2002].

Ito, M. (2007). "Diet Lowers Incarceration Age to 'About 12'." *Japan Times*. (May 26). http://search.japantimes.co.jp/print/nn20070526a1.html [Retrieved March 19, 2008].

Japan Times (2006). "'Lay' Judges Harsher than Pros on Minor Killers." (March 16). http://search.japantimes.co.jp/cgi-bin/nn20060316b8.html [Retrieved March 19, 2008].

Japan Times (2004). "Juvenile Crime Rates Rose in 2003." (February 6). http://search.japantimes.co.jp/cgi-bin/nn20040206a3.htm [Retrieved March 19, 2008].

Japan Times (2002). "Teen Gets Life Sentence For Murder." (March 28). http://search.japantimes.co.jp/print/nn20020328b1.html [Retrieved March 19, 2008].

Japan Times (2000). "Changes in Crime...and Punishment." (September 20). http://search.japantimes.co.jp/cgi-bin/ed20000920a1.html [Retrieved March 19, 2008].

Johnson, D.T. (2002). *The Japanese Way of Justice*. New York, NY: Oxford University Press.

Kakuchi, S. (2005). "JAPAN: Rising Juvenile Violence Linked to Internet." Inter Press Service News Agency. (October 12). http://ipsnews.net/news.asp?idnews=30600 [Retrieved March 18, 2008].

Kangaspunta, K., M. Joutsen & N. Ollus (eds.) (1998). *Crime and Criminal Justice in Europe and North America 1990-1994*. Helsinki: HEUNI, Monsey, NY: Criminal Justice Press.

Kuhn, A. (1998). "Sanctions and Their Severity." In K. Kangaspunta, M. Joutsen & N. Ollus (eds.) *Crime and Criminal Justice in Europe and North America, 1990-1994*, pp. 115-137. Helsinki, Finland: European Institute for Crime Prevention and Control.

Kuzio, T. (2006). "Ukraine Is Not Russia: Comparing Youth Political Activism." *SAIS Review* 26(2):67-83. Johns Hopkins University Press. https://muse.jhu.edu/journals/sais_review/v026/26.2kuzio.html [Retrieved November 27, 2007].

Li, L. (2005). "Legal Reform Likely as Juvenile Crime Rises." *China Daily*, (September 17). http://www.chinadaily.com.cn/english/doc/2005-09/17/content_478587.htm [Retrieved March 20, 2008].

Lindstrom, P. & K. Svanberg (1998). "Victim Offender Mediation in Sweden." In L. Walgrave (ed.) *Restorative Justice for Juveniles: Potentialities, Risks and Problems for Research*, pp.245-260. Leuven, Belgium: Leuven University Press.

Marshall, I.H. (1998). "Operation of the Criminal Justice System." In K. Kangaspunta, M. Joutsen & N. Ollus (eds.) *Crime and Criminal Justice in Europe and North America, 1990-1994*, pp. 54-114. Helsinki, Finland: European Institute for Crime Prevention and Control.

McAuley, M. & K. MacDonald (2007). "Russia and Youth Crime: A Comparative Study of Attitudes and Their Implications." *The British Journal of Criminology*, 47(1):2-22.

Ministry of Health and Social Affairs (2001). *National Report on Follow-Up to the World Summit for Children*. (June) www.social.regeringen.se/inenglish/publications. [Retrieved November 22, 2002].

Ministry of Justice (2000). *Information About the Swedish Prison and Probation Service.* (August) Stockholm, Sweden.

Moriyama, T. (2002). *World Factbook of Criminal Justice Systems: Japan.* www.ojp.usdoj. gov/bjs/pub/ascii/wfbcjjap.txt. [Retrieved November 19, 2002].

Mosher, S. (2004). "Juvenile Crime Fact Sheet." *Human Rights in China.* No. 4, (December 21). http://www.hrichina.org/public/PDFs/CRF.4.2004/JuvenileCrime4.2004.pdf [Retrieved March 21, 2008].

Nakanishi, Y. (2003). "Making Sense of Japanese Juvenile Crime Statistics: Beyond an Economic Approach and Policy Implications." *Radical Statistics*, Issue 81: (Spring). http://www. radstats.org.uk/no081/nakanishi.pdf [Retrieved November 15, 2007].

National Council for Crime Prevention (2007a). *Persons Suspected of Offenses.* (August 8). http://www.bra.se/extra/pod/?action=pod_show&id=16&module_instance=11 [Retrieved March 9, 2008].

National Council for Crime Prevention (2007b). *Persons Found Guilty of Offenses.* (August 8). http://www.bra.se/extra/pod/?action=pod_show&id=17&module_instance=11 [Retrieved March 9, 2008].

National Council for Crime Prevention (2001a). *English Summary: Criminal Statistics 2001.* Stockholm, Sweden.

National Council for Crime Prevention (2001b). *English Summary: Crime Trends in Sweden, 1998-2000.* Stockholm, Sweden.

National Council for Crime Prevention (2000a). *English Summary: Juvenile Robbery in Malmo and Stockholm.* Stockholm, Sweden.

National Council for Crime Prevention (2000b). *English Summary: The Sanction System for Young Offenders.* Stockholm, Sweden.

National Council for Crime Prevention (1999a). *English Summary: Youth, Drugs, and Police Strategies.* Stockholm, Sweden.

National Council for Crime Prevention (1999b). *English Summary: Mediation-The Revelations of Young Offenders.* Stockholm, Sweden.

Negishi, M. & K. Shimizu (2006). "Young Killers at Heart of Capital Punishment Fight." (May 20). http://search.japantimes.co.jp/print/nn20060520f2.html [Retrieved March 19, 2008].

Nikiforov, I.V. (2002). *World Factbook of Criminal Justice Systems: Russia.* www.ojp.usdoj. gov/bjs/pub/ascii/wfbcjrus.txt [Retrieved November 19, 2002].

OJJDP Statistical Briefing Book (2007). Online. Available: http://ojjdp.ncjrs.gov/ojstatbb/crime/ qa05102.asp?qaDate=2006 (Released on December 13.) [Retrieved March 20, 2008].

Osborn, A. (2005). "Russia's Youth Faces Worst Crisis of Homelessness and Substance Misuse since Second World War." *BMJ Publishing* (11 June), 330:1348. http://www.bmj.com/cgi/ content/full/330/7504/1348-b [Retrieved November 14, 2007].

Pridemore, W.A. (2002). "Social Problems and Patterns of Juvenile Delinquency in Transitional Russia." *Journal of Research in Crime and Delinquency*, 39(2):187-215.

Reichel, P.L. (2002). *Comparative Criminal Justice Systems: A Topical Approach*, Third Edition. Upper Saddle River, NJ: Prentice Hall.

Ren, X. (1996). "People's Republic of China." In D.J. Shoemaker (ed.) *International Handbook of Juvenile Justice*, pp. 57-79. Westport, CT: Greenwood Press.

Sarnecki, J. (2006). "Responses to Juvenile Crime: The Swedish System." In E.L. Jensen & J. Jepsen (eds.) *Juvenile Law Violators, Human Rights, and the Development of New Juvenile Justice Systems*, pp. 187-212. Oxford, UK: Hart Publishing.

Sarnecki, J. & F. Estrada (2004). *Juvenile Crime in Sweden: A Trend Report on Criminal Policy, the Development of Juvenile Delinquency and the Juvenile Justice System*. Stockholm University. Department of Criminology. http://www.esc-eurocrim.org/files/youth_crime_in_sweden_sarnecki_estrada_final_version.doc]Retrieved November 1, 2007].

Sarre, R. (1999). "Family Conferencing as a Juvenile Justice Strategy." *The Justice Professional*, (11)3:259-296.

Shestakov, D.A. & N.D. Shestakova (2001). "An Overview of Juvenile Justice and Juvenile Crime in Russia." In J.A. Winterdyk (ed.) *Juvenile Justice Systems: International Perspectives*, Second Edition, Toronto, ON: Canadian Scholars' Press Inc.

Shikita, M. & S. Tsuchiya (eds.) (1990). *Crime and Criminal Policy in Japan from 1926 to 1988*. Tokyo, Japan: Japan Criminal Policy Society.

Shore, H. (1999). "The Trouble with Boys: Gender and the 'Invention' of the Juvenile Offender in Early Nineteenth-Century Britain." In M.L. Arnot & C. Usborne (eds.) *Gender and Crime in Modern Europe*, pp. 75-92. London, England: University College London.

Snyder, H. & M. Sickmund (1995). *Juvenile Offenders and Victims: A Focus on Violence*. Washington, DC: U.S. Justice Department, Office of Juvenile Justice and Delinquency Prevention.

Statistics Canada (2008a). *Persons Charged by Type of Offense*. http://www40.statcan.ca/l01/ind01/l3_2693_2102.htm?hili_none [Retrieved March 9, 2008].

Statistics Canada (2008b). *Court, Youth Cases by Type of Sentence*. http://www40.statcan.ca/l01/ind01/l3_2693_2102.htm?hili_none [Retrieved March 9, 2008].

Statistics Canada (2006a). *Persons Charged by Type of Offense (Rate, youths charged)*. http://www40.statcan.ca/l01/cst01/legal14b.htm?sdi=youth%20crime%20rate [Retrieved November 7, 2007].

Statistics Canada (2006b). *Persons Charged by Type of Offense, by Province and Territory (Canada)*. http://www40.statcan.ca/l01/cst01/legal17a.htm?sdi=youth%20crime%20rate [Retrieved November 7, 2007].

Statistics Canada (2002a). *Youths and Adults Charged by Type of Offense*. www.statcan.ca/english/Pgdb/State/Justice/legal14a.htm [Retrieved October 5, 2002].

Statistics Canada (2002b). *Cases Heard by Youth Courts with Guilty Findings, by Most Significant Sentence*. www.statcan.ca/english/Pgdb/State/Judicial/legal16.htm [Retrieved October 5, 2002].

Sturova M.P. (2001). "The System of Education and Youth Crime." *Russian Social Science Review*, 42(5) (September-October):36-49.

Terrill, R. (2003). *World Criminal Justice Systems: A Survey*, Fifth Edition. Cincinnati, OH: Anderson Publishing Company.

Thomas, J. (2005). "Youth Court Statistics, 2003/04." *Juristat*, 25:4. Canadian Centre for Justice Statistics. http://www.statcan.ca/english/freepub/85-002-XIE/0040585-002-XIE.pdf [Retrieved March 9, 2008].

Umbreit, M. & W. Bradshaw (1997). "Victim Experience of Meeting Adult vs. Juvenile Offenders: A Cross-National Comparison." *Federal Probation*, 61(4):33-39.

UNICEF (2004). Russian Federation: Juvenile Justice. Unicef. http://www.ceecis.org/child_protection/russianfed_juvenile.htm [Retrieved November 16, 2007].

USAID (2007). " Trip Overview for the 'Juvenile Justice' Group, Tomsk Oblast – Washington State, May-June 2007." http://www.ccfrussia.ru/index.php?mod=n_article&n_id=268 [Retrieved November 29, 2007].

USA TODAY (2007). "China Reports Major Juvenile Crime Jump." (December 6) http://www.usatoday.com/news/world/2007-12-06-china-juvenilecrimes_N.htm [Retrieved March 20, 2008].

von Hofer, H. (2003). "Crime and Punishment in Denmark, Finland, Norway, and Sweden – A Summary." *Nordic Criminal Statistics 1950-2000*. Department of Criminology. Stockholm: Stockholm University. http://www.istat.it/istat/eventi/perunasocieta/relazioni/Hofer_rel.pdf [Retrieved November 12, 2007].

Walgrave, L. (1998). "What Is at Stake in Restorative Justice for Juveniles?" In L. Walgrave (ed.) *Restorative Justice for Juveniles: Potentialities, Risks and Problems for Research*, pp. 11-16. Leuven, Belgium: Leuven University Press.

Wang, D. (2006). "The Study of Juvenile Delinquency and Juvenile Protection in the People's Republic of China." *Crime & Justice International*, 22(94):4-13.

Winterdyk, J.A. (2002). "Juvenile Justice and Young Offenders: An Overview of Canada." In J.A. Winterdyk (ed.) *Juvenile Justice Systems: International Perspectives*, Second Edition, pp. 61-102. Toronto, ON: Canadian Scholars' Press Inc.

Wittrock, U. (2006). *English Summary. Criminal Statistics 2005*. National Council for Crime Prevention. Stockholm, Sweden. http://www.ok.cz/iksp/docs/a070611s.pdf [Retrieved November 3, 2007].

Wong, D.S.W. (2001). "Changes in Juvenile Justice in China." *Youth and Society*, 32:492-509.

Yokoyama, M. (2002). "Juvenile Justice and Juvenile Crime: An Overview of Japan." In J.A. Winterdyk (ed.) *Juvenile Justice Systems: International Perspectives*, Second Edition, pp. 321-352. Toronto, Canada: Canadian Scholars' Press Inc.

Yokoyama, M. (2001). "Revision of the Juvenile Law Toward Partial Criminalization in Japan." Paper presented at the American Society of Criminology Annual Meeting in Atlanta, Georgia.

Yokoyama, M. (1997). "Juvenile Justice: An Overview of Japan." In J.A. Winterdyk (ed.) *Juvenile Justice Systems: International Perspectives*, pp. 1-28. Toronto, ON: Canadian Scholars' Press, Inc.

Yue, L. (2002). "Youth Injustice in China." In J.A. Winterdyk (ed.) *Juvenile Justice Systems: International Perspectives*, Second Edition, pp. 103-126. Toronto, ON: Canadian Scholars' Press Inc.

Zalkind, P. & R. Simon (2004). *Global Perspectives on Social Issues: Juvenile Justice Systems*. Oxford, UK: Lexington Books.

Zhao, G. (2001). "The Recent Development of Juvenile Justice in China." In J. Liu, L. Zhang & S.F. Messner (eds.) *Crime and Social Control in a Changing China*, pp. 177-188. Westport, CT: Greenwood Publishing Group.

Contributors' Biographical Information

Peter J. Benekos is Dean of the School of Social Sciences and Professor of Criminal Justice and Sociology at Mercyhurst College. He received his Ph.D. in Sociology from the University of Akron. He has conducted research and published in the areas of juvenile justice, corrections, and public policy. He is the co-author with Alida V. Merlo of *Crime Control, Politics, and Policy*, Second Edition (LexisNexis/Anderson) and *Corrections: Dilemmas and Directions* (Anderson), and "The Nacirema Revisited: A Pedagogical Tool for Teaching Criminological Theory" with Frank E. Hagan, *Journal of Criminal Justice Education*. He is past-president of the Northeastern Association of Criminal Justice Sciences.

Donna M. Bishop is Professor in the College of Criminal Justice at Northeastern University. She received her Ph.D. in Criminal Justice from the State University of New York at Albany in 1982. For over two decades, her research and scholarship have focused primarily on juvenile justice and youth policy. She is the author of one book, over sixty articles, and numerous monographs, including major works on racial and gender disparities in juvenile court processing; juvenile detention reform; and juvenile transfer policy and practice. She has presented her research to legislative committees, judicial groups, public defender and sentencing advocacy groups, juvenile task forces and commissions, as well as academic audiences both in the U.S. and abroad. She has served on the board of the American Society of Criminology; is a former editor of *Justice Quarterly*; currently serves on the editorial boards of five major journals; and is a member of the Advisory Council of the Campaign for Youth Justice. Her current work focuses on the implications of incarceration for adolescent development, the role of organizational factors in justice decisionmaking, the link between features of juvenile correctional institutions and inmate misconduct, and racial stereotyping in the juvenile justice system.

Tory J. Caeti (deceased) was on the faculty in the Department of Criminal Justice at the University of North Texas. He earned his Ph.D. from Sam Houston State University. Dr. Caeti authored numerous articles in the area of juvenile justice in such journals as *Law and Policy, Crime & Delinquency,* the *American Journal of Criminal Law*, and *Criminal Justice Policy Review*. He was co-author of the textbook *Juvenile Justice: Policies, Programs, and Practice*, and co-editor of *Youth Violence and Juvenile Justice: An Interdisciplinary Journal*. Dr. Caeti was a former juvenile correctional counselor in Denver, Colorado and worked on the Serious Habitual Offender Comprehensive Action Program for OJJDP.

Dianne Carmody is Associate Professor in the Department of Sociology and Criminal Justice at Old Dominion University. She earned her Ph.D. in Sociology from the University of New Hampshire. Her research interests are varied, and she has published articles and book chapters on the media portrayal of crime and criminals, juvenile offenders, the criminal justice response to wife assault, school violence, and rape victimization. Her publications have appeared in the *Journal of Marriage and the Family*, *Justice Quarterly*, *Violence and Victims* and *The Journal of Quantitative Criminology*.

Amy C. Eisert is Director of the Mercyhurst College Civic Institute in Erie, Pennsylvania. She received her M.S. in the Administration of Justice from Mercyhurst College. Her research areas include juvenile justice, mental health and juvenile offenders, incorrigibility, and dependent youth.

Eric J. Fritsch is Professor in the Department of Criminal Justice at the University of North Texas. He received his degrees from Sam Houston State University. Dr. Fritsch has authored and co-authored several journal articles, book chapters, and technical reports. Most of his publications focus on juvenile justice, in particular juvenile violence. His articles appear in numerous journals including *Crime & Delinquency*, *Police Quarterly*, *Law and Policy*, *Criminal Justice Review* and the *American Journal of Criminal Law*. He has also co-authored textbooks on juvenile justice, digital crime and digital terrorism, and police patrol allocation and deployment. His areas of interest include organizational assessment, policing, juvenile justice and delinquency, gangs, criminological theory, criminal procedure, and research methods.

Thomas J. Gamble is President of Mercyhurst College, Erie, Pennsylvania and Associate Professor of Criminal Justice and Psychology at Mercyhurst. His earned degrees include the Ph.D. in Social Psychology from the Psychology Department at Syracuse University as well as from the Maxwell School for Citizenship and Public Affairs at Syracuse. He completed postdoctoral studies in child psychology in the Psychology Department at Yale University. His research and publications are in the area of child abuse risk assessment, juvenile detention screening, racial and gender bias, and the application of biological and psychological perspectives to the development of delinquency in the context of the operation of broader social forces.

Frank E. Hagan is Professor of Sociology and Criminal Justice at Mercyhurst College, Erie, Pennsylvania. He holds a Ph.D. from Case Western Reserve University. He is co-author with Marvin Sussman of *Deviance and the Family* (Hayworth, 1988) and author of *Research Methods in Criminal Justice and Criminology* (Sixth Edition, Allyn and Bacon, 2003) and *Introduction to Criminology: Theories, Methods, and Criminal Behavior* (Sixth Edition, Sage, 2007). Other books include: *Political Crime* (Allyn & Bacon, 1997), *White Collar Deviance* with David Simon (Allyn & Bacon, 1999) and with Pamela Tontodonato *The Language of Research in Criminal Justice and Criminology* (Allyn & Bacon, 1998). Dr. Hagan has concentrated much of his research in areas of political, white collar and organized crime. The political crime book includes discussion of the issue of terrorism and counter terrorism.

Richard Lawrence is Professor of Criminal Justice at St. Cloud State University in Minnesota. He received his Ph.D. from Sam Houston State University. Dr. Lawrence is the author of *School Crime and Juvenile Justice*, published by Oxford University Press and the author of more than 30 articles published in journals, books, and encyclopedias.

John Lemmon is Associate Professor of Criminal Justice at Shippensburg University. He received his Ph.D. in Social Work from the University of Maryland. He has 30 years experience working in Pennsylvania's children and youth and juvenile justice systems. His research and teaching interests include the effect of family life on youth deviancy and the clinical treatment of antisocial behavior. Currently, Dr. Lemmon is investigating motivational typologies of juvenile firesetters.

Marilyn D. McShane is Professor of Criminal Justice, University of Houston Downtown. She received her Ph.D. in 1985 from Sam Houston State University. She has taught at the graduate and undergraduate level and has served on a number of national criminal justice professional organization boards. At California State University, San Bernardino she received the faculty Professional Development Award in 1994 and she was Chair of the Department of Criminal Justice at Northern Arizona University. Professor McShane has a consistent record of publication and grantsmanship (more than 50 books and articles, and directed dozens of grants). Her editorial work includes a series of dissertations with LFB Scholarly Publishing and a scholarly monograph series with Greenwood/Praeger. She co-edited the award-winning *Encyclopedia of American Prisons* and is co-editor of the *Encyclopedia of Juvenile Justice*. Her most recent books are *Prisons in America* as well as *A Thesis Guide for Criminology and Criminal Justice* and *Criminological Theory*, Fourth Edition, both of which are coauthored with Frank P. Williams III.

Alida V. Merlo is Professor of Criminology at Indiana University of Pennsylvania. She earned her Ph.D. in Sociology at Fordham University. Previously, she was a faculty member in the Criminal Justice Department at Westfield State College in Westfield, Massachusetts, and a juvenile probation officer and Intake Supervisor in Mahoning County Juvenile Court in Youngstown, Ohio. She has conducted research and published in the area of juvenile justice, criminal justice policy, women and the law, and corrections. She is co-author (with Peter J. Benekos) of *Crime Control, Politics, & Policy*, Second Edition (LexisNexis/Anderson, 2006), co-editor (with Joycelyn M. Pollock) of *Women, Law & Social Control*, Second Edition (Allyn & Bacon, 2006), and co-editor (with Peter J. Benekos) of *Corrections: Dilemmas and Directions* (Anderson, 1992). She is past-President of the Academy of Criminal Justice Sciences (1999-2000) and recipient of the Academy's Founder's Award and the Fellow Award.

Alexis J. Miller is Associate Professor in the Department of Political Science and Criminal Justice at Northern Kentucky University. She received her Ph.D. in Urban and Public Affairs from the University of Louisville. Her research interests include hate crimes, prisoners' rights, criminal justice students, and institutional corrections.

Peggy S. Plass is Associate Professor in the Department of Justice Studies at James Madison University. She received her Ph.D. in Sociology from the University of New Hampshire where she worked in the Family Research Lab. She has done research in the areas of domestic violence, child abduction, and the criminal victimization of children.

Joseph Sanborn is Professor of Criminal Justice and Legal Studies at the University of Central Florida. He received his Ph.D. in Criminal Justice from SUNY Albany in 1984. His research focuses mostly on the processing of juvenile offenders, criminal procedure, and human rights. Dr. Sanborn is the Past President of the Southern Criminal Justice Association and formerly served as the Chair of the Juvenile Justice Section within the Academy of Criminal Justice Sciences (ACJS).

Pamela Tontodonato is Associate Professor in the Department of Justice Studies at Kent State University. She earned her Ph.D. from the University of Pennsylvania, specializing in Criminology. She taught at the University of Northern Iowa in the Department of Sociology and Anthropology prior to coming to Kent State. She has served variously as interim chair and as the Department's undergraduate coordinator, overseeing the B.A. program and advising transfer and regional campus students. Her research and teaching interests include Juvenile Delinquency, Victimology, Violent Crime, Quantitative Research Methods, Criminological Theory, and Criminal Justice Education. She has published recently in the Journal of Criminal Justice Education and is co-author (with Frank Hagan) of *The Language of Research in Criminal Justice and Criminology*.

Ruth A. Triplett is Associate Professor in the Department of Sociology and Criminal Justice at Old Dominion University in Norfolk, VA. She earned her Ph.D. from University of Maryland, College Park. Dr. Triplett's research interests include social disorganization, labeling theory, and the role of gender and class in criminological theory. Her most recent publications are found in the *Journal of Criminal Justice Education*, *Journal of Criminal Justice*, and *Justice Quarterly*.

Richard Tewksbury is Professor of Justice Administration at the University of Louisville. He received his Ph.D. in Sociology from The Ohio State University. Dr. Tewksbury's research interests include institutional corrections, victimization risks assessment, and sex/gender/sexuality issues. He has published widely in criminal justice, sociology, and public health issues. He is co-editor of *Controversies in Criminal Justice Research*.

P.J. Verrecchia is currently Assistant Professor of Behavioral Sciences at York College of Pennsylvania. A former juvenile probation officer, he holds a Ph.D. in Human Development from Marywood University. His research interests include the transfer of juvenile offenders to criminal court, restorative justice, and gender issues in criminal justice.

Frank P. Williams III is Professor of Criminal Justice at the University of Houston-Downtown and Professor Emeritus, California State University-San Bernardino. He received his Ph.D. in 1976 from Florida State University and his specializations are in criminological theory, corrections, fear of crime, drug abuse, methodology, and statistics. He has taught at departments in six universities and has published a substantial number of articles, research monographs, government reports, and books. He has served as a department chair (California State, San Bernardino), doctoral program coordinator (Prairie View A&M), Assistant Director for Research (Sam Houston State University) and directed numerous research projects and two research centers. He has served on/been elected to the boards of national scholarly organizations, chaired a major division of a national organization, and chaired/served on numerous national/regional committees. He has been an editor or deputy/associate editor for several journals and publisher's book and monograph series. He is currently serving as co-editor of two book series, and is most recently co-author with Marilyn McShane of *Criminological Theory*, Fifth Edition (2009), *A Thesis Resource Guide for Criminology and Criminal Justice* (2008), and a three-volume set entitled *Youth Violence and Delinquency: Monsters and Myths* (2008). His most recent sole-authored book is *Statistical Concepts for Criminal Justice and Criminology* (2008).

Index

CPSIA information can be obtained
at www.ICGtesting.com
Printed in the USA
FFOW04n1512201214
9715FF